# Narcos Over the Border

This book takes a hard hitting look at the drug wars taking place in Mexico between competing gangs, cartels, and mercenary factions; their insurgency against the Mexican state; the narco-violence and terrorism that is increasingly coming over the border into the United States; and its interrelationship with domestic prison and street gangs. Analysis and response strategies are provided by leading writers on 3GEN gang theory, counter-terrorism, transnational organized crime, and homeland security.

*Narcos Over the Border* is divided into three sections: narco-opposing force (NARCO OPFOR) organization and technology use, patterns of violence and corruption, and United States response strategies. The work also includes editor's notes, foreword, strategic threat overview, and afterword. Specific topics covered include: narcotics trafficking and street taxation; cartel and gang evolution; Mexico futures; Los Zetas; street and prison gangs; social networking; corruption; firefights, raids, and assassinations; torture, beheadings, and narcocultos; and border violence.

This book was published as a special issue of *Small Wars & Insurgencies*.

**Robert J. Bunker** is CEO of the Counter-OPFOR Corporation, USA. He is an applied theorist focusing on non-state opposing force (OPFOR) research, analysis, and defeat strategies and Epochal Warfare studies. He was the 2006-2007 Futurist in Residence (FIR), FBI Academy, Quantico, VA and has counter-terrorism and red teaming experience. His publications include *Non-State Threats and Future Wars; Networks, Terrorism and Global Insurgency;* and *Criminal-States and Criminal-Soldiers* (all published by Routledge).

# Narcos Over the Border

## Gangs, Cartels and Mercenaries

Edited by Robert J. Bunker

Routledge
Taylor & Francis Group

LONDON AND NEW YORK

First published 2011 by Routledge
2 Park Square, Milton Park, Abingdon, Oxon, OX14 4RN

Simultaneously published in the USA and Canada
by Routledge
270 Madison Avenue, New York, NY 10016

*Routledge is an imprint of the Taylor & Francis Group, an informa business*

This book is a reproduction of *Small Wars & Insurgencies*, vol.21, issue 1. The Publisher
requests to those authors who may be citing this book to state, also, the bibliographical
details of the special issue on which the book was based

Typeset in Times New Roman by Value Chain, India

*British Library Cataloguing in Publication Data*
A catalogue record for this book is available from the British Library

ISBN13: 978-0-415-56072-6 (hbk)
ISBN13: 978-0-415-59725-8 (pbk)

# CONTENTS

# Notes on Contributors

**Matt Begert** has for the last eight years been the operations officer for the National Law Enforcement and Corrections Technology Center-West, a grant-funded field activity of the National Institute of Justice oriented to the efficient and effective use of technology in policing operations and tasks.[*] He is currently a supporting consultant to the Counter-OPFOR Corporation and the Terrorism Research Center as well as a project leader for a corporation in the aerospace industry, a member of the volunteer forces of the San Bernardino (CA) Sheriff's Department, and an executive board member of the National Institute for Urban Search and Rescue. He is a regular officer in the United States Marine Corps, not currently serving, with operational experience in infantry operations, special operations and tactical aviation and logistics as well as instructional experience in basic skills training, aviation weapons and tactics, and red team organization and operation. He has written and spoken on these subjects to law enforcement and public safety audiences throughout the US. He holds a BA in Anthropology and a BS in journalism/mass communications from the University of Kansas and is a graduate of the National Security and Strategic Studies curriculum of the Naval War College.

**Pamela L. Bunker** is a Senior Officer of the Counter-OPFOR Corporation. Her research specializations include extremists, radical environmental and fringe groups, pirates, ritual killings and religious cults. Her works have appeared in edited journals and books, encyclopedias, and subject bibliographies. She is currently working on a co-authored essay on pirates and narco gangs for *The Routledge Companion to the Study of Insurgency and Counter Insurgency*. She graduated from California State Polytechnic University, Pomona with a BS in anthropology/geography and a BS in social science and from The Claremont Graduate University with an MA in public policy with additional post-graduate work completed there in comparative politics and government. Ms. Bunker also holds a Certificate in Terrorism Studies from the University of St. Andrews, Scotland. She has presented to both national and international policing groups and past professional experience includes research and program coordination in university, non-governmental organization (NGO), and city government settings.

**Robert J. Bunker** is CEO of the Counter-OPFOR Corporation. He holds a PhD in political science from the Claremont Graduate University, five other university

---

[*]*Editor's note:* NLECTC-West was subsequently closed after the submission of Matt Begert's co-authored contribution.

degrees, and has undertaken counter-terrorism related training. He is a founding member of the Los Angeles Terrorism Early Warning Group (LA TEW) established in 1996 and has counter-terrorism operational planning experience. Professional experience includes university teaching at the graduate and undergraduate level, red teaming and field exercises, special research projects and consulting for numerous US law enforcement, military, and governmental organizations. He has given over 150 briefings and presentations throughout the US and overseas on terrorism and other non-state threat force related topics. He has over 200 essays and longer publications including the edited works *Non-State Threats and Future Wars* (Routledge, 2002); *Networks, Terrorism, and Global Insurgency* (Routledge, 2005); and *Criminal-States and Criminal-Soldiers* (Routledge, 2008). He has also co-authored, with Stephen Sloan, *Simulating Terrorism II*, forthcoming from Oklahoma University Press. He is currently working on a paper, based on earlier projections and LE/Gov presentations conducted from 2006–09, concerning the terrorist use of body cavity bombs against high-value targets.

**Lisa J. Campbell** is a Senior Intelligence Officer for the California Air National Guard. She is a graduate of the USAF Intelligence Officer Course at Goodfellow Air Force Base, Texas and holds a BS in geology from Cornell College, Iowa. She specializes in wartime air base operability, predictive threat analysis, and anti-terrorism and force protection. Ms. Campbell performs estimates on enemy conventional and asymmetric weapons systems that can be used against military airlift and provides recommendations to military commanders in situations including those taking place during overseas contingency operations. She has written articles and book chapters covering operational assessments of non-state groups, postmodern beheadings, and laser threats. Ms. Campbell is a member of the Los Angeles Terrorism Early Warning Group and has been deployed to Iraq and Afghanistan.

**Paul Rexton Kan** was born in Hong Kong and raised in Hawaii and Australia. He is currently an Associate Professor of National Security Studies at the US Army War College at Carlisle Barracks. He earned his PhD in International Studies from the Graduate School of International Studies at the University of Denver. While finishing his PhD, he was the Deputy Director of the Center for China-United States Cooperation where he coordinated professional exchanges with Chinese officials from the policy institutions linked to the Ministry of Foreign Affairs, the Ministry of State Security, and the People's Liberation Army. He is the author of the recent book, *Drugs and Contemporary Warfare* (Potomac Books, 2009), and was awarded the General George C. Marshall Faculty Research Grant to complete it. He is also the recipient of a Madigan Faculty Writing Award for his article, 'Drugging Babylon: The Illegal Narcotics Trade and Nation-Building in Iraq', published in the June 2007 edition of the journal *Small Wars and Insurgencies*. He is currently working on his next book, *Whiskey Rebellions, Opium Wars and Other Battles for Intoxication*.

**Alberto M. Melis** is Chief of Police (Jefe de policía) of Douglas, Arizona. He was born in Havana, Cuba, came to the US at the age of 11, and resided in South Florida until 2000. He holds a BA in criminal justice from Florida Atlantic University and a MS in criminal justice from Florida International University. He is a graduate of the University of Louisville's Southern Police Institute's Command Officers Development Course, the Federal Bureau of Investigation's National Academy Law Enforcement Executive Development Seminar, and the Police Executive Research Forum's Senior Management Institute for Police at the JFK School of Government at Harvard University. He also has earned nearly 3000 hours of additional law enforcement training. He worked for over 24 years for the Delray Beach Police Department in virtually every position, rising from patrol officer to captain – and during that period he commanded every division of the department. He was responsible for creating the first community policing division to lead the agency into total community policing. He became Chief of Police of Lauderhill in 1997 and he was chosen as Chief of Police for Waco in April 2000. In November of 2007, he was chosen as Chief of Police of Douglas.

**Luz E. Nagle** is a Professor of Law at Stetson University College of Law, Gulfport, Florida. She specializes in the areas of international law and international criminal law. She received her LLD from the Universidad Pontificia Bolivariana, a JD from the College of William and Mary, and an LLM and MA (Latin American studies) from UCLA. Professor Nagle has also been a visiting professor and lecturer at the University of Tampa, the Universidad de Granada in Spain, the Universidad de los Andes, and the Universidad de Antioquia in Colombia. She also serves as an External Researcher in the Strategic Studies Institute of the US Army War College and has been involved in several rule of law reform projects sponsored by USAID and the US Departments of Defense, Justice, and State in Colombia, Panama, and Mexico. A prolific speaker and writer whose body of work probes the realities of foreign policy and the rule of law from a critical perspective that reflects her training and experience in both the Anglo-American and continental law systems, Professor Nagle has published in English and Spanish on four continents, including book chapters, law review articles, and monographs on topics related to international humanitarian law and internal armed conflict, transnational crime, corruption, national security, and rule of law/judicial reform movements. She was honored with the 2009 Freedom Award given by the Florida Coalition against Human Trafficking in recognition of her activism and involvement in training law enforcement personnel and legal professionals about its pernicious effects.

**John P. Sullivan** is a Senior Research Fellow at the Center for Advanced Studies on Terrorism (CAST). He also serves as a lieutenant with the Los Angeles Sheriff's Department; currently assigned to the Emergency Operations Bureau. His immediate past assignment was director of the National TEW Resource Center and is co-founder of the Los Angeles Terrorism Early Warning (TEW) Group. Sullivan holds a BA in government from the College of William and

Mary and a MA in urban affairs and policy analysis from the New School for Social Research. He participated in the Director of National Intelligence's 2006 Summer Hard Problems Program (SHARP) and is a member of the InterAgency Board on Equipment Standardization and Interoperability (IAB). He is also a member of the California Gang Investigators Association and on the board of advisors for the *Small Wars Journal*. Sullivan is co-editor of *Countering Terrorism and WMD: Creating a Global Counter-Terrorism Network* (Routledge, 2006) and *Global Biosecurity: Threats and Responses* (Routledge, 2010*)* and has authored or co-authored works including *Jane's Unconventional Weapons Response Handbook* (Jane's Information Group, 2003), *Jane's Facility Security Handbook* (Jane's Information Group, 2001), *Policing Transportation Facilities* (Charles C. Thomas, 1996), as well as over 100 chapters or articles on terrorism, policing, intelligence, and emergency response.

**Graham H. Turbiville, Jr.** is a Senior Consultant and Researcher for Courage Service, Inc., McLean, Virginia, addressing Department of Defense and Intelligence Community programs dealing with cultural and geographic assessments in several areas of the world, and producing history-based assessments of tribal/clan societies in contemporary war and conflict. Dr. Turbiville was a Senior Fellow with the US Special Operations Command/ Joint Special Operations University (USSOCOM/JSOU) from 2004 until 2009. His USSOCOM/JSOU monograph 'U.S. Military Engagement with Mexico: Uneasy Past and Challenging Future' is forthcoming in late Fall 2009. Earlier, Dr. Turbiville served 30 years in intelligence community analytical and leadership positions at the Defense Intelligence Agency and the Department of the Army. These included as director/chief of long-range and current intelligence offices and directorates, director of a Joint Reserve Intelligence Center, and other assignments dealing with foreign combined arms, security, and special operations forces.

**Phil Williams** is Wesley W. Posvar Professor and Director of the Ridgway Center for International Security Studies, at the University of Pittsburgh. Professor Williams has published extensively in the field of international security. During the last 15 years, his research has focused primarily on transnational organized crime and he has written articles on various aspects of this subject in *Survival, Washington Quarterly, The Bulletin on Narcotics, Temps Strategique, Scientific American, Criminal Organizations*, and *Cross Border Control*. In addition, Dr. Williams was founding editor of the journal *Transnational Organized Crime*. He has been a consultant to both the United Nations and United States government agencies on organized crime and has also given congressional testimony on the subject. He has also focused on alliances among criminal organization, global and national efforts to combat money laundering, and trends and development in cyber-crime. Dr. Williams has edited a volume, *Russian Organized Crime* (London: Cass, 1997), and a book, *Illegal Immigration and Commercial Sex: The New Slave Trade* (London: Cass, 1999). He is also co-editor of a volume on *Combating Transnational Crime* (London,

Cass, 2001). In 2001–02, he was on sabbatical from the University of Pittsburgh and was a Visiting Scientist at CERT/CC Carnegie Mellon University, where he worked on computer crime and organized crime. Over the last few years, he has also served as Visiting Research Professor, Strategic Studies Institute, US Army War College, Carlisle Barracks. Recent works include *From the New Middle Ages to a New Dark Age: The Decline of the State and U.S. Strategy* (2008) and *Criminals, Militias and Insurgents: Organized Crime in Iraq* (2009), both published by the Strategic Studies Institute, US Army War College.

**Sarah Womer** is a Middle East, media, and research analyst with Science Application International Corporation (SAIC). Ms. Womer has looked at extremism in a variety of different forms on the Internet since 2001 and authored a chapter for the *Encyclopedia of World Terrorism, 1996–2002* (M.E. Sharpe, 2003) on Internet and terrorists. Ms. Womer has also been a guest speaker at several conferences and seminars on Middle East issues, extremism on the Internet, and on cultural communications. She spent three years as an instructor teaching analysis, culture, research skills, and media in the contemporary operating environment. She has visited and worked in several Middle Eastern countries and has supported the government in media analysis on a variety of projects.

# Abstracts

*Strategic threat: narcos and narcotics overview*
ROBERT J. BUNKER
This introductory essay provides a strategic overview of the threat posed by the largest Mexican drug cartels (The Federation, Gulf, Juárez, and Tijuana), and affiliated mercenary groups and street and prison gangs, to the United States. Cartel areas of operation in both Mexico and the United States are highlighted along with linkages to affiliated enforcers and gangs such as Los Zetas, the Mexican Mafia (La Eme), and Mara Salvatrucha (MS-13). The illegal economies of these threat groups – ranging from narcotics trafficking through commodities smuggling and theft, extortion and kidnapping, weapons trafficking, and street taxation – is discussed. The trans-operational environments involving US engagement with the Mexican cartels, mercenaries, and their Sureños affiliates is then characterized. Lastly, individual contributions to this work are summarized.

*Cartel evolution revisited: third phase cartel potentials and alternative futures in Mexico*
ROBERT J. BUNKER AND JOHN P. SULLIVAN
Drug Trafficking Organizations (DTOs) – commonly called drug cartels – are challenging states and their institutions in increasingly brutal and profound ways. This is seen dramatically in Mexico's drug wars and the expanding reach of Mexican organized criminal enterprises throughout Latin America and other parts of the world. This essay updates a 1998 paper 'Cartel Evolution: Potentials and Consequences' and examines current cartel and gang interactions. The paper links discussion of cartel phases to gang generations; updates and applies the discussion of third phase cartel potentials to Mexico; and assesses four alternative futures for Mexico, as well as their cross-border implications for the United States.

*Los Zetas: operational assessment*
LISA J. CAMPBELL
Today, analysts of the postmodern era recognize that worldwide conflicts are increasingly influenced by the interaction between terrorists, criminals, gangs, and private armies and that this interaction is a threat to the nation state. Now, a related threat is coming into play – one that involves all of these types of groups being represented at once in a single adversary. One such multifaceted group that is in the forefront is Los Zetas, a band of Mexican cartel enforcers that cannot be easily categorized, assessed, or targeted. Within broad categories of a

multitude of irregular groups, Los Zetas embodies such capabilities as extensive compartmentalized networking, pervasive intelligence and counterintelligence capabilities, amassing of advanced weaponry, brutal tactics, top level military and police training, and the ability to undermine state governments and control large swaths of territory. Los Zetas, if left unchecked and unexamined, could potentially become a great security problem for Mexico, the US, and Central America. This essay provides an operational assessment that explores Los Zetas using various criteria traditionally used by nation state militaries, and more recently by Terrorism Early Warning Groups, to assess opposing forces (OPFOR). The purpose of this operational assessment is to provide a baseline understanding of Los Zetas that would make them less imposing and more targetable.

*Sureños gangs and Mexican cartel use of social networking sites*
SARAH WOMER AND ROBERT J. BUNKER
Narco use of the Internet, specifically social networking sites by Sureños gang and Mexican cartel members, is a rich yet underexplored area of research in open venues because of its sensitive nature. This essay provides overviews of Sureños gang and Mexican cartel use of the Internet by means of viewing and analyzing primary Internet sources linked to purported narcotics groups and their associates. These patterns of use were then compared to more sophisticated Internet use by terrorist groups with similarities and contrasts noted. This essay concludes with a few general observations concerning likely narco Internet use patterns that will emerge.

*Corruption of politicians, law enforcement, and the judiciary in Mexico and complicity across the border*
LUZ E. NAGLE
Mexico is a failing state, languishing under a deeply entrenched system of political corruption that undermines the three branches of government and compromises Mexico's law enforcement and national security capabilities.
This article explores the culture of corruption that pervades the state and frustrates the rule of law in Mexico, examining how the political elites, the judiciary, and police officials embrace corruption as a primary means for career advancement and for acquiring personal wealth. It is an examination of a country overwhelmed by a system of government and commerce that has grown dependent on corruption in order to function. But such a system cannot sustain itself indefinitely, and the signs of the Mexican state's collapse are becoming more apparent in the wake of unprecedented political and social violence at the hands of corrupt actors and Mexican drug lords.

*Firefights, raids, and assassinations: tactical forms of cartel violence and their underpinnings*
GRAHAM H. TURBIVILLE, JR.
This article examines some specific types of narco-generated combat, assault, and brutality that over the last decade have acquired an increasingly organized and

paramilitary character. The planning; training; intelligence and counterintelligence preparation; mobility; communications; type of weaponry; levels of intensity; and sheer audacity substantially exceed the threats with which traditional law enforcement had been trained and equipped to deal. It matches the apt Drug Enforcement Administration description of a 'transition from the gangsterism of traditional narco hit men to paramilitary terrorism with guerrilla tactics'. These methods have become a mainstay in the struggle of narco-traffickers against law enforcement, the military, and to a major degree among the competing drug-trafficking organizations themselves. While the infrastructure and practice of paramilitary violence is established in Mexico in seemingly unprecedented ways, the concern north of the border is its potential transportability. Many law enforcement personnel have compared 1980s Miami – with its running drug firefights, revenge raids, and bloody assassinations by Colombian cocaine traffickers – to Mexican drug violence. There are enough precursors north of the Rio Grande now to make the potential for something analogous more than empty speculation.

### *Torture, beheadings, and* narcocultos
PAMELA L. BUNKER, LISA J. CAMPBELL AND ROBERT J. BUNKER

This essay provides an overview of those incidents of torture and beheadings linked to the Mexican cartels and their mercenary and gang affiliates taking place both within Mexico and the United States. Specific forms of torture are discussed as well as the most likely victims and perpetrators. Beheadings, primarily taking place only in Mexico, are also analyzed with supporting database information provided. The occurrences of torture and beheadings tied to these cartels, both in Mexico and more recently across the border into the United States, beg the question of the context in which they are being conducted. Most cases of torture or beheading are regarded as primarily secular in nature – a terrorist tactic tied to economic or political gain. In an even more macabre twist, however, certain instances have been seen as intertwined with a group's belief system, performed in ritual fashion to fulfil religious or spiritual demands. This suggests that the emergent Mexican *narcocultos* that are evolving may further increase drug war violence to new levels of brutality heretofore unseen.

### *Counter-supply and counter-violence approaches to narcotics trafficking*
JOHN P. SULLIVAN

Narcotics and the drug trade contribute to a range of social ills. Among these are social instability, violence, corruption, and a weakening of the state. A range of criminal enterprises, including transnational gangs and drug cartels are engaged in the global trade in illicit drugs. This essay looks at measures to stem this trade through interventions directed against the drug supply and efforts to limit the violence that results from the drug trade. As such it looks at 'counter-supply' and 'counter-violence' approaches. While it emphasizes the impact on the

Western Hemisphere – the United States and Latin America – it has international implications for global and national security, intelligence, and law enforcement.

*Counter-demand approaches to narcotics trafficking*
ROBERT J. BUNKER AND MATT BEGERT

The illegal narcotics demand in the US is discussed in relation to the products supplied by the Mexican cartels. This is then contrasted with major legal commodities with addictive properties consumed in the US. Overlaps of use are also noted. Traditional, right of center, and left of center counter-demand approaches to narcotics trafficking are also surveyed. All of these approaches represent no-win scenarios for the US with its 'troubled population' of addicted users. Final analysis suggests that a blended counter-demand strategy should be explored based on extinguishing demand, coercing the users, and, to some extent, fulfilling user demand by the provision of prescription narcotics to 'special status' addicts and by means of limited decriminalization of personal marijuana use. Such a suggested strategy would have its own negative elements and should be considered less of a bad choice than the other, even worse, US counter-demand policy options that exist.

# Editor's note

The course of this research project, and its subsequent publication as a special issue of *Small Wars & Insurgencies*, has had a long and tortuous path dating back to early 2008. Rising levels of drug cartel violence in Mexico and the penetration of cartel operatives into the US prompted the editor to solicit funding to study this dangerous trend and the cross-border and homeland security implications it represented. Mexican drug cartel links to street and prison gangs, specifically the Sureños affiliated ones, and mercenary groups, became apparent very early on and were an integral part of the proposed research. Some of these concerns are graphically portrayed in the publication of a National Drug Intelligence Center (NDIC) map in April 2008, which highlights Mexican cartel penetration of US cities (Figure 1).

Unfortunately, initial attempts at securing research funding were unsuccessful and the proposed project languished. Deep frustration over inattention to this growing security threat to the United States, more than anything else, finally prompted the editor to assemble a concerned and dedicated group of close associates who supported the intent and mission of this project despite the time and opportunity costs involved. For contributors, it increased their workloads and meant the use of evenings, weekends, and even vacation time to research and write their essays. Many already have full time jobs in support of law enforcement and the military or are actual law enforcement officers, while others are academics engaged in research on subjects pertaining to military and judicial policy, transnational organized crime, and state corruption. Some of the contributors wear multiple hats.

The research team assembled, the editors of *Small Wars & Insurgencies* were approached with the project proposal in early 2009. Paul B. Rich and Thomas-Durell Young have to be singled out for their immediate support in this endeavor and their quick recognition and acceptance of the theoretical and policy merits of the proposed research project. Much thanks for this from the editor of this book and for the guidance you provided him in the final assemblage of the special issue. The staff at Routledge must also be thanked for their relatively quick decision also to reproduce the edited collection of writings in the form of this follow-on book. This will mark the fourth book in a series of cross-journal edited works that I have had the privilege of publishing with Routledge focusing on non-state, transnational organized crime, and other threat groups.

The numerous contributions made by my wife, Pamela L. Bunker, a contributor to this work, key provider of editorial support, and of course love of my life, must also be acknowledged. Finally, I'd like to give my sincere

Figure 1.    Situation report: Cities in which Mexican DTOs operate within the United States. Source: National Drug Intelligence Center (NDIC), 11 April 2008, http://www. usdoj.gov/ndic/pubs27/27986/appenda.htm#Map

appreciation to each of the contributors to this project, they are the ones who stuck by me, believed in what we were doing, and ultimately made it happen: Alberto M. Melis, John P. Sullivan, Lisa J. Campbell, Sarah Womer, Luz E. Nagle, Graham H. Turbiville, Jr., Pamela L. Bunker, Matt Begert, Paul Rexton Kan and Phil Williams – I give you each my thanks.

This project, once underway, also greatly benefited from two special quarterly meetings of the Los Angeles Terrorism Early Warning Group (LA TEW) – of which a number of the contributors are members – focusing on border security issues with Mexico and on Mexican cartels and gangs. Numerous requests for information (RFI) were also sent out to OSINT (open source intelligence) news groups, including that of the Police Futurists International (PFI), by the editor in support of the project. Important research leads, sources, and ideas were generated by these endeavors and helped to support the project. A warm thank you for all of those who helped in this regard and to all others from the US government, law enforcement, and the military who are vigilant in the defense of our great nation.

Dr Robert J. Bunker
CEO, Counter-OPFOR Corporation
Claremont, CA
USA
October 2009

# Foreword: a view from the Borderlands

Alberto M. Melis

*Douglas Police Department, Douglas, AZ, USA*

The southern border of the United States, with Mexico, is 1,969 miles (3,169 km) long. With 250 million counted people traveling it yearly, it is the most crossed border in the world. It spans 4 US states, 6 Mexican states, 20 railroad crossings, and there are about 30 city pairings along it (US and Mexican cities directly across from each other). About 12 million people live on both sides in the Borderlands. It is a storied area. General Francisco Villa and his troops bivouacked near the volcano, Cerro Gallardo. We know him as Pancho Villa. Aimee Semple McPherson came out of the desert here after her alleged kidnapping. Thornton Wilder wrote in Douglas for a while. These Borderlands are, indeed, the stuff that legends are made of.

The border transverses valleys, deserts, canyons, and mountains. The terrain is beautiful and it can kill you. The Sonoran Desert is 120,000 square miles (311,000 square km). It covers large parts of California and Arizona, as well as Baja California, Baja California del Sur, and Sonora. It is hot, dry, and unforgiving. As I write this, the newspaper reports two bodies found there by one of the humanitarian groups. I was recently contacted by the leader of a mission group near Mexico City on behalf of the family of a young man who had left there to come to the United States. He was several weeks overdue from reporting back. I checked the hospitals, sheriff offices, Border Patrol, and the jails to no avail. People attempt to cross the desert on foot with minimal preparation, thinking that it is just another hike. It is not. Part of the border is marked by the Rio Grande. Or what *we* call the Rio Grande. The Mexicans call it the Río Bravo del Norte. It is all relative, and it is all perspective. This year, 29 people drowned crossing the Rio Grande. With the lessened traffic in 2008, 23 drowned that year. Over the past 15 years, over 5,000 people have died crossing into the United States from Mexico. This is approximately a rate of one death every 24 hours. And while actual crossings seem to have dropped because of the economic downturns, the number of deaths seems to be headed up this year.

In contrast, the northern border of the United States, with Canada, is 5,525 miles long (or 8,891 km) including 1,538 miles (2,475 km) shared with

Alaska. It is the longest common border in the world. While protected at various levels by the US Border Patrol, it is not militarized. There is human trafficking going on there, however, and no doubt narco-trafficking. In terms of money, that seems to pale in comparison with cigarette smuggling as well as problems with soft wood and liquor. By most standards, these are minor compared with the problems across the southern border.

To paraphrase a current saying, I can see Mexico from my backyard. The border or, as it is called in the Borderlands, 'the line' is less than two miles away but I can see the husk of an extinct volcano that is iconic to Agua Prieta in the State of Sonora, which is the city on the other side. I can see the various mountains in Mexico: the Sierra Naideribacachi, the Sierra de Agua Prieta, the Sombrero Mountain, and the cone of the Cerro Gallardo. This is the border with which I am familiar, and which I love. Practically everyone living on the US side is related to someone across the line. Folks worry about the state of the dollar versus the peso, and shop and dine with equal facility on either side – with either pesos or dollars or the ubiquitous plastic. They fret about the outcome of local and national elections. Weddings, baptisms, banquets, concerts, first communions, *quinceañeras,* masses, and funerals are celebrated on either side and attended by residents of both countries. People on the US side will cross to the Mexican side to buy large banners bearing a photo of their children with congratulatory messages to hang in their homes in celebration of graduations.

Old timers and not so old timers talk about the days before the fence when only a rusty barbed wire demarcated the line – and was largely absent for miles. People treated the line as an imaginary construct and not a real thing. Today, one can still find the barbed wire once past the modern protections, and if one drives far enough outside the cities. But in town, the Port of Entry, the sensors, the passport radio chip readers, the automatic auto plate scanners, really just make crossing slower and perhaps more inconvenient. People cross daily. Politicians and high level government officials from Mexico live in this side of the line or have homes here. My wife and I go to a dentist across the line, and I run into him at the grocery store here all the time. Our ophthalmologist practices across the line but his kids attend high school here. In fact, before and after school, there is heavy traffic across the port with children headed across the line in both directions. Yet there are differences.

**The narcotic influx**

The flow of narcotics into the United States is immense and commensurate with the nation's thirst for mind-altering substances. There is an influx of people, weapons, and narcotics across the line but by far the most lucrative on the southern border is narcotics and, of these, the choice is marijuana. We have run into the mules. People want to come to this country and know the dangers present in a desert crossing. They are approached by people who will guarantee their safe and escorted crossing, and perhaps throw in some cash to sweeten the deal.

All they have to do is carry a backpack full of dope when they cross into the United States. If found or believed spotted, their handlers disappear and leave them to face arrest and punishment, or worse, as then they are left alone in the desert with no support. Sometimes we get information that narco-traffickers have put out the word that human smuggling or undocumented alien transiting in a given area needs to stop, as it is attracting too much attention to their planned activities. Sometimes we hear the opposite, that they want increased activity to draw attention to a given area from another area. It is always hard to determine what is information and what is disinformation.

There are so many means of smuggling that are tried. Just last week, Customs Officials intercepted a load at the Port of Entry. A shipment of furniture had been carefully hollowed out and the spaces filled with tightly packed marijuana. One of our detectives saw a flatbed trailer being towed and found it suspicious that the welds holding the bed flooring down to the framing seemed new and shiny. Below the bed flooring, there were hundreds of pounds of marijuana.

We have stopped cars with carefully constructed hidden spaces anywhere from the body to the gas tank. Sometimes the smuggling is at its most basic, where someone runs to the fence from the Mexican side and lobs a long football-like ball to someone on the other side. There was a report this week from Nogales that people were seen in the surveillance cameras throwing softball-sized aluminum foil balls into the US while others were seen collecting the balls. One of the balls was found to contain an assortment of controlled pills. This method continues as it is low cost and high yield. In the days before taller fences, several would jump the fence and scatter in a nice shotgun approach, while only one would be carrying the payload.

There are many ways of getting across, some harder than others. The US government has sued railroads for not doing more to secure their lines. For those attempting it on foot, there are the canyons and then there are the tunnels. There has only been one tunnel on the northern border of the United States, but many have been found on the southern border. Since 1990, 109 tunnels have been found in California and Arizona and, of those, 65 have been between Nogales, Sonora and Nogales, Arizona. Some are sophisticated to the point of having their own ventilation system, and some barely hold up the roof. Then there are the fences that we read so much about, and these fences are easily breached. Those that want to breach them have cut gates in the metal with cutting torches and plasma torches. Often they have been sophisticated enough to put hinges and latches so that the cuts are less visible and then they wipe their tracks clean. They use these 'gates' as their own private point of entry until found and sealed.

Other attempts involve 'drive-throughs'. I have seen the use of car transporters to form a bridge of sorts over the fence, where the transporter is backed to the fence with the vehicles that will make the crossing already loaded, then the ramps are lowered over the fence and the vehicles are driven down. This becomes an effective movable bridge over the fence. These are sophisticated operations with reconnaissance, surveillance, and communications systems.

Worse is the fact that more often than not they have rescue vehicles that will attempt to disrupt the law enforcement operation, recover the personnel, and recover the cargo if possible. We have been fired upon by their guards – although this is considered to be bad for business. They will use decoy vehicles to draw attention, so that the real load can get through, or use the convoy concept so that some will get through. Their vehicles are often 'clones', i.e. they are made to look like official vehicles or even vehicles belonging to local residents, and may be equipped with countermeasures such as wagon wheels. These are metal wheels similar to those of a wagon welded to the rims, inside the tire and not visible so that, when they are spiked by law enforcement, they can still roll and proceed with their attempt to escape back over the line. There are even drive-throughs called suicide runs, where an actual attempt will be made to run the Port of Entry. The POE personnel are well trained in stopping these, and there are some attempts to run the POE the wrong way. In all these cases, the point is to drive into town and then access the highway system. If pursued, they have total disregard for traffic or pedestrian safety, which is, of course, a major consideration for law enforcement.

Finally, planes are being used too – a sort of narco air force. There are the regular planes along with examples of large planes as well as small, private planes being flown. There is a new development in the use of ultralights to transport narcotics. The hope is that because the ultralights are small, slow, and fly low that they will escape detection. They seem to use various methods, one in which the craft lands and is unloaded and another in which the craft does the equivalent of a bombing run and drops its cargo. In some cases, the cargo is readily visible; in other cases, it is painted to match the fuselage or structure of the craft. Various types of ultralights are being used. There have been a few crashes, mostly fatal, of overloaded ultralights. On top of that, marijuana tends to absorb moisture, which increases its weight, and the pilots have little training and are mostly inexperienced. This is a development that is still evolving.

**Violence**

We read about the narcotics influx through the southern border and that there are no cities in the United States where illegal drugs cannot be obtained. Nowhere has the effects of the massive influx been as apparent and visible as in the Borderlands. Here, the violence has been escalating in ever more horrific steps, not seen since the cocaine cowboys of the 1980s or the days of prohibition. The effects are seen at all levels of Mexican society. There is nobody too high to be out of reach, and we worry about the spillover effect. There are many examples, but I want to highlight one in the person of Police Chief Ramón Tacho Verdugo. This is one case that really brought these issues home to those in this area, but it is all too common elsewhere in Mexico.

Chief Tacho was appointed police chief in Agua Prieta in September 2006. He had been chief of detectives of the State of Sonora and then chief in nearby

Cananea. He was larger than life and had recorded *corridas,* the country and western songs of Mexico. He even dressed as a cowboy. About 5 p.m. on 26 February 2007, Chief Tacho was coming out of the police building with some staffers when a Jeep Cherokee and a Jeep Liberty stopped in front and those inside opened fire with automatic rifles. More than 40 rounds were shot at Tacho and one bullet went past him and hit a nearby Red Cross worker. Tacho died 90 minutes later, after emergency surgery, as preparations were being made to airlift him to Tucson. Chief Tacho's brother, Roberto Tacho Verdugo was a chief of police in nearby Naco. He resigned and, in March of 2007, he was arrested while trying to smuggle 59 pounds of marijuana – an interesting coincidence.

Before and since, there have been numerous shootings of police officers in the area and elsewhere, and sometimes just people on the periphery of the narco-trade. On 16 May 2007, about 50 hit men went to Cananea and settled some scores, including the shooting of five police officers. The shootings have been sporadic and at different levels across the Borderlands. Saúl Noé Martínez Ortega, a reporter, was being chased and drove up onto the sidewalk of the police station in Agua Prieta but he was still abducted. His body was later found. Since 2000, 55 reporters have been killed and 8 are still missing. By comparison, although still present, shootings, abductions and violence are much less frequent here than in other areas such as Tijuana or Ciudad Juarez. I travel into Mexico often with my family and I feel safe.

### Broader issues

Police officers are being killed in Mexico on a continuing basis. The Tacho incident was unusual in this area, but similar incidents have been repeated over and over throughout Mexico. Locally, several officers were killed in Agua Prieta before it stopped, probably because of an increase in military presence. This lawlessness has been starting to get attention, although much of it has been watered down by the politically charged issue of undocumented immigration. Meanwhile the trafficking and killings go on.

A great deal has been written on Mexico in anarchy and Mexico on the verge of collapse. I think this is an exaggeration, but unarguably there is much happening and it will worsen before it improves. There is so much money involved that the figures and potential for profit are staggering – staggering even to the point of destabilizing whole economies and changing cultures. This special issue deftly edited by Robert J. Bunker will undoubtedly fill in a lot of the blanks and questions about this complex issue. He has assembled a dedicated team of contributors from academia, and those both involved with, and providing support to, US law enforcement, military, and governmental entities. While readers may not agree with all of the points of view expressed in this work, it will become an important contribution to our understanding of the drug wars taking place in Mexico and a conflict that is increasingly spilling over our southern border.

# Strategic threat: narcos and narcotics overview

Robert J. Bunker

*Counter-OPFOR Corporation, Claremont, CA, USA*

This introductory essay provides a strategic overview of the threat posed by the largest Mexican drug cartels (The Federation, Gulf, Juárez, and Tijuana), and affiliated mercenary groups and street and prison gangs, to the United States. Cartel areas of operation in both Mexico and the United States are highlighted along with linkages to affiliated enforcers and gangs such as Los Zetas, the Mexican Mafia (La Eme), and Mara Salvatrucha (MS-13). The illegal economies of these threat groups – ranging from narcotics trafficking through commodities smuggling and theft, extortion and kidnapping, weapons trafficking, and street taxation – is discussed. The trans-operational environments involving US engagement with the Mexican cartels, mercenaries, and their Sureños affiliates is then characterized. Lastly, individual contributions to this work are summarized.

Over the last few years, the drug war in Mexico has gained increasing attention in both the mass media and in scholarly and policy publications in the United States. The implications of this 'narco-insurgency' for Mexico, the United States, and even for the various Central and South American states where spillover from this conflict continues to wreak havoc should not be understated.[1] Much of the dialogue focuses on the health of the Mexican state and its potential for failure. This author and a colleague have in the past commented on that concern:

> Full scale Mexican state failure would result in even greater levels of criminalization and lawlessness than are already evident in that state. Simply put, if Mexico dies, we will be trapped in a room with a rotting corpse.[2]

Currently, two schools of thought exist on Mexican state failure potentials with each drawing upon well researched and analyzed information sources such as interviews, investigative and intelligence sources, and the Mexican press. In retrospect, quite possibly this 'either/or' debate as to whether or not Mexico is heading towards collapse is the wrong one to focus upon. This is because the actual threat being faced by the US is so alien to modern perceptions of national security that very few scholars and analysts recognize or even understand it. What is proposed here is that Mexico is not on its way to becoming a 'rotting corpse' but potentially something far worse – akin to a body being permanently infected by a malicious virus. Already, wide swaths of Mexico have been lost to the corrupting forces and violence generated by local gangs, cartels, and mercenaries. Such narco-corruption faced few barriers given the fertile ground already existing in Mexico derived from endemic governmental corruption at all levels of society and, in some ways, it even further aided the 'virus' spreading through Mexican society from this new 'infection'. Among its other symptoms, it spreads values at variance with traditional society, including those:

> ... conceivably derived from norms based on slave holding, illicit drug use, sexual activity with minors and their exploitation in prostitution, torture and beheadings, the farming of humans for body parts, the killing of innocents for political gain and personal gratification (as sport), and the desecration of the dead. Concepts such as due process, right to a jury trial, individual privacy concerns, the right to vote, women's rights to literacy, and self-determination, and the personal freedoms that so many Americans take for granted (life, liberty, and the pursuit of happiness) do not exist.[3]

To these above 'symptoms' of this diseased state can also be added a move in affected sectors toward cult-like religions that worship 'saints' and occult figures who validate these values and which promote engaging in blood and ritual sacrifice of one's enemies and their families. While the power and influence of such religions are still relatively weak within this emergent value system, they are beginning to fill a spiritual void for some of the criminal-soldiers of the gangs and para-states that have arisen. For some, dark deities offer protection, wealth, status, women, and a glorious death that others will praise, and, if fortune should have it, immortalize in song (the *narcocorrido*). For others, professing a twisted form of Christianity allows them to glorify the torture and murder of their enemies as 'divine justice'.

The end result of all these trends is that Mexico is becoming an entity that is truly the antithesis of the modern nation-state. Parts of Mexico have already been taken over by the virus which courses through its veins and have embraced its narco-criminal value system. Beyond the pull of demand-side economics, NAFTA (the North American Free Trade Agreement) and the highly developed national highway system, especially the north–south routes, within the US have further helped those in the drug trade transmit this 'narco virus' well into Mexico's neighbors. Territories of the Central and South American states have thereby fallen under its influence along with enclaves – streets, neighborhoods, urban zones, and prisons and jails – within the United States.

It would be both unfair and patently racist, however, to blame Mexico for all of these ills. The interplay between internal and domestic events throughout the Americas with the rise of the early Colombian cartels, the insatiable demand for illegal narcotics in the United States, the civil wars of El Salvador and Guatemala, illegal immigration from the south and the exploitation of cheap labor in the north, and the rise of such gangs as La Eme (The Mexican Mafia), 18th Street, and Mara Salvatrucha (MS-13) in the Los Angeles region, and the subsequent deportation of 'LA style gangsters' back to Mexico and Central America have all, along with numerous other events not mentioned, provided a rich contextual background for where we find ourselves today.

What we now have is a state in which the government is no longer able to govern entire sectors within its sovereign territory and, instead, these areas have been taken by a narco-insurgency and lost to the influence of criminal-based entities. This does not necessarily mean that all of the state will succumb and become that 'rotting corpse' as predicted earlier. Colombia, for example, has previously survived such onslaughts though it has never been the same and now, in many ways, resembles a narco-democracy. Nor, however, does the fact that the state government of Mexico has not succumbed necessarily mean that law, order, and state authority will be ultimately reestablished in these former territories, urban zones, villages, or neighborhoods. Indeed, that seems even more unlikely given this same insurgency has already crossed over the US–Mexican border and has probably been festering internally in the United States for decades with the rise and mass proliferation of street and prison gangs throughout the country. Not to overextend the analogy, but the upshot of this dynamic is that what has crossed over the border and what has arisen domestically are similar infections by the same virus – the Mexican strain is simply far more evolved, powerful, and violent.

## Narcos over and gangs inside the border

Domestic US homeland security concerns from this threat have recently multiplied given the increasing levels of violence on the border along with a concurrent change in the orientation of the Mexican cartels towards their operations inside the United States. The earlier Mexican cartels' policy of tempering overt violence north of the Rio Grande has been slowly eroding. In the past, those numerous incidents of violence that have taken place within, and at times between, the various narcotics distribution networks themselves have generally been discriminate and of little media interest. Offenses such as failure to make payments on money owed, skimming of profits, or shorting of loads have often resulted in the torture and deaths of cartel operatives and their individual prison and street gang contractors but it has been kept between individuals involved in the drug trade. In fact, on many occasions, these individuals are kidnapped inside the US and taken back to Mexico for elimination thus taking it further out of the US public eye.[4]

The cartels' policy has since changed due both to a conscious decision on the part of cartel leadership and an inability to maintain control of the various contractors and freelancers that work for the cartel network. This changing orientation can be seen with an increase in firefights pertaining to drug loads coming over the border and 'firebreak events' such as the June 2008 Phoenix incident in which cartel operatives, dressed as tactical officers, assassinated a Jamaican drug dealer and, in their subsequent escape and evasion attempt, set up an ambush with the intent of killing responding US law enforcement officers. In May 2009, it was reported that Joaquin 'El Chapo' Guzman, head of the Sinaloa Cartel (part of The Federation) had, back in March, given standing orders for cartel operatives to protect drug loads against both rival cartels and US law enforcement *with deadly force if required*.[5] The inability to control parts of the narcotics distribution networks can be seen with the vast number of kidnappings now openly taking place in Phoenix, making it the kidnapping capital of the US. Kidnappings are based on the Sinaloan model which originated as a means to collect on drug debts but later expanded to include kidnappings of legitimate businessmen and merchants. These kidnappings, numbering over 700 in 2007 and 2008 according to police reports (though twice that number are thought to go unreported), appear still to be focused on the collection of drug debts but undoubtedly, in some instances, have shifted to individuals not involved with narcotics distribution or use.[6]

The extent to which the narco threat has evolved and matured can be viewed in two tables pertaining to (1) the dominant Mexican cartels that have arisen, their areas of operation, and the enforcers (gang contractors) that they use and (2) US street and prison (Sureños) gangs affiliated with these cartels. Table 1 is pieced together from various sources and is divided into sections representing the four dominant Mexican cartels: The Federation (Sinaloa), Gulf, Juárez, and Tijuana. The power and fortunes of these cartels continually rise and fall and, in fact, their actual number is even disputed with the Mexican government in the past identifying seven drug cartels rather than recognizing The Federation, which is a larger cartel alliance.[7] For our purposes, we will focus on the four cartels listed because of US governmental and other open source information pertaining specifically to them. The areas of influence within Mexico is listed for each of these four cartels along with a listing of the US states where cartel personnel have been identified as operating.[8] It is assumed that these identifications are only of actual cartel personnel and not of US gang contractors as well, but this is unknown since all specific information pertaining to these identifications is restricted. The final column in this table lists the Mexican enforcers of each of these cartels and their gang contractors (*in italics*). From an OSINT (open source intelligence) perspective, this listing is probably the most comprehensive one so far but undoubtedly errors of omission are present.

The four dominant Mexican drug cartels, their enforcers, and affiliated gang contractors are in violent competition with one another for control over narcotics trafficking routes (*plazas*) into the United States and the markets within. Narcotics sales within Mexico, and into Central America with the continual opening of new markets in the countries of that region, are also now a source of strife and competition. In addition, conflict over auxiliary forms of illegal revenue generation including street taxation, extortion, and kidnapping along with human and arms smuggling is also taking place between the various gangs,

Table 1. Federation, Gulf, Juárez, and Tijuana cartels: areas of operations and enforcers.

| Name | Mexico[a] (areas of influence) | United States[b] (personnel reported) | Enforcers (gang contractors)[c] |
|---|---|---|---|
| The Federation (Sinaloa) | Sonora, Chihuahua, Sinaloa, Durango, Coahuila, Nayarit; US Border from Western Arizona to Juarez/El Paso | Arizona, Arkansas, California, Colorado, District of Columbia, Florida, Georgia, Illinois, Indiana, Iowa, Kentucky, Louisiana, Maryland, Massachusetts, Michigan, Mississippi, Missouri, Nebraska, New Jersey, New Mexico, New York, North Carolina, Ohio, Oklahoma, Oregon, Pennsylvania, Rhode Island, Tennessee, Texas, Virginia | Los Negros, Los Numeros (faction), Los Pelones (Ex Mexican Mil), La Gente Nueva (Mexican LE), Los Lobos (US Citizens), Fuerzas Especiales de Arturo (FEDA), *Barrio Azteca (formerly), Mexicles, Artistas Asesinos, La Eme, Sur-13* |
| Gulf | Michoacan, Veracruz, Tamaulipas, Coahuila; US Border East of Juarez/ El Paso to East of Matamoros | Arizona, Florida, Georgia, Illinois, Kentucky, Louisiana, Maryland, Massachusetts, Missouri, Nebraska, New York, North Carolina, Ohio, Oklahoma, Pennsylvania, South Carolina, South Dakota, Tennessee, Texas | Los Zetas (Ex Mexican SF), Kaibiles (Ex Guatemalan SF), La Familia, Grupo Tarasco, Los Numeros (faction), Los Halcones, *Los Zetitas (Loredo gang members), Texas Syndicate, Mexikanemi, MS-13 (El Salvador), Hermanos Pistoleros Latinos (HPL), Tango Blast* |
| Juárez | Chihuahua, Coahuila; US Border Juarez/EL Paso area | Arizona, Colorado, Georgia, Illinois, Indiana, Kansas, Massachusetts, Missouri, Nevada, New Jersey, North Carolina, Ohio, Oklahoma, Oregon, Pennsylvania, Texas, Wyoming | Los Linces (Ex GAFE), La Linea (State & Local LE), *Barrio Azteca (Currently), Sureños, Syndicato de Nuevo Mexico, Mexican Clique Killers* |
| Tijuana | Baja California; US Border from San Diego to East of Mexicali into Western Arizona | Alaska, California, Massachusetts, Minnesota, Nebraska, Nevada, New Jersey, New York, Ohio, Pennsylvania, South Dakota, Washington | *Fuerzas especiales del Muletas (FEM),* Sicarios (Tijuana street gangs), La Eme, Logan Calle 30, 18th Street, Varrio Chula Vista, Sur-13, Wonderboys, Border Brothers |

[a] Guerreo, Chiapas, Tabasco, Campeche, Yucatan, and Quintana Roo disputed between the Federation and Gulf cartels. STRATFOR, *Areas of Cartel Influences,* 2008; US Drug Enforcement Agency information, adapted by Congressional Research Service (P. McGrath, 2 March 2007).
[b] National Drug Intelligence Center, *Situation Report: Cities in Which Mexican DTOs Operate Within the United States,* ID. 2008-S0787–005, 11 April 2008. See document for the specific cities within these states.
[c] Chris Swecker, Ast. Dir. CID, FBI, *Congressional Testimony,* 17 November 2005; E. Eduardo Castillo, 'Mexican attorney general: Drug cartels recruiting hit men in U.S', signonsandiego.com (20 December 2005); Colleen W. Cook, *Mexico's Drug Cartels,* CRIS Report for Congress, RL34215, 16 October 2007: numerous other OSINT sources including STRATFOR.

cartels, and mercenary groups on both sides of the US–Mexican border. Until recently, the Mexican state generally turned a blind eye to the growing power, influence, and military-type capabilities of the cartels and their allies. Numerous political, judicial, law enforcement, and military officials and reporters had been corrupted and/or killed allowing the cartels freedom of action via their doctrine of *¿plata o plomo?* (silver or lead?). Since late 2006, however, open warfare has broken out between the Mexican drug cartels and the state under the Felipe Calderon administration. With the fighting intensifying, President Calderon recently said, 'It's either the narcos, or the state.'[9] Over 10,000 have died in what has basically become a 'free for all', given the wars raging amongst the cartels themselves and between the various cartels and the Mexican state. The violence levels, however, are, in context, still somewhat restrained given the absence of 'car bombs' as were employed by the Medellín cartel against the Colombian state in that conflict decades ago. Highlighting additional concerns about this internal war in Mexico, it was reported in March 2009:

> The biggest and most violent combatants are the Sinaloa cartel, known by U.S. and Mexican federal law enforcement officials as the 'Federation' or 'Golden Triangle,' and its main rival, 'Los Zetas' or the Gulf Cartel … The two cartels appear to be negotiating a truce or merger to defeat rivals and better withstand government pressure. U.S. officials say the consequences of such a pact would be grave.[10]

These two cartels alone are estimated to have fielded over 100,000 foot soldiers, rivaling the Mexican army which numbers about 130,000.[11] Additionally, the forces of these cartels include former special forces personnel and have access to equipment and weaponry which are in many cases far superior to that fielded by the Mexican state.

Table 2 focuses on US prison and street gangs affiliated with the four major Mexican cartels. Only Sureño (southern) gangs with Mexican and Central American cultural origins have been listed because of their identifiable direct ties to the cartels. Prison and street Norteño (northern) gangs, independent Mexican gangs (e.g. the Fresno bulldogs), black, Puerto Rican, white and other ethnicity prison and street gangs, and all forms of motorcycle gangs have been excluded from this table. The reason for this exclusion is that, while these gangs may benefit from narcotics trafficking inside the United States, they are typically one step removed in the distribution networks and act as retail sub-contractors or second order wholesale suppliers of the narcotics.[12] What is apparent from this table is that the Mexican cartels have at their disposal direct linkages to a gang contractor network encompassing tens of thousands of members. This gang wholesale distribution network is controlled by the prison gangs, such as the Mexican Mafia (La Eme) and Barrio Azteca, who have enforced their will and dictates upon numerous Hispanic street gangs in the United States to increase their power and enrich their pockets.

For instance, all gangs which include the number '13' 'M' in their names are subordinate to La Eme. This also includes the local taxation of gang territories

Table 2.    US prison and street (Sureños) gangs affiliated with Sinaloa, Gulf, Juárez, or Tijuana cartels.[a]

| Name | Type | Reach | Size |
|---|---|---|---|
| Barrio Azteca | Prison | National (Texas, SE New Mexico)[b] | 2000 |
| 18th Street | Street | National (44 cities 20 states) & Mexico, Central America[c] | 30,000–50,000 |
| Hermanos de Pistoleros Latinos | Prison | Local (Texas, Mexico) | 1000 |
| Mara Salvatrucha (MS-13) | Street | National (& Mexico, Central America) | 8,000–10,000 (30,000–50,000 The Americas) |
| Mexican Mafia (La Eme) | Prison | Regional (California, Southwest, Pacific areas) | 200 350–400[b] |
| Mexikanemi (Emi) | Prison | Regional (Texas) | 2000 |
| Florencia 13 (F13 or FX13) | Street | Regional (California, 4 other States) | 3000+ |
| Sureños Gangs (Sur-13; includes Avenues, F13) | Street | National (Mostly California) | 50,000–75,000 |
| Tango Blast | Street-Prison | Regional | 14,000+ |
| Texas Syndicate | Prison | Regional (South-West both sides of the border)[b] | 1,300[b] |

[a] National Drug Intelligence Center, *National Drug Threat Assessment 2009*, December 2008 and National Gang Intelligence Center, *National Gang Threat Assessment 2009*, January 2009.
[b] US Department of Justice, *Attorney General's Report to Congress on the Growth of Violent Street Gangs in Suburban Areas*, April 2008.
[c] Via other OSINT.

to extract revenues from legitimate and illicit businesses operating within the gang's turf. Thereby, each of these gang members can in some way be thought of as a 'foot soldier' who, if given a directive by the Mexican Mafia, have the choice of carrying it out or risk having a 'green light' placed on them and being killed.[13] This would mean that both MS-13 and 18th Street members, increasingly under the control of La Eme, in Central America whose cliques are led by original gangsters or OGs (i.e. originally deported Los Angeles gang members) are to some extent still theoretically (and nominally) under the authority of the Mexican Mafia in California. If they did not follow La Eme dictates, their families and fellow 'homies' in the US could suffer severe consequences ranging from intimidation and beatings to rape, torture, and murder. While actual Mexican Mafia influence in Central America is currently in debate, the street and prison gangs are the same in that region. Mara Salvatrucha (MS-13) and 18th Street dominate and do openly show respect to La Eme.

The national security importance of these close relationships between Sureño prison and street gangs and the Mexican drug cartels is that dangerous internal narco-terrorism potentials now exist for the US homeland depending on the orders gang 'foot soldiers' are given. While this might sound highly implausible, if the Mexican drug cartels and the United States government did in fact engage in open conflict with one another, the Mexican Mafia could possibly side with their cartel allies:

> The Mexican Mafia works with allied gangs in the American Southwest to control large swaths of territory along both sides of the U.S.-Mexican border. These gangs are organized to interact directly with traffickers in Mexico and oversee transborder shipments as well as distribution inside the United States.[14]

With its revenue streams and power threatened, La Eme could draw upon its dominance of the Sureño street gangs to provide support to the Mexican cartels. Failure to provide such 'military aid' if requested – even if it is only symbolic and limited in scope – would not only endanger short-term narcotics trafficking operations but also the long-term relationship between these allies.

The Mexican drug cartels thus possess the very real ability to draw either upon their own mercenaries and employed assassins and bring them into the United States to engage in operations against our government or upon allied domestic prison gangs such as the Mexican Mafia. The latter, in turn, can order subordinate '13' street gang 'foot soldiers' to engage in specific insurgent operations (such as the killing of police officers or judges) on their behalf. This capability combined with the tried and true *¿plata o plomo?* (silver or lead?) doctrine utilized in Mexico, and in Colombia decades before, to intentionally undermine and corrupt the workings of government is a volatile mix. If any real intent to stand up to the US government were ever added to it, Pancho Villa's notorious raid into Columbus, New Mexico in 1916 would look like a Sunday picnic.[15]

It is assumed such potentials have been considered by Homeland Security Janet Napolitano. However, her vague focus on a 'trigger point' concerning spillover of narco-violence from Mexico into the United States fundamentally misses the domestic aspects of the narco-insurgency which could very well emerge.[16] As has been outlined earlier, this 'virus' which has taken parts of Mexico and is spreading values incompatible with those of a healthy democracy is growing on both sides of the US–Mexican border and has extended its network into Central America along with enclaves and territories in South America as well.[17] From a theoretical perspective, it represents the fusion and intersection of third phase cartel and third generation gang concerns that John Sullivan and this author have been researching and writing on now for over a decade.[18]

### The illegal economy of Mexican–US (Sureños) gangs, cartels, and mercenaries

The underworld economy that provides revenues and logistical support to the various gang, cartel, and mercenary groups needs to be touched upon. While narco- and gang-economics are far from an exact science since monetary values are at best estimates and – like much of the other information pertaining to these groups – quickly become restricted in nature, figures are available that provide us a rough overview of what financial resources the narco-cartels and their associates have at their disposal and what the underlying workings of these economies entail. These will provide a reality check as we face the age-old dilemma of balancing a tendency to overestimate our adversaries without consequently and more dangerously underestimating them. We struggled throughout the Cold War in seeking to determine the resources and capabilities of the Soviet Union and our understanding of gangs, cartels, and mercenaries and the various relationships between them is far more primitive.[19] The dynamics of this illegal economy can be seen in Table 3.

Some of the specific commodities and activities addressed in Table 3 should be discussed. Narcotics are and continue to be the major source of revenue for the Mexican drug cartels and are estimated to be in the $14–17 billion dollar range, based on a compilation of the various sources listed in Table 3, although given the illicit nature of the industry they could actually be somewhat lower or even much higher. Marijuana is by far the dominant source of narcotics revenue for the cartels followed by cocaine, methamphetamine, and heroin. Marijuana is highly profitable because it is grown in Mexico as well as inside the US in cartel controlled fields generally concentrated in California, Oregon, Washington, and Arizona but with cultivation expanding eastwards. High potency yields, starter plant cloning, and 90-day shortened growth cycles are adding to the marijuana profit margins.[20]

Cocaine and heroin produced in South America is less profitable than marijuana because the revenues have to be shared with third party cartels and traffickers. It is notable that Colombian heroin production is decreasing while Mexican production and purity has recently increased. These two drugs are worth about half of the marijuana trafficking trade, with most of the value in cocaine sales. Cocaine has seen recent shortages in some US cities because of disruptions in distribution all along the transit chain from Colombia through Central America and Mexico and into the United States due to the Mexican government crackdown, nonetheless, demand for cocaine is still relatively high in the US.[21] Heroin use is generally declining in the US and is more prevalent in the eastern states. The Mexican cartels themselves are attempting to better expand their markets in northeastern US cities.[22] This may be challenging because of the lack of Sureño gangs in those cities though MS-13 and 18th Street gang members are found in many pockets within the US and new distribution potentials with Norteño, Puerto Rican, and other gangs may exist.

In the case of methamphetamine trafficking, about $1 billion in sales take place annually with the bulk of the drugs originating in Mexico. One of the vulnerabilities of this trade is the need to constantly obtain the precursor ingredients needed to 'manufacture' or 'cook up' the narcotics. These precursor ingredients, ephedrine and pseudoephedrine, are being obtained by the Mexican cartels throughout the Americas in a cat-and-mouse game of bypassing import restrictions and required sales reporting via massive small scale purchases

Table 3. The illegal economy of Mexican–US (Sureños) gangs, cartels, and mercenaries.

| Commodity/activity | Monetary value (per year) | Location/direction | Participants |
|---|---|---|---|
| Marijuana | $8.5 billion[a] | Mexico to US, US, Mexico | Cartels & gangs |
| Cocaine | $3.9 billion[a] | 3rd country to Mexico to US, 3rd country to Mexico | Cartels (+ Colombian) & gangs |
| Methamphetamine | $1.0 billion[a] | Mexico to US, US (limited), Mexico | Cartels & gangs |
| Heroin | $0.4 billion[a] | 3rd country to Mexico to US, 3rd country to Mexico, Mexico to US, Mexico | Cartels (+ Colombian) &gangs |
| Illegal immigrants | $2 billion (Arizona)[d] | Mexico to US, 3rd country to Mexico to US | Cartels & gangs |
| Illegal weapons | $0.356–0.730 billion[e] | US to Mexico | Cartels, gangs, & mercenaries |
| Illegal bulk $ & laundering / black market peso exchange (BMPE) / other | $8.6 billion in bank notes.[c] | US to Mexico, US to Mexico to 3rd country | Cartels (+ Colombian) |
| Plaza & gatekeeper taxes (*distribution choke points*) | > $1 billion | Mexico to US, US to Mexico | Cartels |
| Street–prison taxation (extortion) | < $1 billion | Mexico & US | Gangs |
| Kidnapping (*including express*) | < $1 billion | Mexico & US | Cartels, gangs, & mercenaries |
| Commodities, load, & monetary theft | < $1 billion | Mexico & US | Cartels, gangs & mercenaries |
| ALL | **$13.8 billion[a]** **$25–$30 billion[b]** **$18–$39 billion** (includes Colombians)[c] | ALL | ALL |

[a] Mark Stevenson, 'Marijuana big earner for Mexico gangs'. Figures from US drug czar John Walters. Heroin value estimated by subtracting other major narcotics from total estimate.

[b] STRATFOR, 'Organized Crime in Mexico'.

[c] National Drug Intelligence Center, *National Drug Threat Assessment 2009*, December 2008. NDIC estimates.

[d] Josh Meyer, 'Blood money flows by wire to Mexico', A12. Arizona Attorney General estimate of the value of illegal immigrants being smuggled into Arizona each year.

[e] Stohl and Tuttle, *The Small Arms Trade in Latin America*, 15. Mexican government study that suggests 2000 guns are crossing into Mexico each day. Monetary range based on gun values from $500 to $1000. Other OSINT sources also utilized, including a review of *all* US HIDTA region reports available via NDIC.

in Mexico and large 'legal' purchases by front companies in South America and even Southeast Asia. Mexican cartel and gang affiliated 'meth labs' have also existed for years on the US side of the border but some debate rages between local law enforcement and federal government agencies concerning the extent of these operations, especially in California, where the majority of these labs now exist.[23] All four of these forms of narcotics are increasingly being marketed, specifically to teenagers and older children, in Mexico itself to boost domestic profits. They are also being sold in Guatemala and other neighboring countries as the Mexican cartels expand into these regions. The value of these markets can be seen in the more than 6000 deaths in Guatemala alone in 2008 likely linked to gang conflict over the lucrative drug trade.[24]

Mexican drug cartel trafficking of illegal immigrants has multiplied since the 1990s and is now worth at least $2 billion in yearly revenues.[25] Initially, the human smuggling or 'Coyote' trade was the work of independent operators who were taxed by the gatekeepers and other cartel personnel. Over the last 15 years or so, cartel personnel and their gang associates have increasingly dominated this lucrative business and now sometimes maximize their profits by utilizing those individuals smuggled in to carry drug loads, such as bales of marijuana, on their person into the US as they cross over the border. With the domination of this trade by the cartels, smuggled individuals now face even higher incidents of physical abuse and rape, extortion for additional sums of money, or ending up as indentured household servants or forced into prostitution.[26]

Other areas of revenue generation are the illegal smuggling of US weapons and bulk sums of money (laundering US narcotics sale proceeds) into Mexico. Middle-men, specialized organizations, and shell laundering businesses in sectors involving large sums of cash, such as casinos, are utilized to make sure that the drug cartel revenues flow back to Mexico and sometimes down to South America. Billions of dollars generated by illegal narcotics sales in, and human trafficking into, the US must flow back to the major Mexican cartels and, in the cases of cocaine and heroin, back to the third party Colombian baby cartels and narcotics funded rebel groups such as FARC (*Fuerzas Armadas Revolucionarias de Colombia*). Expensive luxury items, real estate, and bulk commodities can also be purchased in order to help launder the narcotics proceeds and are then later resold. Ultimately, the goal is to use financial tricks and ploys, like small bank deposits and wire transfers, to legitimize drug proceeds by getting them into the US and other country's financial systems.[27] In the case of illegal weapons smuggling, the US ATF (Alcohol, Tobacco, Firearms, & Explosives) Bureau 'estimates that 90% of the firearms recovered from crime scenes in Mexico originated in the United States', though this figure is now in dispute.[28] The lucrative aspect of the gun trade is due to the fact that Mexico has very strict gun control laws and no private sector gun stores. The estimated value of the illegal weapons trade is in the hundreds of millions of dollars and includes not only handguns but also assault rifles and, in some past incidents, .50 caliber sniper rifles and grenades.[29]

Sustained community taxation undertaken by street gangs in the US and Mexico is estimated to bring in tens, if not hundreds, of millions of dollars each year. Failure to pay results in property damage, injury, torture, and ultimately death to an individual or his or her loved ones. The racketeering conviction against La Eme member Francisco 'Puppet' Martinez is illustrative of the lucrative potentials of this economy. Martinez ran a taxing crew of the Columbia Lil Cycos, an 18th Street clique in Los Angeles, from his prison cell during the late 1990s:

> ... 18th Street cliques offer protection from rival gangs in exchange for kickbacks from illegal street sales of narcotics, fake green cards, passports or driver's licenses ... the Columbia Lil Cycos also tax illegal vendors. The gang takes a cut from people who sell food, anything counterfeit or anything illegal that goes on in the street.[30]

He brought in as much as $40,000 in a good month from this operation.[31] This was a far cry from the $16,000 earned by his Eme carnal (brother) Alex 'Pee Wee' Aguirre each month. He ran a crew of the 57 Chicos clique of the Avenues gang in Los Angeles during this same time period from his prison cell. His camarada (associate) had about 25–30 names on the tax list which included drug dealers, drug houses, body shops, used car dealerships, and barbershops.[32] This same process of community taxation is taking place throughout Sureños gang turf on both sides of the border and, in lieu of cash, payments in the form of barter (cars, guns, jewelry, drugs), and potentially even services, are accepted. In Tijuana, failure to pay 'taxes' on one's business, which can range from $500 to $23,000 a month, results in arson of the establishment or injury or death to the owner's family.[33] A similar process also exists within US and Mexican prisons, which targets unaligned and vulnerable prisoners. In some instances, it may also incorporate revenues generated from male prostitution.

Unlike taxation, which creates a sustained predatory relationship between the gangs and the communities within which they exist, kidnapping and commodity, load, and monetary thefts are normally one-time affairs. Repeated kidnappings of the same individual or the stealing of the same product from the same location, however, may occur if lucrative. Typically, such targets of opportunity are selected although well-planned operations in order to rip off big drug loads and bulk drug profits (large sums of cash) or to kidnap the children of wealthy individuals are not unheard of. These forms of crimes are far more prevalent in Mexico – with thousands of kidnappings per year – than in the US with the exception of Phoenix, Arizona. Kidnappings in Phoenix are well into the hundreds and primarily focused on those involved in the Mexican drug trade as previously mentioned. Most Mexican kidnappings are of the 'express' or 'virtual' type where one's ATM (automated teller machine) account is emptied out or one's relatives pay a small ransom for a kidnapping that was alleged to have happened or is threatened. High end kidnappings have resulted in ransoms being paid in the low tens of millions (topping out at about $30 million) with settled ransoms more often in the $10,000–30,000 range.[34] Failure to pay results in body parts being cut off the victim and sent to family members as an incentive and in some instances, even when payment is made, the kidnapped individual is found murdered or 'disappears'. Another variant is the Los Zetas practice of using the Internet to lure migrants by means of bogus promises of employment and migration offerings. Those who are then kidnapped and can't come up with money for the ransom demands are sent into prostitution, forced (slave) labor camps, or contribute to the black market organ trade by having a kidney removed.[35] Forced participation in the pornography industry, a variant of the prostitution trade, has also been noted.

General commodities theft, other than that of drug loads, was not initially viewed as a revenue generating strategy by the Mexican cartels but in recent years has been gaining increased media attention. The cause for this increase is probably less an intentional diversification of actual cartel income sources, though such claims have been made, but rather the rise of cartel moonlighters and subcontractors acting as entrepreneurs. Off-duty cartel enforcers, drug runners, kidnapper cells, mercenary contractors, and gang contract personnel can make serious money from bulk thefts. These thefts have not only included cars and trucks but also bulk agricultural goods, industrial loads (in one case a 30-ton roll of steel), and millions of gallons of diesel from Pemex pipelines in the state of Veracruz.[36] In addition, unaffiliated individuals, pretending to be cartel or mercenary members engaging in commodities theft confound the situation. Gangs of armed and hooded men will claim to be from such groups as FEDA (*Fuerzas Especiales de Arturo*) or FEM (*Fuerzas especiales del Muletas*) when in fact they are freelance groups. The same form of deceptive activity also applies to armed groups masquerading as police and military units. This potentially becomes even more ominous when actual police and military groups have gone over to the cartels and engage in commodities thefts while in their duty uniforms.[37]

Some useful statistics and insights emerge from this overview of the illegal economy of Mexican and US (Sureños) gangs, cartels, and mercenaries. On the surface, the monetary value of the illegal commodities and activities engaged in by these non-state groups appear relatively small vis-à-vis Mexican governmental budget revenues and especially minor when compared to those of the United States. If $20 billion is a fair estimate of those specific narco- and gang-economies, it represents only about 7.8% of Mexican governmental budget revenues of $257 billion and 0.67% of US governmental budget revenues of $2.98 trillion. Compared to Mexican and US gross domestic products (GDPs) of $1.1 trillion and $14.3 trillion (2008 estimates), narco- and gang-economic values appear almost meaningless.[38] However, this 7.8% of Mexican governmental budget revenues represented by those narco- and gang-economies, the majority of which flows back as revenues to the Mexican cartels, should not be dismissed lightly.

The cause for concern comes when recognizing that Mexican and US governmental revenues must be allocated to the functioning of numerous state institutions and domestic services and public debt servicing. Further, defense expenditures are dominated by the maintenance of conventional military forces well suited to engagements with other nation-states. These conventional force programs are overwhelmingly based on expensive and complicated warships, aircraft, and tank/artillery/missile systems which are of no value in combating domestic narco- and gang-insurgencies.

Additionally, gang, cartel, and mercenary groups do not have huge bureaucracies, domestic programs, or debt-servicing commitments to contend with and field 'foot soldiers' relatively cheaply – outfitting an enforcer with an assault rifle, armor piercing ammo, grenades, and body-armor can be done for less than $2000. If basic training costs are factored in, an effective criminal-soldier can be produced in three to four months time for about $5000. Further, the majority of the personnel belonging to those groups come from disenfranchised and lower socio-economic groups in inner cities, slums, and poor rural villages with minimal basic costs of living. Also, at least in the US, more than a few of the gang families are on public assistance programs.

The Mexican cartels have a large enough free cash flow to allow them to engage in the ongoing corruption of governmental officials and law enforcement and military personnel by means of bribes or enticements of joining the cartels as employees at better rates of pay. This suggests that gang, cartel, and mercenary groups can translate a higher percentage of their economies (group revenues) into 'criminal-insurgent activities' based on diplomacy-corruption (*plata*) and military-like (*plomo*) capabilities than the nation-state 'law enforcement-military' capabilities needed to counter them. The actual efficiency or force multiplier is unknown (whether 1.25 × to 3 × or even higher) but it helps to explain why these threat groups can operate effectively on smaller budgets when compared to overall governmental revenues.

### US engagement in trans-operational environments

A component of the strategic threat that the Mexican cartels and their associated mercenary and gang affiliates pose to the US is the numerous operational environments in the Western Hemisphere in which they are now being engaged. These six trans-operational environments can be viewed in Table 4. These operational environments can be characterized by the environment itself, the location of the physical threat, the narco-opposing force (NARCO-OPFOR), a typology of the criminal-combatants engaged, and the US responding forces. The most basic environment is that of crime taking place within the US. Local and state law enforcement respond to the threats that exist in this environment – threats which are basically low level street and prison gangs and individual members of the Mexican cartels. The next environment type is that of high intensity crime taking place in the US. This threat is derived from more organized entities such as the Mexican cartels themselves and actual drug trafficking gangs who have access to better weapons and employ more sophisticated tactics.

Table 4. Trans-operational environments involving US engagement with Mexican cartels, mercenaries and Sureños gangs

| Operational environment | Crime | High intensity crime | Homeland security (terrorism and insurgency) | Homeland defense (terrorism and insurgency) | Foreign military support (terrorism and insurgency) | Foreign law enforcement support (high intensity crime) |
|---|---|---|---|---|---|---|
| Physical threat location NARCO-OPFOR | United States | United States | United States | United States | Mexico Latin America | Mexico Latin America |
| Criminal-combatant Typology | Street and prison gangs, individual cartel members 1st GEN. gangs, individual members of more advanced gangs or cartels and mercenary groups | Mexican cartels, street and prison gangs 1st–2nd phase cartels, 2nd GEN. gangs | Mexican cartels, Mexican/US street and prison gangs 2nd–3rd phase (emergent) cartels, 3rd GEN. gangs, narco-terrorists, narco-insurgents, narco-mercenaries, criminal-soldiers | Mexican cartels, Mexican/US street and prison gangs 2nd–3rd phase (emergent) cartels, 3rd GEN. gangs, narco-terrorists, narco-insurgents, narco-mercenaries, criminal-soldiers | Mexican and Colombian cartels, Latin American street and prison gangs 1st–3rd phase (emergent) cartels, 3rd GEN. gangs, narco-terrorists, narco-insurgents, narco-mercenaries, criminal-soldiers | Mexican and Colombian cartels, street and prison gangs 1st–3rd phase (emergent) cartels, 2nd GEN. gangs |
| US responding Forces | Local and state law enforcement | Special LE units and task forces and federal law enforcement (DEA, FBI, ATF) | Federal law enforcement (DEA, FBI, ATF), Department Of Homeland Security (DHS) | US Northern Command, US Army North | US Northern Command, US Army North, US Southern Command, US Special Forces | Special LE units and task forces and federal law enforcement (DEA, FBI, ATF) |

Source: ©Counter-OPFOR Corporation, September 2009.

The responding forces are specialized law enforcement units and task forces and federal law enforcement agencies such as the DEA, FBI, and ATF.

The third operational environment is characterized by threats to US homeland security. This is a new environment that has been created in response to the September 11 attacks and is focused on protecting the US from threats of terrorism and insurgency taking place within its borders. The primary responding forces are drawn from federal law enforcement agencies and components of the still relatively new Department of Homeland Security. Some specialized units created by the larger cities, especially New York and Los Angeles, will also be operating in this environment though, from a support and consequence management perspective, all levels of law enforcement and other responder groups will also be involved. The next operational environment is homeland defense support against terrorism and insurgency taking place on US soil. The military corollary to homeland security with the operating environment and response requirements also articulated since the September 11 attacks. The creation of US Northern Command and US Army North are integral components of the federal military response, with these entities presently providing a stability and support and consequence management support role due to *Posse Comitatus*.

The fifth operational environment is found in Mexico and Latin America and pertains to foreign military support. Specifically the US military is providing allied military forces, predominately the Colombian and Mexican militaries, with the training, resources, and hardware necessary to respond to the drug cartels who are waging campaigns of narco-terrorism and narco-insurgency throughout large swaths of Latin America. This response from the US side falls predominantly upon US Northern Command and US Army North in regards to Mexico and US Southern Command and US Special Forces in regards to Latin America. The final operational environment is also primarily found in Mexico and Latin America. It pertains to foreign law enforcement support to allied nations facing what is generally considered to be an operational environment challenged by cartel, mercenary, and gang generated high-intensity crime. Federal law enforcement agencies and specialized law enforcement units, such as Los Angeles based gang task forces, are principally involved in providing this foreign support.

Of concern with regard to the trans-operational environments the US is engaging in is the lack of any form of comprehensive hemispheric strategy coordinating these multiple efforts. Because the threats are principally non-state, criminal, and more networked than hierarchical in nature, they continue to defy US national security perceptions. This should be somewhat of an amazing occurrence given the recent passing of the eighth anniversary of September 11 but ultimately it is not. The US response to the threats posed by the Mexican (and Colombian) cartels and their mercenary and gang associates is being responded to in a federally mandated 'stove pipe' manner. This is the process the US followed for decades during the Cold War – though an overarching strategy existed – and ultimately yielded victory over the Soviet Union. This same process is now being taken into the twenty-first century and applied to very different types of threats. In this new conflict in the Americas, we are still very much in the opening rounds so caution concerning the future is warranted. At the very minimum, the US critically needs an organizing hemispheric strategy to be developed which coordinates the current 'stove pipe' response.[39] More than likely, however, given the fundamentally different nature of the new non-state threats and opposing networks (the NARCO-OPFOR) developing in the Americas, a hemispheric strategy combined with a new process, drawing upon network response capabilities, will be required to meet this new challenge – a war this author views will be fought over humanity's new forms of social and political organization.

## Overview of the work

The work which follows is divided into three major thematic parts. Part 1 focuses on organization and technology use by Sureños gangs, Mexican cartels, and their hired enforcers. The first essay revisits and revises a 1998 article on drug cartel evolutionary processes. The update links a discussion of cartel phases to the better known third gang generation typology and then turns its eye to a discussion of third phase cartel potentials in Mexico. Lastly, it assesses four alternative futures that could take place in Mexico, as well as their cross-border implications for the United States. Of concern are the potentials for broader 'societal warfare' taking place between state and non-state forces over the value system, ideology, and organizational form of the Mexican state. The second contribution provides a detailed military grade operational assessment of the Los Zetas mercenary organization. This private narco army, or freebooter corporation, is the enforcer component of the Gulf Cartel and has made earlier forms of cartel gunmen totally obsolete. An in-depth analysis is undertaken of Los Zetas capabilities and organizational structures with the intent of providing a reference for friendly forces (the 'good guys') to better know thy enemy. From an open source information perspective, this assessment sets the new standard of our understanding of that narco opposing force (NARCO-OPFOR). The third essay provides a review of Sureños-affiliated gang and Mexican cartel member use of social networking sites. Because of the sensitive nature of these topics, little to no publicly available research has been conducted. Patterns of gang and cartel use identified were then compared to more sophisticated Internet use by terrorist groups with similarities and contrasts noted. The essay concludes with a few general observations concerning likely narco Internet use patterns that will emerge.

Part 2 of the work addresses corruptive (silver; *plata*) and coercive (lead; *plomo*) techniques and methods utilized by the Mexican cartels and their allies. The initial essay is a 'no-holds-barred' look at corruption in Mexico. The primary argument developed by the contributor revolves around the contention that '... corruption IS the institution of government in Mexico and that a long line, generations long, of politicians and officials have merely passed beneath the "yoke" of corruption on their way to acquiring personal wealth and accomplishments. Corruption is a mistress to which nearly all of the political elite of Mexico are seduced.' It is little wonder that the rise of powerful drug cartels, with ample revenues and the ability to offer huge bribes with impunity, have overtaxed a Mexican political system already overly ripe with graft and moral bankruptcy. The second contribution provides a detailed and clinical analysis of cartel violence revolving around firefights, raids, and assassinations. Signature tactical events are discussed along with evidence of a shift from cartel gangsterism into 'paramilitary terrorism with guerrilla tactics'. The sections on the militarization of cartel gunmen and the conflict crossing over the US border are especially relevant to the theme of this special issue. The third essay focuses on the heinous acts, specifically torture and beheadings, and their potential links to the *narcocultos* (narco cults) arising in Mexico. An overview of torture and beheadings conducted by the Mexican cartels, their enforcers, and Sureños gangs on both sides of the Rio Grande is provided. It is followed by a detailed overview of the narcocultos that have arisen and their potentials for ritual torture and sacrifice. Such religious practices would bring a new and unwanted dynamic into the drug wars in Mexico. The current conflict could then be expanded from a criminal insurgency into a conflict between traditional value systems and emergent narco-value systems with quasi-religious and cult-like underpinnings.

The third part of the work discusses response strategies directed at the flow of narcotics coming over the US and Mexico border and their subsequent use. The first essay highlights approaches pertaining to counter-supply policies and operations. They target the actual flow of drugs into the US and the narco-trafficking organizations themselves. Further, counter-violence approaches to gangs and related groups will be discussed in that essay. While innovative options may be provided, such as the use of intelligence networks, they will fall under the counter-supply and counter-violence theme. The second essay focuses on counter-demand targeting and concerns itself with traditional, right of center, and left of center perspectives on illegal narcotics use. From these discussions, a blended counter-demand strategy is explored. It is derived from extinguishing user demand, coercing the users, and to some extent fulfilling user demand by the provision of prescription narcotics to 'special status' addicts and by means of limited decriminalization of personal marijuana use. Such a suggested strategy would have its own negative elements and should be considered less of a bad choice than the other, even worse, US counter-demand policy options that exist.

Following the thematic parts of the work, an afterword is then provided which to some extent plays 'devil's advocate' to many of the criminal insurgency focused contributions and counterbalances them with a differing viewpoint. It compares and contrasts the present situation in Mexico to that of Colombia encountered decades ago when it was locked in a fierce and violent struggle with the Medellín and later Cali cartels and leftist guerillas. That essay advocates the position that Mexico is nowhere near as threatened as Colombia once was and that using the terms 'Colombianization' and 'insurgency' would be improper in describing the drug-related violence presently taking place in Mexico. The essay ends by offering core principles that should be used to respond to the 'high intensity crime' taking place in Mexico.

**Notes**

1. While my usage is in the singular, multiple narco-insurgencies are in actuality being waged by the competing cartels and their networks. Taken together they can be broadly viewed as a larger narco-insurgency being directed against the nation-state form in the Western hemisphere. Recent works on this topic include: Brands, *Mexico's Narco-Insurgency and U.S. Counterdrug Policy*; Sullivan and Elkus, 'State of Siege'; Fleming, *Drug Wars*; and Manwaring, *A Contemporary Challenge to State Sovereignty*. For a view of this of threat to the Mexican state written in Spanish, see Menéndez and Ronquillo, *De Los Maras A Los Zetas*.
2. Bunker and Begert, 'Overview: Defending Against Enemies of the State', xli.
3. Ibid., xxvii. While some of these criminal values may sound questionable, Mexico is now thought to be the second largest producer of child pornography in the world according to some estimates. See Guillermoprieto and Lowrey, 'Popping the Balloon Theory'.
4. As far back as the 1970s, the Colombian cartels had sent operatives into the United States to establish cocaine processing labs and create distribution routes. The disappearance and subsequent killing of cartel personnel, contractors, and any other individuals that crossed the cartels on US soil has thus been discretely going on for almost 40 years. According to Chepesiuk, one early group of these assassins was the Palestinos: 'Santacruz employed a group of hit men who were known as the Palestinos, street-tough Colombians who came from Medellin under the leadership of Julio Palestino. The Cali cartel brought the Palestinos to the United States, and they were suspected of being involved in the killing of numerous people in New York, Chicago and Miami.' See Chepesiuk. *Drug Lords*, 55.
5. Meyer, 'Drug Violence May Bleed into the U.S.', A1, A18–19.
6. Quinones, 'America's Kidnapping Capital', A1, A22–23.
7. Cook, Mexico's *Drug Cartels*, 1.
8. For the actual maps which show the locations where the cartel personnel have been identified as operating, go to National Drug Intelligence Center website (http://ndic.gov) and look for the *Situation Report: Cities in Which Mexican DTOs Operate Within the United States*. Note this means that the *La Familia* cartel will not be highlighted even though it has now become a major player in the Mexican drug wars.
9. Luhnow and Millman, 'Mexican Leader Prepares for Bloodier Drug Wars', 6.
10. Carter, 'EXCLUSIVE: 100,000 Foot Soldiers in Mexican Cartels', 1–5.
11. Ibid.
12. This may be an inaccurate assumption on the part of this author but I would rather err on the side of conservatism in defining the gang contractor groups directly linked to the Mexican cartels. Nothing in the open source literature suggests that this assumption is inaccurate but ties to the Latin Kings have been mentioned in other works.
13. My understanding of La Eme influence, organization, and operations is derived from Rafael, *The Mexican Mafia* and Blatchford, *The Black Hand* and some discussions with law enforcement personnel. Historical context was provided by reading Dunn, *The Gangs of Los Angeles*. Specific attention should be paid to the La Eme mandated gang peace meetings that took place in El Salvador Park in Santa Ana in the Summer of 1992 and at Elysian Park, next to Dodger Stadium, in September 1993. Such meetings mark their ascendancy over the Sureño street gangs in their areas of operation.

14. Burton and West, 'When the Mexican Drug Trade Hits the Border', 4.

15. For information on this raid and some thoughts on the current border war, see Jenkins, 'Savage Struggle on the Border: Part II', 27–8, 29–31.

16. Strohm, 'Homeland Security Chief Defines "Trigger Point" for Border Response', 1.

17. It is interesting that, as the Mexican drug cartels move into Central America, they will presumably link up with the MS-13 and 18th Street prison and street gangs – who function as some of their street gang contractors in the US – which have overrun many of those countries already. These gangs are even more vicious than their Los Angeles brethren. One example is an infamous bus massacre in December 2004 in Honduras that killed 27 people (including children). It was masterminded by Rivera Paz, known as 'El Culiche' (The Tapeworm), leader of the MS-13 gang in Honduras and a deported LA gangster. See Vasquez, 'Mexican Drug Cartels Infiltrating Guatemala', 1; Barrett, 'DEA: Mexican Cartels Migrate', 1; and Ellingwood, 'Mexico's Drug War is Pushing Gangs into Guatemala', A1, A18.

18. See Bunker and Sullivan, 'Cartel Evolution', 55–74; Sullivan and Bunker, 'Third Generation Gang Studies', 1–10.

19. Special thanks to Graham Turbiville for reviewing this analysis and providing insights into the many uncertainties that exist when undertaking it. His lessons learned concerning this process when applied to Soviet military capability were invaluable.

20. National Drug Intelligence Center (NDIC), *Domestic Cannabis Cultivation Assessment 2007*.

21. National Drug Intelligence Center (NDIC), 'Cocaine' section of the *National Drug Threat Assessment 2009*.

22. National Drug Intelligence Center (NDIC), 'Heroin' section of the *National Drug Threat Assessment 2009*.

23. National Drug Intelligence Center (NDIC), 'Methamphetamine' section of the *National Drug Threat Assessment 2009* and National Drug Intelligence Center (NDIC), *National Methamphetamine Threat Assessment 2009*.

24. Ellingwood, 'Mexico's Drug War is Pushing Gangs into Guatemala', A1, A18.

25. While there is valid concern that members of entities hostile to the US, reportedly including Hezbollah personnel, have been smuggled in by these groups, it is safe to say that these are rare occurrences.

26. Meyer, 'Cartels Snatch Coyote Trade', A1, A12.

27. National Drug Intelligence Center (NDIC), 'Illicit Finance' section of the *National Drug Threat Assessment 2009*; and Meyer, 'Blood Money Flows by Wire to Mexico', A12.

28. Embassy of the United States: Mexico, 'U.S. – Mexico at a Glance: Law Enforcement at a glance'. A figure disputed by David Kuhn, a military standoff weapons and counter-terrorism expert. The author has reviewed Kuhn's findings based on an analysis of international weapons transfers to the Mexican cartels. Personal communications with David Kuhn, October 2009.

29. Embassy of the United States: Mexico, Bureau of Alcohol, Tobacco, Firearms & Explosives. 'U.S. – Mexico At a Glance: Combating Illicit Firearms'; and Stratfor.com., 'Mexico: Dynamics of the Gun Trade'.

30. del Barco, 'Feds Aim to Dismantle L.A'.s 18th Street Gang'.

31. Winton, 'L.A. Sues 18th Street Gang Members, Seeking Cash Damages for Pico-Union and Westlake neighborhoods'.

32. Blatchford, *The Black Hand*, 2, 135–41.

33. *El Universal*. 'M3 Report: Gulf Cartel Stealing from Pemex Pipelines!'

34. For some dated, yet good baseline data, see Peters, 'Kidnapping Thrives in Mexico'.

35. *NarcoGuerra Times*, 'Zetas Now Harvesting and Marketing Kidneys'.

36. *El Universal*, 'Mexican Trains, Trucks Hijacked in New Crime Wave', Reuters and 'M3 Report: Gulf Cartel stealing from Pemex Pipelines!' The diesel estimate is based on the seventy companies involved that bought the stolen fuel and the average of 3500 gallons per week delivered.
37. A far more common occurrence, however, is the theft of seized narcotics by uniformed Mexican law enforcement and military personnel operating freelance or under cartel authority.
38. US Central Intelligence Agency, *The WORLD FACTBOOK*. Accessed repeatedly in June 2009 for information pertaining to Mexico and the United States.
39. This fits well with the suggestion that the State Department becomes a 'Department of State and Non-State' as part of its reorganization to address the new threats emerging. See Armstrong, 'Hitting Bottom in Foggy Bottom'.

## Bibliography

Armstrong, Matthew. 'Hitting Bottom in Foggy Bottom'. *Foreign Policy Blog* (11 September 2009), http://www.foreignpolicy.com/articles/2009/09/11/hitting_bottom_in_foggy_bottom?page=full (accessed 12 June 2009).

del Barco, Mandalit. 'Feds Aim to Dismantle L.A'.s 18th Street Gang'. *National Public Radio*, n.d., http://www.npr.org (accessed 12 June 2009).

Barrett, Devlin. 'DEA: Mexican Cartels Migrate'. *Atlanta-Journal Constitution* (16 April 2009), 1.

Blatchford, Chris. *The Black Hand*. New York: William Morrow, 2008.

Brands, Hal. *Mexico's Narco-Insurgency and U.S. Counterdrug Policy*. Carlisle, PA: Strategic Studies Institute, US Army War College, May 2009, 1–61.

Bunker, Robert J., and Matt Begert. 'Overview: Defending against Enemies of the State'. In *Criminal-States and Criminal-Soldiers*, ed. Robert J. Bunker. London: Routledge, 2008.

Bunker, Robert J., and John P. Sullivan. 'Cartel Evolution: Potentials and Consequences'. *Transnational Organized Crime* 4, no. 2 (Summer 1998): 55–74.

Burton, Fred, and Ben West. 'When the Mexican Drug Trade Hits the Border'. *Stratefor.com* (15 April 2009): 4

Carter, Sara A. 'EXCLUSIVE: 100,000 Foot soldiers in Mexican Cartels'. *The Washington Times* (Tuesday, 3 March 2009): 1–5.

Chepesiuk, Ron. *Drug Lords: The Rise and Fall of the Cali Cartel, the World's Richest Crime Syndicate*. Wrea Green: Milo Books Ltd, 2007.

Cook, Colleen W. *Mexico's Drug Cartels*. RL34215. Washington, DC: Congressional Research Service, updated 25 February 2008.

Dunn, William. *The Gangs of Los Angeles*. New York: iUniverse, Inc., 2007.

Ellingwood, Ken. 'Mexico's Drug War is Pushing Gangs into Guatemala'. *Los Angeles Times* (4 June 2009), A1, A18.

*El Universal*. 'M3 Report: Gulf Cartel stealing from Pemex Pipelines!'. Translated from *El Universal* (Mexico City) (19 May 2009), http://www.nafbpo.org (accessed 12 June 2009).

Embassy of the United States: Mexico. 'U.S. – Mexico at a Glance: Law Enforcement at a glance'. n.d., http://www.mexico.usembassy.gov (accessed 10 June 2009).

Embassy of the United States: Mexico, Bureau of Alcohol, Tobacco, Firearms & Explosives. 'U.S.–Mexico At a Glance: Combating Illicit Firearms'. February 2009, http://www.mexico.usembassy.gov.

Fleming, Gary. 'Rusty'. *Drug Wars: Narco Warfare in the 21st Century*, A Producers Journal, 2008, http://www.booksurge.com (accessed 12 June 2009).

Guillermoprieto, Alma, and Annie Lowrey. 'Popping the Balloon Theory'. *Foreign Policy* (April 2009), http://www.foreignpolicy.com (accessed 12 June 2009).

Jenkins, Brian Michael. 'Savage Struggle on the Border: Part II'. *HSToday Magazine* (February 2009), 27–8, 29–31.

Luhnow, David, and Joel Millman. 'Mexican Leader Prepares for Bloodier Drug Wars'. *Wall Street Journal* (28 February 2009), 6.

Manwaring, Max G. *A Contemporary Challenge to State Sovereignty: Gangs and Other Illicit Transnational Criminal Organizations in Central America, El Salvador, Mexico, Jamaica, and Brazil*. Security Issues in the Western Hemisphere. Carlisle, PA: Strategic Studies Institute, US Army War College, December 2007, 1–59.

Menéndez, Jorge Fernández, and Víctor Ronquillo. *De Los Maras A Los Zetas*. Mexico City: Editorial Grijalbo, 2006.

Meyer, Josh. 'Cartels Snatch Coyote Trade'. *Los Angeles Times* (23 March 2009), A1, A12.

Meyer, Josh. 'Drug Violence May Bleed into the U.S'. *Los Angeles Times* (6 May 2009), A1, A18–19.

Meyer, Josh. 'Blood money flows by wire to Mexico'. *Los Angeles Times* (8 June 2009), A12.

*NarcoGuerra Times*. 'Zetas now Harvesting and Marketing Kidneys'. 26 July 2009, http://narcoguerratimes.wordpress.com/2009/07/26/zetas-now-harvesting-and-marketing-kidneys/ (accessed 12 June 2009).

National Drug Intelligence Center (NDIC). *Domestic Cannabis Cultivation Assessment 2007*. Jonestown, PA. No. 2007-L0848–001, 26 February 2007, http://www.ndic.gov (accessed 12 June 2009).

National Drug Intelligence Center (NDIC). *Situation Report: Cities in Which Mexican DTOs Operate within the United States*. Jonestown, PA. ID. 2008-S0787–005, 11 April 2008, http://www.ndic.gov (accessed 12 June 2009).

National Drug Intelligence Center (NDIC). *National Drug Threat Assessment 2009*. Jonestown, PA, December 2008, http://www.ndic.gov (accessed 12 June 2009).

National Drug Intelligence Center (NDIC). *National Methamphetamine Threat Assessment 2009*. Jonestown, PA, December 2008, http://www.ndic.gov (accessed 12 June 2009).

Peters, Gretchen. 'Kidnapping Thrives in Mexico'. *The Christian Science Monitor* (17 September 2002).

Quinones, Sam. 'America's Kidnapping Capital: Mexican Drug Gangs Bring Abduction Epidemic to Phoenix'. *Los Angeles Times* (12 February 2009), A1, A22–3.

Rafael, Tony. *The Mexican Mafia*. New York: Encounter Books, 2007.

Reuters. 'Mexican Trains, Trucks Hijacked in New Crime Wave'. 29 May 2009, 7:43 a.m.

Stevenson, Mark. 'Marijuana big earner for Mexico gangs'. *USA Today* (21 February 2008).

Stohl, Rachel, and Doug Tuttle. *The Small Arms Trade in Latin America*. Washington, DC: Center for Defense Information. March/April 2008.

Stratfor.com. 'Mexico: Dynamics of the Gun Trade'. 24 October 2007.

*Stratfor.com*. 'Organized Crime in Mexico'. 11 March 2008.

Strohm, Chris. 'Homeland Security Chief Defines "Trigger Point" for Border Response'. *Congress Daily* (20 March 2009), 1.

Sullivan, John P., and Robert J. Bunker. 'Third Generation Gang Studies: An Introduction'. *Journal of Gang Research* 14, no. 4 (Summer 2007): 1–10.

Sullivan, John P., and Adam Elkus. 'State of Siege: Mexico's Criminal Insurgency'. *Small Wars Journal* (19 August 2008): 1–12.

US Central Intelligence Agency. *The WORLD FACTBOOK*. n.d., http://www.cia.gov (accessed 12 June 2009).

Vasquez, Patzy. 'Mexican Drug Cartels Infiltrating Guatemala'. cnn.com (5 December 2005), 1.

Winton, Richard. 'L.A. Sues 18th Street Gang Members, Seeking Cash Damages for Pico-Union and Westlake Neighborhoods'. *Los Angeles Times* (9 December 2008).

# Cartel evolution revisited: third phase cartel potentials and alternative futures in Mexico

Robert J. Bunker[a] and John P. Sullivan[b]

[a]Counter-OPFOR Corporation, Claremont, CA, USA; [b]Center for Advanced Studies on Terrorism (CAST), Los Angeles, CA, USA

Drug Trafficking Organizations (DTOs) – commonly called drug cartels – are challenging states and their institutions in increasingly brutal and profound ways. This is seen dramatically in Mexico's drug wars and the expanding reach of Mexican organized criminal enterprises throughout Latin America and other parts of the world. This essay updates a 1998 paper 'Cartel Evolution: Potentials and Consequences' and examines current cartel and gang interactions. The paper links discussion of cartel phases to gang generations; updates and applies the discussion of third phase cartel potentials to Mexico; and assesses four alternative futures for Mexico, as well as their cross-border implications for the United States.

Mexico's drug wars are fertile ground for seeking an understanding of criminal insurgency and the potentials for narco-democracy, or even criminal-state successor, emergence within that country. Mexico and the cross-border region that embraces the frontier between Mexico and the United States are embroiled in a series of interlocking criminal insurgencies.[1] These criminal insurgencies result from the battles for dominance of the 'plazas' or corridors for the lucrative transshipment of drugs into the United States. The plazas such as Tijuana, Ciudad Juárez, and Nuevo Laredo have been the focal points of numerous killings and gun battles.

The cartels battle among themselves and with the police and the military. They have enlisted the support of numerous local and transnational gangs and criminal enterprises including *Mara Salvatrucha* (MS-13), 18th Street, *Los Negros*, and *La Linea*. Corrupt officials fuel the violence, communities are disrupted by constant onslaught of violence, and alternative social structures emerge. Along the border with the US and now deep inside the homeland, cartel operatives and their allies travel freely and have set up a network of stash and safe houses, methamphetamine manufacturing labs, and large expanses of cultivated fields of marijuana protected, in many cases, by snipers and booby-traps. Prison gangs – like *Eme*, the Mexican Mafia, *Emi*, Mexikanemi, Barrio Azteca, and the Texas Syndicate – also play pivotal roles in the allocation of force and influence. The Mexican Mafia alone is able to influence 50,000 to 75,000 members of the Sur-13 street gangs.[2]

Drug cartels are the principal form of organized criminal enterprise that is challenging the Mexican state. They are working in tandem with prison and street gangs and mercenaries to further their agendas. In the process, these cartels and their allies have created 'lawless zones' or criminal enclaves. Examining cartel evolution can help illuminate the challenges to the Mexican state and civil governance posed by criminal gangs and cartels. The authors looked at cartel evolution and related destabilizing potentials in a 1998 paper 'Cartel Evolution: Potentials and Consequences'. [3] That original analysis will be updated in this essay, linked to gang generation research, cartel phase interrelationships with gang generations, and some indications of third phase cartel emergence in Mexico. It will conclude with a discussion of four alternative futures that may come to pass for the drug cartels and the Mexican state as an outcome of the current criminal insurgency now taking place and their implications for the United States.

**Phases of cartel evolution**

In earlier cartel research, three evolutionary phases have been identified (Figure 1).[4] The first two of these phases represent historical patterns of cartel evolution, and the third phase, at that time, represented a projection of cartel evolutionary potentials. For some time, concern has existed that drug cartels, and also some street gangs, have been expanding their reach and morphing into new war-making entities capable of challenging the legitimacy and even the solvency of nation-states. This potential brings life to the prediction made by Martin van Creveld who noted, 'In the future, war will not be waged by armies but by groups whom today we call terrorists, guerrillas, bandits and robbers, but who will undoubtedly hit upon more formal titles to describe themselves.'[5] Such perceptions are in line with one of this work's authors' contentions that a 'War over [human] social and political organization' is taking place as the state transitions into postmodern forms.[6]

During episodes of epochal change, competing state form types, both legitimate (based on the then dominant form) and illegitimate or criminal (based on competitor organizational forms), engage in a conflict that will determine how people ultimately will live and organize themselves and the value and ideological systems that they will hold. Such an epochal war is well underway, with drug cartels representing one of the competitor forms that have emerged. Other competitor forms include the al Qaeda (radical Sunni) and Hezbollah-Iranian (radical Shi'a) religious insurgencies that are currently taking place.

In 'Cartel Evolution: Potentials and Consequences', three cartel phases were identified. The first phase cartel, a hierarchical 'aggressive competitor', and the

| 1st phase cartel<br>**Aggressive competitor** | 2nd phase cartel<br>**Subtle co-opter** | 3rd phase cartel<br>**Criminal state<br>successor** |
|---|---|---|
| Medellín model | Cali model | Ciudad del<br>Este/netwarrior model |
| Hierarchical limited<br>transnational and<br>inter-enterprise links<br>emerging internetted<br>organization | Local (domestic) internetted<br>organization emerging<br>transnational and<br>inter-enterprise links | Global internetted<br>organization evolved<br>transnational and<br>inter-enterprise links |
| Indiscriminate violence | Symbolic violence<br>corruption | Discriminate violence<br>Entrenched corruption<br>(legitimized) |
| Criminal use and provision | Transitional (both criminal<br>and mercenary) use | Mercenary use and<br>provision |
| Conventional technology<br>use and acquisition | Transitional technology use<br>and acquisition | Full spectrum technology<br>use, acquisition and<br>targeting |
| Entrepreneurial limited<br>economic reach | Semi-institutionalized<br>widening economic reach | Institutionalized global<br>economic reach |
| Small Scale Public Profiting | Regional Public Profiting | Mass Public Profiting |
| Limited 'product' focus | Expanding 'product' focus | Broad range of<br>products/activities |
| Criminal entity<br>Emerging netwarrior | Transitional entity<br>Nascent netwarrior | New warmaking entity<br>Evolved netwarrior |

Figure 1.   Phases of cartel evolution.
Source:     Bunker and Sullivan, 'Cartel Evolution'.

second phase cartel, an Internetted 'subtle-co-opter', already existed. Respectively, they provide direct and indirect challenges to the solvency of nation-state institutions. A third phase cartel, a potential 'criminal state successor' was postulated as a future variant. This would be a virtual narco- or criminal-state (kleptocracy). A third phase cartel would occupy a dominant position within a network of TCOs (transnational criminal organizations); that is, it would have gained legitimacy or political influence within the network of state actors and would use and provide mercenaries. This criminal state successor, emerging as a criminal free-state or enclave, may assert itself as a new warmaking entity, challenging contemporary nation-states. The contemporary dynamics of cartel evolution suggest this form indeed may be emerging. Drug cartel evolutionary phases are described as follows:

### First phase cartel (aggressive competitor)

The first phase cartel form originated in Colombia during the 1980s and arose as an outcome of increasing US cocaine demand. This type of cartel, characterized by the Medellín model, realized economies of scale not known to the individual cocaine entrepreneurs of the mid-1970s. This early cartel was an aggressive competitor to the Westphalian state because of its propensity for extreme violence and willingness to challenge the authority of the state directly.

The Medellín model, pioneered by Pablo Escobar, was hierarchical and revolved around Escobar as the kingpin. While other prominent figures maintained their own trafficking operations, they were subordinate to Escobar. This cartel form levied 'cocaine export taxes' on the other major traffickers and by early 1990 initiated 'war taxes' in a life-and-death struggle against the Colombian state.[7] This cartel phase possessed very limited transnational and inter-enterprise links. Structurally, while emerging Internetted channels were apparent, a small leadership cadre dominated this first phase cartel form. Technology use and acquisition by this cartel was conventional in nature. Economic and product limitations on the first phase cartel handicapped its operations. The profits it generated specifically enriched the cartel bosses, their families and retainers, and a few of the local populace in the cartel's immediate sphere of influence. At best, public profiting from the cocaine trade was small scale in nature even with the *apuntada* (stake) system that secretly benefited many of Medellín's elites.

In retrospect, the Medellín model represented a very successful, albeit short-lived, form of criminal entity. Its leadership, while tactically and operationally proficient, was strategically ignorant. Their attempt at directly taking on a Westphalian state, politically and militarily, was both organizationally and individually suicidal as witnessed by the successful decapitation of the top Medellín leadership ranks by governmental forces in the early 1990s. Against the resources and legitimacy of the Colombian state, this emerging netwarrior ultimately was crushed.

### Second phase cartel (subtle co-opter)

The second phase cartel form also originally developed in Colombia, but in this instance was centered on the city of Cali. Unlike their Medellín counterparts, the Cali Cartel was a shadowy organization, and the actual kingpins remained as anonymous as possible. Its organization was more distributed and network-like, relying on terrorist-like cell structures, rather than being hierarchical. Many of its characteristics and activities were dispersed and stealth-masked, which yielded many operational capabilities not possessed by the first phase cartel form. Specifically, it possessed leadership clusters that are more difficult to identify and target with a decapitation attack.

The Cali Cartel was also more sophisticated in its criminal pursuits and far more likely to rely upon corruption, rather than violence or overt political gambits, to achieve its organizational ends. While the majority of the Cali organization was localized in Colombia and the United States, it established increasing transnational and inter-enterprise links to the Russian and Mexican mafias and other groups. This cartel form has also spread to Mexico with the rise of the Mexican Federation, an alliance of the 'big four' mafias based in Tijuana, Sonora, Juárez, and the Gulf. This dynamic is still evolving.

A key difference between the Medellín and Cali models is their respective orientation towards the use of violence. The Cali mafia was far less prone to violence than the Medellín group, and when violence was used, it was more discriminate. Violence thus assumes a more symbolic nature, which, on the surface, makes this cartel form appear to be less of a threat to the Westphalian state than a first phase cartel. In actuality, the threat is more sophisticated and insidious. It relies upon a subtle co-opting approach, wherein premeditated narco-corruption literally erodes the institutions of the state, destroying social and political bonds and relationships. This pattern of narco-corruption is also becoming increasingly advanced in contemporary Mexico where many state institutions have been compromised, allowing this cartel form to graft itself onto pre-existing state structures.

The second phase cartel form is potentially a transitional form as seen in its reliance upon enforcer and operational personnel, such as the Zetas, demonstrating a shift away from mere criminals toward true specialized mercenaries.[8] This cartel phase is also more adaptive in its use of technology and diverse in its range of criminal enterprise. For example, in Mexico, where the cocaine trade was foreshadowed by marijuana and heroin smuggling, synthetic drug products, specifically 'meth' (methamphetamine), have been heavily exploited, transforming the cartels into poly-drug syndicates. While this 'Cali model' represents a far more successful and robust organizational form than the earlier Medellín form, it is a transitional entity. Essentially, the second phase cartel is still a nascent netwarrior.

### Third phase cartel (criminal state successor)

Third phase cartels, if and when they emerge, have the potential to pose a significant challenge to the modern nation-state and its institutions. A third phase cartel is a consequence of unremitting corruption and co-option of state institutions. While this 'criminal state successor' has yet to emerge, warning signs of its eventual arrival are present in many states worldwide. Of current importance to the United States are the conditions favoring narco- or criminal-state evolution in Mexico. Indeed, the criminal insurgency in Mexico could prove to be the genesis of a true third phase cartel, as Mexican cartels battle among themselves and the state for dominance. Essentially, third phase cartels rule parallel polities or criminal enclaves, acting much like warlords.

Thus far, Mexico has not developed into a kleptocracy, but the potential for a 'parallel state'[9] is there, with politicians co-opted by drug syndicates essentially creating a 'state within the Mexican State'.[10] As noted in the 1998 precursor to this essay:[11]

> The majority of Mexican cartels (Gulf, Tijuana, etc.) are seizing political control through co-option rather than emerging as competitors to the state (as in the example of Colombia's Medellín cartel). This allows the cartels to exert greater influence within segments of the 'government.' Rather than being a competitor for political-economic dominance, the cartels seek avenues for enabling their activities. Co-option and corruption are thus aimed at removing the cartels from the limits of state sovereignty. Such corruption and distortion of the state, where criminal organizations are fused to the existing state hierarchy like a parasite or gain local dominance within an exiting state, can potentially lead to the emergence of the third phase cartel acting as a criminal free state or enclave.

Mexico is currently in the thralls of a significant drug war. Since President Calderon's 2006 crackdown on Mexico's four major cartels, the cartel landscape has become increasingly complicated and is stimulating shifts in cartel organization. Prior to the crackdown, four main criminal enterprises dominated the landscape: Tijuana (Arellano-Felix) Cartel, Sinaloa Cartel, Juárez Cartel, and the Gulf Cartel. They fought primarily among themselves. Now they wage war on the state and its security forces as well. Three years into the conflict:

> new armed groups are springing up as the heightened attention has forced old cartels to splinter and evolve. The nascent cartels are ruthless, skilled in military tactics, adept at psychological warfare and eager to expand beyond drug smuggling into other criminal enterprises including extortion, kidnappings for ransom and even software piracy.[12]

Los Zetas and La Familia represent two of these newer and more violent entities.

**Early third phase cartel emergence**

A third phase cartel would dominate a political space such as a criminal enclave, parallel state, or polity – essentially ruling a physical or virtual lawless zone. Criminal enclaves, in many senses, pre-date the emergence of an actual third phase cartel. The earliest development of a viable contemporary criminal enclave was seen in the South American jungle at the intersection of three nations. Ciudad del Este, in Paraguay, is the center of this criminal near free state. Paraguay, Brazil, and Argentina converge at this riverfront outpost. A jungle hub for the world's worst of the worst, a global village of outlaws; the triple border zone is essentially a free enclave for significant criminal activity. Denizens of the enclave include Lebanese gangsters and terrorists, drug smugglers, Nigerian gangsters, and Asian mafias, including the Japanese Yakuza, Tai Chen (Cantonese mafia), Fuk Ching, the Big Circle Boys, and the Flying Dragons. This polyglot mix of thugs demonstrates the potential of criminal netwarriors to exploit the globalization of organized crime.[13]

The blurring of borders – a symbol of the postmodern, information age – is clearly demonstrated here, where the mafias exploit interconnected economies. With the ability to overwhelm governments weakened by corruption and jurisdictional obstacles, the mafias of Ciudad del Este and its Brazilian twin city of Foz do Iguacu demonstrate remarkable power and reach. Terrorism interlocks with organized crime in the enclave, a postmodern free city that is a haven to Middle Eastern terrorists, a hub for the global drug trade, a center of consumer product piracy, and a base for gunrunners diverting small arms (from the US) to the violent and heavily armed drug gangs in the *favelas* of Rio de Janeiro and São Paulo.

The convergence of cartel evolution and the manifestation of Internetted criminal enterprises is so pronounced in this enclave, we called the third phase cartel the Ciudad del Este model.[14] The transnational criminal organizations here demonstrate the potential for criminal networks to challenge state sovereignty and gain local dominance. Such a networked 'enclave', or a third phase cartel embracing similar characteristics, could become a dominant actor within a network of transnational criminal organizations, and potentially gain legitimacy or at least political influence within the network of state actors. Mexico's current battle for the 'plazas' may be an early manifestation of criminal enclave formation on the doorstep of the US – we touch more on this later in this essay.

## Gang generations

Transnational gangs are another state challenger. They are a concern throughout the Western Hemisphere. Criminal street gangs have evolved to pose significant security and public safety threats in individual neighborhoods, metropolitan areas, nations, and across borders. Such gangs – widely known as *maras* – are no longer just street gangs. They have morphed across three generations through interactions with other gangs and transnational organized crime organizations (e.g., narcotics cartels/drug trafficking organizations) into complex networked threats.[15]

Transnational *maras* have evolved into a transnational security concern throughout North and Central America. As a result of globalization, the influence of information and communications technology, and travel/migration patterns, gangs formerly confined to local neighborhoods have spread their reach across neighborhoods, cities, and countries. In some cases, this reach is increasingly cross-border and transnational. Current transnational gang activity is a concern in several Central American states and Mexico (where they inter-operate with cartels).[16]

Transnational gangs can be defined as having one or more of the following characteristics:

(1) criminally active and operational in more than one country;
(2) criminal operations committed by gangsters in one country are planned, directed, and controlled by leadership in another country;
(3) they are mobile and adapt to new areas of operations;
(4) their activities are sophisticated and transcend borders.[17]

| limited | *politicization* | evolved |
|---|---|---|

| local | *internationalization* | global |
|---|---|---|

| first generation | second generation | third generation |
|---|---|---|
| [#] | | |
| turf gang | drug gang | mercenary gang |
| turf protection | market protection | power/financial acquisition |
| [#] | | |
| proto-netwarrior | emerging netwarrior | netwarrior |

| *less sophisticated* | *sophistication* | *more sophisticated* |
|---|---|---|

Figure 2.    Characteristics of street gang generations.
Source:      Sullivan, 'Third Generation Street Gangs'.

The gangs most frequently mentioned in this context are *Mara Salvatrucha* (MS-13) and 18th Street (M-18), both originating in the *barrios* of Los Angeles. In order to understand the potential reach and consequences of transnational *maras,* it is useful to review third generation gang theory.

Traditionally viewed as criminal enterprises of varying degrees of sophistication and reach, some gangs have evolved into potentially more dangerous and destabilizing actors. A close analysis of urban and transnational street gangs shows that some of these criminal enterprises have evolved through three generations – transitioning from traditional turf gangs, to market-oriented drug gangs, to a new generation that mixes political and mercenary elements.

The organizational framework for understanding contemporary gang evolution first was explored in a series of papers starting with the 1997 article 'Third Generation Street Gangs: Turf, Cartels, and Netwarriors'.[18] In these papers, it was postulated that gangs could progress through three generations, influenced by three factors: *politicization, internationalization,* and *sophistication.* This gang form – the 'third generation' gang – entails many of the organizational and operational attributes found with net-based triads, cartels, and terrorist entities. The characteristics of all three generations of gangs are summarized in Figure 2.

The three generations of gangs can be described as follows:

- *Turf: First generation gangs* are traditional street gangs with a turf orientation. Operating at the lower end of extreme societal violence, they have loose leadership and focus their attention on turf protection and gang loyalty within their immediate environs (often a few blocks or a neighborhood). When they engage in criminal enterprise, it is largely opportunistic and local in scope. These turf gangs are limited in political scope and sophistication.

- *Market: Second generation gangs* are engaged in business. They are entrepreneurial and drug-centered. They protect their markets and use violence to control their competition. They have a broader, market-focused, sometimes overtly political agenda and operate in a broader spatial or geographic area. Their operations sometimes involve multi-state and even international areas. Their tendency for centralized leadership and sophisticated operations for market protection places them in the center of the range of politicization, internationalization, and sophistication.

- *Mercenary/political: Third generation gangs* have evolved political aims. They operate – or seek to operate – at the global end of the spectrum, using their sophistication to garner power, aid financial acquisition, and engage in mercenary-type activities. To date, most third generation (3 GEN) gangs have been primarily mercenary in orientation; yet, in some cases they have sought to further their own political and social objectives. A shift from simple market protection to power acquisition is characteristic of third generation activity. A key indicator of gang evolution is internationalization. Transnational gangs in Los Angeles and on the border have been notable in this regard. Cross-border gangs are one consequence of this evolution. The mercenary foray of San Diego's 'Calle Treinta' gang into the bi-national orbit of the Arellano-Felix (Tijuana) cartel is a notable example. Third generation gangs can be considered netwarriors, and networked organizational forms contribute to the rise of non-state or criminal-soldiers.[19]

### Impact of transnational 'third generation' gangs (*maras*)

Like their more sophisticated cartel counterparts, third generation gangs challenge state institutions in several ways. Naval Postgraduate School analyst Thomas Bruneau, paraphrased below, describes five (multi-)national security threats or challenges associated with transnational *maras:*[20]

- They *strain government capacity* by overwhelming police and legal systems through sheer audacity, violence, and numbers.
- They *challenge the legitimacy of the state*, particularly in regions where the culture of democracy is challenged by corruption and reinforced by the inability of political systems to function well enough to provide public goods and services.
- They *act as surrogate or alternate governments*. For example, in some regions (i.e., El Salvador and Guatemala) the 'governments have all but

given up in some areas of the capitals, and the *maras* extract taxes on individuals and businesses.'

- They *dominate the informal economic sector*, establishing small businesses and using violence and coercion to compete unfairly with legitimate businesses while avoiding taxes and co-opting government regulators.
- They *infiltrate police and non-governmental organizations* to further their goals and, in doing so, demonstrate latent political aims.

These factors can be seen graphically in the battle for control of the drug trade in Mexico and can as accurately be applied to the drug cartels themselves as to the *maras*. While Mexico is frequently considered in this light, Mexican cartels and transnational gangs are a destabilizing influence throughout Latin America, and indeed have spread their reach to at least 47 nations abroad.[21] The impact of transnational gangs is particularly acute in Guatemala where MS-13 and 18th Street dominate the local criminal opportunity space, trade with Mexican cartels (including the Zetas and their Guatemalan counterparts the Kaibiles), and hold communities in thrall to their extreme violence. The penetration of organized crime in Guatemala adds a particularly combustive fuel to a mix that includes exceptionally high levels of inequality, very limited opportunities for a large marginalized youth, and the troubling inheritance of a four-decade-long civil war.[22] In some senses, there is a great risk that Guatemala may become subsumed by the criminal 'parallel state' and become a comprehensive criminal enclave.

### Cartel phase interrelationships with gang generations

While both cartel phase and gang generation research have existed for over a decade now, few attempts have been made up to this point to fully link their interrelationships with one another. This is due to the fact that, while gang generation research has flourished, cartel phase research has not. Gang generation research has benefited not only from the continuation of writings by Sullivan, but has also seen Manwaring, Bruneau, Haussler, Bunker, and recently Brands involved in its further development.[23] Cartel phase research, on the other hand, has been noted occasionally in works by Bunker and Sullivan and utilized in a work by Fatic but has not significantly been revisited or further developed.[24] Therefore, this current effort should be considered an exploratory attempt at linking cartel and gang evolutionary interrelationships together.

First phase cartels based on the Medellín model, and functionally obsolete in the Western Hemisphere, died out as an organizational form decades ago because as an 'aggressive competitor' it simply attempted to engage a legitimate state head on. In such a rather simplistic and bloody conflict, the cartel was no match for the raw physical power of the Colombian state. This early cartel phase had at its disposal the resources of what can be considered allied or affiliated first and second generation gangs. The first generation gangs found in Medellín could offer no more than side drug sales (individual retail) and some minimal local (*barrio*) intelligence gathering to this cartel. The majority of street toughs and thugs comprising these basic gangs, who focused on maintaining their turf, were unsophisticated criminals and feared not only cartel enforcers but also the local police. They certainly had no desire to get mixed up in a direct clash between the Medellín Cartel and the Colombian state. Still, many local assassins or *sicarios* were recruited from these very ranks.[25] In most instances, these unsophisticated criminals were provided basic weapons (pistols) and transportation (scooters) by the cartel to engage in their hits.

The second generation, or drug gangs, found in Medellín were more sophisticated and market driven in nature, with the gangs themselves engaging in both retail and some wholesale drug sales. Since these gangs were focused on developing and protecting drug markets, they were far better funded, organized, and armed than the first generation gangs. They represented more sophisticated barrio foot soldiers who could better augment and support Medellín Cartel enforcers. These gang members thus had better opportunities to become cartel contractors, or actual employees, and generally became better educated in their business and coercive practices by their association with Medellín personnel, although the model promoted by Escobar and the other kingpins was one of sheer force and terror – the indiscriminate use of a mailed glove backed up by clumsy attempts at diplomacy, blatant politicking, and the ineffective and limited use of corruption.

Second phase cartels, based on the Cali and later Mexican cartel model, represented the next phase in the evolutionary progression of drug cartels. This cartel phase, known as that of the 'subtle co-opter', is more balanced and nuanced in its strategies and criminal approaches. The cartel form burrows into society and government by means of unrelenting corruption backed up by the discriminate and targeted use of force. Manwaring expands on this 'cocktail mix' process, first described by the authors, which is able to '... challenge the de jure security and sovereignty of a given nation'.[26] The relationship of the Cali Cartel to the first generation gangs in this instance appears not to be much different than that of the Medellín Cartel – though little interest would exist in using unsophisticated and unreliable turf gang members as cartel enforcers. It is far better to utilize them as neighborhood lookouts that could augment the impressive Cali intelligence apparatus. This apparatus utilized taxi cab networks, corrupted officials, and the ability to statistically determine opposing Colombian government activities by means of sophisticated analysis of phone and other records derived from the use of an actual IBM AS/400 super-computer.[27] With shadowy and out of the limelight bosses sporting monikers like 'The Chess-player' and 'El Señor', the Cali organization relied far more upon its brains than on the barrel of a gun. The subsequent influence on the drug gangs in its areas of operation would be to mandate a more discriminate use of force – unnecessary violence draws unwanted attention and is bad for business. It is far better to co-opt a local police officer than kill him and throw him into a ditch, though some brutal beheadings and chainsaw killings transpired and were used selectively to further cartel business. Actual mercenary use and provision arose during this era but was still somewhat constrained in its size and impact.

Much of the Cali model, given its great success, helped to influence the Mexican drug gangs and groups involved in the transshipment of Colombian cocaine through Mexico into the US. These, and similar groups, were the ones that would later evolve in the larger Mexican cartels. Where Colombia and Mexico greatly differ, however, is in the size and scope of second phase cartel operations and societal reach. Cali is but one city in Colombia and, while the Cali Cartel had some influence and reach into other Colombian cities and transnational linkages into numerous other countries, even deploying hit men in the US, the operational space it maneuvered in was much smaller than that occupied by the Mexican cartels.[28] Some basic statistics suggest that Mexico now has over 1500 of its cities infiltrated by the cartels[29] and 450,000 individuals directly working in jobs related to drug trafficking and cultivation.[30] If this number were multiplied by 4.5, which would yield an average family size in Mexico, then over 2,000,000 individuals (workers and their dependents) would benefit directly from narco related activities. If the expanded economic influence of this activity, the purchasing of goods and services by the narco families from others in Mexican society, were then factored in, the mass societal profiting would be even larger. If every individual who is directly benefiting from narco profits is multiplied by 1.6 (a typical output multiplier), to reflect expanded narco economic influence, then an estimated 3,200,000 individuals in Mexican society are now dependent on narcotics trafficking for their livelihood. It is unknown if the endemic bribery of law enforcement, judges, and governmental officials (at all levels) has been factored into the drug trafficking numbers. Also the various cartel, mercenary, and gang networks are involved in numerous other economic activities – from street taxation, kidnapping, and extortion through bulk thefts and human trafficking. Whether the individuals involved in these criminal pursuits are being factored into the 450,000 baseline is unknown. Probably this is not the case with regard to gang taxation of street vendors, businesses, and many of the other economic activities peripheral to narcotics trafficking. What these very basic and rough numbers suggest is the reach and penetration of the second phase cartels and their gang affiliates into Mexican society is significant and on a magnitude not witnessed in Colombia with either the first phase Medellín Cartel or the more evolved and successful second phase Cali Cartel.

Still, Mexican cartel relationships with first and second generation gangs appear to follow the Cali model. First generation gangs are of little utility other than providing the occasional promising recruit and functioning as street intelligence as in the case of *Las Ventanas* (teen informants on bicycles) utilized by the Zetas. Drug gang members, on the other hand, have some smarts, are a bit more disciplined, already view the drug trade as a business, and also tend to be older and more mature. These gang members can function as dealers, protect the local drug markets, and possibly even serve as contract enforcers. More dedicated and dependable members of these gangs will be recruited and trained by the cartels to function as actual foot soldiers, bodyguards, or take on other roles. Third generation gangs have power in their own right with their transnational links, mercenary-like perspectives, and ability to generate money via street taxation and other means. While probably not quite on par with a second phase cartel, such as the Tijuana Cartel because of its immense wealth and sophistication, a group like the Mexican Mafia or MS-13 would not be totally in a subordinate and subservient role. This is especially true given the fact that if a Mexican cartel member is extradited or captured in the US and faces prison time, he will be looking to those and similar groups to ensure his personal safety.

Probably of more interest now are the developing roles and relationships between third generation gangs and what could be emerging third phase cartel characteristics, or actual third phase cartel elements, in Mexico. In many ways, a process of collinear evolution is now taking place. As has been seen, a certain segment or percentage of gangs, cartels, terrorists, and other non-state threats are all evolving into more and more capable and deadly entities. While the majority of such groups remain in their steady state, devolve, die off, or are absorbed by other groups, a select subset of others will naturally evolve. This process will of course be compressed in 'wartime' as is being witnessed by the conflict environment now evident in Mexico and in other contested regions of Latin America such as Guatemala. As third generation *mara* groups, such as MS-13 and 18th Street, continue to come into contact with and create linkages to the various second phase and emergent third phase Mexican cartels, it is expected that they will influence those cartels and, in turn, be influenced even more greatly by them. While some scholars have recognized 'gangs as primitive states',[31] this very primitiveness, in relationship to the more organized drug cartels, means that the less evolved entity will gain more in its transactions with the more evolved one.

A similar process of cross-pollination has existed for decades between and among terrorist groups with the more advanced organizations and nodes tutoring the less sophisticated ones. This has been noted with both the use of weaponry and the use of tactics and is one reason why IRA members have been found providing training to insurgents in Colombia and why al Qaeda terrorist cells from dozens of countries and cultures now mutually support one another. Such a process, at the organizational level, has also been witnessed with the deportation of Los Angeles gangsters to Central America, bringing their unique gang forms with them which then took hold and flourished locally.

In this age of increasing globalization, divergent non-state threat group forms involved in narcotics trafficking thus will readily influence one another. A developing case in point is that the Mexican cartels now need better trained, more dedicated, and ultimately more deadly foot soldiers to compete with one another and the military. As a result, mandatory basic training camps of many months duration are now being implemented. This will have implications not only for the mercenary contractors that presently exist but also for the affiliated gangs. Many of these early gang contractors initially helped to usher in new levels of brutality with their willingness to escalate the violence and, if need be, engage in torture for their criminal employers. Quite possibly, the heyday of the Mexican Mafia, *Calle Treinta* (Logan Heights), and later MS-13 and 18th Street hit men operating in Mexico is coming to a close.[32] Then again, the more advanced third generation gangs may simply adapt to this new 'battlefield' reality and increase their 'military-like' capabilities if they wish to remain relevant and useful allies to the more evolved Mexican cartels. Another concern is that in form and function, although not in origin, the Zetas can be considered very much like third generation gangs. The potentials for cartel enforcers, mercenaries, and affiliated street and prison gangs to further merge and blend together into hybrid combinations now readily exists. Such criminal–soldier blending quickly would defy our still rather primitive typologies of the non-state threat groups opposing us. Such events would also result in new threat entities not yet anticipated.

## Third phase cartel potentials in Mexico

It is well accepted that criminal organizations, particularly drug cartels and transnational gangs, are becoming increasingly networked in terms of organi-zation and influence. As these groups evolve, they challenge notions of the state and political organization. States are, at least in the current scheme of things, entities that possess a legitimate monopoly on the use of violence within a specified territory. A third phase cartel, criminal free-state or criminal enclave, could challenge that monopoly, much the same as warlords within failed states.

As previously discussed, the current situation in Mexico may shed light on these processes. Mexico is consumed by a set of interlocking, networked criminal insurgencies – where the cartels battle the legitimate state and challenging 'parallel states' alike. Daily violence, kidnappings, assassinations of police and government officials, beheadings, and armed assaults are the result of violent combat between drug cartels, gangs, and the Mexican police and military. The cartels vying for domination of the lucrative drug trade are seeking both market dominance and freedom from government interference. Tijuana, Ciudad Juárez, and other border towns are racked with violence. Increased deployments of both police and military forces are stymied in the face of corrupt officials who chose to side with the cartels.

The drug mafias have abandoned subtle co-option of the government to embrace active violence in order to secure safe havens to ply their trade. This *de facto* 'criminal insurgency' threatens the stability of the Mexican state. Not satisfied with their feudal outposts in the Mexican interior and along the US–Mexico frontier, the cartels are also starting to migrate north to the United States and Canada and south throughout Central America even, to the Southern Cone, setting up business in Argentina, and across the South Atlantic to West Africa. Money fuels global expansion and transnational organized crime has learned it can thrive in the face of governmental crisis.

The cartels are joined by a variety of gangs in the quest to dominate the global criminal opportunity space. Third generation gangs – that is, gangs like *Mara*

*Salvatrucha* (MS-13) that have transcended operating on localized turf with a simple market focus to operate across borders and challenge political structures – are both partners and foot soldiers for the dominant cartels. Gangs and cartels seek profit and are not driven by ideology. But the ungoverned, lawless zones they leave in their wake provide fertile ground for extremists and terrorists to exploit. Further, gangs and cartels always have the latent potential to morph and become ideologically captured by a charismatic leader or cause.

Stemming from these above trends, the greatest third phase cartel potentials in Mexico are now emerging from the fringe narco groups which are becoming more socially active and attempting to replace traditional values and ways of living with their own ideologies and value systems. The older people within their areas of control become re-socialized into a new value system while those born into it know no other reality and readily accept the prevailing narco status quo. Older cartels such as the Tijuana, Sinaloa, and Juárez organizations likely will remain within the second cartel phase and even have the potential of devolving into more first phase cartel patterns of behavior if trapped and cornered in a last stand against other cartels and federal Mexican forces. While these cartels environmentally modify their surroundings and the peoples who inhabit them with their illegal activities, this is a second order effect and by no means a primary consideration in their planning. The violence itself is secular in nature, it furthers their criminal activities and no more – killing and torture are part of the business plan for market domination and being decked out in tactical gear and fancy adornments is the epitome of machismo and narco-coolness.

Where the trends become more worrisome and threatening is with groups such as La Familia and those elements of Los Zetas and others who cross the line, tying their killing and torture to religious intent. These are second generation cartels and network clusters who have the very real potentials of evolving into 'new warmaking criminal entities'. The emergence of such an entity would be by no means a phenomenon unique to Mexico – concerns over criminal syndicates forming a para-state in the Balkans were expressed by Fatic in 2004.[33] Even earlier the hypothetical BLACKFOR (Black Force), a networked non-state 'new warmaking entity', was envisioned in 1998 along with criminal-state successors emerging out of the cartel evolutionary process revisited in this essay.[34] Tie-ins also exist to the threats posed by the 'Black Spots' work later undertaken by Stanislawaki in 2004 and expanded into an academic research program.[35] These are regions where state sovereignty has been compromised. They are commonly characterized by the following elements:

- Lack of effective state dominance
- Dominance by illicit organizations
- Transnational illicit activities that may be considered as breeding and exportation of insecurity
- Existence of informal rules governing the area
- Existence or high potential of criminal-terrorist nexus[36]

Such self-governed criminal enclaves (known as 'Zones of Impunity' in Mexico)[37] and the increasing level of conflict in Mexico are further facilitating projected forms of cartel evolution. Conflict and bloodshed increases organizational innovation and mutation of entities because of its Darwinian nature. Advances in military systems, such as army modernization, are relatively slow in peacetime because no immediate imperative for change – that of possibly dying on the battlefield – exists to spur on evolution. The cartel wars in Mexico and their ensuing arms, organizational, and doctrinal races – initially promoted by the introduction of the Zetas into the conflict – thus have turned it into an experimental crucible. Of note are the historical parallels to Early Modern Europe wherein a band of dynastic and still emergent Westphalian-states were locked into endless cycles of warfare – these entities co-evolved each other and became the dominant street fighters of the age beating out empire, city league, and medieval fief to usher in the dominant social and political form of the Modern world.

One byproduct of a similar process now taking place in Mexico is the rise of La Familia, which has its origins traced back to the 1980s. In its early days, it was a vigilante group helping to protect the poor from drug dealers, kidnappers, and other criminals.[38] At some point, it became co-opted by the very criminals it was intended to oppose and was allied for a time to the Gulf Cartel and the Zetas. This entity, based in Michoacán, represents a hybrid fusion of criminal drug enterprise and Christian evangelical beliefs to such an extent that is has become a social, religious, and criminal movement all rolled into one. This mutation or cartel morphing is actively promoting the development of a parallel state in its operational areas, which include the states of Michoacán, Guerrero, Mexico, and Jalisco, based on its own unique narco-cult value systems.[39] Still relatively small, La Familia is heading towards third phase cartel status with its evolved political aims and social plans. These aims and plans include building up a social base by means of providing social services, offering protection to the poor and disenfranchised, ideological indoctrination (especially to addicts in rehab centers), and developing long term patron–client relationships with politicians and political groups who are attempting to run for public offices.[40] The religious nature of this group with its emphasis upon 'divine justice' and overtly insurgent-like activities, competing for the hearts and minds of the locals with a corrupt Mexican state, is in some ways analogous to those characteristics and activities undertaken by the Taliban in Afghanistan and Pakistan or the Lord's Resistance Army in the Congo, Sudan, and Uganda.

Another byproduct of this process can be found in the glorification of the drug trafficking lifestyle through the worship of 'narco-saints' such as Santa Muerte and Jesus Malverde. This injects another ideological component into the ongoing criminal insurgencies and helps to fundamentally alter their character. In its most extreme forms, tied to some members of the Zeta mercenaries and quite probably to some other cartel enforcers, such worship is becoming linked to practices involving ritual sacrifice involving torture, maiming, and beheading. While only an extremely small fraction of Santa Muerte incidents have been reported to involve ritual sacrifices and related practices, they are extremely troubling. At least one call for 'holy war' in defense of narco-shrines to Santa Muerte has been uttered since the Mexican government began a campaign in 2009 to destroy dozens of them.[41] Some individual Santa Muerte adherents, drawn from the Zetas, Gulf, and possibly even the Juárez cartels, thus have also begun to cross the firebreak from second phase to third phase cartel status with a significant co-option of value systems as evidenced by their acceptance of what many would consider 'darkside' religious beliefs.

## Alternative futures

The interlocking criminal insurgencies in Mexico, and broader 'societal warfare' potentials between state and non-state forces over the future value system, ideology, and organizational form of the Mexican state, do not paint an overly rosy picture for those living south of the Rio Grande. Still, the future is not written for Mexico, and today's pessimistic perspectives may conceivably change to more hopeful and optimistic ones.[42] With this in mind, the near-term trajectory and four alternative futures for Mexico are discussed below. These alternative futures range between the overly pessimistic through the overly optimistic. Each one will be characterized briefly, analyzed from the perspective of its probability of occurrence (improbable through high probability), and examined for its potential implications for the United States.

### *Mexico in the near term: the narco-insurgencies continue*

In the near term (the next three to five years), the ongoing narco-insurgencies in Mexico are expected to rage on much as they have done over the last few years. The half dozen or so major cartels (Juárez, Sinaloa, Tijuana, Gulf, Los Zetas, and La Familia) will continue to engage in conflict with each other over the lucrative plazas and other key routes and territories of Mexico and with deployed Mexican military forces. The weaker Juárez and Tijuana cartels always have the potential to be further marginalized, merge, or simply be absorbed by the stronger cartels. The Mexican police forces themselves are becoming increasingly inconsequential to the drug wars after being severely co-opted by the various cartels and literally outgunned in the streets. Corruption is rampant throughout the Mexican political and judicial system and this will not change. This is basically a 'stalemate' situation though, on the margins, more 'Zones of Impunity' may come into being as 'criminal-enclaves' or the process may begin to reverse itself with more territories coming under Mexican state authority. What is expected is that the levels of violence pertaining to the ongoing narco-insurgency will increase before they then begin to subside, if they subside at all. For the United States, this means that cartel operatives, enforcers, and their affiliated gang contractors will continue to do a robust business. Whether the levels of narcotics trafficking violence continue to increase along the border and over it because of newer cartel policies of engagement with US law enforcement is unknown, but this is quite likely.

### *Future 1: criminal-state successor(s)*

This future represents the extremely pessimistic and long-term end state for Mexico in which it is overrun by the Mexican cartels and their network of mercenary and gang associates. Increasing numbers of the populace will directly profit and identify with the developing narco-value system and view the Mexican federal system as a corrupt and hated police state. The centralized government of Mexico collapses under the weight of its own corruption, economic debt, and an increasingly unpopular drug war that compromises the integrity of its military and discredits its political parties. With state failure comes the division of the country into a patchwork of criminal free-states and enclaves dominated by fully developed third phase cartels which are, in turn, backed up by allied third generation gangs. Such a future would require the US to fully militarize its southern border against the threat of a hostile 'new warmaking network' of criminal-states. It also would result in a counter-insurgency campaign actively being conducted to stop the spread of the narco-value system within the United States and the establishment of full-blown criminal-enclaves north of the Rio Grande. Mass migration attempts from Mexico into the US and calls for humanitarian intervention by the international community result in added layers of dilemma for American policy makers. While this sounds like a doomsday scenario – and it is – the actual probability of occurrence of *Future 1* is improbable. The US simply would not allow this future to take place and, at the point it appeared the narco-insurgencies in Mexico were edging towards this path, the US would become involved increasingly in the conflict. To some extent this is of course already the case, with the US for some time now directly working where it can with the Mexican government. Initially, this would be in the form of economic and other indirect forms of aid such as the $1.4 billion multi-year Mérida Initiative, including further training and outfitting of Mexican counter-insurgency units.[43] If the criticality of the situation in Mexico continued to deteriorate, more direct forms of US military and law enforcement participation undoubtedly would be implemented, including the deployment of US forces directly into northern Mexico if warranted.

### *Future 2: Mexican state victory*

The second future focuses on the highly optimistic end of the spectrum of future potentials for Mexico. This is a future wherein the Mexican state is able systematically to defeat and dismantle all of the dominant opposing second and emergent third phase cartels either all once, a couple at a time, or in some sort of sequential order. With these victories comes a suppression of narcotics trafficking in Mexico to the point whereby it becomes a relatively low level and manageable law enforcement problem. This conceivably would be coupled with either transshipment of narcotics shifting outside of Mexico to the Caribbean or a major reduction in both US, and now Mexican, demand for illegal narcotics. Mexican governmental suppression of human trafficking, gang taxation, and other criminal economic elements would also be implemented, as would a concerted effort to implement reforms and clean up corruption in the Mexican political system. For the United States, this would be the best of all possible futures with a secure, stable, and fully democratic Mexico on its southern border and the threat of well-armed drug cartels, mercenaries, and second and third generation Sureño gang affiliates diminished, if not totally eliminated. The probability of such a rosy end state, as in *Future 2*, actually taking place in Mexico is now improbable. The opportunity fully to eliminate the narco threat groups, before they became entrenched in Mexican society, was likely missed several decades ago. Even the elimination of one or more major cartels now only creates a temporary supply gap in the illegal drug market. Such gaps get filled quickly by preexisting and new drug trafficking organizations that arise who will immediately penetrate any illegal markets left vacant. This scenario would build from the strength of Mexican civil society, cultural institutions, and current efforts towards reinforcing a stable democracy. Whether the corruption in the Mexican political system also can be reformed significantly – without dismantling the system itself – is another issue.

### Future 3: narco-democracy emergence

Depending on one's perspective, this is either a slightly optimistic or slightly pessimistic projection of an alternative future for Mexico. Regardless of one's viewpoint, such a future is likely one of the two that will now take place. In this future, much like that of *Future 2*, the dominant second phase and emergent third phase Mexican cartels are defeated and dismantled by Mexico with varying levels of US support. However, rather than a clear-cut victory, what immediately arises domestically in Mexico is a patchwork of dozens upon dozens of baby cartels and second generation drug gangs who replace their large-scale trafficking operations with small-scale and niche-focused operations. Under duress, network organizational forms will devolve into smaller and smaller clusters and nodes as a defensive measure – this took place in Colombia decades ago with the elimination of the Medellín and Cali cartels and is still a valid narcotics trafficking response to a similar situation taking place in Mexico. This would be equivalent to taking four to six major cancer tumors (e.g., the dominant Mexican cartels) in a host (e.g., Mexico) that are threatening to kill it and atomizing them so that they are spread out irrevocably through the body politic. This results in the metastasizing of drug cartel nodes and cells throughout Mexican society and the Mexican political system being subjected to a 'condition' that will not kill it but also one that is endemic and slightly crippling. The Mexican government would then remain on the continued lookout for new dominant cartels attempting to emerge and immediately suppress them. Given the already high levels of corruption in Mexico, many of these baby cartels and drug gangs would strike deals and even merge and fuse to attributes of the Mexican state at the federal, state, and local levels. What we end up with is the emergence of some sort of narco-democracy where violence levels eventually subside and Mexican society writ large, especially its elites, benefits from illegal narcotics trafficking. It is debatable if the state co-opts the drug traffickers or the drug-traffickers ultimately co-opt the state – quite possibly both sides reach a tactical agreement of some sort and end up in an uneasy yet stable marriage of convenience. For the United States, this is not the perfect future that it had hoped for but, on the other hand, it is a far better outcome than some of the other potential drug war alternate futures that could have taken place. The illegal narcotics flow into the United States from Mexico will, of course, continue to take place unabated, however, due to the lack of dominant cartels, periodic drug shortages in US cities may become more pronounced. The probability of occurrence of *Future 3* is in the medium range and pretty much evenly split with that of *Future 4*.

### Future 4: the Mexican dark renaissance

This alternative future for Mexico is on the pessimistic side of the continuum and, like *Future 3*, has a very good chance of taking place over the longer term. This future is a formalization of the near-term scenario which is a status quo projection of the current reality in Mexico. While the US provides economic and military support to Mexico, it is limited in scope, and though helping to keep the Mexican state from failing, does not fully tip the balance towards defeating the narco-insurgencies taking place in various regions of that country. This future is somewhat reminiscent of a high medieval or renaissance era Italy with a patchwork of zones of control and influence being projected by competing city-states and other entities. In this twenty-first century narco-generated scenario, the Mexican state, in name anyway, will be in control of all of Mexico as it is today and will be viewed as a sovereign nation. Foreign diplomats, the United Nations, news reporters, and others will carry on as if nothing has changed and Mexican governmental authority remains unquestioned. In actuality, the Mexican state will only be in control of the Mexican federal areas, key urban centers, and strategic facilities such as major ports, airports, oilfields, refineries, energy generation, food production, and major highway systems. Other parts of the country will have become institutionalized as criminal enclaves and para-states belonging to third phase cartels, such as La Familia, and third generation gangs, such as Mara Salvatrucha, and their organizational descendants. Even in these regions, Mexican governmental apparatus and symbols may be apparent but such institutions will have been thoroughly penetrated, corrupted, and are no more than window dressing or a political charade. For many citizens of Mexico, living under La Familia or similar criminal-state rule may be no better or no worse than that of living in the Mexican federal zones. Without political reforms, the Mexican governmental system remains corrupt and its legitimacy threatened, and while it supports more traditional values over those of the various narco-ideologies that have emerged, it caters more to the needs of the elites than those of the peasants and peoples of the street. For the United States, this results in its being presented with Byzantine-like dilemmas and tradeoffs in its relations with the Mexican state, criminal enclaves, and para-states now in existence. It also justifies the need to enhance security on its southern border, developing high intensity policing and quick reaction force (QRF) capabilities to blunt drug loads, escorted by offensive cartel forces, coming by land, air, or through tunnels under the border. Sporadic narco and criminal enclave development in the US must also now be monitored and guarded against. An extreme variation of this scenario would be the continued expansion and entrenchment of Mexican cartel reach into Central America.[44] In this variant, Guatemala, El Salvador, and other states also become 'hollow' and the cartels dominate 'parallel states' within their borders; potentially linking these enclaves into a narco-confederation. The probability of occurrence of *Future 4* is in the medium range and pretty much evenly split with that of *Future 3*.

Of these two likely alternatives, the United States should actively promote *Future 3: narco-democracy emergence* in Mexico and bring all elements of national power to bear to see that it, rather than its darker alternative, becomes the future reality. While this may sound like an a priori admission of defeat, it is not. For decades now in the Americas, a select group of both drug cartels and gangs respectively have evolved through various phases and generations. Over time, they have gotten increasingly more networked, sophisticated, and deadly and are actively mutating into new war-making entities. The fact that these groups are not 'states,' and therefore not recognized as 'real national security threats' by *de jure* states, is meaningless. Something could have been done about it back in the 1980s, or maybe even in the 1990s in the case of Mexico, but the process and threat were not identified and basically have been ignored. It is potentially too late to achieve the highly desirable *Future 2: Mexican state victory* over the narcos – the best we can hope for at this point is to bolster a somewhat stable, democratic, and politically less-corrupt Mexico suffering from a narco 'condition' that will not kill it but at the same time endemically weakens it. This should be viewed as a stabilizing option, until enhanced steps to build the rule of law and strengthen societal institutions are realized. This is perhaps the best current option for Mexico and acknowledges the *realpolitik* required in the war over social and political organization now upon us.

## Notes

1. See Sullivan and Elkus, 'Red Teaming Criminal Insurgency', 'State of Siege', and 'Plazas for Profit'; and Sullivan, 'Criminal Netwarriors in Mexico's Drug Wars'.
2. Sur stands for *Sureños* (Southerners) and 13 for the letter M (*Eme*) and that means that those street gangs are subordinate to Mexican Mafia (*Eme*) authority.
3. Bunker and Sullivan, 'Cartel Evolution', 55–74.
4. Few works have been produced on the potential for cartel evolution. In addition to the original paper 'Cartel Evolution: Potentials and Consequences', see Fatic, 'The criminal syndicate as para-state in the Balkans', 137–56.
5. Creveld, *The Transformation of War*.

6.   Bunker, 'Epochal Change', 15–25.
7.   Clawson and Lee III, *The Andean Cocaine Industry*, 47. See also Cañon, *El Patrón*, 20, 129.
8.   Logan, 'Los Zetas'.
9.   See Briscoe, 'The Proliferation of the "Parallel State"'.
10.  Paternostro, 'Mexico as a Narco-democracy', for an early discussion of the emergence of criminal enclaves in Mexico.
11.  Bunker and Sullivan, 'Cartel Evolution'.
12.  Hawley, 'Bold New Cartels Emerging in Mexico'.
13.  Ibid.
14.  Ibid.
15.  Sullivan, 'Maras Morphing', 487–504 for a detailed discussion of the current state of *maras* and third generation (3 GEN) gangs worldwide.
16.  Sullivan, 'Transnational Gangs'.
17.  Franco, 'The MS-13 and 18th Street Gangs', 2.
18.  Sullivan, 'Third Generation Street Gangs', 95–108.
19.  Sullivan, 'Gangs Hooligans, and Anarchists', 99–128 for a discussion of the analysis underlying this section.
20.  Bruneau, 'The Maras and National Security in Central America'.
21.  Llorca and Bajack, 'AP Impact'.
22.  Casas-Zamora, "Guatemalastan": How to Prevent a Failed State in our Midst'.
23.  See Sullivan and Bunker, 'Third Generation Gangs', 1–10 for a discussion of 'third generation' gang literature. A newer contribution is Brands, 'Third-Generation Gangs and Criminal Insurgency in Latin America'.
24.  See, for example, Sullivan, 'Future Conflict' and notably Fatic, 'The Criminal Syndicate as Para-state in the Balkans', 137–56.
25.  Salazar, 'Young Assassins of the Drug Trade'.
26.  Manwaring, *A Contemporary Challenge to State Sovereignty*, 20.
27.  The computer seized in 1994 was valued at one million dollars. See Chepesiuk, 'The Fall of the Cali Cartel'.
28.  This comparison does not take into consideration the guerilla FARC group which suggests that second phase cartel evolution and mutation is alive and well in Colombia with that hybrid guerilla-cartel entity's larger spheres of operation than those achieved by the Cali Cartel.
29.  Logan, 'Mexico'.
30.  Lacey, 'In Drug War, Mexico Fights Cartel and Itself'.
31.  Skaperdas and Syropoulos, 'Gangs as Primitive States', 61–82.
32.  Early participation of individual Mexican Mafia members as hit men for the Mexican cartels is not well known. See Rafael, *The Mexican Mafia*; and Blatchford, *The Black Hand*.
33.  Fatic, 'The Criminal Syndicate as Para-state in the Balkans', 137–56.
34.  Bunker, *Five-Dimensional (Cyber) Warfighting*, 1–42; and Bunker and Sullivan, 'Cartel Evolution', 55–74.
35.  Stanislawski, 'Transnational "Bads" in the Globalized World', 155–70 and 'Para-States, Quasi-States, and Black Spots', 366–96.
36.  Email correspondence concerning the characteristics of Black Spots with Dr. Bartosz Stanislawski, October 17, 2008.
37.  Lovelace, 'Foreword', iii–iv; and Manwaring, *A 'New Dynamic' in the Western Hemisphere Security Environment*, ix.
38.  Logan and Sullivan, 'Mexico's "Divine Justice"'.
39.  Ibid. See also Bunker et al., 'Torture, Beheadings and Narcocultos', in this work for additional information on La Familia.

40.   Sullivan and Elkus, 'Mexican Crime Families: Political Aims and Social Plans'.
41.   This synopsis is drawn from the Narcocultos section of Bunker et al., 'Torture, Beheadings and Narcocultos', found in this work.
42.   An excellent background debate on Mexican failed-state potentials, narco related conflict, and futures for that country can be found in Ronfeldt's Two Theories blog. See 'Why Mexico May NOT Fall Apart – and a Way to Think about it' and 'Mexico Plagued by Myriad Interlaced Netwars – a TIMN Analysis'.
43.   The bulk of the security cooperation money will go to Mexico with some also earmarked for Central America and the Caribbean. See Johnson, 'The Merida Initiative'.
44.   See Logan and Sullivan, 'Costa Rica, Panama in the Crossfire'.

## Bibliography

Blatchford, Chris. *The Black Hand*. New York: William Morrow, 2008.

Brands, Hal. 'Third-Generation Gangs and Criminal Insurgency in Latin America'. *Small Wars Journal* (4 July 2009), http://smallwarsjournal.com/blog/2009/07/third-generation-gangs-and-crim/ (accessed 12 June 2009).

Briscoe, Ivan. 'The Proliferation of the "Parallel State"'. Working paper, FRIDE: Fundación para las Relaciones Internacionales y el Diálogo Exterior (October 2008), http://www.fride.org/publication/511/the-proliferation-of-the-parallel-state (accessed 12 June 2009).

Bruneau, Thomas C. 'The Maras and National Security in Central America'. *Strategic Insights* 4, no. 5 (May 2005), http://www.ccc.npps.navy.mil/si/2005/May/bruneauMay05.pdf (accessed 12 June 2009).

Bunker, Pamela L., Lisa J. Campbell, and Robert J. Bunker. 'Torture, Beheadings and Narcocultos'. *Small Wars and Insurgencies* 21, no. 1 (2010): 145–78.

Bunker, Robert J. 'Epochal Change: War Over Social and Political Organization'. *Parameters* 27, no. 2 (Summer 1997): 15–25.

Bunker, Robert J. *Five-Dimensional (Cyber) Warfighting*. Carlisle, PA: Strategic Studies Institute, US Army War College (10 March 1998), 1–42.

Bunker, Robert J., and John P. Sullivan. 'Cartel Evolution: Potentials and Consequences'. *Transnational Organized Crime* 4, no. 2 (Summer 1998): 55–74.

Cañon, Louis M. *El Patrón: Vida y Muerte de Pablo Escobar*. Bogotá: Planeta, 1994.

Casas-Zamora, Kevin. '"Guatemalastan": How to Prevent a Failed State in our Midst'. *Mexidata* (1 June 2009), http://www.mexidata.info/id2285.html (accessed 12 June 2009).

Chepesiuk, Ron. 'The Fall of the Cali Cartel'. *Crime Magazine: An Encyclopedia of Crime* (21 October 2006), http://www.crimemagazine.com/06/calicartel,1021-6.htm (accessed 12 June 2009).

Clawson, Patrick L., and Rensselaer W. Lee III. *The Andean Cocaine Industry*. New York: Palgrave MacMillian, 1998.

Creveld, Martin van. *The Transformation of War*. New York: The Free Press, 1991.

Fatic, Alexsandar. 'The Criminal Syndicate as Para-state in the Balkans: is the "New War-Making Criminal Entity" a Reality?'. *South-East Europe Review for Labour and Social Affairs*, no. 4 (2004): 137–56.

Franco, Cindy. 'The MS-13 and 18th Street Gangs: Emerging Transnational Gang Threats?'. *CRS Report for Congress*. Washington, DC: Congressional Research Service (RL34233) (2 November 2007).

Hawley, Chris. 'Bold New Cartels Emerging in Mexico'. *Arizona Republic* (30 August 2009), http://www.azcentral.com/arizonarepublic/news/articles/2009/08/30/20090830lafamilia.html (accessed 12 June 2009).

Johnson, David T. 'The Merida Initiative'. Congressional Testimony, Subcommittee on State, Foreign Operations, Related Programs of House Committee on Appropriations, Washington, DC (10 March 2009), http://www.state.gov/p/inl/rls/rm/120225.htm (accessed 12 June 2009).

Lacey, Marc. 'In Drug War, Mexico Fights Cartel and Itself'. *New York Times* (29 March 2009), http://www.nytimes.com/2009/03/30/world/americas/30mexico.html.

Llorca, Juan Carlos, and Frank Bajack. 'AP Impact: Mexican Drug Cartels Expand Abroad'. Associated Press (21 July 2009), http://abcnews.go.com/International/wireStory?id=8137836 (accessed 12 June 2009).

Logan, Samuel. 'Los Zetas: Evolution of a Criminal Organization'. *ISN Security Watch* (11 March 2009), http://www.isn.ethz.ch/isn/Current-Affairs/Security-Watch/Detail/?id=97554&lng=en (accessed 12 June 2009).

Logan, Samuel. 'Mexico'. *Southern Pulse* (Tuesday, 9 June 2009).

Logan, Samuel, and John P. Sullivan. 'Mexico's "Divine Justice"'. *ISN Security Watch* (17 August 2009), http://www.isn.ethz.ch/isn/Current-Affairs/Security-Watch/Detail/?lng=en&id=104677 (accessed 12 June 2009).

Logan, Samuel, and John P. Sullivan. 'Costa Rica, Panama in the Crossfire'. *ISN Security Watch* (7 October 2009), http://www.isn.ethz.ch/isn/Current-Affairs/Security-Watch/Detail/?lng=en&id=106768 (accessed 12 June 2009).

Lovelace, Douglas C. 'Foreword'. In Max Manwaring, *A 'New Dynamic' in the Western Hemisphere Security Environment: The Mexican Zetas and other Private Armies.* iii–iv. Carlisle, PA: Strategic Studies Institute, US Army War College, September 2009.

Manwaring, Max G. *A Contemporary Challenge to State Sovereignty: Gangs and Other Illicit Transnational Criminal Organizations in Central America, El Salvador, Mexico, Jamaica, and Brazil.* 1–59. Carlisle, PA: Strategic Studies Institute, US Army War College, December 2007.

Manwaring, Max G. *A 'New Dynamic' in the Western Hemisphere Security Environment: The Mexican Zetas and other Private Armies.* 1–52. Carlisle, PA: Strategic Studies Institute, US Army War College, September 2009.

Paternostro, Silvana. 'Mexico as a Narco-democracy'. *World Policy Journal* (Spring 1995).

Rafael, Tony. *The Mexican Mafia.* New York: Encounter Books, 2007.

Ronfeldt, David. 'Why Mexico May NOT Fall Apart – and a Way to Think about it'. Theories blog (Monday, 30 March 2009), http://twotheories.blogspot.com/2009/03/why-mexico-may-not-fall-apart-and-way.html (accessed 12 June 2009).

Ronfeldt, David. 'Mexico Plagued by Myriad Interlaced Netwars – a TIMN Analysis'. Two Theories blog (Friday, 27 February 2009), http://twotheories.blogspot.com/2009/02/mexicos-potential-plagued-by-myriad.html (accessed 12 June 2009).

Salazar, Alonzo. 'Young Assassins of the Drug Trade'. Street Children: Latin America and the Caribbean, NACLA Report on the Americas, May–June 1994, http://pangaea.org/street_children/latin/colokid.htm (accessed 12 June 2009).

Skaperdas, Stergios, and Constantinos Syropoulos. 'Gangs as primitive states'. In *The Economics of Organized Crime*, edited by Gianluca Fiorentini and Sam Peltzman, 61–82. Cambridge, MA: Cambridge University Press, 1997.

Stanislawski, Bartosz H. 'Transnational "Bads" in the Globalized World: The Case of Transnational Organized Crime'. *Public Integrity* 6, no. 2 (Spring 2004): 155–70.

Stanislawski, Bartosz H., ed. 'Para-States, Quasi-States, and Black Spots: Perhaps not States, but not "Ungoverned Territories"'. *International Studies Review* 10, no. 2 (June 2008): 366–96.

Sullivan, John P. 'Criminal Netwarriors in Mexico's Drug Wars'. *GroupIntel* (22 December 2008), http://www.groupintel.com/2008/12/22/criminal-netwarriors-in-mexico's-drug-wars/ (accessed 12 June 2009).

Sullivan, John P. 'Future Conflict: Criminal Insurgencies, Gangs and Intelligence'. *Small Wars Journal* (31 May 2009), http://smallwarsjournal.com/blog/journal/docs-temp/248-sullivan.pdf (accessed 12 June 2009).

Sullivan, John P. 'Gangs Hooligans, and Anarchists: The Vanguard of Netwar in the Streets'. In *Networks and Netwars: The Future of Terror, Crime, and Militancy*, edited by John Arquilla and David Ronfeldt. Santa Monica: RAND, 2001.

Sullivan, John P. 'Maras Morphing: Revisiting Third Generation Gangs'. *Global Crime* 7, no. 3–4 (August–November 2006): 487–504.

Sullivan, John P. 'Third Generation Street Gangs: Turf, Cartels, and Net Warriors'. *Transnational Organized Crime* 3, no. 3 (Autumn 1997): 95–108.

Sullivan, John P. 'Transnational Gangs: The Impact of Third Generation Gangs in Central America'. *Air and Space Power Journal – Spanish Edition* (Second Trimester 2008), http://www.airpower.au.af.mil/apjinternational/apj-s/2008/2tri08/sullivaneng.htm (accessed 12 June 2009).

Sullivan, John P., and Robert J. Bunker. 'Third Generation Gangs: An Introduction'. *Journal of Gang Research* 14, no. 4 (Summer 2007): 1–10.

Sullivan, John P., and Adam Elkus. 'Mexican Crime Families: Political Aims and Social Plans'. *Mexidata* (Monday, 27 July 2009), http://mexidata.info/id2344.html (accessed 12 June 2009).

Sullivan, John P., and Adam Elkus. 'Plazas for Profit: Mexico's Criminal Insurgency'. *Small Wars Journal* (26 April 2009), http://smallwarsjournal.com/blog/2009/04/plazas-for-profit-mexicos-crim/ (accessed 12 June 2009).

Sullivan, John P., and Adam Elkus. 'Red Teaming Criminal Insurgency'. *Red Team Journal* (30 January 2009), http://redteamjournal.com/2009/01/red-teaming-criminal-insurgency-1/ (accessed 12 June 2009).

Sullivan, John P., and Adam Elkus. 'State of Siege: Mexico's Criminal Insurgency'. *Small Wars Journal* (19 August 2009), http://smallwarsjournal.com/blog/journal/docs-temp/84-sullivan.pdf (accessed 12 June 2009).

# Los Zetas: operational assessment

Lisa J. Campbell*

*146^th Airlift Wing, Channel Islands Air National Guard Station, CA, USA*

Today, analysts of the postmodern era recognize that worldwide conflicts are increasingly influenced by the interaction between terrorists, criminals, gangs, and private armies and that this interaction is a threat to the nation state. Now, a related threat is coming into play – one that involves all of these types of groups being represented at once in a single adversary. One such multifaceted group that is in the forefront is Los Zetas, a band of Mexican cartel enforcers that cannot be easily categorized, assessed, or targeted. Within broad categories of a multitude of irregular groups, Los Zetas embodies such capabilities as extensive compartmentalized networking, pervasive intelligence and counter-intelligence capabilities, amassing of advanced weaponry, brutal tactics, top level military and police training, and the ability to undermine state governments and control large swaths of territory. Los Zetas, if left unchecked and unexamined, could potentially become a great security problem for Mexico, the US, and Central America. This essay provides an operational assessment that explores Los Zetas using various criteria traditionally used by nation state militaries, and more recently by Terrorism Early Warning Groups, to assess opposing forces (OPFOR). The purpose of this operational assessment is to provide a baseline understanding of Los Zetas that would make them less imposing and more targetable.

Los Zetas, the most infamous Mexican cartel enforcers, have set the bar for the next escalation in hostile transnational group activities. This group has become a security problem not just for Mexico, but for the US and countries in Central America as well. The Zetas, along with newer groups that are emerging and following their lead – paramilitaries that are small, smart and mobile – are thought of as smarter and better strategists than the Mexican military itself. The Assistant US Attorney General, following the July 2009 US indictments on major cartel leadership, including Zeta leaders, was quoted as saying that ' . . . the most effective way to disrupt and dismantle criminal organizations is to prosecute their leaders and seize their funding'.[1] This same approach, while successful in the

---

*The views expressed here do not represent those of the US Air Force, Department of Defense, or the US Government.

past, may not be effective enough against Los Zetas or successor groups like them. The operational assessment set forth below reveals how Los Zetas differ from traditional drug cartels, past and present. The assessment may serve as a baseline study for US friendly forces to plan future operations, including Intelligence Preparation for Operations (IPO) and other analytical framework used for locating the Zetas and for detecting any changes to them. In the US, early detection of indications of Los Zetas activities and movement is especially critical, before they can control new terrain, subvert local governments, or corrupt or coerce *people*, potentially creating ungovernable spaces.

The Zetas began in the late 1990s, when the Gulf Cartel leader Osiel Cárdenas Guillen began to recruit from the Mexican Army's Groupo Aeromovil de Fuerzas Especiales (GAFE), elite airborne Special Forces who are trained for the purposes of locating and apprehending drug cartel members.[2] Cárdenas Guillen hired these elites to become an inner circle of protection for him and to perform other vital functions for the Gulf Cartel, such as 'enforcement' of drug trafficking activities. The original Zetas numbered approximately 31, including the top recruit, Lieutenant Arturo Guzmán Decena, who brought the others with him, all enticed by substantially greater salaries than those paid by the Mexican government. While in the GAFE, Guzmán Decena was known as 'Z1', a radio callsign, which became the Zetas' name.[3]

By 2003, the Zetas had trained an additional 300 members or so for the protection of the Gulf Cartel leadership. In 2005, the Zetas began to hire into their ranks Kaibiles, Guatemalan Special Forces known for their extreme Special Forces training in jungle environments as well as for their brutal tactics.[4] In 2007, Cárdenas Guillen was extradited to the US; prior to this the Gulf Cartel had a four- or five-ring-deep security detail for the top leaders, with the Zetas remaining in the inner rings.[5] Following Cárdenas Guillen's extradition, the Zetas' organizational structure changed. For instance, they separated themselves from the control of the Gulf Cartel while rising to top leadership positions. Further, below their still hierarchical leadership, the Zetas, for security reasons, began to adopt networked properties. Within their network, Los Zetas instituted a compartmentalized cell structure to limit the information that any one member of the organization knows about his associates.

Today, it is believed that the Zetas and the Gulf Cartel are largely one and the same, or at least operate parallel to or in cooperation with one another.[6] In mid-2009, the US indicted 10 Gulf and Zeta top leaders and renamed them together as *The Company*, offering $50 million total in rewards for information leading to their capture.[7] While the relationship between the Zetas and the Gulf Cartel remains unclear, what is evidenced is that the Zetas act like a competitive cartel while at the same time contracting themselves for hire to other major drug trafficking organizations in Mexico.[8] The Zetas also take on the functional characteristics of many types of organizations today, including insurgencies, nation-state militaries, corporations, irregular warfare units, terrorists, and organized crime. Most distressing are the similarities the Zetas have with third generation gangs and the national security threats they pose.[9]

To assess the Zetas and reveal their operational significance while cataloging and describing their unique characteristics, the following analytical criteria were used: Operational areas; Composition; Disposition; Strength figures; Tactics; Training; Logistics; Recruitment; Criminal brand naming; Intelligence and operations security; Administrative; Morale; Weather, enemy, terrain; and Most dangerous enemy courses of action.

**Operational areas**

The Area of Interest (AI) is comprised of general areas worldwide where Los Zetas may be operating either with their own members or through surrogates. The AI serves as a big picture reference for friendly forces and includes far-reaching areas where Los Zetas' drug, human, and weapons trafficking or other illicit business activity occurs or will potentially occur. Because much is unknown about the extent of Los Zetas' reach, the AI is speculated, at best, to include all of the US and Canada, Mexico, Central and South America, the Caribbean (including Cuba), Europe (Spain), West and North Africa, and Asia. The AI, or each individual AI, also includes everything from major cities to very small towns in the US, nodes where final destinations of drug shipments are but the Zetas' footprint is not yet proven.

The geographic Area of Operation (AO) encompasses those areas where friendly forces counter Los Zetas or prepare for operations against them. The AO includes most of Mexico, the US/Mexican border; southern to northeastern US, including Arizona;[10] and Central America and parts of South America, where many of Los Zetas drug transshipment routes begin. Within these territories, the AO includes ground (urban, rural, and jungle environments), the littoral coasts, airspace, space, and cyberspace. Airspace is from ground level up to and including medium flight altitudes; space, to the extent of the US and Mexican government's ability to use satellite and Unmanned Aerial Vehicle (UAV) imagery to detect activities of Los Zetas. Cyberspace, while it cannot be graphically depicted like the other components, is critical to defining the AO, and includes websites such as YouTube where much evidence may be found on Los Zetas or those websites where Los Zetas conduct illicit business and which will lend support to friendly forces intelligence collection.[11]

**Composition**

As a result of ongoing indictments of Los Zetas leadership and recent (2007–09) military offensives by the Mexican government in Gulf Cartel/Los Zetas territory, the organization of the Zetas is in flux. The complex and irregular composition of Los Zetas reflects both a hierarchy and a network. Los Zetas composition is best understood when arranged into two areas: Operations (Figure 1) and Intelligence (Figure 2).[12] There is a reasonable level of confidence

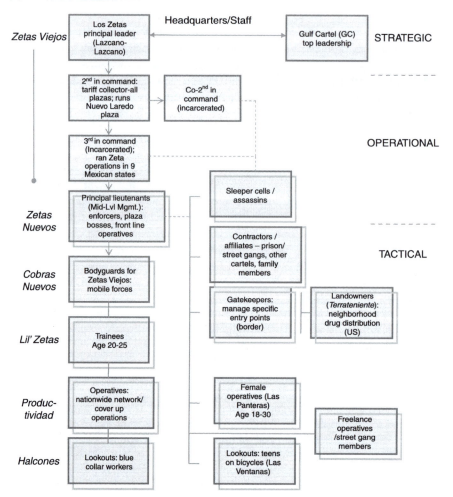

Figure 1.    Los Zetas composition: operations.
Note: The use of STRATEGIC, OPERATIONAL AND TACTICAL in this figure are to provide a reference for friendly forces (the 'good guys') to understand and relate Zetas' overall operations to traditional levels of operations.

that Figures 1 and 2 reflect the functions, activities, and organizational tasks of the Zetas, as well as what may be concluded from a wide array of media and government assessments regarding their components. Irregular armed groups like the Zetas are always developing and shifting and continuing efforts must be made to adjust, correct, or update information on the Zetas, their components, and their relationships. The Zetas' organization as set forth on paper portrays only a snapshot in time. The utility of illustrating and defining their organizational composition is that, within such an illustration, exploitable weaknesses or *centers of gravity* may be more readily found.

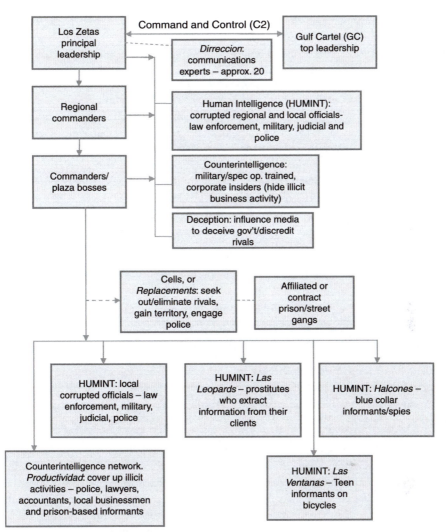

Figure 2. Los Zetas compostion: intelligence.

Top Zeta leaders, or *Zetas Viejos*, are of the original Zetas; with the eventual elimination of all original members, the top leadership will evolve. These top leaders have specific roles and are assigned to regions. Zetas Viejos have their own bodyguards and accountants, and any number of police, officials, lawyers, and businessmen on the payroll and under their influence. The top leader of Los Zetas, Herbierto Lazcano Lazcano,[13] currently shares leadership of the Gulf Cartel with two Gulf Cartel leaders. Lazcano is in charge of the Los Zetas enforcement organization – its primary role. The number two leader of Los Zetas is a plaza commander in Mexico who controls numerous transportation and distribution cells in the US.[14]

Next in the chain of command are the Principal Lieutenants, referred to as *Zetas Nuevos*; they are the enforcers, trained to perform in the most brutal and lethal manner. Their ranks include Mexican military deserters, former policemen, family members of Los Zetas, and Kaibiles. The Zetas Nuevos operate on the front lines, taking orders from the Zeta Viejo commander under whom they serve. They are often plaza bosses, assigned to a slice of operational territory. Relative to longstanding insurgencies or cartels, they are frequently killed or captured, often by the Mexican military.[15]

Those that serve under plaza bosses are the remaining main-body Zetas, also frequently captured or killed. These subordinate Zetas may be newly trained recruits and trained regulars who are integrated into the system by being assigned to a Zeta Nuevo in a particular territory. The young, frontline male operatives average 20 years of age – similar to their Mexican army counterparts. A women's 'division' exists as part of the Zetas; the women are typically aged 18–30.[16]

The Zetas network is a layer of their organization and is composed of a wide variety of cells at all levels. Cell functions include seeking out and eliminating rival drug and alien smuggling groups; gaining or regaining plaza territory; seeking out people owing the cartel money for lost, stolen, or seized drug loads or profits; kidnapping personnel who do not pay, or kidnapping for extortion purposes. Los Zetas cells include a sleeper version; upon notification, a sleeper cell may perform any of the aforementioned and are often hired as (sleeper) assassins. One such assassination cell, a three-man team, was revealed and captured in the US.[17] Similar to cells, within the Zetas there are rings; a ring of truck hijackers captured in March 2009 was found to be working under the auspices of the Zetas.

Other key elements of the Zetas network are the individuals who perform a variety of functions that fall under either operations or intelligence. The Zetas intelligence infrastructure includes numerous, perhaps thousands, of individual operatives that act as spies or lookouts in Mexico; collectively these individuals are early warning, cover-up, or deception operations networks for the Zetas. Some of these operatives have titles – the *Productividad* are nationwide and are a sub-network of the cartel composed of businessmen (white collar) who operate in place to cover up illicit operations of Los Zetas. The lookouts, or *Halcones*, are individuals ranging from business owners (blue collar) to youths who patrol the streets of Mexico and can signal (early warning) or provide information (intelligence collection) to the Zetas.[18] On the operational side of the Zetas' organization, individuals are specialized contractors and freelance operatives hired from a pool of affiliated gangs and family members in both the US and Mexico. The Zetas are said to be allied with the Beltran Levya Organization, Carrillo Fuentes Organization (aka Juárez Cartel), and the Arellano Felix Organization. These cartel alliances while they last are auxiliary forces for the Zetas (and vice versa), containing pools of individuals for hire for ad hoc or contract jobs. US gangs, including prison gangs who are affiliated with or hired by Los Zetas are the Mexican Mafia, MS-13, Texas Syndicate, Hermanos Pistoleros Latinos (HPL), Barrio Azteca, Valluco Soldiers (TX), Mexikanemi, Tri-City Bombers, and the Latin Kings.[19] There are also a number of 'regular guys off the street' who are contracted by Los Zetas. Other individuals or small groups affiliated with the Zetas include anti-Castro Cuban-Americans and Guatemalan smugglers.

Like their gang and cartel affiliates, individual Los Zetas often have multiple names, or AKAs, which may confuse analysts when attempting to conduct in-depth reconstruction of the Zetas' composition. Names beginning with 'L' plus a number are used for bodyguards or drivers. Higher numbers indicate lower rank (with the exception of those leaders who choose to keep their original names even as they move up in rank). The Zetas also have nicknames, for example, *El Winnie Pooh*, *El Talibán*, or Lazcano's *The Executioner*. As a group, Los Zetas are also referred to as *The Zetas Organization*, *The Company* (US only), and *FECG* (*Fuerzas Especiales del Cartel del Golfo*; Special Forces of The Gulf Cartel). The latter designation was found on a Zetas shield patch on tactical shirts in a Zeta safe house.[20]

**Disposition**

Los Zetas, headquartered in Nuevo Laredo, primarily operate in the northern and eastern Mexican states. Nuevo Laredo, located very near the US border represents an approximate 120-mile northwest shift along the border from Matamoros, where the Gulf Cartel, their originator, still keeps its primary hub. Having essentially two headquarters, both strategically placed just across the border from the US and with access to major shipping freeways (e.g. Highway 35 from Nuevo Laredo), is perhaps an overlooked advantage of the Zetas/Gulf Cartel. Having two hubs allows them redundancy of command and control as well as control of alternate access routes directly into the US. Throughout Mexico, Los Zetas are reportedly operating in more than 20 states, and possibly have a presence in all 31. In the US, Los Zetas are active in Texas and Arizona and, to a lesser known degree, in Oklahoma, Georgia, Alabama, and Tennessee. Across the eastern half of the US, the Zetas have a shadowy existence in many states, which may at best be assessed as co-located with reported Gulf Cartel operational areas, illustrated by the National Drug Intelligence Center's (NDIC) 2008 Situational Report.[21]

The Zetas' presence in Mexico is in stark contrast to their presence in the US – as overt in Mexico as it is shadowy in the US. In Mexico, Los Zetas' territories have various standings: they are either established and controlled, in dispute with rivals, or shared among rivals. Zetas' areas, often well-known smuggling corridors or *plazas,* are segregated into operational territories, each with a leader. Some evidence suggests that Los Zetas are accomplishing this type of area distribution in the US as well, particularly in Texas. The Rio Grande area in

Texas is assessed to have been divided by the Zetas into operational territories each with an assigned leader. These territories must correlate to those under the Zetas' control across the border in Mexico creating a narco-trafficking continuum.

The Zetas try to limit their time in the US to avoid being arrested by authorities, who are by-and-large not corrupt.[22] Los Zetas' presence in the US includes high ranking members and their hired assassins, who have access to a variety of weapons there. Some ranking members of Los Zetas have familial ties in the US, near the US/Mexico border, and in major cities further from the border. These familial ties allow for natural safe havens and storage facilities and, as a result, more operational freedom for drug traffickers. The number two leader of Los Zetas, Miguel Angel Treviño-Morales, according to investigative analysis, controls numerous transportation and distribution cells located in North Texas. Several members of Treviño-Morales's immediate and extended family have resided in the northeastern Texas area for many years, including Dallas/Fort Worth. His family connections there provide Treviño-Morales with a safe operating environment based on intimate knowledge and trust. The resulting freedom of movement allows him to further the drug trafficking operations of the Gulf Cartel and Los Zetas.[23]

To facilitate their drug trafficking operations through the US, the Zetas contract US gangs. Gangs hired by Los Zetas are either locals or they have a more permanent presence than the Zetas; US gangs often maintain chapters and use their members along the border with Mexico to facilitate drug transshipments to other parts of the state(s).[24] The Zetas' presence in US cities, towns, or suburbs whether permanent, temporary, or by association with contracted gangs or individuals, is often affirmed only when a crime or a sting operation occurs. In August 2008 in Alabama, Los Zetas were suspected to be involved in a multiple homicide event. In August 2009, at least 16 people including US citizens were arrested in Houston, McAllen, Brownsville, and Edinburg, Texas as well as Nashville, Tennessee and West Palm Beach, Florida in a federal drug trafficking and money laundering sting operation. Those arrested are believed to be linked to the Zetas. Other multi-state drug distribution arrests have occurred in the US that have involved regular citizens, including college students, a massage therapist, firefighters and others – each connected to the Zetas. The crimes of Los Zetas and those of their affiliates and contractors help to expose their suspected presence as reality, bringing them into *humanspace* where they might otherwise be invisible to law enforcement. It is also possible that with their many contractors, the Zetas themselves are not required to have much of a footprint in the US in order for their drug distribution operations to succeed.

Changes in enemy dispositions are often indicators requiring further scrutiny and intelligence collection. Los Zetas are increasingly moving south of Mexico and are operating in the northern and eastern provinces of Guatemala, including Guatemala City. This move south by the Zetas is an evasive one in response to increased military pressure by Mexico and to increased airborne and maritime surveillance of narco-trafficking by several countries in the region. But the Zetas' move is also an offensive one that facilitates arms transfers of military-style weapons into Mexico to fight their opposition there. Los Zetas are increasingly reported in areas outside of Mexico. Since at least 2007, in addition to Guatemala, Los Zetas have been establishing networks and routes in Honduras, Belize, Costa Rica, and Panama.[25]

## Strength figures

Los Zetas are estimated to have 300–350 core members (there are other estimates which place this number much lower, at 100–200).[26] By some accounts there are now some 2000 extended members, a number that is thought to be growing.[27] Core members include the remaining original Zetas plus follow-on, mid-level members and trainees. Extended members most likely include the various auxiliary forces, contractors, family members, and other support personnel at their disposal – particularly the large numbers of corrupt Mexican police that act as a force multiplier for the Zetas.

The Zetas use some of their forces as reserves – and they have a kind of replacement system. It is thought that with the capture or killing of any high ranking Zeta member, business would continue as usual as soon as the next day. In part, the overlapping, parallel association the Zetas have with the Gulf Cartel makes them less affected by losses. When Los Zetas are placed in a defensive posture by federal forces targeting their plazas, they respond by mobilizing additional personnel to the area being targeted. These reserve personnel are likely pulled temporarily from another plaza under the Zetas' control. The Zetas' leader of the McAllen-Mission, Texas plaza, Jaime Gonzalez Duran, aka *El Hummer*, ordered additional personnel to the plaza to regain control of it and to engage law enforcement *if confronted*. The reserves, or *replacements* ordered by Gonzalez Duran were believed to be armed with assault rifles, bulletproof vests, and grenades, and occupied safe houses throughout the McAllen area.[28]

The weapons and equipment of Los Zetas, like those of insurgencies and terrorist groups, are impossible to count and track due to their dispersed and non-permanent nature (Table 1).[29] Unlike insurgencies, the Zetas have unlimited funding with which to purchase more weapons, including more advanced types. In November 2008, the capture of Jaime Gonzalez Duran and the simultaneous raid of three Zeta safe houses in Reynosa, Tamaulipas yielded the largest weapon seizure in the history of Mexico. The combined caches held 540 assault rifles, 287 grenades, 2 M72 LAW rocket launchers, 500,000 rounds of ammunition, 67 ballistic vests, 14 sticks of TNT, and more.[30] The Zetas are reported to be storing similar weapons in Guatemala, and Zetas operating there are said to be well-organized, have plenty of money and arms, and are well prepared to protect their acquired territories.

## Tactics

Los Zetas' tactics reflect their many operational modes. On a given day or in a given territory, the Zetas operate like an insurgency, state military, paramilitary,

Table 1.    Weapons and equipment of Los Zetas (known or suspected)

| Category | Description |
| --- | --- |
| **Weapons** | M-16 |
| | AK-47 |
| | AR-15 with Aimpoint sights |
| | AR-180 (found in Zeta cell leader's cache) |
| | MP5 Submachine gun |
| | .50 cal sniper rifle /including armor piercing capability |
| | M-60 |
| | 9 mm pistols |
| | .38 Super pistol |
| | .45 caliber pistol |
| | Colt .223 |
| | Five-Seven semi-automatic pistol |
| | PS90 (Belgian made) |
| | Revolvers |
| | Rocket Launchers |
| | Fragmentation hand grenades |
| | 40 mm grenades |
| | M-72 Anti-tank rockets |
| | AT-4 Anti-tank rockets |
| | RPG-7 grenade launchers |
| | Anti-aircraft guns (found in Guatemala) |
| | Surface-to-air missiles |
| | Machetes |
| | Bazookas |
| | Anti-personnel mines |
| | Claymore mines |
| | Chinese-made antitank rocket |
| | Paintball weapons (for training) |
| | Machetes |
| | Bowie knives |
| | Axes |
| | Paddles (used to beat foes or to discipline troops, some found w/the letter "Z" on them) |
| **Explosives** | TNT |
| | Dynamite |
| | Military grade explosives |
| **Equipment** | Tactical/commando-style uniforms |
| | Police and military uniforms (complete, incomplete and/or outdated sets). Manufacturing of uniforms has been discovered |
| | Night vision devices |
| | Armored vests |
| | Kevlar ballistic helmets |
| | Gas masks |
| | Vehicles (cars, trucks, SUVs—including many stolen) |
| | Armored vehicles |
| | Motorcycles |

Table 1 – *continued*

| Category | Description |
|---|---|
| | Boats |
| | Small aircraft |
| | Helicopters |
| **Communications Equipment** | Radio transmitters |
| | Walkie-Talkies |
| | Voice over Internet Protocol |
| | Broadband satellite instant messaging |
| | Text messaging |
| | Encrypted messaging |
| | Two-way radios |
| | Scanner devices |
| | Modern wiretapping equipment |
| | High-frequency radios with encryption and rolling codes |

terrorist group, organized criminal enterprise, cartel, gang, or business; their varying nature explains why they have been called many different things by media and investigative reporters attempting to categorize them (Table 2). Zeta tactics go beyond those of other postmodern armed groups in terms of their 'extremeness' – outright gruesome torture and killings, mass killings, skilled use of high-caliber weapons, and the practices of occultism and death saint worship to name several. Zeta tactics will likely continue to evolve and develop based on their circumstances – their operational freedom of movement and the emergence of similar competitive groups who will raise the bar by using more extreme tactics than the Zetas.

Los Zetas' operations in Mexico are brazen and out in the open, in great contrast to how they operate in the US. In the US, one will not see groups of 20 or more operatives in a convoy of bulletproof trucks, as has been observed in Mexico. On the US side of the border, the Zetas as enforcers conduct stealthy kidnappings and assassinations. By contrast in Mexico, the Zetas engage in very bloody street fights; they willingly announce their presence and claim responsibility for their acts. And collateral damage is not an issue for the Zetas; women, children, and bystanders often become victims in their firefights. Trademark tactics of the Zetas are those of swarming – conducted in vehicles for both assassinations and for theft of goods from commercial trucks – and their frequent wearing of military or police uniforms as disguises for unimpeded access to their targets.

Los Zetas have many tactical advantages in their operational territories, one being the easily fueled fear of their widespread presence among the people in Mexico. The Zetas' extreme tactics – including torturing, beheading, and sometimes mutilation of bodies – contribute to the spread of this fear and also to the success of the Zetas.[31] Body parts are left as gruesome displays often with

Table 2.    Tactics[a]

| Category | Tactic used (known or reported) | Location |
| --- | --- | --- |
| **Insurgency** | Use of disguises for access to target(s) | US, Mexico |
| | Killing of high-level officials | Mexico, Central America |
| | Disruptive tactics, e.g., place threatening phone calls to businesses to disrupt/delay business | Mexico |
| | Suppression of journalism | Mexico |
| | Computer-hacking | Mexico |
| | Threat calls via cell phone or police radio networks | Mexico |
| | Suborning of officials | Mexico, Central America |
| | Corruption of street police, border patrol agents | US, Mexico, Central America |
| | Expose rivals via internet | Global |
| | Swarming tactics (when attacking in vehicles) | Mexico |
| | Coordinated prison breaks | Mexico |
| | Seizing territory using extreme violence | Mexico, Central America |
| | Compartmentalization of cells in the network | US |
| | Use of insiders to facilitate operations | Mexico, Central America |
| **Military/ paramilitary** | Wearing of dark clothing, blackening faces when conducting operations | Mexico |
| | Use of lookouts | Mexico |
| | Cross-border killings | US, Mexico |
| | Direct engagement with military in firefights | Mexico |
| | Combined arms attacks, e.g., grenade tossing in conjunction with automatic firearms (used defensively and offensively) | US (uncommon), Mexico, Central America |
| | Commando-style raids | US, Mexico |
| | 'Take no prisoners' approach to outright battles | Mexico, Central America |
| **Terrorist** | 'El Guiso'[b] | Mexico |
| | Torture, beheading, mutilation | Mexico, Central America |
| | Kidnapping for torture, killing, exploitation | Mexico, Central America |
| | Mass graves, burning or dissolving bodies (in vats of lye) to dispose of evidence | Mexico |
| | Feeding bodies to lions | Mexico |
| **Organized crime/cartel/ illicit business** | Contract killings | US, Mexico, Central America |

Table 2 – *continued*

| Category | Tactic used (known or reported) | Location |
|---|---|---|
| | Purchase of cellular phone codes of intended targets, directly from their phone company | Mexico |
| | Hijacking trucks to steal goods ('urban piracy') | Mexico |
| | Kidnapping for debt collection or extortion | US, Mexico, Central America |
| | 'Silver or lead' offerings (a no choice bribe) | US border, Mexico |
| | Use of overkill on assassination targets (e.g. 40 or more rounds on one target) | Mexico |
| | Double-tap style assassination | US, Mexico, Central America |
| | Armed robbery | Mexico |
| | Bribery, intimidation | Mexico |
| | Use of the internet to lure individuals into kidnap-for-profit situations | Central America |
| | Hostile takeovers of drug markets | Mexico |
| | Same-day assassinations provided by sleeper cells | US, Mexico |
| | Use of spotters to observe commercial loading docks for future theft operations | Mexico |

[a] Tactics used by the Zetas are derived from multiple news and analysis sources.
[b] 'El Guiso', or 'stew' is a form of torture/killing and/or body disposal whereby the Zetas place sometimes live captives in a barrel filled with diesel and light it on fire. For purposes of torture, they often add chunks of iron for added heat.

notes, both to claim responsibility and at the same time threaten a specific group or individual with more of the same. No one who gets in the way of the Zetas is exempt from this tactic, which has been used on rivals, journalists, civilians, police, military, and government officials. The strategic advantages of using torture, beheadings, and mutilation for groups like Los Zetas are evident, and the tactic will likely continue.

Another tactic that allows Los Zetas strategic gains is the suppression of media, an Information Warfare (IW) tactic that is a high priority. Los Zetas actively suppress journalists with a mixture of physical aggression, threats and intimidation, and killings. In 2008, overall cases against media personnel in Mexico were assessed at approximately 31.8% physical aggression, 21% threats and intimidation, and 5.3% killings. Also in 2008 in Mexico, there were 223 attacks on freedom of expression and information, 85.1% of which targeted journalists and 14.9% targeted media outlets.[32] For Los Zetas, their efforts to suppress the Mexican media result in incorrect or under-reporting on Los Zetas; the consequences are such that investigative or intelligence collection efforts against the Zetas become complicated, and regular citizens are less likely to form opinions against the Zetas.

Another form of Information Warfare employed by the Zetas is their creative use of the Internet. They lure migrants from Central America with false employment and migration offerings through the use of website advertisements. When the unsuspecting targeted immigrants cross the southern Mexican border, they are then kidnapped and held until they come up with money. Without money they are sent into prostitution, forced labor camps, or forced to donate a kidney for resale.[33] Other uses of the Internet are for targeting rivals by threatening them or revealing personal information on them, or hacking into websites of journalists. Another form of IW that the Zetas employ is through their access to police radios, which they use to broadcast messages or intent, sometimes with music, and sometimes just prior to their killing of a police officer. They may also use police radios for deception operations in order to mislead local police.

The suborning of officials of all kinds is inherent to the Zetas' model and a necessary part of staying in business. As much as 15% of cartel money goes toward corruption of police, military, and government officials. Tactics used in the corruption of officials include the use of threats and intimidation tactics such as *plato or plomo*, whereby the individual is given a choice of taking money or meeting certain death; other tactics include intimidation of family members, cash payoffs, or other bribes such as sex. Through these tactics, Los Zetas have made significant inroads to the government at local and state levels and are said to be running parallel governments in many of their plaza territories.[34] Officials the Zetas can't corrupt are killed. In 2009 they threatened to take the life of the president of Guatemala.[35] In February 2009, several Zetas, including the Cancun police chief, were arrested for the torture and murder of retired General Mauro Enrique Tello in Cancun, to prevent him from setting up an elite counter-drug operation there.[36]

**Training**

Many of the skills the Zetas acquired in their original GAFES training included rapid deployment, aerial assaults, marksmanship, ambushes, intelligence collection, counter-surveillance techniques, prisoner rescues, sophisticated communications, and the art of intimidation. Many of these skills, while probably not passed to the next generation Zetas with the same degree of proficiency, are still evident in recent Zeta activities. Recent highly coordinated prison breaks conducted by the Zetas suggest that many high-level capabilities remain. The *Zetitas, Zetillas,* or *Lil Zetas* are next-generation Zetas who do not have the same level of training as the originals but are considered to be of a more brutal mindset.

Los Zetas have a number of training camps in Mexico and Guatemala and possibly in the US. The camps are designed for recruits as young as 15–18 who receive training for approximately six months.[37] The Kaibiles are employed by the Zetas as trainers at these camps for the purpose of giving *Lil Zetas* the necessary skills to conduct Zeta operations. The Zeta trainees are trained like

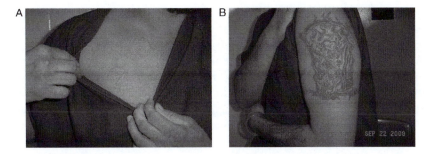

Figure 3.    Photos taken of a Zeta arrested in Memphis, TN, September 2009.
Note:    A. The image on the left is that of 'Z' branded on the Zeta's right chest and was
done after initial training was completed in Mexico on a large ranchero.
B. The image on the right is that of 'The Grim Reaper' on the Zeta's left arm. Zetas
can have a Santa Muerte or Grim Reaper tattoo and are encouraged to pray to Santa
Muerte for protection and success. The Zetas discourage tattoos that cannot be
covered. Hence, the tattoo on the lower left arm was done since the Zeta's
incarceration in Memphis and would not have been permitted by his superiors.
Source: US Law Enforcement.

soldiers, with high-powered weapons; they are taught to torture, and those who
cannot make it as a torturing killer are given another trade. After training is
completed, branding with the letter 'Z' may take place. Tattoos, which can be
concealed, are also allowed (see Figures 3a and 3b). Training camps in the US,
speculated to exist, serve different training purposes than camps in Mexico, an
indication that training conducted may be reflected in the local operational
environment. Texas-based Zeta trainees are reportedly taught home invasions,
firearms, and ways to run vehicles off the road in order to kidnap occupants who
owe drug debts. Kidnappings and home invasion robberies are increasingly
occurring in Phoenix, Arizona, as well as Texas.

## Logistics

Los Zetas must ensure that their trafficked drugs get to their final destinations
without interference, but they must also ensure that the cash received for them
makes its way back to their management in Mexico. Logistics, defined in
business terms, which includes the management of cash flows, applies as much to
Los Zetas as logistics defined in military terms does. A highly effective logistics
system is crucial for any successful organization, business, or military – one that
can rapidly move materiel or persons to where they need to go. Los Zetas are no
different. What the Zetas have to their advantage are their many logistical options
for trafficking and smuggling, with plenty of redundancies for both routes and
means of transportation. Where they encounter obstacles to the flow of their
product, they use an alternate or find a new route or means.

Logistics for Los Zetas' drug trafficking operations from origin to final
destination may be understood best if assessed in three separate phases: from

South and Central America through Mexico, from the US–Mexican border into the US, and throughout the US. Drug shipments that originate in South America, particularly Colombia and Venezuela, are shipped via boats, aircraft, and automobiles to Central American countries and on into Mexico. The Zetas may employ one or more transportation means (air, land, or sea) in a series of short clandestine hops until they reach Mexico. For this first phase, the drugs are like wholesale goods – they are cheaper and are shipped in bulk. Through Mexico, the drugs are shipped northward using well-known drug corridors shared or controlled by the Zetas. Many drugs are grown or manufactured in Mexico; drug shipments that can originate in Mexico versus farther away in Central America represent a shorter logistics tail for Los Zetas and thus an advantage for them.

In a second phase, movement of drugs across the border into the US involves a different set of logistics requirements. The Zetas often use commercial trailers on major roadways to get across the border undetected; alternatively, they will use commercial rail cars. Near the Rio Grande river crossing that connects Nuevo Laredo, Mexico with Laredo, Texas, the Zetas are said to maintain a network of boats and rafts along the river to help move drugs into the US.[38]

At some point upon reaching the US, the drugs go from wholesale bulk shipments to small retail packages for distribution – a third logistics phase. The drugs are repackaged in cities such as Houston for further shipment within the US. Los Zetas use a variety of means to get drugs to their final destinations. The highway network that runs from Mexico throughout the US is ideal for drug trafficking – there is little law enforcement scrutiny placed on vehicles beyond the border areas. San Antonio is a major facilitating drug transshipment center for the Zetas; it is far enough away from the border and has many major roadways that connect with other major roadways. In South Texas, drug trafficking organizations, likely including the Zetas who are dominant in the area, are also known to use commercial bus lines and commercial mail and package delivery services to ship drugs within the US.[39]

The Zetas must also move personnel (trafficked humans or their own personnel for operational purposes), arms, and cash, including bulk cash shipments. Often, arms and cash require storage, even if temporary. Storage areas for Los Zetas commonly include ranches, homes of wealthy drug-traffickers, or warehouses. Logistics for Los Zetas weighs heavily on their getting their money. Assessing logistics for conventional militaries assumes their funding is from state sources. Because money-making is what the Zetas are about, their illicit businesses will be factored into the operational assessment as a subset of logistics. In Mexico, the Zetas extract money from both legitimate and black market businesses. Sources of 'black revenue' include bordello operators, bars, and restaurants. The following are known illicit businesses of the Zetas, which range from large-scale to very small-scale operations:[40]

- Transport cargo theft
- Auto theft

- Home invasion robbery
- Extortion of street vendors
- Charging other groups a tariff for passage through Zeta/Gulf Cartel territory
- Gun, drug, and human smuggling
- Sexual exploitation
- Forced labor camps
- Money laundering
- Kidnapping for ransom
- 'Prepaid' assassinations
- Collection of protection money from business owners, bars, table dance joints, gambling houses, and other illicit or black market businesses
- Arms procurement (via hired *Los Mañosos*)
- Harvesting and marketing of human kidneys
- Oil siphoning and selling via Mexican front companies
- Corporate equipment theft and resale
- Paying small-time farmers to grow poppies (Guatemala) and to move contraband into Mexico
- Illegal CD/DVD marketing

Where the Zetas are moving their operations in Guatemala, logistics nodes are emerging.[41] Guatemala itself may be a new warehouse for the Zetas, where they can store and repackage drugs, stockpile weapons, and hide drug money. Evidence of criminal groups hiding money has been found in growing foreign reserves in Guatemala's central bank as recently as early–mid 2009. Los Zetas are also setting up airstrips and warehouses in remote parts of the jungle.[42] The end result of their move to Guatemala may be more security for the Zetas' products as a tradeoff to longer routes to the US – but overall, have increased chances of revenue gain.

### Recruitment

To perpetuate and grow their transnational businesses and replace their personnel losses, Los Zetas need to recruit continuously into their ranks. Newer generation Zetas are recruited from a virtually unlimited pool of federal and local law enforcement agencies, Mexican and Guatemalan military and special forces, and, increasingly, regular citizens, including Guatemalans and Americans. While Guatemalan citizens are often forced into working for the Zetas, the Americans have a choice. The ideal Zeta recruit is young, corruptible, and is a potential killer who can easily blend in with his intended operational area.[43] Young recruits are actively sought by Los Zetas in places such as nightclubs across the US border in Mexico where they are easily lured in; they are highly susceptible to the offer of money, or *bling*, and the need for respect. Youth, including children, are also sought after and easily recruited in poor small villages in internal Mexico. Los Zetas are using the Internet to recruit and ads soliciting workers have appeared for short periods at a time in the classified sections of newspapers in northern Mexico, possibly linked to Los Zetas. In April 2008, the news media captured images of what appeared to be a Zeta recruitment banner hung across a major thoroughfare in Nuevo Laredo before Mexican federal troops removed it. The banner, written in Spanish, translates as: 'Operative group "The Zetas" wants you, soldier or ex-soldier. We offer a good salary, food and benefits for your family. Don't suffer anymore mistreatment and don't go hungry. We won't give you instant noodle soup.'[44]

## Criminal brand naming

There are indications that Los Zetas have become a brand name, or *criminal brand*, due to widespread fear of their ruthlessness and seeming omnipresence.[45] Gangs and thugs who willingly call themselves Zetas know it is a useful tool for exerting control over their opponents by sparking fear in them. Evidence of Los Zetas as a criminal brand is reflected in the current estimates of their numbers, which range widely. For comparison, in the Caucasus region of Russia, Chechens in effect became a brand name throughout the country – so ruthless and notorious were they that they were petitioned by other gangs to use their 'brand name' in return for a cut of their proceeds.[46] Like the Chechens, the Zetas are notorious for their ruthlessness and brutality, including in the US and even where they may not be. As far away as Twin Falls County, Utah, an arrested man was proclaimed to be 'a member of Los Zetas' by his nephew.[47] Claims like the one in Utah may create dilemmas for local law enforcement. In a more conceptual example of criminal branding, the Zetas have their own seal: *Los Unicos*, or *The Only Ones*, a logo of a black horse surrounded by four Zs; they reportedly order vendors to sell pirated CDs and DVDs which have this logo on them. Allegedly they even have their own brandy in a Z-shaped bottle.[48]

## Intelligence and operations security (OPSEC)

The Zetas' intelligence network is said to be 'without equal in the Americas' by the Mexican Procuraduria General de La Republica (PGR, their Attorney General's office).[49] The intelligence network functions as an early warning system that ranges from youth observers on the streets to intelligence operatives using sophisticated techniques with high-tech equipment. All information collected is funneled somehow through the Zetas' network. The Zetas also employ counterintelligence cells that monitor law enforcement activity and rival cartel operations. Information gathered via surveillance activities is used by the Zetas to plan their own timing of operations and routes for smuggling attempts. In Texas where Zeta intelligence gathering activity is known to occur, the use of cell phones by Zetas or their contractors is prevalent.[50] OPSEC is used by the Zetas and was probably originally very good due to the level of their military training. Several known OPSEC practices used by the Zetas include their use of multiple phones or rotating or dropping phone numbers on a regular basis to avoid law enforcement detection. Another known OPSEC practice bears resemblance to some gangs; Zetas who are victims of cartel violence will not reveal information on their assailants to avoid further scrutiny by law enforcement of their own involvement in cartel activities. Further, Zeta leaders indicted in 2009 spoke code on the phone when discussing cartel business.

### Administrative

The Zetas/Gulf Cartel, aka *The Company,* have sophisticated record keeping programs to track shipping, employment, payroll, and payments made to law enforcement officials, as well as payments received and owed. Many captured Zetas have been accountants for key Zeta leaders, suggesting there are many of them. The US Drug Enforcement Administration (DEA) has said that, although the Zetas were originally based on military lines, the cartel has been built into a business structure, with quarterly meetings, business ledgers, even votes on key assassinations. According to a 2009 US indictment of four top leaders of *The Company*, alleged discussions occurred by those leaders regarding:[51]

- Supply infrastructure
- Debt collection
- Pricing for drugs in specific areas
- Bonus structures for individuals working at the *plazas*
- Drug concealment during transportation
- Methods of shipment from Mexico to Texas
- Seizures of shipments and their locations along the US–Mexico border

### Morale

Los Zetas go to great lengths to retrieve the bodies of their fallen comrades-in-arms, including removing them from graveyards. The intent of such acts is to enhance esprit de corps among the ranks. The Zetas also honor their dead. They not only honor their own dead, they worship a 'death saint'. In what might be called a religious practice, they call upon Santa Muerte, or Saint Death, to ensure an honorable death – death itself being inevitable. The Zetas know they are disposable, thus carrying with them images or figures of such as Santa Muerte may provide them with a morale boost while on paths to their own demise.[52] Another form of 'troop morale' for the Zetas lies in the significant wealth they are able to amass even at the lowest ranks, and their subsequent ability to purchase whatever they want for themselves and their families.

### Weather, enemy, terrain (WET)

Weather affects operations for both the Zetas and the US and Mexican efforts to detect them. Zetas likely use the cover of darkness for many of their operations, especially those in the US.[53] While it is unknown if the Zetas are so savvy, their knowledge of potential weather effects on US satellite imagery or UAV feeds that might pick up trafficking activity could affect Los Zetas timing of operations.

Terrain is a heavily used asset by Los Zetas; it forms the basis for their logistics and trafficking operations. They use the vast amount of land on both sides of the US–Mexican border to transfer drugs or humans with little chance of being detected. They use almost every component of terrain: oceans, littoral coasts, rivers, major to minor roadways, urban and rural environments, buildings,

Table 3.  Strengths and weaknesses of Los Zetas

| Strengths | Weaknesses |
| --- | --- |
| Ability to amass weapons | Dilution of quality of training |
| International expansion & networking | Decreased OPSEC as numbers grow |
| Own/operate state-of-the-art equipment (including communications) | Decreased trust among ranks as numbers grow – more vetting required |
| Intelligence gathering | Vulnerability to rival cartel hits, takeovers |
| Built-in redundancies (routes and means of transportation) | Leaders vulnerable to becoming drug users or addicts |
| Justification for actions: use of cult-behavior, death saint worship to justify brutal, criminal acts; lack of remorse. | The larger the cache, shipment or operation, the more susceptible to detection, capture |
| Ability to outgun, out-man Mexican, US police & border officials, even some Mexican military | Greater administrative requirements as numbers grow |
| Diversification – taking on multiple illicit businesses | Many Zetas captured or killed |
| Top level military training (from GAFES, Kaibiles) | Zetas lose most gun battles with the Mexican military |
| Unlimited funding | Risk of factions (e.g., La Familia Michoacana) |
| Use of corrupted police force as force-multiplier | |
| Ability to bribe and corrupt officials of all kinds | |
| Ability to compartmentalize cells within the network | |
| Integrate family into the organization | |
| Advantages from criminal branding | |
| Ability to survive, adapt and regenerate (even when hit hard by governmental forces) | |
| Ability to manipulate weak nations | |

airspace, jungles, border tunnels, to only name some. Use of a wide variety of terrain, in addition to enabling trafficking operations allows the Zetas to set up training camps, conduct planning, and secure weapons caches. Much more should be studied on the use of terrain and the cultural aspects benefiting the Zetas operations and their potential for global spread.[54]

## Most dangerous enemy courses of action (COA)

There are too many worst case options to name that could occur on US soil. The most significant courses of action concern Los Zetas making greater inroads into the US by doing the same things they do in Mexico, only by implementing them more slowly. Many Zeta activities in Mexico are already being transferred to US soil and include linking up with criminal gangs, taking advantage of the prison system, amassing weapons,[55] and, although more difficult in the US, corrupting border law enforcement, government officials, and corporations. Accompanying these activities would be more brutal acts and more overt firefights in the US. Over time, if these tactics were to be successful, the Zetas would begin to control portions of US territory. Open source indications of drug trafficking organizations linking up with terrorist groups such as Hezbollah to learn bomb-making techniques would certainly be an escalation and another possible COA for Los Zetas. Techniques such as vehicle-borne improvised explosive devices (VBIEDs) and explosively formed projectiles (EFPs) would allow for targeting of government buildings, vehicles, and personnel, at the same time outdoing their cartel rivals.[56] The more layered the potential COAs are upon one another, the more dangerous the situation becomes for the US and Mexico.

The Zetas are by no means invincible; they face the same range of threats faced by any guerilla group, both internally and externally (Table 3). But so far the Zetas have shown that they can withstand significant losses and adapt, continue to operate, and even expand their businesses and shift their operations into other countries, especially countries with weak governments. More importantly, they have led the way for other groups like them to emerge, often through similar beginnings such as enforcers for warring cartels. The danger of these new groups that have emerged is that they are already equally as brutal and act even more strangely than the Zetas, they operate on their own terms, and are even becoming cartels of their own.[57] The worldwide drug trafficking business is a brutally competitive one; it now requires the formation of enforcer groups that must continue to escalate their tactics. The Zeta brand just may be the ultimate inspiration for postmodern criminal groups worldwide.

## Notes

1.  Schiller, 'Turning in Drug Boss Could be Worth $5 million'.
2.  Freeman, 'State of Siege', 3.
3.  Recent works on the history of Los Zetas include: Grayson, 'Los Zetas'; Southern Pulse, 'Inside Los Zetas'; and Logan, 'Los Zetas'. Much of this information is traced

to a Procuraduria General de La Republica (PGR) report that was obtained by a writer who published a synopsis in *El Universal*. See Gomez, 'Inside the "Zetas"'.

4.  Cook, 'Mexico's Drug Cartels', 7–8.
5.  Logan, 'Los Zetas'.
6.  Burnett, 'Mexico's Ferocious Zetas Cartel Reigns through Fear'. For background on the Gulf Cartel, see Brophy, 'Mexico: Cartels, Corruption and Cocaine'.
7.  US Drug Enforcement Administration, 'Alleged Mexican Cartel Leaders, Associates Targeted'.
8.  Beittel, 'Mexico's Drug-Related Violence'.
9.  See Sullivan, 'Transnational Gangs'.
10. National Drug Intelligence Center (NDIC), 'Map 4'.
11. Roig-Franzia, 'Mexican Drug Cartels Leave a Bloody Trail on YouTube', A01.
12. For additional information on the Los Zetas organizational structure, see Manwaring, 'A "New" Dynamic in the Western Hemispheric Security Environment, 19–22.
13. US Drug Enforcement Administration, 'DEA Fugitive: Lazcano-Lazcano, Heriberto'.
14. Information on positions within the Zetas organization may be found at: Grayson, 'Los Zetas'; and *Southern Pulse*, 'Inside Los Zetas'.
15. See Grayson, 'Los Zetas' and *Southern Pulse*, 'Inside Los Zetas'.
16. Ibid.
17. Lavandera, 'Police: US Teens were Hitmen for Mexican Cartel'.
18. *Southern Pulse*, 'Inside Los Zetas'.
19. For a general overview, see National Gang Intelligence Center (NGIC), 'Gang Relationships with DTOs and Other Criminal Organizations'. Gang relationships to Los Zetas were determined by governmental and news reports.
20. *El Porvenir*, 'Detain armed commando in Guadeloupe'.
21. National Drug Intelligence Center (NDIC), 'Map 4'.
22. Concerns for corruption taking place on the US side of the border are ongoing. See Miller, 'The Mexicanization of American Law Enforcement'.
23. North Texas High Density Drug Trafficking Area (HIDTA), *Drug Market Analysis 2009.*
24. South Texas High Density Drug Trafficking Area (HIDTA), *Drug Market Analysis 2009, 5.*
25. For more on the Zetas moving south into Guatemala, see the following: Ellingwood. 'Mexico under Siege'; Beaubien, 'Mexico Drug Violence Spills into Guatemala'; and *NarcoGuerra Times*, 'Good Morning, Guatemalastan'.
26. Brands, 'Mexico's Narco-Insurgency and US Counterdrug Policy', 8.
27. *The History Channel*, 'To Torture or to Kill?'.
28. Carter, 'FBI warns of Drug Cartel Arming'.
29. Numerous news reports exist on these weapons. Most of these weapons are military grade and obtained via the international black market. See Ellingwood and Wilkinson, 'Drug gangs are winning the arms race', A1, A16–A17.
30. Sanchez, 'Mexican Drug Cartels Armed to the Hilt, Threatening National Security'.
31. This includes burning the victim in a barrel or throwing him or her into a vat of acid. These are variations of *guiso* (human stew) making. For a narco-video confession of captured Zetas, see Corchado and Samuels, 'Video offers brutal glimpse of cartel'.
32. *Latin American Herald Tribune*, 'Foundation: 17 Journalists Killed in Mexico in 18 Months'.
33. *NarcoGuerra Times*, 'Zetas Now Harvesting and Marketing Kidneys'.
34. It would not be surprising if the Zetas ultimately try to become a legitimate political entity; Cárdenas, the Gulf Cartel leader who first brought the Zetas into his inner

circles, is known for his currying favor with the poor by lavishing children with thousands of dollars' worth of toys, cakes, and milk.

35. McDermott, 'Mexican Cartel Threatens Guatemala President'.
36. Booth, 'Warrior in Drug Fight Soon Becomes a Victim'.
37. Rosalito Reta, a US citizen recruited by the Zetas as a teen, was trained for six months at a ranch in Mexico.
38. Schiller, 'FBI: Texas Drug Cell Trains on Own Ranch'.
39. North Texas High Density Drug Trafficking Area HIDTA, *Drug Market Analysis 2009*.
40. The Zetas, like other cartel groups, are rapidly expanding beyond drug trafficking and exploiting new revenue sources. News reports include National Association of Former Border Patrol Officers, 'Gulf Cartel stealing gas from Pemex pipelines!'; Rosenberg, 'Mexican Trains, Trucks Hijacked in New Crime Wave'; *NacroGuerra Times*, 'Zetas Now Harvesting and Marketing Kidneys'; and Associated Press, 'Feds: Mexican Drug Cartels Sold Stolen Oil to US Refineries'.
41. Associated Press, 'DEA: Mexican Cartels Push South'.
42. Vasquez, 'Mexican Drug Cartels Infiltrating Guatemala'.
43. All of the major Mexican drug cartels have been recruiting US citizens as assassins for years now. See Castillo, 'Mexican Attorney General: Drug Cartels Recruiting Hit Men in US'.
44. There are two schools of thought on the Zeta recruitment banner that was subsequently taken down by Mexican authorities: One, that it was a brazen and open recruitment attempt. A second school of thought is that the Zetas' banner, although deemed authentic, was posted in response to 'wanted' signs posted by the Mexican government on three Zeta members, that the Zetas' response was a way of thumbing their nose at the government and not for recruitment purposes. Additionally, the phone number listed on the banner reportedly did not exist when dialed. See Hawley, 'Mexico Cartels Post "Help Wanted" Ads.'.
45. See http://samuellogan.blogspot.com/2009/03/zetas-as-criminal-brand-name.html and http://www.chron.com/CDA/archives/archive.mpl?id=2009_4715303.
46. Galeotti, '"Brotherhoods" and "Associates"', 175.
47. Jackson, 'Utah Man Accused of Getting Minors Intoxicated'.
48. *RadioQuintana Roo*, 'Brandy Launches the Zetas'.
49. See Gomez, 'Inside the 'Zetas, They are Trained in Coahuila'.
50. South Texas High Density Drug Trafficking Area (HIDTA), *Drug Market Analysis 2009*.
51. US Drug Enforcement Administration, 'Alleged Mexican Cartel Leaders, Associates Targeted in Newest Effort to Combat Drug Trafficking Organizations'.
52. Freese, 'The Death Cult of the Drug Lords'.
53. Night time capabilities include the use of night vision goggles. See Johnson, 'The Merida Initiative'.
54. A somewhat dated, yet useful, general work in this regard is Eskridge, 'The Mexican Cartels and their Integration into Mexican Socio-Political Culture'.
55. For example, see Schiller, 'FBI: Texas Drug Cell Trains on Own Ranch'.
56. Not only is an arms race taking place between the competing Mexican cartels but weapons use is also evolving. The use of military hand grenade attacks are increasingly noted in press reports. Future cartel use of vehicular bombs, anti-tank mines, thermobaric weapons, and shaped charge weapons must now be considered. As early as 2002, near Fabens, Texas, the use of a laser in a counter-optical role against a US border patrol helicopter, most likely by Zeta personnel, was confirmed. See Bunker, 'Terrorists and Laser Weapons Use', 445.

57.  La Familia Michoacan has wreaked havoc in Michoacan state, Mexico, infiltrating and threatening the state government. In 2009, the US government designated both Los Zetas and La Familia as kingpin organizations along with other major Mexican drug cartels.

## Bibliography

Note: numerous OSINT (open source intelligence) documents, predominantly news reports and some analytical briefs, were utilized in the creation of the figures and tables accompanying this essay. These sources were vetted and cross-referenced by the author and then the products produced underwent subject matter expert review. These sources are not reflected in this bibliography (*The Editor*).

*Associated Press*. 'DEA: Mexican Cartels Push South'. *MSNBC.com* (15 April 2009), http://www.msnbc.msn.com/id/30229942.

*Associated Press*. 'Feds: Mexican Drug Cartels Sold Stolen Oil to US Refineries'. *Khou.com* (10 August 2009), http://www.khou.com/topstories/stories/khou090810_mh_drug-cartels-stolen-oil.c93ada51.html.

Beaubien, Jason. 'Mexico Drug Violence Spills into Guatemala'. National Public Radio (1 June 2009), http://www.npr.org/templates/story/story.php?storyId=104789349.

Beittel, June S. 'Mexico's Drug-Related Violence'. CRS Report for Congress R40582. Washington, DC: Congressional Research Service, 27 May 2009.

Booth, William. 'Warrior in Drug Fight Soon Becomes a Victim'. *The Washington Post* (9 February 2009), http://www.washingtonpost.com/wp-dyn/content/article/2009/02/08/AR2009020802388.html.

Brands, Hal. 'Mexico's Narco-Insurgency and US Counterdrug Policy'. Carlisle, PA: Strategic Studies Institute, US Army War College, May 2009.

Brophy, Stephanie. 'Mexico: Cartels, Corruption and Cocaine: A Profile of the Gulf Cartel'. *Global Crime* 9, no. 3 (August 2008): 248–61.

Bunker, Robert J. 'Terrorists and Laser Weapons Use: An Emergent Threat'. *Studies in Conflict & Terrorism* 31, no. 5 (May 2008): 434–55.

Burnett, John. 'Mexico's Ferocious Zetas Cartel Reigns through Fear'. National Public Radio (2 October 2009), http://www.npr.org/templates/story/story.php?storyId=113388071.

Carter, Sara A. 'FBI Warns of Drug Cartel Arming'. *The Washington Times* (26 October 2008).

Castillo, E. Eduardo. 'Mexican Attorney General: Drug Cartels Recruiting Hit Men in US'. *Associated Press* (20 December 2005).

Cook, Colleen W. 'Mexico's Drug Cartels'. CRS Report for Congress RL34215. Washington, DC: Congressional Research Service, 16 October 2007.

Corchado, Alfredo, and Lennox Samuels. 'Video Offers Brutal Glimpse of Cartel'. *The Dallas Morning News* (1 December 2005), http://www.dallasnews.com/sharedcontent/dws/dn/latestnews/stories/120105dnintdvd.1277f911.html.

Ellingwood, Ken. 'Mexico Under Siege: Drug Violence Spilling into Guatemala'. *Chicago Tribune* (3 June 2009).

Ellingwood, Ken, and Tracy Wilkinson. 'Drug Gangs are Winning the Arms Race'. *Los Angeles Times* (Sunday, 15 March 2009): A1, A16–A17.

*El Porvenir*. 'Detain armed commando in Guadeloupe' (Tuesday, 18 August 2009). Translation of 'Detienen a comando armado en Guadalupe'. http://www.elporvenir.com.mx/notas.asp?nota_id=331441.

Eskridge, Chris. 'The Mexican Cartels and their Integration into Mexican Socio-Political Culture'. Huntesville, TX: Office of International Justice, Inc., 2001.

Freeman, Laurie. 'State of Siege: Drug-Related Violence and Corruption in Mexico'. Special Report. Washington, DC: Washington Office on Latin America (WOLA), 2006.

Freese, Kevin. 'The Death Cult of the Drug Lords: Mexico's Patron Saint of Crime, Criminals, and the Dispossessed'. Fort Leavenworth, KS: Foreign Military Studies Office, 12 September 2005.

Galeotti, Mark. '"Brotherhoods" and "Associates": Chechen Networks of Crime and Resistance'. In *Networks, Terrorism and Global Insurgency*, edited by Robert J. Bunker, London: Routledge, 2006.

Gomez, Francisco. 'Inside the "Zetas", they are Trained in Coahuila'. *El Universal* (17 August 2008). Translation of 'Los Zetas por dentro; los entrenan en Coahuila'. http://www.vanguardia.com.mx/diario/noticia/seguridad/nacional/los_zetas_por_dentro;_los_entrenan_en_coahuila/209970.

Grayson, George W. 'Los Zetas: The Ruthless Army Spawned by a Mexican Drug Cartel'. *Foreign Policy Research Institute*, May 2008.

Hawley, Chris. 'Mexico Cartels Post "Help Wanted" Ads.' *USA Today* (24 April 2008), http//www.usatoday.com/news/world/2008-04-24-mexicocartels_N.htm.

*The History Channel*. 'To Torture or to Kill?'. Gangland series, Season 3, Episode 11, 29 November 2008. 45 Minutes. Also available on http://www.YouTube.com.

Jackson, Andrea. 'Utah Man Accused of Getting Minors Intoxicated'. *Times-News* (13 May 2009), http://www.magicvalley.com/articles/2009/08/05/news/local . . . / 167766.txt (Information cached on Google.com).

Johnson, David T. 'The Merida Initiative'. Remarks to the Subcommittee on State, Foreign Operations, Related Programs of House Committee on Appropriations. Washington, DC, 10 March 2009. http://www.state.gov/p/inl/rls/rm/120225.htm.

*Latin American Herald Tribune*. 'Foundation: 17 Journalists Killed in Mexico in 18 Months'. (3 August 2009), http://www.laht.com/.

Lavandera, Ed. 'Police: US Teens were Hitmen for Mexican Cartel'. *CNN*, Laredo, Texas (13 March 2009).

Logan, Samuel. 'Los Zetas: Evolution of a Criminal Organization'. *ISN Security Watch* (11 March 2009).

Manwaring, Max G. 'A "New" Dynamic in the Western Hemispheric Security Environment: The Mexican Zetas and Other Private Armies'. Carlisle, PA: Strategic Studies Institute, US Army War College, September 2009.

McDermott, Jeremy. 'Mexican Cartel Threatens Guatemala President'. *Telegraph.co.uk* (2 March 2009), http://www.telegraph.co.uk/news/worldnews/centralamericaand thecaribbean/guatemala/4928428/Mexican-cartel-threatens-Guatemala-President. html.

Miller, Judith. 'The Mexicanization of American Law Enforcement'. *City Journal* (Autumn 2009), http://www.city-journal.org/2009/19_4_corruption.html.

*NarcoGuerra Times*. 'Good Morning, Guatemalastan'. (28 June 2009).

*NarcoGuerra Times*. 'Zetas Now Harvesting and Marketing Kidneys'. (26 July 2009).

National Association of Former Border Patrol Officers. 'Gulf Cartel Stealing Gas from Pemex Pipelines!'. M3 Report. Nafbpo.org. 20 May 2009. Translated from *El Universal* (Mexico City), 19 May 2009.

National Drug Intelligence Center (NDIC). 'Map 4: Cities Reporting the Presence of Mexican DTOs Affiliated with the Gulf Coast Cartel', in *Cities in which Mexican DTOs Operate within the United States*. US Department of Justice. Situation Report, Product No. 2008-S0787-005, 11 April 2008.

National Gang Intelligence Center (NGIC). 'Gang Relationships With DTOs and Other Criminal Organizations', in *National Gang Threat Assessment 2009*. Product No. 2009-M0335-001, January 2009.

North Texas High Density Drug Trafficking Area (HIDTA). *Drug Market Analysis 2009*, National Drug Intelligence Center (NDIC), US Department of Justice (DOJ), Product No. 2009-R0813–021, April 2009.

*Radio Quintana Roo*. 'Brandy Launches the "Zetas"' (23 March 2009). Translation of 'Lanza Brandy de los "Zetas"', http://radioquintanaroo.com/lanza-brandy-de-los--zetas/.

Roig-Franzia, Manuel. 'Mexican Drug Cartels Leave a Bloody Trail on YouTube'. *The Washington Post* (9 April 2007): A01.

Rosenberg, Mica. 'Mexican Trains, Trucks Hijacked in New Crime Wave'. *Reuters* (29 May 2009), http://in.reuters.com/article/governmentFilingsNews/idINN2644884820090528.

Sanchez, Matt. 'Mexican Drug Cartels Armed to the Hilt, Threatening National Security'. *Fox News* (4 February 2009), http://www.foxnews.com/story/0,2933,487911,00.html.

Schiller, Dane. 'FBI: Texas Drug Cell Trains on Own Ranch'. *Houston Chronicle* (19 May 2009).

Schiller, Dane. 'Turning in Drug Boss Could be Worth $5 Million'. *Houston Chronicle* (20 July 2009).

South Texas High Density Drug Trafficking Area (HIDTA). *Drug Market Analysis 2009*, NDIC, US DOJ, Product No. 2009-R0813–031, February 2009.

*Southern Pulse*, 'Inside Los Zetas'. *Security in Latin America*, 14 January 2009, http://www.southernpulse.com.

Sullivan, John P. 'Transnational Gangs: The Impact of Third Generation Gangs in Central America'. *Air and Space Power Journal*, Spanish version (1 July 2008).

US Drug Enforcement Administration. 'Alleged Mexican Cartel Leaders, Associates Targeted in Newest Effort to Combat Drug Trafficking Organizations'. News Release, 20 July 2009. http://www.justice.gov/dea/pubs/pressrel/pr072009.html.

US Drug Enforcement Administration. 'DEA Fugitive: Lazcano-Lazcano, Heriberto'. nd., http://www.justice.gov/dea/fugitives/houston/LAZCANO-LAZCANO.html (accessed 30 October 2009).

Vasquez, Patzy. 'Mexican Drug Cartels Infiltrating Guatemala'. *CNN.com* (5 December 2008), http://www.cnn.com/2008/WORLD/americas/12/05/guatemala.safe.haven/index.html.

# Sureños gangs and Mexican cartel use of social networking sites

Sarah Womer[a] and Robert J. Bunker[b]*

[a]SAIC, San Diego, CA, USA; [b]Counter-OPFOR Corporation, Claremont, CA, USA

Narco use of the Internet, specifically social networking sites by Sureños gang and Mexican cartel members, is a rich yet underexplored area of research in open venues because of its sensitive nature. This essay provides overviews of Sureños gang and Mexican cartel use of the Internet by means of viewing and analyzing primary Internet sources linked to purported narcotics groups and their associates. These patterns of use were then compared to more sophisticated Internet use by terrorist groups with similarities and contrasts noted. This essay concludes with a few general observations concerning likely narco Internet use patterns that will emerge.

This open source review of Sureños affiliated gang and Mexican cartel member use of social networking sites will provide a baseline of narco opposing force (NARCO-OPFOR) patterns of use. Sureños use analysis builds upon recently identified patterns, while Mexican cartel member research will venture into new and for the most part previously unexplored territory. Little to no publicly available research has been conducted on these topics because of their sensitive nature. Overall this type of endeavor is one of looking at primary Internet sources linked to purported narcotics groups and their associates. The actual Internet research itself undertaken was passive in nature. This methodology utilizes a subtle and non-intrusive approach whereby keyword searches are conducted using Internet search engines. Hits are generated and then the unique individual user addresses on the various social networking sites being focused upon are viewed and analyzed. These 'rhetorically supportive' cyber portals, in turn, then provide links to other purported narco cyber addresses, homepages, and websites. At no time was forced entry attempted into any of these links – such as defeating password protection by means of hacks or social engineering attempts (e.g. actively gaining key information via online deceit by creating and utilizing a user alias); both of which would not only be academically unethical for this venue but also quite possibly illicit activity in their own right. Instead, already open doors were simply walked

---

* The views expressed in the author's contribution to this work do not represent SAIC.

through by the researchers and the information contained behind the various portals observed, analyzed, and then commented upon. None of the online identities were contacted directly to validate whether or not they were actual members of a gang, cartel, or enforcer group. Appropriate measures were also undertaken by the researchers to maintain necessary cyber-security protocols. Comparisons of these groups were subsequently made to known terrorist Internet and social networking use patterns with similarities and contrasts noted. Finally, a few general observations concerning likely future Sureños and Mexican cartel Internet use patterns are then discussed.

## Sureños related gangs

Sureños and affiliated gang use of the Internet and World Wide Web has been recognized for some time now and is routinely exploited by local law enforcement gang investigators and other gang suppression personnel. Typically, gang members will brag about their exploits on open social networking and other sites or even incriminate themselves concerning graffiti tagging and other criminal activities. Research on gang use of the Internet above the local level is almost non-existent or, if undertaken by groups such as the multi-agency National Gang Intelligence Center (NGIC) and the MS-13 National Gang Task Force, is highly sensitive in nature. Open literature on gang cyberspace presence is found in two federal gang threat assessments, and then mentioned only in brief generic overviews, and in general publications such as newspapers and online blogs.[1] Current perceptions, found in the *2009 National Gang Threat Assessment*, are that:

> Gang members often use cell phones and the Internet to communicate and promote their illicit activities... Internet-based methods such as social networking sites, encrypted e-mail, Internet telephony, and instant messaging are commonly used by gang members to communicate with one another and with drug customers. Gang members use social networking Internet sites such as MySpace, YouTube, and Facebook as well as personal web pages to communicate and boast about their gang membership and related activities.[2]

### Historical use

A general baseline of Internet use, found in the *2005 National Gang Threat Assessment*, states that gangs:

- continue to use web sites to notify members of meetings and event dates;
- advocate political platforms on web sites;
- use web sites that often include photos, tattoos, and gang hand signs; and
- have sites that may have bulletin boards or chat rooms where members can post messages or 'shout-outs' to identify cliques or chapters of the gangs in various cities.

That work also mentions that basic forms of operational security (OPSEC) were even then being followed by gangs to protect themselves from rival gangs and law enforcement monitoring:

- Many of these sites are now becoming password-protected, member only-sites.
- Gang websites or postings may contain false information intended to mislead other gangs and law enforcement.[3]

Also noted, in another publication, was the amateurish posting of the warning 'law enforcement is forbidden to enter' at some gang sites as an unsuccessful legal ploy to block gang investigators from viewing them.[4]

Historical research on Internet use by Sureños and related gangs is limited. Research conducted in early 2007 by one of the authors in collaboration with other researchers focused primarily on MS-13 gang presence on a small sampling of 10 social networking sites. Keyword searches initially utilized were 'MS-13', 'Sur-13', 'Mara Salvatrucha', 'Salvatrucho', and 'Los Sureños' with secondary links followed to individual homepages and postings as the research branched out from the initial word search hits. A very sizeable MS-13 presence, including affinity individuals (what appears to be middle and a few upper-middle class teens with gang friends), was evident on YouTube, Xanga, and MySpace. Blackplanet, Pbase, and Migente each had only one unique hit with a Canadian locale hit highly in question – though since that time it has become evident that MS-13 members now operate in Canada. Sites with no MS-13 presence were Vox, Ning, Sphere, and Facebook. Those no hit sites, along with the three single hit sites, did not have MS-13 presence for a number of reasons including cost barriers to use, yuppie or non-Hispanic orientations (such as Blackplanet), 'tech geek' focus, or overt gay user presence. Social networking sites are much like a 'cyber neighborhood', and MS-13 members and affinity hangers-on appear uncomfortable operating within some of those neighborhoods. MS-13 and Sureños related postings and images from the three main sites show the following activities:

- Propaganda/glorification of MS-13 and individual cliques in both English and Spanish videos set to rock music.
- Video of Sur-13 members in Queens, New York sitting on the curb while being jammed (questioned) by law enforcement purported to be ICE (Immigration and Customs Enforcement).
- Two jump-in (gang initiation) videos of MS-13 members.
- A video of a MS-13 member in a fist-fight with a rival gang member.
- Rest in peace (RIP) memorials to MS-13 members killed.
- Video of MS-13 members riding in a car with guns and music.
- Two short hand-coding (throwing gang signs) videos of poor quality.
- Numerous blogs and social networking pages of text and chit chat in English, Spanish, and what could be considered Ganglish (a mixture of both languages and street gang speak).
- Neighborhood pictures which included gang graffiti and images of gang members (with and without their faces covered).

- Videos containing threat postings and cartoon images of Norteños (N-14) being shot and their colors (red bandanas) being burned.
- F-13 (Florencia Threse) members wearing dog tags in a picture posted alongside that of a room containing an arsenal of weapons including assault and sniper rifles, numerous clips, an M203 Grenade Launcher, and a defensive (fragmented body) hand grenade.[5]

### Present use

The 2007 Sureños and MS-13 focused social networking research has been updated in this section and also includes a key word search for the18th Street Gang. Besides the initial sites searched, four more sites – Hi5, Bebo, Multiply, and Linkedin – were reviewed. Searches have also been conducted for dedicated gang and member only sites, including those potentially password protected. These searches took place primarily in July 2009 and included over 200 individual cyber portal and user views. Social networking sites devoid of Sureños, MS-13, and 18th Street affinity and gang presence are Vox, Sphere, Blackplanet, Pbase, and Linkedin. The Multiply site had only one usable search hit and the homepage reviewed was one of the strangest encountered. It purports to originate out of the Philippines and calls for an alliance between the True Brown Style (TBS) 13 gang and other Philippine based gangs with the La Mara Salvatrucha 13 gang. Pictures of TBS 13 gang members and MS-13 gang members in separate photos are posted on the page.[6] On the Migente site, Sureños gang presence is non-existent and older Sur-13, MS-13, and Florencia 13 affinity activity that was attempted has since ceased.

Ning was surprising in that it now has a couple of active clusters of Southside x3 (LA Sur-13) and Sureños (Sur Siders) affinity wannabees, gang associates, and probably a few actual gang members on them. Pictures of interest included gang members holding a sawed off shotgun and what appears to be a silver plated submachine gun (which makes that photo somewhat questionable)[7] and a coffin draped with blue bandanas. South Side glorification videos set to rock music were also present on one of the homepages. The Sureños gang affinity presence now on Facebook was quite surprising since none was noted in the review of a couple of years ago. Heavy Mara Salvatrucha user topical interest exists on this site with at least half a dozen groups with over 1000 members in them. Deeper analysis suggests that actual gangster and associate use on this site is extremely limited at best and the vast majority of the participants are aspiring members from both the US and foreign countries. Sur-13 group interest was much smaller and slightly more gang oriented. Overall, the sheer size of this site and its more global middle to upper class orientation makes it unattractive to gang use. The smaller Hi5 and Bebo sites both contain small clusters of users who identify with the Sureños and MS-13. The 18th Street Gang has only a couple of minor hits regarding professed associates or members with one image of a heavily tattooed individual calling himself a 'Ms 13 puto killer' making threats in Ganglish.

For the most part, the orientation on these sites was toward chit chatting, dating, and gang lifestyle glorification with the usual poses with gang signs, tattoos, gang paraphernalia, and a few photos with members posing with semi-automatic pistols.

The three main sites with Sureños and related gang presence, YouTube, Xanga, and MySpace, were once again reviewed. Xanga is now empty of this form of gang activity. The other two sites were still quite active and had basically the same types of activities as noted two years ago.[8] Eighteenth Street Gang and associate user presence also noted. Additional items of interest were:

- Photo after photo of gang hand signs, blue bandanas, graffiti, tattoos, and numerous pictures of gang members with pistols, shotguns, assault rifles and weapons mixes such as a machete and a machine pistol and an assault rifle and a pistol on the various homepages.
- Most, though not all, of the MySpace pages were set on friends only viewing.
- Dozens of videos posted ranging from gang, clique, and individual glorification through spray painting on walls, hand signing, the taunting and threatening of rivals, fist fights with rivals, and new gang member jump-ins (gang initiations).

The general consensus is that gang recruiting on the Internet is still not fully understood by researchers:

> On MySpace, Facebook and YouTube, there are plenty of pages and videos of gangsters from the 'red' and 'blue' teams. But even though there are media articles dating back to 1996 that talk about gangs recruiting new members on the Internet, officials say it's an area that is still relatively new to them and the prevalence of gang recruitment on the Web is still unknown.[9]

The FBI did, however, earlier equate more passive Internet activities 'MS-13 often recruits new members by glorifying the gang lifestyle (often on the Internet, complete with pictures and videos) ...' as recruitment measures.[10] An extreme example of an active recruitment measure would be a Los Zetas narco-banner hung under a freeway underpass in Mexico providing a telephone number for those seeking employment.[11] This suggests that differing views exist over just how gang recruitment Internet activities are defined. With regard to Sureños and related gangs, the open source analysis suggests that recruitment is still done at the neighborhood level and that joining a gang is a lifestyle choice rather than a job or profession, though postings by aspiring gang members asking how to join MS-13 and related gangs were viewed in a number of the social networking sites. Propaganda and perception management was highly evident at the various sites with the use of symbols, graffiti, music, and multimedia promoting gang culture widespread. Alcohol and marijuana images and use references were also quite common.

**Mexican drug cartels**

Like the Sureños and affiliate gangs, Mexican drug cartel members will brag about their organizational affiliation and will often incriminate themselves by posting information about drugs or other illicit activities. In addition, the cartels advertise themselves as a culture, religion, and way of life. A notable difference is that many of the Mexican drug cartel member web pages advertise their affiliation as a profession with an income, in addition to a group membership. Mexican drug cartels have symbolic logos, banners, posters, and other visual propaganda that is similar to what would be seen on a terrorist web site, such as FARC or al Qaeda, although not as evolved. Research studies on Mexican drug cartel use of the Internet are minimal. However, there is limited information about their Internet use in English and Spanish news stories and blogs. Mexican drug cartels have used the Internet for some time and cartel online videos started to become popular as early as 2005, if not earlier.[12] The most prevalent use of the Internet by Mexican drug cartels members, aspiring cartel members, and supporters appears to be propaganda and social networking. However, drug cartels have also posted threats and intended targets. For example, in December 2006 Mexican singer Valentin Elizalde was indirectly threatened on the Internet by alleged cartel members and supporters prior to his assassination. The threats were in response to an anti-cartel PowerPoint presentation which was posted on YouTube and was accompanied by his music. Similarly in August 2006, a Monterrey investigator was killed after having threatening messages posted online.[13] Mexican drug cartels appear to not only be active in cyberspace but are promoted and emulated by online drug cartel enthusiasts, who either role play as cartel members or pose as them. On 19 September 2009 the online *El Sol de Cuernavaca* newspaper ran a feature story entitled 'The Popularity of Another Drug', by Miguel Angel Rojas García. In the story he notes that drug cartel organizations, like Loz Zetas, have gained ground beyond drug trafficking to a grassroots level and are often depicted online as the 'Robin Hoods' of the 'XXI century' versus violent criminal organizations.[14]

This section on Mexican drug cartels on the Internet will look at some present and evolving use patterns that will later be compared and contrasted to Sureños gangs and terrorist use of the Internet. The observations and findings in this section were conducted from reviewing over 250 cyber venues that claimed to be affiliated and/or members of a Mexican drug cartel and from online cyber actors that are emulating and/or promoting cartels. Initial utilized keyword searches included 'Cártel del Golfo', 'Cártel D Zetas', 'Cártel Z', 'Los Zetas', 'Cartel De Sinaloa', 'El Sinaloense' and 'Cártel', 'Cártel de Tijuana', 'Cártel de Matamoros', 'Cártel de Tamaulipas', 'Cártel de Juárez', and 'La Familia Michoacana' with secondary venues followed to drug cartel cyber-locations as the research expanded from the initial keyword searches. Some of the more popular cartels (and sub-groups) on the Internet were the Sinaloa Cartel, the Gulf Cartel and Los Zetas, the Juárez Cartel, the Tijuana Cartel, and La Familia Michoacana.

The venues that appeared to have the largest drug cartel presence were MySpace and YouTube. There were some supporters and claimed drug cartel members present in Facebook, Hi5, Bebo, and Migente. There did not appear to be any notable overt presence of Mexican drug cartels in Twitter, Multiply, Vox, Sphere, Blackplanet, Pbase, Ning, or Linkedin. A primary limitation to the research is that the authors did not contact the self-claimed cartel members to confirm membership status, and some reviewed identities may be wannabes and/or posers pretending to be in a drug organization. Interestingly, there were several groups that claimed to be virtual role-playing cartels in online games and virtual communities. For example, as of 30 August 2009, *World of Warcraft* had a small grouping of players who called themselves 'Los Zetas'. There was also a virtual Los Zetas Gulf Cartel group present in Habbo Hotel which only had four members since its establishment on 24 January 2009 with the motto 'Zetas only Wear this badge. Cartel del Golfo. Loyalty Forever'.[15] There were also a few Habbo Hotel profiles in which the individual emulated a cartel. For example, one member described himself as 'Zetas Hitman' and stated that 'I work for the Zetas'.[16] There were also several virtual role-play cartels in Second Life. Some of the virtual Second Life cartels were 'Cartel de Juarez', 'Cartel de Juarez Jefes', 'Cartel of Cali', '$$Tijuana Locos Drug Cartel$$', '$$Compton Cartel$$', and '$$Garza West Cartel$$'. Following is a sample description.

### Second Life member description of Cartel De Juarez

'Originally modeled on the RL Cartel of northern Mexico, is now a private underground family built around the SL activities of a group gathered by Darko and Paris Cellardoor in SL's first year. Ad Hoc activities and resources of the group are dedicated to spreading the love and backing up of the la Familia. CHOLOS POR VIDA! The group is no longer admitting members.' The symbol for the group is the message Cartel de Juarez with a marijuana leaf underneath followed by 'The first official cartel party of 2005 Saturday 29@ 7PM PST'. The group appears to have 75 SL members.[17]

The online gaming and drug cartel virtual communities appeared to be people who were emulating the cartels and role-playing versus actual members. However, there were several MySpace pages in which the person claimed to be in or supportive of a particular cartel but that also engaged in online gaming. One of the games that appeared to be popular with these individuals was *Mafia Wars*. *Mafia Wars* is a social game by Zynga that is currently available via MySpace, Facebook, Tagged, Yahoo, and IPhone.[18]

### Drug cartels on MySpace

MySpace had several hundred pages dedicated to Mexican drug cartels. Most of the overt advertised cartel members in MySpace were self-described as male, from middle school age through 30 (most in the late teens to mid 20s,) and

Christian (two viewed profiles stated they were Muslim and several did not provide a religious preference). Most stated that they lived in Mexico, Texas, California, or Arizona and often provided the name of the city or area that they reside in. There were several self-proclaimed drug cartel members who stated that they lived in other locations, such as Chicago, Illinois, or Alabama. Of additional interest is that, while some self-proclaimed cartel members choose to make their MySpace profile private, many do not. Overt deception was used on some of the MySpace pages. For example, a participant may post a photo of a young man as an identity and list his age as 99 years old. Surprisingly, several self-claimed cartel members would overtly list their occupation as a drug cartel. One identity even stated in his profile under 'occupation' that he was a 'narco-trafficker'. Multiple individuals proudly displayed alleged photos of themselves with a gun (some with a ski mask and others without) and/or drugs. A few participants also posted other basic cartel equipment, such as bulletproof vests and walkie-talkies. Some individuals would borrow a popular photo of a known cartel member, or another person, in place of a self-photo as an OPSEC precaution. Many of the MySpace pages also had posted photos and images advertising illegal drugs (in some cases possibly the participant's drugs), primarily marijuana and cocaine. One participant even posted a video on his page on how to make cocaine. Most of the viewed pages had a drug cartel theme that represented the identity's claimed organizational affiliation and some would use a pre-made drug cartel MySpace layout from a freeware site (Figure 1). There were notable common logos, banners, and symbols used to represent various cartel affiliations. A few profiles also indicated the person's claimed rank within the cartel. For example, one individual stated that he was in Laredo, Texas and that he was in 'Los Zetas Juniors'. The popularity of the pages varied from some individuals listing five friends to 1,488 friends. Often the listed friends of a particular MySpace member cartel page would lead to additional self-claimed

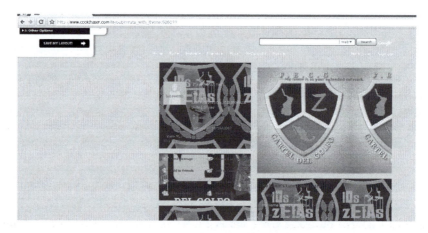

Figure 1.    Los Zetas MySpace template that was advertised on Coolchaser.com.

members of cartels. It was common for self-claimed MySpace cartel members to mashup with other services such as the MySpace mobile phone function and YouTube. There were even some self-claimed online cartel members that would play online games together such as *Mafia Wars* via MySpace to pretend that they were in a different mafia or cartel in addition to their self-claimed cartel membership.

### Drug cartels on YouTube

Mexican drug cartel presence directly and/or indirectly on YouTube appears to be common and has been noted multiple times in the mass media. The videos range from propaganda for or against a particular cartel to execution and operational videos. The topic in and of itself is very popular on YouTube, and most of the videos receive high hits with some videos receiving over 990,000 views. Like MySpace, multiple YouTube pages have been set up by individual subscribers claiming to be cartel members. In addition to posting videos, the self-claimed cartel member will often post a photo, cartel affiliation, logo, screen name, and list of friends that will often lead to other self-proclaimed cartel members and supporters. One primary difference between the cartel use of MySpace and YouTube is that multiple self-claimed cartel members on YouTube show an alleged self-photo with a gun but also blur out and/or cover their face to hide their identity (Figure 2); this practice seems to be less common in MySpace.

### Drug cartels in and on other cyber venues

In addition to YouTube and MySpace drug cartel members, aspiring gang members, and supporters did appear to access and use other social networking sites and forums, such as Hi5, Bebo, FaceBook, and FunForMobile, but to a lesser extent; they also use photo and image sharing sites such as Fotolog and PhotoBucket. Both the Fotolog and Photobucket sites appeared to contain some fairly self-incriminating photos, such as marijuana crops, individuals with different types of guns, and even two individuals sitting and smoking a joint. In addition, there were a few overt indications that drug cartel members and supporters may use Internet Relay Chat Clients (IRC.) For example, in 2008 one IRC site had the following group 'CaRtEl Del GOLFO'. The drug cartels may be using more advanced methods of communication but are not openly advertising it on the Internet. However, MySpace, YouTube, and other social networking venues provide ample opportunity for self-claimed drug cartel members to communicate with each other.

### Comparison of online gangs, drug cartels, and terrorists

Sureños gangs, Mexican drug cartels, and online terrorists, such as the Revolutionary Armed Forces of Colombia (FARC), Hamas, and al Qaeda, are

Figure 2.    Sample image from a page dedicated to a drug cartel by a YouTube member. The image shows an individual with a blacked-out face sitting on a couch with two AK-47 and AR15 type weapons. As of 2 October 2009, he had 318 friends and 48 subscribers in YouTube.

distinctly different in the way that they utilize the Internet, but there are some similarities. Most similarities indicate that self-claimed online terrorists, Sureños gang members, and Mexican drug cartel members perceive themselves as an online community, organizational culture, and way of life with religious and spiritual tones (and in some cases a blatant distortion of a religion). First, both Mexican drug cartels and Sureños gangs use online graffiti as a form of identification and communication. Interestingly, although al Qaeda does not use gang graffiti, there was one online member in YouTube who was in favor of al Qaeda-like ideologies and who also used crude gang-like graffiti and language. The individual had also posted al Qaeda videos on his YouTube page. This was exceptional, but it showed that online gang and terrorist cultures can merge and/or morph, and there is a possibility that al Qaeda-like ideologies could be picked up by gangs and/or gang-like members. All three categories use identifiable posters, banners, symbols, music (or songs), and in some instances poetry to represent organizational affiliation. Another similarity was the depiction of child indoctrination into a criminal organizational culture. Online terrorists, like al Qaeda and Hamas, have training videos that depict young boys going through paramilitary style training and indoctrination. Sureños gangs and Mexican drug cartels do not appear to have these types of online training videos, but some do post pictures of their children and some of the viewed self-claimed members are middle school to high school aged boys. In addition, one MySpace page that showed support for a Mexican drug cartel also showed a picture of a toddler aged boy wearing a red Spider-Man T-shirt with what looked to be a real gun on his waist. The image was strikingly similar to some of the pictures that are posted online of children being dressed in support of Hamas. There was also an MS-13 MySpace page in which a toddler aged boy was dressed in similar colors and gang paraphernalia to the man who was tying his shoes, and it is fairly common for Sureños gang members to dress their kids up in their colors. On the topic of online gaming and virtual role-playing there appeared to be more similarities between Sureños gangs and Mexican drug cartels versus terrorist organizations. For example, there appeared to be individuals who emulated and role-played groups like MS-13 and the Gulf Cartel. However, there also appeared to be self-claimed members of MS-13 and drug cartels who were playing online games. From the viewed websites, there were not any noted self-claimed terrorists from Hamas or al Qaeda playing online games, but there were individuals who were playing games with terrorist characters and/or role-playing as a terrorist. Another similarity between all three categories is the use of religion as part of the organizational online indoctrination. Religious-based terrorist organizations are markedly different in that they place the foundation of their ideology on a distorted misinterpretation of a religion, and that is the primary justification for the organization's existence. However, there were multiple self-claimed Sureños gang member social networking pages which depicted a picture of a pistol, the gang's color, and a crucifix in a manner reminiscent of some images on terrorist websites which depict an AK-47 on top or under a Qur'an. For Mexican drug cartels, it was common to find pages in which the individual promoted Jesus Malverde, who is often described as the patron saint of drugs and/or drug traffickers. Some of these postings would even include a full propaganda poster with the image of Jesus Malverde depicted as a patron saint with halo-like light over his head superimposed over a marijuana leaf. In addition, all three venues glorified their perceived 'martyrs' although at different levels of technical sophistication. For example, as noted earlier, MS-13 posts RIP memorials, there are videos that glorify dead drug cartel members, and al Qaeda and Hamas both post 'martyrdom' videos, poems, posters, and other types of propaganda glorifying dead members. All three categories utilize online social networks to promote their ideologies and organizations, although the actual social networking platforms may differ, and in some cases shift, as one platform becomes more popular for a particular group. One platform that appears to be popular with all three categories is YouTube, although there are other platforms that have all three categories present. YouTube has member-posted promotional videos for all three categories, and when a YouTube video is taken down, or a member is removed, the individual will often shift and rename the information within the same social networking platform, or in some cases will relocate to a different platform. All three categories have different levels of indoctrination and initiation videos in addition to advertisement-like propaganda. One similarity between Mexican drug cartels and organizations like al Qaeda which has been reported by multiple news agencies is the posting of execution videos and images.

A distinct difference between terrorist organizations and the other two categories is the level of technical sophistication and the fact that it is common for terrorist organizations to have an entire domain and website allocated to the organization, whereas the Sureños gangs and drug cartels appear to be more active on free-hosting platforms, such as MySpace. From the reviewed websites, Mexican drug cartels and Sureños gangs do not appear to post materials for paramilitary-style training, explosives, or other instructive technical operational information overtly. Although they will, as noted earlier, sometimes post incriminating information, such as weapons, drugs, meet-ups, and/or posted threats. However, multiple terrorist organizations have individuals who are in ideological support and/or who belong to the organization that provide online training, classes, and instructions. Another noted difference was that some terrorist websites and self-claimed terrorists will post hacking instructions (and in some instances cyber targets) and different types of software to maintain their operations. If these types of postings are used by drug cartels and Sureños gangs, they were not apparent from the reviewed sample population. Finally, some terrorist organizations, like al Qaeda and Hamas, appear to have a more evolved and advanced use of the Internet. This advanced use is most likely related to how long they have been using it, their formalized organizational structures, their funding, and global reach. For example, Hamas has official spokespeople who are employed primarily to speak to the mass media, and they have official online published articles and editorials. Al Qaeda has had websites on the Internet since at least 1995–96, such as the defunct Azzam.com website. One possible future evolution is that, as Sureños gangs and drug cartels become more adept with the Internet and more established as criminal enterprises and grassroots movements, they may shift toward patterns similar to current terrorist use. For example, Mexican drug cartels do appear to have a grassroots public relations outreach effort. Over time, this effort may evolve to having a more formalized structure. In addition, although no overt hacking activities were noted with the Sureños gangs and Mexican drug cartels, there is a possibility that it could be adopted as criminal elements are always looking for the newest tactic to evade law enforcement and to make money. Terrorist, Sureños gangs, and Mexican drug cartel use of the Internet will most likely continue to grow as a natural evolution of criminal elements keeping up with the newest communication mediums and technologies. The different ways, venues, and tactics of use will most likely shift and evolve over time to reflect the organizational growth structures and as the organizations learn new techniques.

**Acknowledgements**

Special thanks to Gus Frias for comment and review of an earlier draft of the Sureños gang use of social networking sites section of this essay.

**Notes**

1. These include Papachristos, 'Gang World'; KETV, 'Gangs Take Graffiti To Internet'; Glazer, 'Authorities Say Gangs Using Internet'; and Borunda, 'Street gangs use Web sites to promote their agendas'.
2. National Gang Intelligence Center, 'Gang Communications' section of the *National Gang Threat Assessment 2009*.
3. National Alliance of Gang Investigators Associations, *2005 National Gang Threat Assessment*, 4.
4. See KETV, 'Gangs Take Graffiti To Internet'.
5. Begert, Sullivan, and Bunker, 'MS-13 and Improvised Online Communication Networks'.
6. No reciprocal MS-13 member contact from the Americas was noted, so multiply.com should also at this time be considered devoid of use though an open invitation for MS-13 to ally with Philippine street gangsters is troubling.
7. Wes McBride, a noted gang researcher and retired law enforcement professional, was contacted concerning the image. Street gang members do not typically pose with submachine guns, especially silver-plated ones, which look like they came from a Hollywood movie.
8. Begert, Sullivan, and Bunker, 'MS-13 and Improvised Online Communication Networks'.
9. Information from the 19th annual Utah Gang Conference. Reavy, 'Gangs recruit new members via Internet, officials say'.
10. FBI Website, 'The MS-13 Threat: A National Assessment'.
11. The actual intent of hanging the banner is in dispute and may have been undertaken for psychological warfare purposes against the Mexican government. The number on it reached a taped recording.
12. Patterson (quoted), 'Mexican Cartel War Spreads to the Internet'.
13. *San Antonio Express News*, 'Singers Slaying was Posted in Advance'.
14. García, 'The Popularity of Another Drug'.
15. Review of overt profiles and groups on http://www.habbo.com.
16. Zeta Hitman Profile, Habbo Hotel, profile created on 24 June 2009, http://www.habbo.com.
17. Review of overt group profiles on http://www.secondlife.com.
18. *Mafia Wars* description from the Zynga website, http://www.zynga.com/games/index.php?game=mafiawars.

**Bibliography**

Hundreds of cyber venues – unique Internet addresses – linked to purported Sureños gang and Mexican drug cartel and enforcer affiliated individuals (including aspiring members, groupies, and role players) were utilized in this essay. Due to individual privacy concerns, tradecraft, and operational security issues pertaining to information collected from these venues, no specific Internet addresses will be listed (*The Authors*).

Begert, Matt, John P. Sullivan, and Robert J. Bunker. 'MS-13 and Improvised Online Communication Networks'. Presentation, *STEP 2007 IOCN Conference*, 21–22 February 2007. McLean, VA., invitation only.

Borunda, Daniel. 'Street Gangs Use Web Sites to Promote their Agendas', *El Paso Times* (Friday, 28 July 2006), http://www.elpasotimes.com/news/ci_4105310 (link is dead but mirrored on other sites).

*FBI Website.* 'The MS-13 Threat: A National Assessment', 14 January 2008, http://www.fbi.gov/page2/jan08/ms13_011408.html.

García, Miguel Angel Rojas. 'The Popularity of Another Drug'. *El Sol de Cuernavaca* (18 September 2009), http://www.oem.com.mx/elsoldecuernavaca/notas/n1330773.htm.

Glazer, Andrew. 'Authorities Say Gangs Using Internet'. *The Washington Post* (6 July 2006; 9:25 p.m.), http://www.washingtonpost.com/wp-dyn/content/article/2006/07/06/AR2006070600886.html.

KETV. 'Gangs Take Graffiti to Internet: Lincoln Police Monitor Gang Web Sites'. POSTED: 8:59 p.m. CDT 11 August 2005, UPDATED: 9:10 am CDT 12 August 2005, http://www.ketv.com/news/4841356/detail.html.

National Alliance of Gang Investigators Associations. *2005 National Gang Threat Assessment*. Grant Number 2003-DD-BX-0311, US Department of Justice, Bureau of Justice Assistance (BJA), http://www.ojp.usdoj.gov/BJA/what/2005_threat_assesment.pdf.

National Gang Intelligence Center. *National Gang Threat Assessment 2009*. Johnstown, PA, January 2009, http://www.usdoj.gov/ndic/pubs32/32146/activities.htm.

Papachristos, A. 'Gang World'. *Foreign Policy*, n.d., http://www.foreignpolicy.com/story/files/story2798.php (retrieved 14 April 2005).

Patterson, Kent (quoted). 'Mexican Cartel War Spreads to the Internet'. *Red Orbit* (11 April 2009), http://www.redorbit.com/news/technology/1669268/mexican_cartel_war_spreads_to_Internet/.

Reavy, Pat. 'Gangs recruit new members via Internet, officials say'. *Deseret News* (Thursday, 2 April 2009; 11:45 p.m. MDT), http://www.deseretnews.com/article/705294818/Gangs-recruit-new-members-via-Internet-officials-say.html.

*San Antonio Express News.* 'Singers Slaying was Posted in Advance' (6 December 2009), http://www.mysanantonio.com/entertainment/MYSA120306_01A_narco_Internet_34fd8de_html911.html.

# Corruption of politicians, law enforcement, and the judiciary in Mexico and complicity across the border

Luz E. Nagle[1]

*Stetson University College of Law, Gulfport, FL, USA*

Mexico is a failing state, languishing under a deeply entrenched system of political corruption that undermines the three branches of government and compromises Mexico's law enforcement and national security capabilities. This article explores the culture of corruption that pervades the state and frustrates the rule of law in Mexico, examining how the political elites, the judiciary, and police officials embrace corruption as a primary means for career advancement and for acquiring personal wealth. It is an examination of a country overwhelmed by a system of government and commerce that has grown dependent on corruption in order to function. But such a system cannot sustain itself indefinitely, and the signs of the Mexican state's collapse are becoming more apparent in the wake of unprecedented political and social violence at the hands of corrupt actors and Mexican drug lords.

Lawlessness south of the United States–Mexico border is nothing new. A culture of crime and banditry has long existed throughout the northern Mexican states and the southwestern United States and has benefitted from geographical homogeneity, terrain favorable to criminal activities, impoverished communities easily attracted to enrichment through nefarious means, and a folklore mentality that celebrates the exploits of larger-than-life characters existing outside the law – glorified in music and legend as much for way they met violent deaths as for the way in which they lived. The *narcocorridos* sung in cantinas on both sides of the border chronicle the brazen exploits of drug traffickers who have assumed exalted places among the pantheon of outlaws stretching back to Pancho Villa, Pascual Orozco, and even Geronimo.[2]

The modern precursors to the drug cartels operating along the US–Mexico border were established through familial ties during the Depression of the 1930s when groups living on the both sides of the border began moving people and contraband back and forth between the two countries.[3] Over the ensuing decades, the violence and wealth attached to the modern cartels has reached mythical proportions. The proliferation of the transborder crimes of trafficking in drugs,[4] human beings, weapons, false documents, pharmaceuticals, and other various forms of contraband might be less prolific were it not for the high level of corruption among officials at all levels of the Mexican government, and a massive web of drug cartels, money launderers, and shady businessmen who profit from corruption on both sides of the border.[5] Corruption in Mexico is not so much a symptom of illegality as much as it is a time-honored method by which successive groups of political and business elites amass influence and vast wealth on their rise to becoming Mexico's power brokers, and are then replaced by another group of elites who through proven means of corruption, amass influence and vast wealth on their own rise to the top.

## Political corruption in Mexico

Corruption in Mexico has been defined as an abuse of the public trust to gain a private benefit.[6] On a more basic level, however, corruption represents not a failure of law, per se, but a lack of political will to hold accountable those individuals who would seek personal gain through illegal means.[7] All too often in Mexico, those who have the power to hold corrupt actors accountable to the law and to the nation are themselves corrupt.

Under the long control of the Partido Revolucionario Insitucional (PRI), the government of Mexico developed and solidified a centralized structure with an ineffective federal system, an authoritarian political scheme with a strong president and weak and subservient legislative and judicial branches. Such an arrangement allowed the government to cultivate a blueprint of corruption and a lack of accountability by asserting widespread clientelist controls over the Mexican people. The PRI has portrayed itself as a system observing democratic principles and adherence to the rule of law while, at the same time, discretely preserving the political and economic prerogatives of a core group of power brokers and individuals and families intensely tied to Mexico's corporate monopolies and underworld criminality. As part of its political facade, the Mexican government has signed several international instruments to combat corruption. Among these instruments are the United Nations Convention against Corruption,[8] the Inter-American Convention against Corruption,[9] and the OECD's Convention on Combating Bribery of Foreign Officials in International Business Transactions.[10] Yet, Mexico is among nations having poor enforcement capabilities for combating corruption because political corruption is a crucial mechanism in the nation's unique style of government. Corruption actually aids in maintaining an equilibrium of sorts for the Mexican political and business systems and serves to undermine the potential of the organizations and economic forces to endanger the system.

Corruption also contributes to alleviating the demands imposed by Mexico's social classes by relieving the government of fiscal duties to provide the jobs and social services necessary to safeguard the civil society. The political system is designed to curtail questions about governmental policies and their goals.

Corruption is so deeply entrenched in Mexico that the goals of the system or the policies of government cannot be questioned. In fact, blaming failures of the system on individuals' ambition and offering up the occasional sacrificial lamb gives the government an easy and sustainable method for the government to control problems that could become politically explosive.[11] The quandary is that a government based on corruption as a means of getting things done cannot indefinitely sustain itself without the attendant harms associated with corruption overwhelming the capacity of the political system to hold those harms in check – unemployment, political discontent, failure of the legal system, economic crisis, inflation, and crime.

At the same time that political corruption in Mexico forms one of the underpinnings of government and business, Mexicans seem to both deride and relish the soap-opera-like scandals involving dramatic accusations and allegedly plausible evidence of pervasive corruption at all levels of government uncovered by the heroic efforts of clay-footed reformers and ideologues leading sporadic and often little more than ceremonial anti-corruption campaigns.[12] The PRI's control of Mexico for most of the last century was accomplished through a great deal of corruption, and in no small measure positioned the opposition candidate, Vicente Fox, to use fighting corruption as one of the main planks of his reform-oriented campaign for the presidency following the scandal-ridden administrations of his predecessors.[13] But even Fox, too, was tied to his own brand of corruption, known as 'blue corruption', the characteristics of which were described as modernizing all forms of *caciquism*.[14]

Recent data, however, suggests that corruption has not abated appreciably in Mexico under the successive reform-minded administrations of Vicente Fox and Felipe Calderón and their National Action Party (PAN), particularly in areas where organized crime asserts hegemony.[15] While Mexico has a legal framework in place to fight corruption, the Global Integrity Index for 2007 gave a 'Weak' rating to Mexico based on an index of integrity measurements compiled for more than 50 countries.[16] Data compiled by Transparency International also indicates that Mexico languishes behind many other nations in how the level of corruption is perceived there, and the 2008 Corruption Perception Index of 180 nations placed Mexico in 72nd place.[17]

As had been said, 'Corruption is not a characteristic of the system in Mexico. It is the system.'[18] It runs deeply throughout the cultural, historical, political, and social fabric of the nation, and emanates from an imbalance of the social, government, and business forces that confers to the Mexican state and its representatives a virtual monopoly on opportunities to achieve personal wealth and upward mobility. Such a structural asymmetry foments a peculiar pattern of generalized extortion[19] and a sense that it is easier to resort to corruption to get ahead than to work diligently and patiently to succeed based on merit, skill, and integrity. The Mexican state dictates the opportunities for upward mobility and the opportunities to advance almost exclusively through corrupt means form an important ingredient of state power. This condition emerges from internal attributes comprising the fundamental structure of Mexican government and the role a class of political elites (which for many decades was only the PRI) plays in controlling the laws and procedures of a heavily bureaucratic system.[20] To get ahead, an aspiring 'servant' of the state must early on reconcile himself to the fact that corruption equals advancement and that one has to pay to play. The fact that corruption in government nevertheless undermines public confidence and creates a malaise of indifference and cynicism by the vast majority of Mexican citizens is irrelevant.

Corruption in Mexico has been so widespread and so persistent for so long that some believe the source of corruption is physiological in nature. According to one analyst, 'corruption seems to be part of our DNA'.[21] To excuse corruption as being part of the psychological or genetic fabric of the nation is an easy cop out. Paying into corrupt circumstances, however, is due more to practicality and reality rather than to genetic predisposition.[22] Corruption is not hereditary; it is a learned behavioral trait based on many factors, including necessity, pragmatism, fear, ambition, and hubris.

## Elements of corruption among law enforcement

### Unchecked greed and ambition

Hubris may be a dominant element of corruption among the commanders of Mexico's law enforcement agencies, and the poster child for hubris and arrogance within the officer ranks of the police forces would have to be Major General Arturo 'El Negro' Durazo Moreno,[23] whose rise to prominence on the coattails of his childhood friend, President José López Portillo, became the stuff of which legends are made. Over the course of four decades, Durazo parlayed his rise to the top spot within the Departamento de Policia y Tránsito (police and transportation enforcement) into an empire of wealth and influence that utterly belied his official earnings of $350 per month.

Durazo was both an enabler and an enforcer. He was linked to the torture and disappearance of suspected subversives during the Dirty War of the 1970s and 1980s, and his reputation for brutality gave him a panache that no one in government dared to challenge. His utter lack of restraint and excess was symbolized in the hilltop estate he built in the resort town of Zihuatanejo called *El Partenon*, an imposing residence modeled on classical Greek architecture and a profusion of tackiness.

Durazo elevated political corruption to an art form unsurpassed in Mexico during the late twentieth century and used his political connections and the power of his office to reward allies and punish anyone who might stand between his ego and his desires. Among the many stories circulating about Durazo is one in which when told that he would need 150 workers to complete timely construction of a palatial home he envisioned, replied that he would have 650 policemen on the job site ready to begin work the next day. Related to this was the manner in which he acquired the land on which to build the home by offering the landowners lucrative and important jobs in the police for their sons and daughters in exchange for a fair price for the land. Later, he would tell the landowners that their children had been caught doing illegal acts on the police force and that if the landowners reneged on turning over their land as agreed, he would have their sons and daughters jailed for a very long time.

Durazo was instrumental as well in creating celebrity in Mexico among the nation's most political elites. He is credited with having financed and promoted the rise to stardom of the popular Mexican singer Luis Miguel and brokered highly lucrative business arrangements between powerful businessmen, drugs lords, and politicians. In the mid-1980s, Durazo also arranged summits among Mexico's leading drug lords that became known as the Empire of Evil and provided for their security. His excess contributed in no small measure to a deepening economic crisis in the central government and, when President Miguel de la Madrid came to power in 1982 on a mandate to change economic policy and moral reform, Durazo was among the prize targets to be investigated and ultimately charged with corruption, weapons smuggling, and crimes of extortion. He was subsequently arrested under an Interpol warrant in Los Angeles, California in 1984, extradited to Mexico, convicted, and imprisoned for eight years until released for good behavior and medical reasons.[24] While his assets were seized by the government, controversy continues over the actual disposition of Durazo's wealth and who in the government may have subsequently benefited from his misfortune.[25]

Durazo's collusion with underworld criminals is not at all unique among Mexican officials as indicated in the following report:

> When Sinaloa drug cartel leader Hector 'El Guerro' Palma was arrested by the military in June 1995, he was at the home of the local police commander; the majority of the armed men protecting him were federal judicial police. Subsequent investigations revealed that Palma had bought off the senior federal judicial police commanders in Guadalajara with several $40 million payments.[26]

### *Poor public perception*

With police officials such as Durazo gaining such notoriety, it is little wonder that 80% of the Mexican population believes that police are generally corrupt[27] and that at any time a police officer might attempt to shake a civilian down in some way. Mexican children learn early on from older family members not to trust police or any Mexican authorities.[28] Even American tourists in Mexico have known for decades that carrying extra money specifically to pay off police officers who may detain them is a requisite for travel south of the border.

Contrary to the United States where television and film portray police officers and detectives as larger-than-life heroes and guardians of society, Mexican police have long been portrayed in telenovelas and on the big screen as corrupt and incompetent oafs or sinister antagonists. Such stereotypes, justified or not, contribute to the negative perception that police do not investigate reports of crimes and, in many instances particularly those involving crimes against women and children, further victimize the victims or protect those individuals, such as corrupt labor managers, unethical manufacturers, brothel and nightclub owners, and racketeers who exploit women and children.

### *Poor compensation and benefits*

Corruption among police forces is due primarily to the inability of most Mexican police officers to earn a living wage and benefits that would possibly dissuade them from pursuing illicit activities. Among Mexico's 350,000 police officers working among 1,661 local, state, and federal law enforcement agencies,[29] thousands earn less than $250 per month. There is abundant anecdotal evidence of how the combination of inadequate legal compensation and a powerful drug underworld provides many opportunities for police to use their positions for easy, if not often risky, personal enrichment. Some have described police agencies as syndicates designed to funnel money upward to police supervisors from patrolmen who shake down prostitutes and run protection rackets to make their payments.[30]

As recently as June 2009, 93 Mexican police in the central Mexican state of Hidalgo were arrested on corruption charges for being on the payroll of the Zetas, the paramilitary enforcers of the Mexican drug cartels. Some officials arrested in the operation were receiving as much as $225,000 per month.[31] In the small town of La Junta in northern Mexico, police officers earn about $1,000 per month yet many wear fancy clothes, drive nice cars, and carry expensive weapons.[32] The cops who try to be honest run grave risks to their personal safety and have little hope for advancement in their careers when police supervisors and officials are on the take from drug traffickers. When one detective tried to question some of his colleagues about their affluence on such low salaries, someone tried to set him up for a bribery attempt involving an investigation in which he had transferred two suspects from a jail cell to the police station. An anonymous caller told the detective, 'You transferred some of my guys who work for me. And I want you to let me know every time you go to see them.'[33] The detective knew that drug traffickers paid cooperative police officers $3,000 up front and an addition $2,000 each time a cop tipped the traffickers off on impending raids or provided other intelligence. Two weeks later the detective's family was threatened, and when he went to his supervisor to ask for protection, the supervised ignored him and said there was nothing he could do. The detective then fled with his family to the United States to request political asylum.

In such a climate of corruption, honest police officers have almost no hope of doing their jobs with integrity and with support from supervisors. The only alternatives for many who go into law enforcement with a desire to help their community and nation are to buy into the corruption or get out, which often entails leaving the country altogether. The problem with going north, however, is that most police officers do not qualify for asylum in the United States because their claims are not on the required grounds of political persecution or persecution for being a member of a protected class.

Like many professionals in Mexico, adequate salaries to live on and to support a family are elusive. The number of Mexicans migrating illegally to the United States each year for work opportunities would suggest that employment in Mexico is in a constant state of crisis. Economic studies undertaken in the latter part of this decade, however, indicate that Mexico's unemployment rate is actually significantly lower than unemployment figures in France, Germany, and the United States.[34] The problem is that the peso has little buying power in an economy where 40% of Mexican citizens live below the poverty line. In fact, reportedly, 'The poverty class in Mexico may have more in common with homeless Americans than they do with poor Americans.'[35] Yet, as of January 2009, the official daily minimum wage set by the Mexican government for Mexico City and cities along the US–Mexico border is only 54.80 pesos ($4.18) per day,[36] compared to a minimum hourly rate across the border in the United States of $7.25 in Arizona, $8.00 in California, $7.50 in New Mexico, and $7.25 in Texas.[37]

Drug traffickers operating throughout Mexico have little hesitation in spending a lot of money buying off local law enforcement because the difference between the benefit drug lords reap to pay bribes and the huge benefit corrupt officers receive is so vastly disproportionate. A study by the Autonomous National University in the late 1990s indicated that drug traffickers spent somewhere in the area of $500 million per year on bribes, more than double the annual budget of Mexico's Attorney General's office.[38] Five hundred dollars paid to a policeman making less than that in a monthly salary to look the other way on any given day is a pittance to drug traffickers who will make millions on the successful result of that bribe. Moreover, the fear factor of not accepting an offered bribe goes a long way as well. According to one police officer interviewed recently, 'If they (drug traffickers) offer you 500 dollars a day, well it's pretty tempting, and if you say no, they kill you. So we're in a pretty tough position, huh?'[39]

The extreme amount of money passed around by drug cartels to buy up police officers and police commanders creates highly contentious competition among law enforcement, particularly between local and federal police, who have been known to engage in shootouts for control of key posts along drug trafficking corridors, and between 'police operating as law enforcers and police operating as law breakers'.[40]

Officials in the Mexican government have also engaged in franchising arrangements with law enforcement agencies in which, in exchange for producing results in the war on drugs, the official receives generous kickbacks from law enforcement commanders and federal prosecutors for appointments to profitable postings along border trafficking corridors and major drug production areas.[41] In other words, the officials in charge of anti-drug policies and prosecutions strive for a balance of showing success in fulfilling the mandates given to them by whichever president is in power while using corruption within the system for personal enrichment by regulating the amount of seizures that occur on their watch – enough to make it look like they are accomplishing something, but not enough to eat into the drug traffickers' profit margins.

Mexican police officers in the northern states on average earn a far lower monthly salary than their American counterparts just across the border. Using 2005 figures, Shirk notes that Mexican police offers in Tijuana earn $300–600 monthly compared to roughly $4600 per month earned by police in the neighboring community of Chula Vista, California. Granted, the costs of living are very different between San Diego County and Baja California, however, the salaries paid to American police officers demonstrate the commitment of local government in the United States to pay a professional salary in exchange for professional work and adherence to professional standards. As Shirk points out, 'That to me shows the investment we are willing to make in a professional police force. It's not just giving a guy a gun and a badge and saying, "Go out and do a good job".'[42] Moreover, a beat cop on the streets of Tijuana, just like a patrolman in San Diego, will take his cues from the top officials in his department. If he sees bribery and corruption as a means for advancement and survival within that law enforcement infrastructure, then he might not be expected to do otherwise – especially in communities where economic conditions are stressed and societal circumstances suppress the ambitions of individuals from humble backgrounds to climb up the social and economic ladder.

Because a Mexican police officer's salary and compensation benefits are generally insufficient to live on comfortably and to make police work a career vocation, there is a mindset among police officers that they are expected to use extortion to augment their salaries. The government tacitly looks the other way with a nod and a wink at this longstanding practice because it reduces pressure on law enforcement budgets to provide the officers a decent living wage and it contributes to the perpetuation of a patronage system that has its roots deeply embedded in Latin American culture.

Allowing officers to step outside the bounds of integrity to obtain greater compensation actually aids in the retention of experienced police officials and reduces pressure on officials higher up the chain of command or in other branches of government from worrying too much about being held accountable for their own corrupt activities. If everyone is on the take, then no one is going to upset the system, and no one is going to overturn the rice bowl of a colleague.

A noted American travel photographer tells the anecdote of a photo shoot that was done at the home of the mayor of a desirable Mexican Riviera resort town back in the 1980s in which the opulence of the mayor's hillside mansion overlooking the Pacific Ocean surprised even the photographer's seasoned experiences. When asked by the photographer how it was possible for the mayor to live so lavishly on a modest government salary, the mayor replied, with a conspiratorial grin, that that he enjoyed generous political support and that his constituents expected the mayor to demonstrate affluence and success. It was a tradition, the mayor said, that citizens take pride in the exalted status of their public officials, and that it gave Mexicans the ambition to reach high in the pursuit of their own dreams.

Corruption creates its own equilibrium and a symbiotic relationship develops between government officials and law enforcement. Each side knows that as long as they leave each other alone to pursue their own forms of corruption, then everyone will generally be happy. The trouble develops when outside influences interfere with that balance in the relationship, such as an investigation launched by a political rival, a directive from central government, or pressure from a foreign entity such as the United States government, the World Bank, or some particularly effective (and likely very lucky) anti-corruption watchdog.

### Few opportunities for career advancement

Mexico is a collection of states, similar to the United States' federation of states. Along Mexico's 2,100-mile-long northern border, more than 12 million people reside in communities on both sides of the border.[43] Most residents are dependent on trade and industries that rely on the exploitation of skilled and unskilled labor, and more than 70% of the population resides in 14 sets of twin cities such as San Diego–Tijuana; Nogales, Arizona–Nogales, Sonora; El Paso–Juarez; Loredo–Nuevo Loredo; and Brownsville–Matamoros. The population of the region has more than doubled since 1980, creating severe pressure on the existing physical infrastructure and the environment. However, Mexico City is very much the center of the nation culturally, intellectually, politically, and economically, with few exceptions. The best and brightest of Mexicans living along the northern frontier have lacked opportunities to develop careers and prominent livelihoods along the northern states and invariably head to Mexico City, Monterrey, Guadalajara, or the United States to pursue their professional aspirations. The dramatic increase in violent crime in border cities has exacerbated this problem and, as affluent and professional class Mexicans flee the border cities especially north into the United States, the jobs their presence in the border economies create and sustain are lost. Highly educated Mexicans from prestigious Mexican universities have emigrated to lucrative jobs in technology and business in Northern Texas and California, many doing so under claims of asylum. According to one estimate, 14,000 of the estimated 19,000 Mexicans who hold doctoral degrees reside in the United States.[44] Another report notes that 20,000 Mexican professionals emigrate yearly, at a loss of nearly $7 billion in earnings to boost the Mexican economy.[45] Asylum claims in El Paso, Texas jumped from 12 in 2005 to 80 in 2008. Kidnappings targeting the professional class and corruption among law enforcement play prominently in the decision to leave border cities. According to one case worker in El Paso, 'We're seeing complete families fleeing from our sister city Juarez. They are middle-class business people.... Their loved ones are being kidnapped, and they are asking extremely high amounts of money.'[46]

For a time, the growth of maquila industries along the US–Mexico border in the early 1990s held promises of prosperity for both blue collar and white collar Mexicans. But the region's economic sluggishness due to a downturn in the global economy over the last decade and significant mounting environmental problems associated with maquila plants contributed to a downturn for many manufacturing operations and their subsequent removal to China and other Asian and Latin American destinations.[47] Jobs are precious along the US–Mexico border and, in maquilas, securing a job and career advancement has in many instances been subject to corruption among labor management and labor unions.

Many police officers have very little formal education; some lack even a high school education and are functionally illiterate, and because higher paying positions in law enforcement require administrative and management proficiency and analytical skills, most police officers have no hope of advancing into higher paying and more prestigious positions. Their only alternative is to go on the take. While this creates a culture of corruption in law enforcement, it also relieves law enforcement agencies of the financial burden of training its officer corps and paying higher salaries as police officers progress in seniority. Moreover, just because better educated police may occupy management positions and have better training and skills sets does not mean they are less susceptible to corruption. In a culture of corruption, the higher up receive large bribes commensurate with the responsibilities they carry in their work that must be overcome by drug traffickers and others seeking to subvert the law.

### Poor training and education

In late 2008, Mexican President Felipe Calderón admitted that an evaluation of 56,000 local, state, and national Mexican police officers indicated that 49% of them were unqualified to do their jobs and incapable of combating the drug cartels.[48] Mexican police are woefully undertrained and under-prepared to assume law enforcement responsibilities. One police officer recently interviewed studied up to the third year of secondary school and then took a one-month-long course to become a police officer. His salary after eight years on the force is only $460 per month. One month of police training may include some physical training, rudimentary training in the law, ethics, and human rights, personal defense tactics, and handling weapons.[49]

In contrast, Mexico's national police force, the 15,250 member Federal Preventive Police, also known generically as *federales*, is comprised of 10,000 members of the army and navy, and the remainder from the Federal Investigations Agency.[50] Recruits to this force must have a high school diploma and undergo at least three months of formal police training. Their salaries are around $1,000 per month. Yet, even while they might be considered higher on the ladder of law enforcement, the *federales* are still susceptible to corruption as corruption is ingrained in the system and its members are still subject to the same forms of bribery or extortion by drug traffickers and other criminal elements.

When a police officer was told that his counterparts in the United States make more than $3,000 per month and go through rigorous academy training and follow-up training for at least two years, the officer noted, 'That's why they're respected there, while here in Mexico people just give us dirty looks.'[51] In such a climate of disrespect and lack of career potential and professional development, how can anyone think that corruption among law enforcement can be combated?

At least one government official has tried to turn things around through unconventional thinking. In the small town of Nezahualcoyotl outside Mexico City, Mayor Luis Sanchez thought that the best way to improve the public perception of his police force and make his officers more professional, ethical, and better at communication was to force them to read.[52] Beginning in 2005, all 1,100 officers were required to read one book each month. Failure to do so results in forfeiture of career advancement.[53] The officers receive reading lessons, if needed, and select their readings from a recommended list. They are tested and graded on their readings and on six other proficiency requirements, including physical training, ethics, and law enforcement. The mayor believed that by requiring his police officers to read, '70% of whom have no more than eighth-grade educations', they would be less rude to citizens, gain manners, and be more welcome in the areas they patrol.[54] In addition to requiring reading, the mayor also provisioned his officers with new uniforms, police cars, and even a new helicopter. Over the course of two years of improving working conditions and implementing better policing techniques, the mayor reported a 20% reduction in crime.[55]

Perhaps by gaining a moral compass through literature and other 'civilizing' influences, police officers may be more resistant to corruption. On the other hand, exposure to literature championing greater human ideals and self-esteem might also cause them to rethink the manner in which they are so poorly paid and trained and create dissent and rebellion in the ranks.

Resistance to change among the old guard is also an impediment to rooting out corruption – a condition by no means exclusive to Mexico. Referring to the reading requirement instituted by Mayor Sanchez, one officer noted, 'The majority of us are confused because other mayors have come and made promises that haven't been fulfilled.'[56] However, another officer, one of the 10% of the police who has a high school education, was more hopeful that while people don't read much in Mexico, perhaps forcing the police to do so might awaken cultural interests among the police force.[57]

### *Poor management and squandering resources*

Police corruption is further exacerbated simply by poor management of resources and faulty policing. At the national law enforcement level, President Calderón has spent the better part of the last two years tweaking and reorganizing the national system of public security. But his administration has not done the necessary cleaning out of the agencies known for inefficiencies and corruption. One critic of Calderón's reforms notes that the model upon which the reforms are based prevails only in African nations and that 'such a model is viewed as one of the most archaic in the world by nations like Italy, France, Germany, Colombia and El Salvador'.[58] A major problem with Calderón's reform concerns the political character of Mexico, since the local and state government entities 'are instruments of power by mayors and governments designed to serve their political interests and parallel powers, such as narcotrafficking, and not to serve the society'.[59] In fact, recently reorganized and unified national police are no better off than prior to Calderón's meddling. After removing 284 police officers, the replacements are less well trained, management is described as chaotic, and the ground is more fertile for corruption. For example, one Igor Labastida was appointed Director of Trafficking and Contraband in the Department of Regional Security after that position had been relocated from the Department of Intelligence. Labastida was shortly thereafter assassinated, and it was revealed that he was being investigated for links to the Sinaloa Cartel.[60]

Beat cops have not been well managed by their agencies, either. The traditional method of patrolling a town was little more than a process of turning loose a poorly educated officer with a badge and a gun to go out and wander the streets without any particular method of patrol or supervision. Such a lack of command and control created abundant opportunities for police officers to cross the line and get into situations of compromise or to become involved in nefarious activities with de facto impunity.

One way to reduce corruption and begin to alter negative perceptions by the public toward the police is to curtail an officer's ability to roam freely around a jurisdiction. Some police chiefs have begun to limit patrolmen to a specific area in order to monitor better their work performance and hold them accountable when problems arise or complaints are made. This could include limiting patrol areas to a certain number of square blocks or square kilometers within a jurisdiction and placing vetted supervisors out in the field to monitor the activities of patrols under their charge. Limiting the amount of time a patrolman is out on the street and rotating them through shifts and around a precinct also reduces the opportunities for police officers to be exposed to potential situations for bribery and corruption. Another possible aid to curb bribery and corruption would be to implement the kinds of community policing methods employed in the United States which have proven successful in improving police relations with the public.

Fundamental to combating corruption is the need to ensure that fiscal resources allotted to local law enforcement actually get from the federal and state government to the destination agencies and are properly used. A significant body of research suggests this does not occur in Mexico even as the Mexican government, in the face of mounting public demand and protest, has drastically increased federal resources for law enforcement, particularly along the northern border. In 2005, the federal government allotted $500 million in funding to state and local law enforcement agencies, a 32% increase over the prior year. But monitoring of the dissemination of the funds indicates that the money did not reach many of the destination agencies. Instead, Mexican state legislatures diverted the funds elsewhere in a process that is characterized as 'inevitably political'.[61] According to the same Mayor Sanchez who implemented the reading requirement for his officers, not 'a single cent' of additional funding from the central government was making its way to his law enforcement organization.[62] Instead, he was forced to divert funds for other municipal projects to increase police spending by 50% in order to give new police officers a starting salary of $700 per month.[63] He and Amador, his police chief, also radically reorganized patrolling methods. Instead of roaming freely, officers have 50-block coverage zones from which they are not supposed to stray.

**Military deployments in the war on drugs**

In the 1990s, the Mexican government undertook to train special forces units to combat drug traffickers under the false belief that their specialized training and elite status would render them impervious to corruption. Instead, the soldiers took their special forces training and fire power, deserted en masse over to the drug cartels, and formed a violent paramilitary-styled illegal armed group called the Zetas. The wholesale defection of these highly skilled fighters dealt a demoralizing and strategic blow to the Mexican government and raised the level of violence, particularly in border towns, to heights never before seen in modern Mexico.

In another incident in 1991, Mexican army members opened fire on 10 federal judicial police attempting to arrest smugglers and confiscate their shipment of 800 pounds of cocaine at a small airfield in Veracruz. Seven policemen were killed and the traffickers escaped. Aerial surveillance of the operation by United States Customs showed that the army was protecting the traffickers.[64]

Despite the loss of elite military personnel and an abundance of evidence that army personnel and their commanders are as easily corrupted as local police, President Calderón persists in insisting that because solders are better trained, more disciplined, and less prone to corruption, they are better suited to disrupt drug cartel operations and seize illicit firearms.[65] He continues to order the deployment of army units into areas along the US–Mexico border to fight the growing drug wars between the cartels and between cartels and the Mexican government and to replace local law enforcement whose ties to drug traffickers render them incapable of fulfilling government mandates to fight the drug war. However, the lingering issue of low pay for high risk (an enlisted soldier's average monthly pay is $400 per month) has resulted in many soldiers deserting over to the ranks of cartel 'private armies' throughout Mexico between December 2000 and November 2006.[66] Many of the defectors go from earning a few hundred dollars a month to more than $100,000 per month as cartel enforcers.[67]

**Corruption in the judiciary**

Corruption, inefficiency, and the lack of transparency form a widespread and structural phenomenon that continues to be key problems in Mexico's justice system.[68] The nation's entire judicial system is near collapse due in large part to corruption among its key members: the judicial police officers and judges.[69] Contrary to what analysts may argue, judicial corruption is grounded more in economics and politics than in Mexico's civil law tradition. According to a United Nations study, 'the legal traditions *per se* (civil vs. common law) are not a significant factor in the determination of justice-sector corruption'.[70] Corruption in the judiciary is fomented by weak accountability, lack of transparency, lack of oversight and imposition of disciplinary measures, and a flimsy participation by the civil society in the affairs of justice.[71] Not only does the judicial system fail to punish corrupt judges, it also fails to protect them from corruption.[72] Rather, the system rewards corrupt judges, and if they are dismissed for corrupt acts, they are nearly assured of reinstatement through the constitutional system of *amparo*.[73] Moreover, the agency responsible for protecting the integrity of the judges' decisions, the Federal Judicial Council (CFJ), refuses to take action against corrupt judges even in the face of evidence showing connections with drug cartels and court decisions denouncing judicial 'ineptitude and lack of knowledge of criminal law'.[74]

Out of 67 countries studied, Mexico ranked among the lowest in quality of justice-sector resolutions,[75] and a report by a United Nations Special Rapporteur estimated that between 50 and 70% of Mexican judges were corrupt.[76] Collusion between judges and organized crime and the penetration of drug cartels in the judicial system in order to influence judges' decisions and to manipulate them in their favor have been widely publicized. Yet, it was not until 2008 that the Supreme Court of Mexico acknowledged judicial corruption as a problem in their country.[77]

Corruption of the judicial takes the form of drug cartels bribing and/or threatening judges with *plata o plomo* (silver or lead) – a choice between a bribe or a bullet.[78] However, Mexican drug lords were, in the past, more or less content to penetrate the police and politicians or pay prison officials to allow escapes from jail. The recent targeting of judges raises questions about whether the killing of judges is a response to an actual government crackdown on the cartels, a 'clear sign of decomposition of previous relationships between organized crime and corrupt officials', or a move to emulate Colombian drug cartel tactics of killing judges as a method of doing business by intimidating and terrorizing the judiciary and the general public.[79] Moreover, if Mexican judges have been labeled 'judges of the traffickers',[80] then why would the judiciary be targeted for violence? One reason may have to do with the making of alliances since judges involved in narcotrafficking cases seem to become faithful to a particular drug cartel. Such is the case of Judge Jose Luis Gómez Martinez who has absolved several cases implicating members of the Sinaloa Cartel. In one case, he declared innocent two people accused of transporting $7 million in cash and $500,000 in jewelry and watches for the Sinaloa Cartel. His decisions, which patently violated the criminal procedural code, not only triggered complaints by the Attorney General's Office, but prompted the Attorney General to launch its own investigation. Regardless of any investigation, the defendants remain free and the judge has not been sanctioned even though an appeals court reversed the decision and found the defendant criminally liable.[81] In another case of judicial corruption, the Mexican army detained in Nuevo Laredo a group of 18 hit men loyal to the Sinaloa Cartel. They were found to be in possession of 28 long guns, 2 handguns, more than 10,000 rounds of ammunition, 12 grenade launchers, 18 hand grenades, smoke grenades, bulletproof vests, and equipment reserved for military use. Judge Gómez set them free, arguing lack of evidence of their involvement with organized crime.[82] In a third case, Judge Gómez ordered the freedom of the son of one of the Sinaloa Cartel's leaders, Archivaldo Iván Guzmán Salazar, after the son was accused of money laundering and murdering a Canadian tourist.[83]

Judicial corruption provides fertile ground for all types of crimes, but the biggest winners have been the drug cartels, who themselves become the de facto law in the areas of the national territory under their control. Drug cartels invest millions of dollars in corrupting judges and other public officials in order to advance their illegal ventures,[84] and they depend on criminal syndicates, corruption, intimidation, and brutal violence to protect their interests.[85]

Corrupt judges allow powerful criminals to work unobstructed and to occupy ungoverned space.[86] Moreover, judicial authorities lack respect in light of the actions and inactions taken by judges. Corrupt judges have damaged the image of such an important institution because even if many judges have been accused of corruption with evidence produced by the news media, they continue in their positions, representing justice and objectivity in manners that are little more than a sham.[87] Moreover, Mexico's corrupt judges endanger the society by putting out on the streets dangerous delinquents, kidnappers,[88] murderers,[89] rapists,[90] and the foot soldiers of organized crime.[91]

Due to the relentlessness of the press in reporting on corruption and the experiences Mexican citizens have had in judicial proceedings, public trust in the justice system is very low and discontent very high. More than 80% of Mexican citizens interviewed considered the judicial system corrupt and in the pockets of the elite. Many Mexican citizens perceive judges as a 'mafia', an institution established only for the benefit of those with no money who must use their judicial positions to maneuver into a patronage-fueled system in which cronyism, family ties, and wealth count more than merit.[92] At the same time, however, the civil society is not innocent in judicial corruption; citizens prey on the judicial weak system and exploit structural inefficiencies to obtain personal gain to the extent that one in three people using the court system in Mexico has paid a bribe to gain favorable rulings.[93]

## Poor enforcement against corruption

Those who engage in corrupt practices in Mexico know there is very little risk of being held accountable for their conduct. They know that the numbers favor their ability to avoid prosecution. According to Eduardo A. Bohorquez of Transparencia Mexicana, corruption is not endemic as much as it is epidemic.[94]

The persistence of corruption among law enforcement is due to a lack of desire by the Mexican government to stop it. Corruption actually benefits the Mexican government in much the same manner as remission benefits the Mexican government and the Mexican economy. Remissions from the United States back to Mexico from Mexican nationals take a great deal of pressure off the Mexican government to create jobs and provide better social services and improve the standards of living for its citizens. Every dollar sent to Mexico from the United States to sustain a Mexican family is one less dollar the Mexican government has to spend to take care of its citizens. In the same way, corruption takes financial pressure off the Mexican government to pay higher salaries to law enforcement officials and to increase expenditures to professionalize police forces. If the government knows that Mexican police make money on the side through nefarious means to make up for their shortfalls in salaries, then there is little incentive for the government to increase salaries and compensation. In a way, sustaining corruption in Mexico is a matter of cost-benefit analysis. Corruption is economical feasible as long as the balance between corruption and lawlessness is not upset, and it seems obvious that the Mexican government believes that the collateral damage caused to the state by corruption among law enforcement is not so damaging to the economy and society as to necessitate changing the status quo. The problem is that violence has now spun out of control due to the decades of laissez faire attitudes the government has taken toward combating corruption and the solutions are costing a great deal more in political and economic capital than could have been anticipated.

The only sure way to curtail law enforcement corruption is to make the penalty for corrupt practices far greater than the rewards are worth. Police officers caught and convicted for corruption should face lengthy prison sentences and forfeiture of their assets. They should be vetted periodically and constantly monitored for signs that they are crossing the line into illegal activities. The higher the position a corrupt actor occupies in law enforcement, the more severe should be the penalties and sanctions imposed. The approach should be one of a carrot and a stick. In order to become a police officer, one must take a solemn oath to protect the public trust and to serve the rule of law. By taking on the mantle and responsibilities, a police officer will be required to have an education, will go through a rigorous police academy training program, and will be subject to satisfying continuing education as a requirement for career advancement. Police officers will be paid a living wage that allows them to provide a solid middle class livelihood for themselves and for their dependents. Advancement will be based on merit and performance. The job of a police officer must become one of pride and honor rather than a means to get rich through illegal activities. If a police officer is expected to risk life and limb in the service of the community, then the worth of that officer must be validated through a good salary, generous benefits, training, and a development of pride in one's work and in one's position in the community. To break that public trust through corrupt acts should mean not only loss of freedom, loss of assets, and loss of a career, but loss of honor.

Only by changing the mindset of what it means to be a police officer can corruption be addressed. Instead of a police officer in Tijuana or Matamoros looking enviously at what his counterpart across the border makes in salary and benefits, that same officer should feel pride in knowing that he makes a similarly good living, that his work matters, and that he occupies an important position in the civil society. If the self-worth of a Mexican police officer equates to that of police professionals in the United States, there can be a dramatic alteration along the border in the way law enforcement operates. But there has to be a will to do so and, for that, there needs to be a large stick looming over the heads of all those, from the newly badged patrolman up to the chief of police and higher, who know that if they are caught committing corrupt acts, their freedom will be taken from them, their savings and assets will be taken from them, and their pride and standing in the society will be taken from them.

## Complicity across the border

The extreme level of violence along the US–Mexico border due to fighting between drug traffickers and between the government and drug traffickers grows because so much money is at stake. But drug trafficking and the corruption that allows the drug lords to persist is not just a Mexican problem. Without complicity in moving extreme amounts of drugs and money into and out of the United States, there would be no drug trafficking problem or a drug war raging at the present time.

There must be corruption across the border in the United States, according to President Calderón, who recently stressed that it is impossible to transport tons of cocaine across the border into the United States without complicity by some American authorities.[95] As evidence, Calderón pointed out that 90% of the weapons used in the current drugs violence originated from among the more than 11,000 gun shops in towns and cities close to the US–Mexico border.[96] The United States' government has long been vigilant of the potential for corruption among the nation's Customs and Border Protection officers, and has periodically established FBI-led Border Corruption Tasks Forces to investigate allegations of officers taking bribes from Mexican smugglers. One recent investigation led to the arrest of a decorated Customs inspector for colluding with a smuggler of illegal aliens (known as *coyotes*). The inspector pleaded guilty to accepting nearly $100,000 in bribes and sexual favors from a female smuggler and was sentenced to five years in prison and a $200,000 fine.[97] The pressure brought on border inspectors and officers to succumb to corruption is growing due to increased smuggling along the border and more money being made by smugglers and drug traffickers. Federal officers interviewed for a PBS Frontline report in 2008 acknowledged that there have been over one hundred similar arrests since 2003 and that, at the time of the interview, there were nearly 200 open investigations of corruption among US border officers and inspectors along the US–Mexico border.[98] In another case of corruption across the border, an INS employee was bribed by the drug trafficker to transport drugs into the United States on INS buses used for deporting illegal aliens back to Mexico.[99]

In the end, it is not the individuals on the ground north of border that get caught up in the allure of easy money in exchange for looking the other way. The individuals most to blame for their complicity with corruption in Mexico are the politicians and policymakers in Washington, DC, who have allowed their Mexican counterparts to get away with illegality for decades. The US government has utterly lacked the courage and resolve to put whatever Mexican administration that is in power in its place and to demand accountability, transparency, and adherence to the rule of law. Bullies will stay bullies, until someone stronger comes along to put them in their place and expose them for the coward they are. Only the United States can make Mexico change. Unfortunately, the policymakers in Washington are either reticent or scared to upset the relationship between the United States and Mexico and all that relationship entails with regards to international commerce and the economies of both nations. Mexico will not change its ways from within. It would take concerted and unrelenting discipline imposed on Mexico by the United States government to effect change in the level of corruption in Mexico.

## Conclusions

Corruption is a self-sustaining dynasty in Mexico, through which a steady, unbroken stream of politicians, businessmen, judges, and police pass beneath its yoke. Some are caught and become sacrificial lambs to make it seem as if whatever government is in power is taking action to fight it. Some of those caught don't care because they can use political connections and back room deals to escape justice.[100] Some anti-corruption efforts are merely good theater, such as occurred in 2006 when the Mexican government claimed to have terminated 945 federal employees and suspended 953 more following investigations into public corruption.[101] As recently as May 2009, Mexican federal law enforcement arrested 10 mayors and 18 local officials in the northwestern state of Michoacan on charges of collusion and providing intelligence information to the La Familia Cartel.[102] No one ever seems to know much about the outcomes of such highly publicized busts, or whether the wrongdoers forfeit their ill-gotten assets. And who is to say that the mayors will not be replaced by another band of corruptible officials, or that the individuals leading the investigations and conducting the purges are not simply clearing out the ranks in order to put their own people and systems of corruption into place? The Mexican government is little more than corrupt actors replacing corrupt actors so that the more things appear to change; the more things stay the same. The faces change, but the system of corruption remains sacrosanct and unbreakable.

Impunity or near-impunity also contributes to the laissez-faire attitudes of corrupt politicos, judges, and civil servants. Even if they are caught and convicted for corruption, their punishments are a joke. When the Clinton administration was considering Mexican certification or decertification in the drug war, a political imprimatur having significant economic impact for Mexico, the Mexican government promptly arrested and jailed a high level Juarez cartel king pin, Oscar Malherbe de Leon. Yet, even before the ink was dry in Washington, another high level money launderer, linked to the Salinas administration, simply walked out of jail, 'despite the fact that his jail cell had apparently consisted of six rooms with telephones and fax machines so that he could keep in touch with his business associates'.[103] Corruption also serves as the price of buying one's freedom in Mexico by paying out mega bribes to stay out of jail or to preserve one's life.[104] One achieves wealth and status through corruption, with enough money, corruption buys freedom, protection from accountability, an air of indignation (hubris), and the ability to use national sovereignty as a shield for criminality.[105]

In a nation where one's origins and familial connections determine one's place in the society, the opportunities for someone to make something of oneself are severely limited by a rigid caste system. Advancement through corrupt means is the only realistic avenue for an enterprising individual from humble origins to get ahead, or for a member of the political and economic elite to rise higher in power and wealth. It would take a massive breakdown and reordering of Mexican society to free Mexico from corruption's stranglehold. But the individuals who have the capacity to lead such a drastic reform are the same individuals who would have the most to lose from doing so.

At some point, the Mexican government and the Mexican people may come to terms with the idea that while corruption greases the wheels, its detrimental effects eventually erode the capacity of the state to govern. More likely, the system of rule by corruption will keep grinding along, spitting out the unlucky from time to time, while carrying the Mexican state forward in a tenuous ebb and flow of deceit, intrigue, and criminality.

## Notes

1. *Author's note*: I was once a judge in one of the most corrupt court systems in the world, the judiciary of Colombia. No matter how hard I strived to defend the rule of law and to dedicate my skills and energies to my job, I was often overwhelmed by a level of corruption and ineptitude ingrained in the system that rendered me powerless and discouraged. The police under my authority were paid off by the drug lords to tamper with or lose evidence. They would line up outside the gate of the local drug lord's estate on holidays to receive monetary gifts for their 'service to the community'. Witnesses were routinely threatened into silence or disappeared all together. The cases against drug traffickers or corrupt influential members of the community that I did manage to adjudicate were often overturned when sent up to the higher court, or simply went away. When I refused efforts to bribe me, I was threatened and attempts were made on my life. When my family came under threat,

I had no choice but to resign my judgeship and leave Colombia. As I have conducted my research for this article, I see so many startling parallels with what I experienced in Colombia in the 1980s. I notice the same methods of corruption and criminality at work and all the ingredients to fuel its proliferation: massive amounts of drug money available to pay bribes, political branches linked to drug traffickers and serving economic and political elite, poor compensation for police and civil servants, socio-economic conditions that encourage individuals to pursue criminal activities in order to survive and get ahead, and above all, hubris – imbued in all the corrupt politicians and officials who smugly believe they are above the law and untouchable. Mexico is so broken and damaged by corruption that no number of reform programs or re-engineering of the systems affected can fix Mexico unless the civil society willingly demands drastic changes and is ready itself to change the culture of corruption embedded in it. Fixing corruption entails taking measures that would be so disruptive to the political and cultural status quo that doing so would bring the Mexican state as we know it to its knees. Who knows if someone will be willing to commit political suicide to risk the fallout that would result with what would essentially be a draconian political revolution? Mexico is not a state afflicted with corruption, but rather a state of corruption ruling the fate and fortunes of a beleaguered nation.

2.  See Hamilton, 'The Story of Narcocorridos' at part 5, p. 1.
3.  Robinson, *The Merger*, 253.
4.  After the crash of the Mexican peso in 1994, drugs surpassed oil as the prime source of currency in Mexico. Ibid.
5.  See International Relations and Security Network, *Guns Galore*, and also Stewart and Burton, 'A Counterintelligence Approach to Controlling Cartel Corruption'.
6.  See Samuels, 'In Mexico, Culture of Corruption Runs Deep' (quoting Eduardo A. Bohorquez of Transparencia Mexicana, the leading organization monitoring corruption in Mexico, who defined corruption as taking a mandate from a public group and acting on one's own behalf).
7.  Raul Salinas de Gortari gained immense wealth through corrupt means through his political connections with his brother, President Carlos Salinas de Gortari. The corruption scandals attached to the Salinas family still haunt Mexican politics. Among the many stories, one involves Raul's wife, Paulina Castanon de Salinas, who was arrested in Switzerland attempting to withdraw $84 million from an account in the name of one of Raul's aliases. When asked why she didn't withdraw a little at a time, her reply was, 'I was taking a little at a time'. See Robinson, *The Merger*, 259.
8.  Ratified by Mexico on 20 July 2004, available at http://www.unodc.org/unodc/en/treaties/CAC/signatories.html.
9.  Adopted 29 March 1996 and ratified by Mexico on 27 May 1997, available at http://www.oas.org/Juridico/english/treaties/b-58.html.
10. Ratified by Mexico on 27 May 1999, available at http://www.oecd.org/dataoecd/4/18/38028044.pdf.
11. Morris, *Corrupción y Política en México Contemporáneo*, 62.
12. One might recall the embarrassment of General Jose de Jesus Gutierrez Rebollo, Mexico's drug czar, arrested for accepting bribes from high level drug lords not ten weeks after his appointment to the post and not two weeks after United States Drug Czar General Barry McCaffrey called him 'an honest man' and 'a guy of absolute integrity'. See Meisler and Shogren, 'Mexico Told U.S. Nothing of Probe into Drug Czar', A20.
13. For a comprehensive description of the programs and legislation implemented during the Fox administration, see Trejo, 'El diseño de la política anti-corrupción

del gobierno federal de México, 2000–2006', and also Berrondo, *Federal Law of Transparency and Access to Public Government Information.*

14. Ledo, 'Mexico: La corrupción azul', *El Universal.* Curiously enough, *El Universal* newspaper was owned at this time by Carlos Ahumada, a political opponent of Vicente Fox, who himself was charged in 2004 with corruption of government officials. Caciques were indigenous rulers and minor nobility of the cultures who occupied much of pre-colonial Mexico, whose system of loyalties were of a nature similar to the patron/client system of ancient Roman origin.

15. For a comprehensive chronicle of events regarding corruption in Mexico since 1994, see Global Integrity's *2006 Country Reports Timeline for Mexico.*

16. See *Mexico: 2007*, at Global Integrity. Among the categories measured for which Mexico show a weak ranking were Media, Judicial Accountability, Whistle-blowing Measures, Privatization, Taxes and Customs, Business Licensing and Regulation, Anti-corruption Agency, Access to Justice, and Law Enforcement. The results were based on 290 integrity indicators tracked over a 10-year period and included peer review perspectives and on-the-ground journalist reports. Of 100 points possible in the index, the legal framework to fight corruption ranked a fairly strong 87 out of 100, but the actual implementation ranking was a dismal 39 out of 100, which suggests an all-too-familiar condition in weak and failing states that even when there may be laws on the books to combat corruption and crime, without a monitoring and law enforcement capability to give laws teeth, corruption will continue to flourish.

17. See Transparency International, *2008 CPI Table.* Mexico tied with Bulgaria, China, Macedonia, Peru, Suriname, Swaziland, and Trinidad and Tobago. Those Latin American states scoring better than Mexico in the Index were Chile (23rd), Uruguay (23rd), Costa Rica (47th), El Salvador (67th), and Colombia (70th). Denmark ranks first on the index for lowest perceived corruption, while the United States ranks eighteenth, tied with the UK, Belgium, and Japan.

18. DePalma, 'How a Tortilla Empire Was Built on Favoritism'.

19. Morris, *Corrupción y Política en México Contemporáneo*, 63.

20. Such a noteworthy example is the case of an Argentine industrialist, Carlos Ahumada, who emigrated to Mexico as a teenager in 1975. He started out washing car windows on the street and rose to riches through various business schemes and bribery networks among high ranking politicians. A newspaper account of his rise and downfall paint a picture of corruption typical of politics and business in Mexico. When he was charged with corruption, he produced a series of videotapes he had scrupulously made of his bribery transactions with government officials, and his ties to political notables, including the former mayor of Mexico City and presidential hopeful, Andres Manual Lopez Obrador, resulted in a number of politicians going underground and scrambling to concoct plausible denials of collusion in Ahumada's corruption activities. See O'Boyle, 'Contracting trouble', and Dellios, 'Shots Add Twist to Race in Mexico', C10.

21. Samuels, 'In Mexico, Culture of Corruption Runs Deep'.

22. Ibid., citing Dr. David Shirk at the University of California San Diego, who notes that, 'Mexicans who go to another country behave the way the laws and rules of that country dictate. We have 20 million Mexicans in the U.S., and I don't think they're bribing the police'.

23. Durazo was given this rank by López Portillo despite having never served in the military.

24. Durazo then lived quietly in retirement and died in 2000.

25. Other than bringing down Durazo's empire, De la Madrid, himself the subject of many accusations of corruption, could do little to break up the level of corruption

among the powerful elite during the Portillo years because the excessiveness was so tied to the presidency and the central government that many individuals, including the head of Mexico's petroleum monopoly PEMEX, Jorge Diaz Serrano, escaped accountability for complicity in political corruption.

26.    Andreas, 'The Political Economy of Narco-Corruption in Mexico', 160, 162.
27.    Cevallos, 'Police Caught between Low Wages, Threats and Bribes'.
28.    Samuels, 'In Mexico, Culture of Corruption Runs Deep', citing John Bailey of Georgetown University, who posits that distrust of Mexican police officers, 'is deeply learned sitting at the table listening to one's parents'.
29.    Cevallos, 'Police Caught between Low Wages, Threats and Bribes'.
30.    Such realities of working in a corrupt system are made known to the police officers early on in their academy training, such as it is. Some police officers themselves have criminal backgrounds and view police work as a way to utilize their criminal skills for earning money through corrupt means. See generally Botello et al., *Policía y Corrupción*.
31.    Associated Press Worldstream, 'Mexico Detains 93 Police in Corruption Probe'.
32.    Becker, 'Mexico under Siege', A1.
33.    Ibid. The article also reports about the newly appointed police chief of La Junta who was offered cash and a new car by men who said the gifts came from an aide to the mayor. In exchange, he was expected to issue bogus calls for assistance from federal police in order to create a diversion so that drug shipments could cross the border. If he refused, he would be killed and his family harmed. He refused, and after his family was threatened, he took them to El Paso to request political asylum.
34.    See The Stray Dodger, 'The Economic, Political, and Institutional Causes of Crime in Mexico', citing Central Intelligence Agency, *World Factbook 2006*.
35.    Ibid. On the plus side, Mexicans are generally ahead of many other developing nations in terms of literacy and health.
36.    Black, 'Mexico Raises 2009 Daily Minimum Wage Below Inflation Rate', noting that the raise is still 1.7 percentage points below the current annual inflation rate.
37.    See US Department of Labor Wage and Hour Division, 'Minimum Wage Law in the States – July 1, 2009'.
38.    Andreas, 'The Political Economy of Narco-Corruption in Mexico', 160, 162.
39.    Cevallos, 'Police Caught between Low Wages, Threats and Bribes'.
40.    Andreas, 'The Political Economy of Narco-Corruption in Mexico', 160, 162. Some postings have even been auctioned off to the highest bidder from within corrupt law enforcement agencies.
41.    Ibid., citing the case of Salinas de Gortari's top anti-drug prosecutor, Mario Ruiz Massieu, who in 1994 received a million dollars in kickbacks from federal police commanders and prosecutors to gain lucrative assignments.
42.    Samuels, 'In Mexico, Culture of Corruption Runs Deep'.
43.    Frey, 'The Transfer of Core-Based Hazardous Production Processes to the Export Processing Zones of the Periphery', 317, 319.
44.    See Corchado, 'Mexico Sees "Brain Drain" As the Brightest Go North', citing a report by the International Organization for Migration.
45.    Isla, 'Commentary: Bilingual is Better, Especially on Borders'.
46.    Pinkerton, 'Drug Violence: Affluent Fleeing Crime in Mexico', A1, according to Elvia Garcia, outreach coordinator for the Paso Del Norte Civil Rights Project in El Paso.
47.    Frey, 'The Transfer of Core-Based Hazardous Production Processes to the Export Processing Zones of the Periphery', 317, 324.
48.    *London Daily Mail Online*, 'Half of My Country's Police Aren't Up to the Job, Says Mexican President Locked in Bloody Fight with Drug Cartels' (in a written

response to questions from legislators). The same article reported on the charging of a police commander and a drug cartel member in the kidnapping and murder of 24 men outside Mexico City, believed to have been rival drug traffickers.

49. Cevallos, 'Police Caught between Low Wages, Threats and Bribes'.
50. Ibid.
51. Ibid.
52. Kraul, 'Mexican Cops Get a Required Reading List', A3.
53. Ibid.
54. Ibid.
55. It is interesting to note that his predecessor as mayor presided over a notoriously corrupt administration and police force, and subsequently went to jail for corruption.
56. Kraul, 'Mexican Cops Get a Required Reading List', A3.
57. Ibid.
58. Ravelo, 'Las policies: Improvisación, caos, desastre', citing eminent legal scholar Eduardo Buscaglia.
59. Ibid.
60. Ibid.
61. Kraul, 'Mexican Cops Get a Required Reading List', A3.
62. Ibid.
63. Ibid.
64. Andreas, 'The Political Economy of Narco-Corruption in Mexico', 160, 164.
65. Government Accountability Office (GAO), *Firearms Trafficking*, 51. According to the report, 'in late 2008, President Calderon's administration terminated around 500 officers on Tijuana's police force and brought in the military to fill the gap until new officers who had been sufficiently vetted could be hired and trained'.
66. Cevallos, 'Police Caught between Low Wages, Threats and Bribes'.
67. Ibid.
68. US Department of State, *2008 Human Rights Report: Mexico*.
69. There are many honest and hard working judges, prosecutors, and judicial police officers who try their best to do their job. But they are often marginalized and overwhelmed and must preserve their own careers and livelihoods.
70. See Transparency International, *Global Corruption Report 2007*, 15.
71. An adversarial system alone cannot change a culture of corruption. Such a system can produce a more efficient, predictable and sometimes equitable process, but changes must occur in the Mexican political system and society as a whole.
72. Menendez, *Mexico: The Traffickers' Judges, Global Corruption Report 2007*, 77.
73. Trejo, 'Inaceptable Reinstalen a Jueces Corruptos; Nazario', Amparo is a constitutional remedy that allows judicial protection of constitutional rights against any government action, including judicial decisions. See Fix-Zamudio, *Introduccion al Estudio de la Defensa de la Constitution en el Ordenamiento Mexicano*.
74. Menendez, *Mexico: The Traffickers' Judges, Global Corruption Report 2007*, 77.
75. See Transparency International, *Global Corruption Report 2007*, 15.
76. United Nations Special Rapporteur, *Independence of Judges and Lawyers*, published as a 52-page report challenging the independence and effectiveness of Mexican judges.
77. *El Universial*, 'Reconoce Suprema Corte corrupción en jueces'.
78. Judges threatened by drug cartel tend to take the bribe instead of being killed. See Sullivan, 'Mexican Judges' Climate of Fear', A16.
79. In November 2001, two federal judges were killed by an AK-47. Until then, the police officers, politicians, and informants were targeted while the judiciary

remained largely untouched by organized crime. See Sullivan, 'Mexican Judges' Climate of Fear', A16.

80. Menendez, *Mexico: The Traffickers' Judges, Global Corruption Report 2007*, 77.

81. In April 2005, Judge Gómez Martínez presided over the case of Olga Patricia Gastelum Escobar and Felipe de Jesus Mendivil Ibarra, both accused of transporting $7 million in cash and $500,000 in jewelry and watches for the Sinaloa Cartel. The judge cleared Gastelum of wrongdoing, and the sentence was tarnished by many irregularities. Violations included notifying the prosecutor's office 24 hours after the defendant was freed from prison, when under article 102 of the Mexican Code of Criminal Procedure, such 'decisions cannot be executed without first notifying the public prosecutor'. Ibid.

82. Ibid.

83. Ibid.

84. The trial of Garcia Abrego, head of the Gulf Cartel, revealed the freedom he had to operate, due to the millions of dollars in bribes he paid to members of the Mexican Justice Department, to deputy attorneys general, and to law enforcement officials. According to a testifying witness, Luis Esteban Garcia Villalón, a Federal Ministry agent, and Javier Coello Trejos, a deputy attorney general in the General's office, obtained monthly installments of $1.5 million. See Thorpe, 'Anatomy of a Drug Cartel'.

85. The United States won a forfeiture judgment of $8 million claimed to be bribe money from narcottraffickers in Mexico and stashed in Texas banks by Mario Ruiz Massieu, who served twice as a Deputy Attorney General and who in 1994 supervised federal police and anti-drug operations. Swiss officials confiscated more than $132 million from drug traffickers' bribes deposited in banks by Raul Salinas de Gortari, brother of President Carlos Salinas de Gortari. See Golden, 'In Breakthrough, Mexican Official Testifies in Texas'.

86. According to Thomas A. Constantine, the administrator of the United States Drug Enforcement Administration, the Mexican cartels learned from the Colombian Cali Cartel that the only manner organized criminal syndicates prosper is by corrupting officials and intimidating citizens. See Constantine, *Interviews*.

87. Trejo, 'Inaceptable Reinstalen a Jueces Corruptos; Nazario'.

88. The ex-employee accused of kidnapping and killing the victim went free. See Aviles, 'Marti pide castigo para jueces corruptos'. Before the investigation was completed, Judge Gustavo Ramirez Avila freed a criminal accused of aggravated armed robbery. Trejo, 'Inaceptable Reinstalen a Jueces Corruptos; Nazario'.

89. Judge Maria Claudia Campuzano freed a man who killed US businessmen. According to the prosecutor's office, the judge described the killer as 'a modern Robin Hood who doesn't only rob and distribute what he obtains in the robbery, but gives all the money to his sidekicks without any profit for himself'. See Sheridan, 'Mexican Judge Frees Men Held in American's Killing'. See also Fix-Fierro, 'La reforma judicial en Mexico, de donde viene? A donde va? Reforma Judicial' (describing how two judges accepted money to free a murderer).

90. In 1988 Supreme Court Justice, Ernesto Diaz Infante, after receiving $500,000 pressured Magistrate Judge Gilberto Arredondo to liberate a man who had raped a child. See Cacho, 'El buen juez por casa empieza'. See also Hughes, 'Law and Disorder', 10.

91. According to the Court, judges not only act corruptly but collude with organized crime. See also Fix-Fierro, 'La reforma judicial en Mexico, de donde viene? A donde va? Reforma Judicial'. See also Allende, 'Reconoce Suprema Corte corrupción en jueces'.

92. Corruption by patronage limits more 'the competitiveness of politics and responsiveness of government than to threaten their viability'. See Elliot, 'Corruption as an International Policy Problem'.
93. Menendez, *Mexico: The Traffickers' Judges, Global Corruption Report 2007*.
94. Samuels, 'In Mexico, Culture of Corruption Runs Deep'.
95. See BBC interview, 'U.S. Graft Adds to Mexico's Woes'.
96. Ibid.
97. See PBS Frontline Report, 'Mexico: Crimes at the Border'.
98. Ibid.
99. The drug dealer shipped cocaine to Houston, and a Joe Polanco, a former INS officer, coordinated with friends in the INS to place the drugs on the bus. INS vehicles were always waved through checkpoint at Sarita. See Thorpe, 'Anatomy of a Drug Cartel'. For an additional list of instances of border corruption in Texas, see Grits for Breakfast, 'Border Corruption Runs Amok'.
100. Among the most notorious instances of near impunity is the case of Raul Salinas de Gortari, who salted away hundreds of millions of dollars during his brother's administration, and was arrested in connection with the 2004 murder of a rising politician, José Francisco Massieu. Despite significant evidence in the case, which was investigated by Massieu's brother, Raul Salinas was acquitted a year later. Massieu resigned and fled Mexico to be reunited with $7 million deposited in his bank account in Texas amid accusations that he had been bought off by the Salinas brothers to make the case go away. See Robinson, *The Merger*, 259.
101. Government Accountability Office (GAO), 51.
102. Castillo, 'Mexico Detains 10 Mayors for Alleged Drug Ties'.
103. Robinson, *The Merger*, 260.
104. Robinson, *The Merger*.
105. Ibid. (quoting US Senator Charles Grassley, who expressed his frustration with Mexico's unwillingness to extradite drug traffickers). The remarks were in reaction to the Clinton administration caving into President Zedillo's indignation over the US-led anti money-laundering operation in Mexico which uncovered three of Mexico's largest banks laundering more than $157 million worth of drug profits – the largest anti-money laundering operation ever.

## Bibliography

Allende, Carlos Aviles. 'Reconoce Suprema Corte corrupción en jueces'. *El Universal* (29 November 2008), http://www.eluniversal.com.mx/notas/559292.html.

Andreas, Peter. 'The Political Economy of Narco-Corruption in Mexico'. *Current History* (April 1998), 160–2, 164.

*Associated Press Worldstream*. 'Mexico Detains 93 Police in Corruption Probe' (29 June 2009).

Aviles, Carlos. 'Marti pide castigo para jueces corruptos'. *El Universal* (15 October 2008), http://www.el-universal.com.mx/nacion/162963.html.

BBC interview. 'U.S. Graft Adds to Mexico's Woes' 30 March 2009, http://news.bbc.co.uk/2/hi/americas/7971335.stm.

Becker, Andrew. 'Mexico under Siege'. *Los Angeles Times* (15 June 2009), A1.

Berrondo, Diana Hierro. *Federal Law of Transparency and Access to Public Government Information*, Numero 8, at 1–3, Julio–Agosto 2002, http://www.funcionpublica.gob.mx/doctos/g8_ew.pdf.

Black, Thomas. 'Mexico Raises 2009 Daily Minimum Wage Below Inflation Rate'. *Bloomberg.com* (19 December 2008), http://www.bloomberg.com/apps/news?pid=20601086&sid=axTODZx0rUwU.

Botello, Nelson Arteaga et al. *Policía y Corrupción: El caso de un municipio en México.* San Rafael, Mexico: Plaza y Valdes, 1998.

Cacho, Lydia. 'El buen juez por casa empieza'. *lydiacacho.net* (15 December 2008), http://www.lydiacacho.net/categoria/articulos/page/2/.

Castillo, E. Eduardo. 'Mexico Detains 10 Mayors for Alleged Drug Ties'. *Huffington Post* (27 May 2009), http://www.huffingtonpost.com/2009/05/27/mexico-detains-10-mayors_n_208011.html.

Central Intelligence Agency, *World Factbook 2006*, http://www.cia.gov/cia/publications/factbook/index.html

Cevallos, Diego. 'Police Caught between Low Wages, Threats and Bribes'. *International Press News Service* (7 June 2009), http://ipsnews.net/print.asp?idnews=38075.

Constantine, Thomas A (DEA Administrator). *Interviews*, PBS online, n.d., http://www.pbs.org/wgbh/pages/frontline/shows/mexico/interviews/constantine.html.

Corchado, Alfredo. 'Mexico Sees "Brain Drain" as the Brightest Go North'. *Dallas Morning News*, No. 1, 2008.

Dellios, Hugh. 'Shots Add Twist to Race in Mexico'. *Chicago Tribune* (7 June 2006), C10.

DePalma, Anthony. 'How a Tortilla Empire Was Built on Favoritism'. *New York Times* (15 February 1999), http://www.nytimes.com/1996/02/15/world/how-a-tortilla-empire-was-built-on-favoritism.html?pagewanted=all.

Elliot, Kimberly Ann. 'Corruption as an International Policy Problem: Overview and Recommendations'. In *Corruption and the Global Economy*, edited by Kimberly A. Elliot. Washington, DC: Institute for International Economics, 1997.

*El Universal.* 'Reconoce Suprema Corte corrupción en jueces' (29 November 2008), http://www.eluniversal.com.mx/notas/559292.html.

Fix-Fierro, Héctor. 'La reforma judicial en Mexico, de donde viene? A donde va?, Reforma Judicial'. *Revista Mexicana de Justicia*, 262, no.26 (2003), http://works.bepress.com/hector_fix_fierro/.

Fix-Zamudio, Héctor. *Introduccion al Estudio de la Defensa de la Constitution en el Ordenamiento Mexicano*. Mexico City, Mexico: Universidad Nacional Autónoma de México, 1994.

Frey, R. Scott. 'The Transfer of Core-Based Hazardous Production Processes to the Export Processing Zones of the Periphery: The Maquiladora Centers of Northern Mexico'. *Journal of World-Systems Research*, 9, no. 2 (Summer 2003): 317–54. Available at http://jwsr.ucr.edu/archive/vol9/number2/pdf/jwsr-v9n2-frey.pdf.

Global Integrity. *2006 Country Reports Timeline for Mexico*, http://www.globalintegrity.org/reports/2006/Mexico/timeline.cfm.

Global Integrity. *Mexico: 2007*, http://report.globalintegrity.org/Mexico/2007.

Golden, Tim. 'In Breakthrough, Mexican Official Testifies in Texas'. *New York Times* (15 July 1998), http://www.nytimes.com/1998/07/15/world/in-breakthrough-mexican-official-testifies-in-texas.html.

Government Accountability Office (GAO). *Firearms Trafficking: U.S. Efforts to Combat Arms Trafficking to Mexico Face Planning and Coordination Challenges.* Report GAO-09–709, Washington, DC, June 2009.

*Grits for Breakfast.* 'Border Corruption Runs Amok: New Cash for Border Cops Should go to Internal Affairs', 22 April 2006, http://gritsforbreakfast.blogspot.com/2006/04/border-corruption-runs-amok-new-cash.html.

Hamilton, Denise. 'The Story of Narcocorridos – Right or Wrong'. *Los Angeles Times* (27 February 2002).

Hughes, Sallie. 'Law and Disorder'. *Mexico Business* (April 1995), 10.

International Relations and Security Network. *Guns Galore*, http://www.isn.ethz.ch/isn/Current-Affairs/Special-Reports/Desperation-Route/Armed-for-Corruption.

Isla, Jose de la. 'Commentary: Bilingual is Better, Especially on Borders'. Scripps Howard News Service, 8 April 2009.

Kraul, Chris. 'Mexican Cops Get a Required Reading List'. *Los Angeles Times* (7 March 2005), A3.

Ledo, Porfirio Muñoz. 'Mexico: La corrupción azul'. *El Universal* (15 June 2006), http://www.offnews.info/verArticulo.php?contenidoID=4871.

*London Daily Mail Online*. 'Half of My Country's Police Aren't Up to the Job, Says Mexican President Locked in Bloody Fight with Drug Cartels', 28 November 2008, http://www.dailymail.co.uk/news/worldnews/article-1090137.

Meisler, Stanley, and Elizabeth Shogren. 'Mexico Told U.S. Nothing of Probe into Drug Czar'. *Los Angeles Times* (22 February 1997), A20.

Menendez, Jose Fernandez. *Mexico: The Traffickers' Judges, Global Corruption Report 2007*, Transparency International, http://www.transparency.org/global_priorities/other_thematic_issues/judiciary.

Morris, Stephen D., ed. *Corrupció. Política en México Contemporáneo*, Delegación Coyoacán, Mexico: Siglo Veintiuno Editores, 1992.

O'Boyle, Michael. 'Contracting trouble: Soccer Team Owner, Lover of PRD Leader and Wheeler-and-Dealer Extraordinaire, Carlos Ahumada Stands at Center of Videotaped Corruption Scandal'. The Free Library, n.d., http://www.thefreelibrary.com/Contracting+trouble:+soccer+team+owner,+lover+of+PRD+leader+and...-a0142107497.

*PBS Frontline Report*. 'Mexico: Crimes at the Border'. Video, 24:41 minutes, n.d., http://www.pbs.org/frontlineworld/stories/mexico704/video/video_index.html.

Pinkerton, James. 'Drug Violence: Affluent Fleeing Crime in Mexico'. *Houston Chronicle* (9 March 2009), A1.

Ravelo, Ricardo. 'Las policies: Improvisación, caos, desastre'. *Demócrata Norte de Mexico* (17 August 2008), http://democratanortedemexico.blogspot.com/2008/08/las-policas-improvisacin-caos-desastre.html.

Robinson, Jeffrey. *The Merger: The Conglomeration of International Organized Crime*. Woodstock, NY: The Overlook Press, 2000.

Samuels, Lennox. 'In Mexico, Culture of Corruption Runs Deep'. *San Luis Obispo Tribune* (29 December 2005).

Sheridan, Mary Beth. 'Mexican Judge Frees Men Held in American's Killing'. *Los Angeles Times* (6 January 1998), http://articles.latimes.com/1998/jan/06/news/mn-5374.

Stewart, Scott, and Fred Burton. 'A Counterintelligence Approach to Controlling Cartel Corruption'. Stratfor Global Intelligence, http://www.stratfor.com/weekly/20090520_counterintelligence_approach_controlling_cartel_corruption.

*The Stray Dodger*. 'The Economic, Political, and Institutional Causes of Crime in Mexico', 14 February 2008, http://www.associatedcontent.com/article/600191/the_economic_political_and_institutional.html?cat=49.

Sullivan, Kevin. 'Mexican Judges' Climate of Fear'. *Washington Post* (19 November 2001), A16, http://www.latinamericanstudies.org/drugs/mexican-judges.htm.

Thorpe, Helen. 'Anatomy of a Drug Cartel'. *Texas Monthly* (January 1998), http://www.texasmonthly.com/preview/1998-01-01/feature3.

Transparency International. *Global Corruption Report 2007*, http://www.transparency.org/global_priorities/other_thematic_issues/judiciary.

Transparency International. *2008 CPI Table*, http://www.transparency.org/news_room/in_focus/2008/cpi2008/cpi_2008_table.

Trejo, Daniel Gómez. 'Inaceptable Reinstalen a Jueces Corruptos; Nazario'. *Argomexico.com* (19 January 2009), http://www.argonmexico.com/ultimas/inaceptable-reinstalen-a-jueces-corruptos-nazario.html.

Trejo, Jiménez. 'El diseño de la política anti-corrupción del gobierno federal de México, 2000–2006'. *Observatorio de la Economía Latinoamericana*, No.99 (2008), http://www.eumed.net/cursecon/ecolat/mx/2008/lajt5.htm.

United Nations Special Rapporteur, *Independence of Judges and Lawyers*, 2004, http://unispal.un.org/unispal.nsf/1ce874ab1832a53e852570bb006dfaf6/c10b0148aecdd 27585256e53006de6d2?OpenDocument.

US Department of Labor Wage and Hour Division. 'Minimum Wage Law in the States – July 1, 2009'. http://www.dol.gov/esa/minwage/america.htm.

US Department of State. *2008 Human Rights Report: Mexico*, http://www.state.gov/g/drl/rls/hrrpt/2008/wha/119166.htm.

Wald, Elijah. *Narcocorrido: A Journey into the Music of Drugs, Guns, and Guerrillas*. New York: Rayo, 2001.

# Firefights, raids, and assassinations: tactical forms of cartel violence and their underpinnings

Graham H. Turbiville, Jr.

*Courage Services, Inc., McLean, VA, USA, Department of Defense Consultant, and Associate Fellow, Joint Special Operations University, MacDill Air Force Base, FL, USA*

This article examines some specific types of narco-generated combat, assault, and brutality that over the last decade have acquired an increasingly organized and paramilitary character. The planning; training; intelligence and counter-intelligence preparation; mobility; communications; type of weaponry; levels of intensity; and sheer audacity substantially exceed the threats with which traditional law enforcement had been trained and equipped to deal. It matches the apt Drug Enforcement Administration description of a 'transition from the gangsterism of traditional narco hit men to paramilitary terrorism with guerrilla tactics'. These methods have become a mainstay in the struggle of narco-traffickers against law enforcement, the military, and to a major degree among the competing drug-trafficking organizations themselves. While the infrastructure and practice of paramilitary violence is established in Mexico in seemingly unprecedented ways, the concern north of the border is its potential transportability. Many law enforcement personnel have compared 1980s Miami – with its running drug firefights, revenge raids, and bloody assassinations by Colombian cocaine traffickers – to Mexican drug violence. There are enough precursors north of the Rio Grande now to make the potential for something analogous more than empty speculation.

Violence in varying levels and forms has been a feature of the US–Mexico frontier from the time a border was formally established in 1848, following the treaty of Guadalupe Hidalgo. Challenges to the sovereignty of the US and Mexican Republics – political or economic; government sanctioned or tacitly permitted; and those which are often a consequence of criminal enterprise – have also characterized the frontier over 160 years of shared history. Today, Mexico and the United States are allies, major trading partners, and friends, jointly facing criminal and transnational threats that fundamentally affect the national security of each republic and the stability of the region. These threats are most acute and intense near the US–Mexican frontier area, but manifest themselves elsewhere in both countries as well.

A decade into the twenty-first century, the single largest vector of border violence is indisputably narco-trafficking. Among other measures, Mexican President Felipe Calderón's estimates that 9,000 narco-linked murders had occurred from 2006 to April 2009 underscore this. Other estimates suggest that the number will have exceeded 11,000 by early 2010.[1] Despite the endemic corruption in Mexican law enforcement organizations, it is instructive to remember that some 10% of overall casualties are being incurred by police and military personnel in the performance of their duties.[2] US security officials point to advances in cross-border law enforcement cooperation and the beginnings of success in generous and innovative security assistance programs, and assert that little of the extreme violence that has characterized northern Mexico in recent years has spilled over into the United States.

Regrettably, many of these judgments and expectations are undermined by less optimistic assessments of northern Mexico's operational environment. Some Border Patrol organizations and individuals challenge the idea that the US and Mexico 'are gaining the upper hand in the battle against drug cartels'. They note that interagency cooperation among US security organizations at the working level is still characterized by in-fighting. In addition, despite various cooperative initiatives, trust among US–Mexican law enforcement officers often remains problematic.[3] Anecdotes from individual officers abound and, at higher levels, US drug enforcement and other law enforcement commentators have cited the leakage of sensitive US information from Mexican police sources to the specific trafficking targets in drug cartels. Two decades of police reforms – including President Calderón's recent intense and courageous efforts – have failed to clean up endemic corruption.[4]

The many dimensions and complexities of Mexican drug trafficking, its associated violence, and other debilitating impacts are addressed throughout *Narcos Over the Border*. This article examines some specific types of narco-generated combat, assault, and brutality, which over the last decade have acquired an increasingly organized and paramilitary character. The planning, training, intelligence and counterintelligence preparation, mobility, communications, type of weaponry, levels of intensity, and sheer audacity substantially exceed the threats with which traditional law enforcement had been trained and equipped to deal. It matches the apt Drug Enforcement Administration description of a 'transition from the gangsterism of traditional narco hit men to paramilitary terrorism with guerrilla tactics'. These methods have become a mainstay in the struggle of narco-traffickers against law enforcement, the military, and to a major degree among the competing drug-trafficking organizations themselves. Emblematic of the strength of narco-violence, they constitute three, sometimes overlapping 'tactical' forms that account for a substantial number of deaths and the infliction of other narco-trafficking costs:

- Firefights (*Tiroteos*), featuring planned or – more frequently – sudden armed urban or rural encounters that in some ways are quite analogous to military meeting engagements. Their outcomes depend on the quality of firepower, basic weapons skills, situational awareness, protective equipment, practiced responsiveness and training, willingness to engage, and an ability to terminate or withdraw before reinforcements arrive.

- Assassinations (*Asesinatos*), which depend for success on target identification and surveillance together with the selection of timing, effective attack means, transport, approach, and safe egress. They may claim only the targeted victim, but as often as not employ such substantial firepower that bodyguards, drivers, colleagues, family members, and unfortunate bystanders are among the casualties. Firearms, grenades and explosives, torture, and mutilation have been among the means used. For Mexican drug trafficking organizations, specific targets have covered an array of rival members and leadership, security force members and commanders, journalists, and public officials, including on at least one occasion, planning to assassinate the President of Mexico.
- Raids (*Incursiónes* or *Invasiónes Repentinas*), featuring tactical actions executed with varying degrees of skill that involve travel to a target with the aim of the freedom of captured or imprisoned comrades, the elimination of opposing personnel, destruction of facilities or goods, and general carnages carried out for revenge or intimidation. Raids are a specific subject taught and studied in Mexican military-educational and training facilities, with tactics, techniques, and procedures that transfer well via deserters for drug paramilitary use.

Before addressing the origin, practice, impact, and practitioners of these narco-militant attack forms in further detail, three recent illustrations from late-spring to mid-summer 2009 better illuminate the above terms and the actions they denote. While carried out with frequency and with a now-familiar sameness inside Mexico, what might be termed 'signature' actions, reflect all too typical violent engagements. They also point to a shifting balance between security forces and paramilitaries and the potential for their being precursors of more widespread crossover violence. Despite countless variations and participants, as the second decade of the new millennium begins, there are basic capabilities that have shifted in fundamental ways:

### A *signature firefight*

Police and military drug raids and arrest attempts have long generated shoot-outs between law enforcement targets and security forces. As drug cartels and gangs have acquired high-powered weaponry, these have become increasingly dangerous for law enforcement elements who may find themselves outmatched. In these cases, at least, measures may be taken to isolate areas and targets to prevent collateral damage. However, the mobile, widespread, and confident presence of armed narco-trafficking gang members or their paramilitary associates has created the potential of provoking unexpected armed clashes in routine vehicle stops and checks by police, which may be in the middle of busy city streets or residential areas.

As a consequence, when Federal Police agents attempted to stop a suspicious vehicle in the middle of a Veracruz, Michoacán business and tourist district on a July 2009 afternoon, they found themselves suddenly engaged in a high intensity firefight. The men they attempted to detain are now believed to have been an 'armed commando' unit of the *La Familia* drug cartel. The subsequent firefight involved automatic weapons, hand grenades, and a vehicle chase in the middle of the populated Veracruz 'old district' neighborhood. The exchange of fire, *La Familia's* employment of grenades, and the vehicle chase extended to several streets. It left five vehicles in flames, at least two cartel members dead, and another wounded and captured. At least four police and bystanders were wounded. Such encounters are not daily occurrences in every Mexican city, but in urban areas where drug cartel activity is centered, they have become far from infrequent.[5]

## A *signature raid*

In mid-July 2009, the capacity of at least some cartel paramilitary arms to launch multiple attacks on designated targets – including those of substantial size and government affiliation – was demonstrated in the Mexican state of Michoacán. Despite being at war with the rival Gulf Cartel, the attacks by the militarized *La Familia* drug-trafficking paramilitary were aimed at police, other security forces who presented themselves, and especially Federal law enforcement intelligence assets. The well equipped and mobile narco-enforcement and trafficking group called *La Familia* dispatched heavily armed teams to strike five Federal police stations and a Lázaro Cárdenas port-city guest hotel much used by Mexican Federal officials and police. The assaults were closely timed, underscoring a good measure of coordination and planning. The 'raiders', in a familiar approach, traveled in armored SUVs, and used automatic weapons and grenades.

They killed five police officers, two soldiers, and wounded a number of others at the attack sites with bullets and shrapnel. A group striking Federal police stations in the state capital (Morelia) and the paramilitaries that attacked the hotel were estimated to have some 50 personnel. Perhaps the most memorable aspect of La Familia's strikes, however, was the discovery of 12 murdered, blindfolded, and tortured off-duty police intelligence officers, piled disdainfully by a road. President Calderón dispatched another 5500 troops to the Pacific coast state to join the 2800 soldiers deployed there.[6] The raid, typical of others earlier throughout Mexican trafficking areas, had the goals of revenge for earlier action against the organized crime group, coercion intended to slow enforcement, the infliction of damage on Federal enforcement and intelligence-gathering capabilities, and building further on a reputation for brutality and formidable capabilities that may intimidate rivals.

## A *signature assassination*

The assassination dimension of narco-violence has been a staple of Mexican drug trafficking organizations and gangs as long as they have existed. Targets constitute, variously, senior law enforcement personnel, crusading journalists, hostile and outspoken political figures, rival drug trafficking leadership and members, and those who betray the organization as informants or thieves. They have included Catholic clergy as well. While often still marked by greater-than-necessary firepower and overkill, not to mention fatal collateral damage for anyone in the area, more recently they have reflected more careful planning and better target intelligence. The May 2009 assassination of a Juárez drug cartel mid-level leader, Jose Daniel Gonzalez Galena, was accomplished quickly and in front of the target's home in an up-scale residential neighborhood. The eight close-range shots were heard by neighbors including the city police chief who lived nearby.[7] What was unusual about the assassination was its location in El Paso, Texas, and that the former cartel officer reportedly had become an informant for Federal law enforcement. A rise in the number of murders involving low-level Mexican traffickers and informants in the US has been noted in border cities and other US locations. More senior figures have been killed on US territory as well. This assassination was notable for the eventually arrested assassins. Juárez Cartel traffickers in Mexico had effectively recruited a small team of El Paso residents to conduct surveillance and support. The actual shooter, as alleged with his arrest, was a US army soldier stationed at nearby Fort Bliss, raising a concern about cartel military recruitment. As senior and mid-level cartel leadership have acquired legal residency status in safer US locations just over the border, and with cartels adjusting their recruitment of US-based assassins analogous to those in Mexico, some US specialists anticipate more assassinations like that of Gonzalez.[8]

The strong US commitment to end such destructive and destabilizing kinds of violence inside Mexico, and to forestall their increased appearance and spread north of the border, has been slow in coming despite 15 years of growing indicators and warnings. Border law enforcement, border residents, and elements of some national intelligence agencies pointed to a changing and more dangerous border environment. During this time, Mexican drug trafficking was undergoing profound changes. Specialized Mexican drug criminals originally concerned with facets of receipt, transportation, and distribution of drugs for Colombian cartels, developed into fully established drug trafficking organizations in their own right. A number of smaller independent drug trafficking groups remained operating as well. In the mid-1990s, violence was serious and badly policed, but largely thuggish, undisciplined, and of a familiar type.

Growing competition among more fully developed Mexican cartels, the need to counter Mexico's increasing military-supported law enforcement initiatives, and a flood of narco-dollars, became a catalyst for the development of more capable 'protective' forces. This led to the marriage of drug cartels and organic or associated paramilitary groupings that has fundamentally changed the security environment in Mexico and beyond its borders. The effectiveness of the firefights, raids, and assassinations that comprise some of the most serious and destabilizing drug violence, owe much to the appearance and evolution of paramilitary components. While the 'genealogy' of Mexican paramilitaries is a topic that exceeds the space available here, a brief look at the military links to the development of diverse paramilitary skills and a rich military and police recruiting base is instructive.

## The militarization of cartel gunmen: enhancing tactical competence and effectiveness

The rapid formation of criminal paramilitaries powerful enough to challenge the authority of a state and advance the agendas of private economic or criminal interests is far from a phenomenon limited to Mexico. Analogies have abounded in states with weakened institutions around the world. In Mexico, this was an unintended consequence of the Government's rapid military transformation and expansion intended to combat enduring low level guerrilla activities and growing drug trafficking violence. New, elite drug-fighting units – well-trained but too quickly vetted – defected to form criminal paramilitary cadres or remained on duty to establish a substantial recruiting base for continuing cartel inducements. This 'pool' of trained personnel proved vulnerable to innovative recruiting efforts by drug criminal able to tempt poorly paid servicemen, discharged contract soldiers, and especially deserters whose numbers grew with the size of the armed forces and the dangers and difficult conditions of active service.

### *Force restructuring, special operations force expansion and cartel recruiting*

More specifically, Mexican concerns about international and regional terrorism in the mid-1980s were added to the already realized threats of drug cultivation, trafficking, and a still-moribund-but-stirring insurgent activity. A 1986 military initiative resulted in the creation of a Rapid Response Force (*Fuerza de Intervención Rápida*), which by 1990 had become the first Airmobile Special Forces Group (*Grupos Aeromóviles de Fuerzas Especiales* – GAFE), a prototype of initially company-size mobile light infantry units with advanced and specialized training in desert, mountain, and jungle operations. The reappearance of several guerrilla groups in southern Mexico in 1994 added a final incentive to sweeping military transformation. These multiple threats served as a catalyst for a 1995 defense transformation plan – the *Mexican Army and Air Force Development Plan* – which designated 'the fight against drug trafficking' as a specific military tasking in which the military had already begun to participate more directly.[9]

The reorganizing Mexican Army was to be based in substantial measure 'on green berets, commando units, elite forces, [and] assault troops'.[10] As a consequence, the implemented plan saw the number of GAFE's grow rapidly and exponentially. The then company-size GAFE units were deployed in many states around the country, credited in some reports with four in Chiapas, three in Guerrero, and two each in Tabasco, Puebla, Oaxaca, and Veracruz.[11] In a further expansion of special forces type units, the Sedena (Ministry of National Defense) announced in late summer 1999 that it was forming 36 Special Forces Amphibious Groups (*Grupos Anfibios de Fuerzas Especiales* – GANFE's) for counterdrug operations. These were Marine-like counterparts to the GAFES, under Army command, which have been tasked to carry out riverine and coastal type operations.[12] They proved susceptible to cartel recruiting, as well. The Paratroop Rifle Brigade (*Brigada de Fusileros Paracaidistas* – BFP) brigade constituted another elite component of Mexico's force structure known to have contributed to cartel paramilitaries.

Special operations training was provided by experienced foreign armies including the Guatemalan *Kaibiles* special operations forces, employed throughout Guatemala's long communist insurgency. Kaibiles, regrettably, also came to the recruiting attention of Mexican drug traffickers.[13] The mandated Special Forces Command (Corps) (*Cuerpo de Fuerzas Especiales*) had been created in 1997 and the Special Forces School (*Escuela de Fuerzas Especiales*) was established in 1998. Army GANFE continued to be developed.[14] For the US, GAFE training programs in 1997 and most of 1998 were important in helping prepare the new force in tactical skills and in human rights issues. Training took place mainly in the US at Fort Bragg, North Carolina and Fort Benning, Georgia, where the most appropriate training resources and personnel were located.[15] In addition, Naval and Naval Infantry (Marine) special forces were created in 2001 in the form of two Navy Special Forces Groups (*Grupas de Fuerzas Especiales*), along with training facilities and foreign instruction. In addition to the Navy Special Forces, per se, in 2001 the Navy also formed Amphibious Reaction Forces (*Fuerzas Reacción Anfibia*) within the Marine forces.[16]

But the performance of GAFE and GANFE in particular proved disappointing in some cases. Some GAFE personnel were implicated in torture and illegal detentions, and were reportedly parceled out for roles other than those for which they were trained.[17] Overall, special operations force training had been well enough conceived and implemented. However, the force was expanded so rapidly that the 'special' qualifications of candidates suffered. As in the case with so many rapidly expanded military, police, and other security organizations in many countries including the US, personnel quality suffered. It was in the late 1990s, in particular, as special operations force numbers ballooned, that unit members began to desert in larger numbers and to prove themselves susceptible to far better payment and the romanticized narco-culture that attracted many young men.

By as early as 1996, individuals who had served in early versions of these units and been discharged or deserted had made their way by chance or recruitment to employment within the ranks of some drug trafficking group enforcement arms. Drug cartel recruits had for some time included former

Mexican federal, state, and local police officers, often set adrift in periodic police corruption purges or simply attracted by better pay. Lessons learned from Colombian cartel associates had long since demonstrated the advantages of hiring 'specialists' in firearms, explosives, tactics, and training including foreign specialists that ranged from the IRA to the Tamil Tigers.

While origin stories and myths abound, it is generally accepted that a watershed in Mexican paramilitary recruitment was reached in the very late 1990s with the defection of a GAFE officer named Arturo Guzmán Decena (since killed) who brought with him two and a half dozen fellow GAFEs, a number that has gained acceptance through repetition and its apparent government origin. They formed – with other military and police recruits as well as civilian thugs – the now infamous group called the Zetas (attributed variously to Guzmán's radio codename, because Z as in Zetas stood for the 'last ones', or the 'Z' insignia on a uniform). They became the enforcement arm of the Gulf Cartel, first maintaining some level of semi-independence, then becoming autonomous with other loose affiliations, and subsequently spinning off cells and new components that served as paramilitaries and drug trafficking factions in their own right.[18]

It is clear from subsequent commentary and official statements that something of the Zetas had been known by the Mexican authorities before they emerged for more public consideration. Among the earliest dates in which Zetas were reported in the media was October 2001, a year or two after their establishment as a force that was substantial and cohesive enough to justify the name. At that time, a man named Jaime Morales Navarro had been linked to a shadowy criminal organization reported to be called 'Zetas' and associated with the Gulf Cartel. He was charged with possessing a military weapon, public endangerment, and probable theft. At that time, the full paramilitary nature and function of the group – thought to be located primarily at Matamoros in Tamaulipas State – was not well understood. Concurrently, it was suggested (inaccurately) that the Zetas operated in six-man groups that distributed and monitored drug sales. Since this information came from the Federal Attorney General's Office, it apparently reflected a limited official knowledge of Zeta missions and capabilities.[19] Over the next several years, their paramilitary nature became more than clear as they came to be considered largely militarized cartel gunmen.

As is often the case with the development of traditional insurgent groups, greater differentiation and specialization appeared. While subject to varying interpretations, Zeta subcomponents reportedly include combatants sometimes referred to *sicarios* in the Colombian fashion; elements charged with conducting oversight of selected drug trafficking zones; children, teenagers, and others, such as taxi drivers, conducting street surveillance and warning; communications monitoring and electronic eavesdropping specialists who sit on police and military tactical transmissions and routine radio traffic as well as playing key planning roles for operations; and bookkeeper/administrators who manage resources of all types; and other reported elements whose designations and missions are rendered variously.[20]

By the early 2000s, other rival drug trafficking organizations at least augmented their armed cadres with greater numbers of former military and police personnel. It is important to recall that over the last 15 years, many thousands of Mexican police personnel in Federal, state, and municipal law enforcement organizations have been dismissed for criminal offenses. It is clear that many of these men made their way into drug trafficking organizations, links that in some cases already existed from the time the discharged officers served.

Cartel manning – beyond the popularly cited GAFEs – is also fueled by discharged servicemen from a variety of units leaving after serving out their contract, conscripted personnel in some limited draft categories who leave service, and deserters who are present in large numbers. In the formative stages of Zeta's existence from 2000–03, nearly 50,000 soldiers had deserted.[21] While some reports assert that military deserters numbered as high as 150,000 in the six years preceding April 2009, other suggest that since the late 1990s to early 2009, some 100,000 personnel and 1,000 GAFE soldiers have fled.[22]

It is worth emphasizing that drug paramilitaries are far from static organizations. They change in composition and membership in accord with the successes and failures of their own operations and those of the drug organizations they support. Perhaps the greater source of change, however, is the short lifespan of cartel soldiers who are killed, disabled, arrested, or frightened away by their rivals, security forces, and sometimes violent internal disputes. As a consequence, there is a continuing demand for recruits that sometimes becomes especially acute with mass arrests, casualties, or special needs. Zetas, for example, recruited a 13-year-old male to work as a killer – a romanticized *sicario* as he imagined himself. He was required to, and did, execute a disobedient group member in a Laredo, Texas bar in 2004 as his career introduction.[23]

Serving military officers are recruited by drug cartels for roles other than as fighters or trainers and may remain in place at their units. In June 2009, Mexican authorities charged 10 army officers with providing information to the Pacific Cartel (Sinaloa Cartel) on planned military actions against the narco-traffickers. The cartel – also known as the Joaquin 'El Chapo' Guzman organization – demonstrated a capability to acquire intelligence that could serve in tailoring their own operations. In May 2009, a dozen soldiers were charged with collaborating with Zetas from the Gulf Cartel.[24] Other examples abound.

Both the military and uniformed police agencies have claimed that crimes, assaults, and human rights violations attributed to them have been carried out by narco-traffickers wearing army or police gear. For narco-paramilitaries, of course, the advantages of such deception are aimed at advancing their operations and delaying or preventing identification. Many uniforms and pieces of equipment are stolen, captured, or purchased from corrupt security force personnel. A newer dimension, however, surfaced in late July 2009 with the discovery of a small secret Juárez facility that fabricated a range of uniforms and tactical gear that was intended for sale to drug traffickers and other criminals. The clandestine fabricating facility was well equipped with camouflaged and other fabric, uniform patterns, industrial sewing machines and other items.[25]

### What defectors brought to the fight

As regards the main topic of this paper – firefights, raids, assassinations, and the skills and resources underlying their effectiveness – the appearance and development of militarized enforcement arms with varying concentrations of military or police cadres have clearly provided enhanced capabilities. Mexican military training materials and US training curricula for Mexican military personnel receiving instruction under assistance programs highlighted the nature of basic and more advanced military skills addressed. It would be a mistake and a gross exaggeration, of course, to credit any group with all of the features noted below, or with the capacity always to apply such skills evenly and adequately if they are present.

Some commentators, steeped in Mexican literature and history have pointed to the 1915 Mariano Azuela novella *Los de Abajos* when characterizing the impact of the drug wars.[26] Usually rendered in English as *The Underdogs*, the work described the deterioration of discipline and the pointless killings, betrayals, destruction, and disappearance of morality in Mexican irregular forces during the Revolution. Since drug paramilitaries had already pledged themselves morally bankrupt and profit-oriented criminal enterprises, devolution is a constant factor in group cohesion and conduct. There is no doubt, however, that in unevenly applied ways, and in various combinations, the military characteristics set out below – introduced by former military and security force members – have made paramilitary criminal groups more lethal and able to challenge Mexico's Federal security forces in ways not credited earlier:

- Combatants trained in the employment of light infantry and some low-end crew served weaponry including an array of fully and semi-automatic assault rifles; high-powered arms like the devastating .50 caliber Barret rifle; compact personal defense weapons like the P-90 Herstan automatic weapons; offensive and defensive grenades of various types including 40 mm grenade launchers; explosives of various types; shoulder-launched anti-tank weapons; and land-mines/IEDs among other armaments;
- Intelligence gathering capabilities including extensive HUMINT surveillance networks, radio and telephone intercept means, target assessment concepts and approaches, and informants providing positive intelligence;
- Offensive and defensive counter-intelligence capabilities including the most brutal forms of intimidation and coercion;
- Extensive knowledge of the tactics, techniques and procedures of police and the military;
- Communications means including cell phones, satellite phones, walkie-talkie style and other radios, computers, GPS systems, etc;

- Deception and information management/propaganda capabilities and resources;
- Transportation resources that include SUVs, pick-up trucks, cars, and aircraft as well as training in offensive and defensive driving; training camps facilities, and 'train-the-trainer' programs to instruct recruits not possessing requisite skills;
- Effective recruiting approaches ranging from covert inducements to overt advertising in videos, banners, and fliers;
- Cadres possessing measures of discipline enabling small groups to execute plans more complex that traditional criminal gunmen; and
- Training approaches and some facility in conveying military 'tactics, techniques and procedures' to group members.

These skills and resources have helped transform the enforcement arms of some drug trafficking organizations into what approaches the capabilities of military small units which are able to bring their capabilities to bear in the kinds of firefights, raids, and assassinations that now help define Mexico's operational environment in some areas, and which are appearing more frequently north of the border as well.

### Firefights, raids, and assassinations: Mexican internal clashes and targets across the border

While substantial drug violence has been a factor in Mexico's public safety environment for more than two decades, in 2003 mounting drug violence was marked by attention-getting incidents that signaled something of a change. In some ways, these 2003 armed clashes changed the paradigm of narco-violence even though there had certainly been more horrendous criminal events with greater loss of life. The change was the far more visible step forward in the earlier noted 'transition from the gangsterism of traditional narco hit men to paramilitary terrorism with guerrilla tactics'. The events – including an assortment of spontaneous and planned firefights, raids, and assassinations – marked the greater maturation of drug cartel paramilitaries. It highlighted an increase in their armaments and capabilities to the point where they could openly challenge organized security forces, and an overlay of corruption and compromise that continues to taint domestic and international cooperation in fighting the power of cartel leaders and organizations.

### *The streets of (Nuevo) Laredo*

Coming off more than 50 drug killings the year before, the 2003 New Year in Nuevo Laredo was marked by the assassination of a police officer and the wounding of another. Shortly thereafter, a clash between rival drug trafficking groups – one a new, small, short-lived outfit called 'Los Texas' and the other unidentified – attracted security force attention. Some 11 Los Texas traffickers were arrested when surrounded by responding Mexican Army troops. Several groups, large and small, were probing for control and business advantages, a process exacerbated by the arrest of the Gulf Cartel chief, Osiel Cardenas Guillen. This was a warm-up to several years of intense violence in the city.[27]

Prominent among the 2003 clashes was a firefight in the middle of Nuevo Laredo (Tamaulipas State) the sister city to Laredo, Texas just north on the Rio Grande. After some three to four years of existence in which their role in Gulf Cartel drug violence had gained some relatively limited public notice, an associated paramilitary emerged as a force with capabilities substantial enough to challenge organized security forces. In addition, they had a confidence and lack of scruples that did not flinch at conflict in the midst of a heavily populated urban area. More than that, the identity and affiliation of the various paramilitary components was a bit fuzzy for law enforcement; the exact course of events less than fully understood and highly variable; and police reliability more than questionable. In other words, it was a fine microcosm of an operational environment that would become more familiar and deserves addressing despite its confusion.

The firefight took place at night on 31 July, reportedly lasting 40 minutes. Nuevo Laredo municipal police, according to their initial statements, tried to stop several vehicles carrying an estimated 20 individuals. The caravan turned out to be a heavily armed tactical group that the Tamaulipas Sate Prosecutor's office said were the so-called *Comando Negro* (Black Command) group. They asserted that it was a component of the Zetas, which was suspected of area kidnappings and murders. They were armed with automatic weapons reserved for the military of the AK-47 or AR-15 type. They quickly engaged the police with automatic small arms fire and launcher-fired grenades. Police reports said that the Zetas also had a probable .50 machinegun but could not confirm that it was fired.

Municipal Police, it was claimed, were outgunned and called for military assistance and the help of Federal Police. Reported casualties from the fight varied, but suggested several police and Zetas were killed and others wounded.[28] However, the account soon changed in most aspects. Rather than a firefight between municipal police and Zetas, the shootout resulted from a running a firefight between the Zetas and pursuing Black Command gunmen who worked not for Zetas, but the rival Joaquin 'El Chapo' Guzman Cartel. The *Comando Negro* members did not catch the Zetas, but instead ran into patrolling Federal Investigative Agency officers the (AFI). The AFI, it became clear, had taken over key city patrolling duties since nearly 200 Nuevo Laredo Municipal Police members had been suspended during an investigation of their suspected ties with drug traffickers. Three of the alleged drug traffickers were killed, and six wounded *Comando Negro* group members were arrested. Among the strange dimensions was the presence of the Federal Prosecutor's Office 'Coordinator' in the Zeta force, voluntarily traveling with the fleeing paramilitary. Fearing for his safety, he had called for Federal security force help. Both he and his brother-in-law were arrested.[29] All of this created some dismay on both sides of the border.

Amidst the varying reports and interpretations of the incidents, there was an area of common agreement. This was that the paramilitaries possessed weaponry, confidence, and willingness to engage opposition including federal forces with heavy firepower. Such incidents gained momentum in Nuevo Laredo during 2003 and continued for three years at high levels, when other regions gradually replaced that border city as areas of the hottest conflict and reporting. In Nuevo Laredo, some combination of exhaustion, uneasy stasis among competing drug criminals, and a possibly corruption-based balance with security force enforcement following a major 2005 Federal crackdown, gave the city a degree of respite. The strife accounted for ending the lives of several hundred people, mostly drug traffickers but many police officers and commanders as well.

Retrospectively, the probable explanation for a suddenly greater visibility for drug paramilitaries in Laredo and elsewhere was their maturing capability coming at the same time as decisions by major and minor groups to take on competing organizations more actively. As plausible reporting suggests – from Mexican court testimony given by a protected witness – Joaquín Guzmán's Sinaloa Cartel made a deliberate decision to confront and defeat the Gulf Cartel's Zetas in the summer of 2003. Infrastructure and security preparations were made in advance with the 15–20 houses rented with 15 mattresses in each. The lodgings were to house some 200 Sinaloa gunmen, who some referred to as the *Comando Negro* paramilitary. A senior Guzmán deputy, quoted in August 2003 as declaring that 'the war for Nuevo Laredo has begun', appeared to be correct.[30]

Some volumes would be required to document and discuss paramilitary engagements from 2003 onward in Nuevo Laredo alone, which by no means was the scene of the worst drug violence in the most recent years. Collectively, they constitute a dreary list of lost lives, resources, societal cohesion, and institutional stability. Some selected incidents of firefights, raids, and assassinations, however, illustrate the capabilities of various paramilitaries as they have developed and asserted themselves.

### Capability and audacity on display

What seemed to be a daring raid to free imprisoned drug trafficking prisoners was a hallmark of some cartel paramilitary action. By early 2004, the Federal police and military had arrested some 20 drug traffickers including a number of Zeta members being held at a penitentiary at Apatzingan, Michoacán. On 7 January, some 30 armed men rushed the prison and in an action rather vaguely documented at the time – no shots being fired – effected the freeing of the imprisoned criminals. The Attorney General's office identified some of the assault group as Zeta members and it seemed a remarkable success. The following year, however, after an investigation, 18 prison staff members were arrested for complicity in the operation, suggesting that the paramilitary's ability to bribe or coerce state employees was as effective as their application of violence.[31]

An April 2009 kidnapping and assassination of a municipal police director, a senior Municipal official, and a citizen in Urique, Chihuahua marked the practiced and almost casual acts of violence used to rid criminal organizations of troublesome government and police leadership who pressed them too hard. The deaths served additionally as a proven means of coercing others into cooperation or at least inaction, particularly at the municipal level where police establishments have become thoroughly penetrated. There were no suspects and the rapid time between seizure and execution suggested that ransom had not been a motivation. The two officials had received death threats earlier, and the lack of any announcements or claims over the deaths indicated that the goal of the assassins had quietly been met. In short, the quick, fatal episode seemed to constitute a business decision effectively carried out.[32]

In July 2009, 25 paramilitary gunmen carried out a carefully planned nighttime raid on the home of a vocal 36-year-old American anti-kidnapping commentator in a small town in Chihuahua State. As is not infrequently the case, they wore Mexican Army uniforms and, in the increasingly and gratuitously brutal attacks, violently abused his wife in full view of his five children. The man was abducted, along with a friend at the scene, and both were found tortured and murdered in the town of Flores Magon some 30 miles away. The paramilitaries, of unknown association, left a banner at the scene warning other activists who protested their activities.[33]

In addition to targeting competitors, law enforcement, and the Mexican military, drug cartel paramilitaries also go after journalists who expose their dealings. In August 2005, a law enforcement task force in Baja California arrested a gunman who had assassinated the *Tijuana Zeta* journalist and co-editor Francisco Javier Ortiz Franco in June 2004. One of the arrested assassins worked for senior leaders of the Arellano Felix Cartel. The investigative journalist was leaving his home for an appointment when he was shot several times from a passing vehicle, suggesting at least adequate target reconnaissance surveillance and a well-prepared plan.[34]

By 2007, assassination concerns among US newspaper editors in some border cities resulted in the far more careful employment of investigative journalists inside Mexico and the withdrawal of at least one reporter. One US editor was so concerned about the safety of a reporter who had written more than 100 articles on the cartels – including the Nuevo Laredo violence addressed earlier – that he had arranged to conceal his location.[35]

The ability to react quickly and with surprising effectiveness has been demonstrated on a number of occasions. In September 2008, in the city of Monterrey, several armed gang members were arrested by local police while traveling in an unlicensed vehicle, and loaded into a squad car for transport and further questioning. However, en route to the station the patrol car was reportedly intercepted by two other vehicles containing an armed paramilitary grouping. They stopped the police car, freed the arrested gang members, tied up the police officers, and departed with their freed gang members. When a substantial period of time had passed with no word from the arresting officers, dispatched units eventually found them tied up in the back of their car. The circumstances here do seriously raise the unfortunate question of collusion on the part of the police officers who lost the prisoners. In any case, since there were now no suspects in custody, the identities of the rapidly responding paramilitary gang remained unknown – but the ending was an unusually peaceful one.[36]

That was not the case in Nuevo Leon, where a July 2009 convergence of security force–paramilitary violence left a confusing wake of loose ends. The episode began with the abduction of two men and their immediate execution for reasons which likely involved cartel rivalries but which were not immediately determined. Police, by chance, appeared shortly afterward, discovering the handcuffed bodies in the back of a pick-up truck. The murderers, who were fleeing the scene in several SUVs as the police arrived, encountered a Federal Police patrol a short distance away. A 20-minute shootout ensued, which wounded a number of people including bystanders. It left four of the paramilitary shooters dead at the scene. They were found to have police radio monitoring equipment in addition to their weapons. Searches of the area turned up an armored Escalade SUV with grenades and an AR-15 inside, and a Windstar minivan full of bullet holes. The many unknown dimensions surrounding this episode were to be examined by Federal investigatory bodies, a course that generally indicates no resolution will be forthcoming.[37]

During early June 2009, the first part of a weekend resulted in at least 23 people killed in drug violence in the states of Baja California, Chihuahua, Michoacán, and Durango. This was followed by a series of firefights in Guerrero State, in and near aging resort of Acapulco, involving the Beltran Leyva drug trafficking organization. An Army force had been deployed to the Acapulco tourist district upon receiving reports that armed men were in the area. Acapulco has been not only the site of some of the most brutal narco-violence, but in an area near continuing Popular Liberation Army guerrilla activity and other groups as well. When an Army patrol spotted a suspicious SUV and ordered it to stop, the occupants responded with automatic weapons fire and a chase through downtown Acapulco developed. In the developing firefight, with additional paramilitary members, some 18 people were killed, including an Army captain and 16 cartel gunmen, with at least nine soldiers wounded and five more gunmen arrested.[38]

### Crossing the border

Several of many instances of cross-border violence were noted above. To these could be added other crimes against US citizens, property, and interests to include those stemming from border crossings by armed groups, the coercion and even murder of US citizens such as has occurred in Arizona on the Tohono O'odom Indian Reservation, and occasional clashes with law enforcement and citizens. The January 2009 grenade attack on a Texas bar used by US law enforcement officers ended well when the military grenade failed to explode. US and Mexican investigators determined that the grenade was from the same manufacturing lot as those discovered in a weapons cache near Monterrey. Other grenades from the lot had been used against the US consulate in Monterrey, Mexico and against a Mexican television station.[39] This was one in a growing array of minor and major incidents north of the Rio Grande involving identified or probable Mexican drug trafficking interests.

Beginning more frequently in the mid-1990s, US border law enforcement began to take greater notice of shots fired from across the Rio Grande. The Border Patrol and other police agencies believed that these were not the occasional shots that have long been a feature of border life, but actions undertaken by drug traffickers angry at more rigorous patrolling and arrests. Stories, given credence by many in law enforcement, began to circulate that drug trafficking organizations were willing to pay $10,000 to obtain the home address of a Border Patrol agent.[40] Since that time, rising drug violence in Mexico and incidents of border spillover have raised more seriously the concern that clashes and killings like those that occur daily in Mexico may be transferred at increasing levels onto US territory.

In the last decade and a half – and particularly in the last several years – drug violence directed against illegal and legal US residents from Mexico involved in trafficking have boosted the crime rates of many border cities. These encompass the unholy trinity of 'killings, kidnappings, and home invasions' in a number of border cities, including the widely reported elevation of Phoenix, Arizona into the top kidnapping city in the United States.[41] The US policing term 'home invasion' describes what in Phoenix is actually a raid organized to kill, abduct, or coerce people; seize contraband; and assert territorial control. For cities like Phoenix, in a familiar parallel, police departments have become more militarized and received training that enable them to engage criminals with automatic weapons, grenade launchers, body armor, and improved skill levels. The August 2009 arraignment of members of the Mexican drug, kidnapping, and murder group *Los Palillos* (the Toothpicks) in San Diego, highlighted what had been a four-year period of brutal drug-related murders, abductions, and torture, including the killing of a police officer.[42] Far more than border cities are threatened, however, Atlanta being a case in point. Drug violence in that city has so far involved limited attacks among drug gang members, as they have in some of the other 195 or more US cities having a Mexican drug trafficking cartel presence.[43]

The consequence of this is to establish an infrastructure that will likely serve as a vector for future drug violence that extends beyond border areas. There are already models for addressing existing and potential north-of-the border Mexican drug trafficking violence. They lie in the rich body of assessments of 'ethnic' crime as it appears in many parts of the world.[44] Émigré population bases typically form the sea in which criminals of the same ethnic or nationality group swim. While the US has many ethno-national criminal organizations, Mexican drug trafficking organizations bring an extraordinarily high level of violence to their criminal endeavors and a willingness to target obstructions outside the immediate community. They also have proven skills in using the near-endless amounts of drug money available to fuel official corruption. Growing levels of US enforcement corruption along the border demonstrates this, as does the recent recruitment of a US soldier assassin addressed above.[45]

Few modern states experience such violent and destabilizing episodes at the frequency they occur in 2010 Mexico. With robust US security assistance and support from other countries, Mexico continues to seek combinations of approaches that can slow, badly damage, and eventually reduce to minimal levels the drug trade before it destroys Mexico. The Mexican military – at the center of the struggle – is attempting to improve forces and the tactical and operational concepts governing their employment against drug violence and infrastructure. The dangers of continued skill transference from security forces to drug trafficking organizations is well understood, but so far an unavoidable risk. As 2010 begins, extraordinary levels of violence in Mexico and the basic business of selling drugs continue apace. What had been the creep of violence across the US border appears to be quickening, with departures from the familiar, limited patterns of most other ethnic crime marked by the degrees of violence and rapid metastasizing of émigré criminal groups around the country.

**Conclusions**

The firefights, raids, and assassinations that characterize so much of Mexican drug trafficking violence are actions that require a measure of organization, planning, and equipping to be successful. Wartime and contingency force experience is replete with examples of regular military units around the world which have failed to complete tactical actions that Mexican drug paramilitaries sometimes execute with notable effectiveness. Drug paramilitaries clearly owe much of their real and perceived lethality to cadres recruited from among Mexico's special operations forces, regular military, police, and other security personnel.

The changes that began in drug paramilitaries at the turn of the twenty-first century accord with the arrival of the first major military recruiting of exceptionally well-trained uniformed soldiers and officers. In the years since, drug paramilitaries have often evidenced the tactical competence, weapons skills, communications, transportation, and surveillance capability, and intelligence gathering and counter-intelligence capability that smaller regular armies may not themselves possess. While acting on behalf of a major world evil, they have evidenced a rough, robust confidence and willingness to engage in daring operations that too often have confounded security forces intended to stop or punish them.

As notable as paramilitary capabilities may appear, much of that effectiveness is owed to the 'force multiplier' of endemic corruption. Ubiquitous bribery and coercion of major and minor officials in security and other institutions by drug trafficking organizations opens police road blocks; unlocks prison doors; renders police and security forces blind, deaf, and speechless; reveals military and police plans for pending actions; and purchases not-guilty judgments or dismissals in the Mexican judicial system. It buys lists of informants and facilitates the dissemination of disinformation. Applied brutality and reward also gains a measure of silence and cooperation from citizens. Drug paramilitary employment of informants and the use of squads of street-level observers generate continued information of value. Collectively, this constitutes a penetration of Mexican society that presents a daunting challenge.

While the infrastructure and practice of paramilitary violence is established in Mexico in seemingly unprecedented ways, the concern north of the border is its potential transportability. Many law enforcement personnel have compared 1980s' Miami – with its running drug firefights, revenge raids, and bloody assassinations by Colombian cocaine traffickers – to Mexican drug violence. There are enough precursors north of the Rio Grande now to make the potential for something analogous more than empty speculation. Incidents of cross-border violence; a Mexican narco-trafficking presence in nearly 200 US cities raising local crime rates; limited but increasing corruption among US border law enforcement; and the successful recruitment of US residents to commit capital murder, suggest cross-border criminality could expand apace without stronger countermeasures. In that environment, outbreaks of narco-violence analogous to 1980s' Miami – or the more widespread firefights, raids and assassinations of Mexican cities – seem more than possible.

### Notes

1. *Newsmax.com*, 'Mexico's Calderón Rejects Joint Drug Raids with U.S' and Caldwell, 'Military Chief: No Plan to Ramp up Border Presence'.
2. Beittal, 'Mexico's Drug Related Violence', 14.
3. *CongressDaily*, 'Union head: Border is Far from Secure'.
4. Rosenberg, 'U.S. Anti-Drug Information Leaked to Mexico Cartels'.
5. El Universal.com.mx, 'Mexican Policemen Clash with Armed Commando in Veracruz'.
6. City and Vulliamy, 'Drugs "Taliban" Declares War on Mexican State' and EFE Press Service, 'Violencia y narcotráfico en México: 15 cadáveres en una carretera de Michoacán'.
7. Caldwell, 'Drug Lieutenant Slain on East Side Allegedly Was Confidential Informant'.
8. Ibid. and Caldwell, '16-Year-Old Arrested in Cartel Shooting in El Paso'. Among the specialists is Shannon O'Neil at the Council on Foreign Relations, who is currently preparing a study on US–Mexican relations.
9. Reyna, 'The Enemy is Also Within', Part II, 21.
10. Reyna, 'The Enemy is Also Within', Part I, 42–4.
11. Aranda, 'La Paz en Chiapas pasa por la desmilitarización'.
12. Aranda, 'Participan 26 mil militares en la actividad; de 95 a la fecha han muerto 65'.
13. Mandujano, 'Militares Mexicanos Se Entrenan en Escuela *Kaibil*'.
14. *La Prensa,* 'Goodbye to the Barracks' and Medellín, '1,382 Elite Soldiers Have Deserted'.

15. Center for International Policy. 'Just the Facts: Mexico'. See pertinent years in the multi-year compilation of data.
16. Medellín, 'Reactivan hoy Fuerza Naval del Pacífico; tendrá 3,130 elementos'. See also the official Semar website at http://www.semar.gob.mx/fuerzas/golfo/fuernavgo.htm for a brief description of the Amphibious Reaction Forces.
17. Nájar, 'De soldados a policías, el mapa nacional'; and Farah and Moore, 'Elite Anti-Drug Troops Investigated in Mexico'.
18. Gutiérrez, 'El sofisticado ejército del narco' and the fine recap article by Becerra, 'A to Z of Crime – Mexico's Zetas Expand Operations'.
19. Office of the Attorney General of the Republic, Bulletin 673/0.
20. See Becerra, 'A to Z'; and 'Los Zetas tienen "ejército" de espionaje', http://www.planoinformativo.com/nota.php?id=21915 for varying interpretations. The names *Halcones, Ventanas, Expertos*, and other designations are often applied to these grouping, but the rather confused and changing reporting on their names and complications suggests that the information is less than authoritative.
21. *El Universal*, 'Number of Army Desertions Worries Mexican National Security Expert'.
22. Rodriguez, 'Army Desertions Hurting Mexico's War on Drugs'; Becerra, 'A to Z of Crime'; and Reyez, 'Mercenarios en el Ejército Mexicano'.
23. Fleming, 'Drug Wars: The Next Generation'.
24. *El Universal*, 'Subordinate Officers Allegedly Provided Pacific Cartel with Information on Sedena Counternarcotics Operations'.
25. Borunda, 'Soldiers seize fake military gear being produced at Juárez factory'.
26. Azuela, *Los de Abajo*.
27. *El Universal*, '11 Suspected Narco Traffickers Arrested in Nuevo Laredo'.
28. 'Mexico: Army, Police, Drug Traffickers Fight Pitched Battle in Nuevo Laredo', as translated by a government service.
29. *El Universal*, 'Army Patrols Strategic Points in Nuevo Laredo, Tamaulipas State'; and Gomez and Monge, 'Mexican Army Units Patrol Nuevo Laredo after Friday Night Shootout'.
30. Walker, 'U.S. to Reopen Consulate Despite Cartel Turf War'.
31. *La Voz de Michoacán*, 'Prison Personnel Responsible for Apatzingan Jailbreak Sentenced'; and *Channel 11 Television*.
32. *El Diario*, 'Ejecutan a oficial mayor y a director de Policía Municipal'.
33. US Embassy, Mexico City, 'Anti-kidnap Activist, Relative Murdered in Northern Mexico Submitted'.
34. *La Frontera*, 'Coordination Group Apprehends Journalist's Assassin'.
35. Roig-Franzia, 'Americans Covering Mexico Drug Trade Face Assassination Threat'.
36. Mexico City Embassy, Press Summary.
37. *Milenio Television*, 'Milenio Noticias'.
38. EFE News Service, '18 Die in Shootout between Gunmen and Army in Mexico'.
39. Kocherga, 'Evidence Links US, Mexico grenade attacks'.
40. Billingsley, 'Mexican Drug Lords Trying to Gun Down U.S. Border Patrol'.
41. Caldwell, 'Mexican drug violence spills over into the US'.
42. Office of the District Attorney, County of San Diego, 'DA Announces Charges Against Violent Kidnapping and Murder Crew'.
43. *Newsmax.com*, 'Atlanta Reeling under Mexican Drug Cartel Violence'.
44. Kleinknecht, *New Ethnic Mobs*. Among the many specialized studies of ethnic crime, this provides a good summary and overview.
45. Mendoza and Sherman, 'Busts of Corrupt US Border Police Rise as Smugglers Seek More Protection'; and Cable News Network (CNN), 'Documents: Slain Cartel Member Feared for His Life'.

## Bibliography

Aranda, Jesús. 'La Paz en Chiapas pasa por la desmilitarización' [Peace in Chiapas Through Demilitarization], *La Jornada* (28 May 1999).

Aranda, Jesús. 'Participan 26 mil militares en la actividad; de 95 a la fecha han muerto 65' [2,600 Military Personnel Participated in the Activity; 65 Killed from 95 to Date], *La Jornada* (August 1999).

Azuela, Mariano. *Los de Abajo*. Mexico City: Fondo de Cultura Economica, 2007.

Becerra, Oscar. 'A to Z of Crime – Mexico's Zetas Expand Operations'. *Jane's Intelligence Review* (26 January 2009).

Beittal, June S. 'Mexico's Drug Related Violence'. *Congressional Research Service*, no.7–500 (27 May 2009), 14.

Billingsley, K.L. 'Mexican Drug Lords Trying to Gun Down U.S. Border Patrol'. *The Washington Times* (2 June 1997).

Borunda, Daniel. 'Soldiers Seize Fake Military Gear Being Produced at Juárez Factory'. *El Paso Times* (27 July 2009), http://www.elpasotimes.com/ci_12920523.

Cable News Network [CNN]. 'Documents: Slain Cartel Member Feared for His Life'. August 2009, http://www.cnn.com/2009/CRIME/08/12/cartel.murder/index.html.

Caldwell, Alicia A. 'Mexican Drug Violence Spills over into the US'. Associated Press, 9 February 2009.

Caldwell, Alicia A. 'Military chief: No Plan to Ramp up Border Presence'. *Newsvine.com*, 17 April 2009, http://www.newsvine.com/_news/2009/04/17/2697918-military-chief-no-plan-to-ramp-up-border-presence.

Caldwell, Alicia A. 'Drug Lieutenant Slain on East Side Allegedly was Confidential Informant'. *El Paso Times* (29 July 2009).

Caldwell, Alicia A. '16-Year-Old Arrested in Cartel Shooting in El Paso'. ABC News, 12 August 2009, http://abcnews.go.com/US/wireStory?id=8309831.

Center for International Policy. 'Just the Facts: Mexico'. September 2006, http://www.ciponline.org/.

Fleming, Rusty. 'Drug Wars: The Next Generation'. CNN, 5 August 2009, http://ac360.blogs.cnn.com/2009/08/05/drug-wars-the-next-generation/.

Channel 11 Television, 7 January 2004, as translated in FBIS LAP20040107000029.

City, Jo Tuckman and Ed Vulliamy, 'Drugs "Taliban" Declares War on Mexican State'. *The Guardian* (19 July 2009), http://www.guardian.co.uk/world/2009/jul/19/la-familia-drugs-trade-mexico.

*CongressDaily*. 'Union head: Border is Far from Secure'. 9 July 2009, http://www.GovernmentExecutive.com.

EFE News Service. '18 Die in Shootout between Gunmen and Army in Mexico'. 7 June 2009, as translated in the government translation FEA20090608861189.

EFE Press Service. 'Violencia y narcotráfico en México: 15 cadáveres en una carretera de Michoacán' [Violence and Narco-Trafficking in Mexico: 15 Bodies on a Michoacán Highway], 14 July 2009.

*El Diario*. 'Ejecutan a oficial mayor y a director de Policía Municipal' [A Senior Official and Municipal Police Director Executed], 4 April 2009, http://www.eldiariodechihuahua.com.mx.

*El Universal*. 'Number of Army Desertions Worries Mexican National Security Expert'. 18 August 2003, as translated in LAP20030818000093, http://www.el-universal.com.mx/pls/impreso/edicion_impresa.portada.

*El Universal*. 'Los Zetas tienen "ejército" de espionaje' [The Zetas have an Espionage Army], 3 December 2007 http://www.planoinformativo.com/nota.php?id=21915.

*El Universal*. 'Subordinate Officers Allegedly Provided Pacific Cartel With Information on Sedena Counternarcotics Operations'. 14 June 2009, as translated by a Government service in LAP20090615036002.

*El Universal.* '11 Suspected Narco Traffickers Arrested in Nuevo Laredo'. 4 February 2003, as translated by a Government service in LAP20030205000040.

*El Universal.* 'Army Patrols Strategic Points in Nuevo Laredo, Tamaulipas State'. 3 August 2003 as translated in FBIS LAP20030804000010.

*El Universal.com.mx.* 'Mexican Policemen Clash With Armed Commando in Veracruz'. [Television Feed] 15 July 2009, http://www.eluniversal.com.mx/noticias.html, and translated transcript in LAM20090715049001.

Farah, Douglas, and Molly Moore. 'Elite Anti-Drug Troops Investigated in Mexico'. *Washington Post* (9 September 1999).

Gomez, Francisco, and Gaston Monge. 'Mexican Army Units Patrol Nuevo Laredo after Friday Night Shootout'. *El Universal* (3 August 2003), as translated in FBIS LAP20030803000022.

Gutiérrez, Alejandro. 'El sofisticado ejército del narco' [The Narco's Sophisticated Army], *Proceso* (18 January 2004).

Kleinknecht, William. *New Ethnic Mobs: The Changing Face of Organized Crime in America.* New York: Free Press, 1996.

Kocherga, Angela. 'Evidence Links US, Mexico Grenade Attacks'. 11 News Border Bureau, 17 February 2009, http://www.txcn.com/sharedcontent/dws/txcn/houston/stories/khou090212_mh_mexico_grenade_attacks.c16c1da.html.

*La Frontera.* 'Coordination Group Apprehends Journalist's Assassin'. 5 August 2005, as translated in FBIS LAP20050805000057.

*La Prensa.* 'Goodbye to the Barracks'. 4 June 2004, No. 1321.

*La Voz de Michoacán.* 'Prison Personnel Responsible for Apatzingan Jailbreak Sentenced'. 20 August 2005, as translated In FBIS LAP20050822000052.

Mandujano, Isaín. 'Militares Mexicanos Se Entrenan en Escuela *Kaibil*' [The Mexican Military Trains at the *Kaibiles* School], *Proceso* (29 September 2005), http://www.proceso.com.mx/getfileex.php?nta=34060.

Medellín, Jorge Alejandro. 'Reactivan hoy Fuerza Naval del Pacífico; tendrá 3,130 elementos' [Pacific Naval Force Reactivated Today; It will have 3,130 Personnel], *El Universal* (2 August 2001).

Medellín, Jorge. '1,382 Elite Soldiers Have Deserted'. *El Universal* (28 March 2004), http://www.eluniversal.com.mx/noticias.html.

Mendoza, Martha and Christopher Sherman. 'Busts of Corrupt US Border Police Rise as Smugglers Seek More Protection'. *Associated Press*, 9 August 2009.

'Mexico: Army, Police, Drug Traffickers Fight Pitched Battle in Nuevo Laredo'. 1 August 2003, as translated by a Government service in LAP20030801000122.

Mexico City Embassy, Press Summary, September 2008.

*Milenio Television.* 'Milenio Noticias'. 15 July 2009, as translated by a government service in FEA20090717871472.

Nájar, Alberto. 'De soldados a policías, el mapa nacional' [From Soldiers to Police, the National Map], *La Jornada* (15 August 1999).

*Newsmax.com.* 'Mexico's Calderón Rejects Joint Drug Raids with U.S.' 10 March 2009, http://www.newsmax.com/newsfront/eu_britain_mexico/2009/03/30/197540.html.

Newsmax.com. 'Atlanta Reeling under Mexican Drug Cartel Violence'. 10 March 2009, http://www.newsmax.com/newsfront/atlanta_mexico_drug_gangs/2009/03/10/190259.html.

Office of the Attorney General of the Republic, Bulletin 673/0. Press Release. Mexico City, 6 October 2001.

Office of the District Attorney, County of San Diego, 'DA Announces Charges against Violent Kidnapping and Murder Crew'. Press Release, 13 August 2009.

Reyez, José. 'Mercenarios en el Ejército Mexicano' [Mercenaries in the Mexican Army], *Contralinea* (12 July 2009).

Reyna, Ignacio Rodriguez. 'The Enemy is Also Within: The Army of Rangers and Green Berets'. [Part I of a three-part series], *El Financiero* (25 September 1995), 42–4, as translated in FTS19950925000048.

Reyna, Ignacio Rodriguez. 'The Enemy is Also Within' [Part II of a three-part series], *El Financiero* (26 September 1995), as translated in FBIS-LAT-95-194, 21.

Rodriguez, Rey. 'Army Desertions Hurting Mexico's War on Drugs'. *CNN.com*, 11 March 2009, http://www.cnn.com/2009/WORLD/americas/03/11/mexico.desertions/index.html.

Roig-Franzia, Manuel. 'Americans Covering Mexico Drug Trade Face Assassination Threat'. *Washington Post* (14 July 2007).

Rosenberg, Mica. 'U.S. Anti-Drug Information Leaked to Mexico Cartels'. Reuters, 15 January 2009, http://www.reuters.com/article/topNews/idUSTRE50E7E220090115.

US Embassy, Mexico City, 'Anti-Kidnap Activist, Relative Murdered in Northern Mexico Submitted', 9 July 2009.

Walker, Lynne. 'U.S. to Reopen Consulate Despite Cartel Turf War'. 6 August 2005, Copley News Service, http://www.derechos.org/nizkor/corru/doc/laredo.html.

# Torture, beheadings, and narcocultos

Pamela L. Bunker[a] , Lisa J. Campbell[b] and Robert J. Bunker[a]*

[a]Counter-OPFOR Corporation, Claremont, CA, USA; [b]146th Airlift Wing, Channel Islands National Guard Station, CA, USA

This essay provides an overview of those incidents of torture and beheadings linked to the Mexican cartels and their mercenary and gang affiliates taking place both within Mexico and the United States. Specific forms of torture are discussed as well as the most likely victims and perpetrators. Beheadings, primarily taking place only in Mexico, are also analyzed with supporting database information provided. The occurrences of torture and beheadings tied to these cartels, both in Mexico and more recently across the border into the United States, beg the question of the context in which they are being conducted. Most cases of torture or beheading are regarded as primarily secular in nature – a terrorist tactic tied to economic or political gain. In an even more macabre twist, however, certain instances have been seen as intertwined with a group's belief system, performed in ritual fashion to fulfill religious or spiritual demands. This suggests that the emergent Mexican narcocultos that are evolving may further increase drug war violence to new levels of brutality heretofore unseen.

The use of torture and beheading in narcotics trafficking in Mexico has now become a common occurrence because of the violent nature of the enterprise, the large sums of money at stake, and the animosities that develop between competitors, between traffickers and the authorities, and between traffickers and anyone else considered a threat to them or their business operations. Typically, the larger the stakes and amounts of money involved, the greater the propensity for violence and torture. As drug wars break out over lucrative markets, smuggling routes, and transshipment points and as governmental crackdowns take place, the use of torture also increases as a component of an operational environment characterized by low intensity conflict and narcoterrorism. Because many of the police forces and judicial systems in Mexico have been corrupted and compromised and therefore arrest and prosecution rates are extremely low, the

---

* The views expressed here do not represent those of the US Air Force, Department of Defense, or the US Government.

probability of ever being brought to justice is almost non-existent for most individuals and groups engaging in killings, torture, and beheadings.[1]

On the American side of the border, the legal system still partially serves as a deterrent to incidents of torture due to the severe penalties and special circumstances that these incidents add to state and federal crimes. Still, such repercussions are becoming irrelevant, as more incidents of torture have begun to take place on American soil as the drug wars spill over the border and as cartel and gang culture exerts a greater influence on the prisons and the streets.

The groups engaging in torture and beheadings on both sides of the US–Mexico border include the Mexican drug cartels, their enforcers and mercenary forces, and their prison and street gang sub-contractors and allies such as the Mexican Mafia (La Eme) and thousands of Sureños (Sur 13) foot soldiers. So many incidents of torture and maiming have now taken place in Mexico that a new and tragically unique lexicon is developing to describe the horrific crimes being carried out:

- *Decapitado:* decapitation.
- *Descuartizado:* quartering of a body.
- *Encajuelado:* put body in car trunk.
- *Encobijado*: body wrapped in blanket.
- *Entambado*: body put in drum.
- *Enteipado*: eyes and mouth of corpse taped shut.
- *Pozoleado (also Guisado)*: body in acid bath, looks like Mexican stew.[2]

An additional dimension to these incidents of torture and beheadings is the secular and religious context in which they are being conducted. Torture and beheadings are typically employed for political and economic gain, as a cold and calculated means to wage psychological warfare and terrorism against ones opponents, and even as a form of twisted sport for some. These are all secular motivations. Of concern is the added dimension of cults and other corrupted forms of spirituality tied to the Mexican cartels and their increasing relationships to such heinous and barbaric acts. While still found in only a minority of incidents, the use of ritualistic torture and beheading portends the rise of a religious component in the drug wars. These bad omens are not without their own concerns for they have the potential of further expanding the current conflict from that of a criminal insurgency into a conflict between traditional value systems and emergent narco-value systems with quasi-religious and cult-like underpinnings.

## Torture

In Mexico, well over 5500 people have died in the drug wars during 2008 alone with Mexican TV broadcasts, web sites, and newspapers awash in images of violence. Typically, these deaths are attributed to small arms fire from pistols, rifles, and assault weapons. While many of the targeted individuals are shot numerous times as an outcome of street battles and gunfights, assassinated with extreme prejudice (e.g. the narcocorrido singer Valentín Elizalde 'Golden Rooster' who promoted the Sinaloa cartel was shot 20 times[3]), or executed with a shot to the back of the head at point blank range, none of these occurrences can be considered outright torture. No ready statistics exist concerning rates of torture as a percentage of killings or incidents of torture in which the victim was not killed as in a kidnapping where the brutalized individual was then released. The following passage from a recent article on the Mexican drug wars may help in making one such estimate:

> When I lived in Mexico, the occasional gang member would turn up executed, maybe with duct-taped hands, rolled in a carpet, and dropped in an alley. But Mexico's newspapers itemized a different kind of slaughter last August [2008]: Twenty-four of the week's 167 dead were cops, 21 were decapitated, and 30 showed signs of torture.[4]

If these numbers can be considered a norm then about 18% of the victims were tortured, which would come out to about 1000 people for 2008. Due to sampling error and the unreliability of making such inferences, such a number would have to be considered only an upper threshold. That same year, about 190 beheadings took place in Mexico,[5] and it is reasonable to assume, based on the above August 2008 statistics and common sense, that more people will be torture-killed than beheaded, although beheading can be considered an extreme form of torture if the victim is beheaded while still alive. This would place the probable range of incidence of 'torture-killings' in the Mexican drug wars well above 200 and somewhere below 1000 – with a mean of 600 – as a conservative estimate for 2008 only. Based on this estimate, the use of torture for intimidation and extortion-only purposes would reasonably be projected to be well into the thousands of incidents. Physical injuries such as bruising from punching and kicking, the breaking of a bone, or knife lacerations would all fall into this category. Kidnapping and abduction would be required to take place prior to many of these torture-killing or 'torture-intimidation' incidents with some sort of safe house, ranch, or out-of-the-way location being utilized to engage in the actual act of torture itself.

Physical torture can be short in its duration and last for minutes or can be a drawn-out process and last for hours, possibly even days in some rare cases. DEA Special Agent Enrique 'Kiki' Camarena was torture-killed over the course of two days in March 1985 at the El Bufalo marijuana ranch in Chihuahua. He ultimately died of injuries suffered from a crushed skull.[6] More than nine hours of the torture sessions were taped by the killers and culminated with the DEA agent's death.[7] Longer instances of torture would fall more into traditional forms of kidnappings with starvation, beatings, and sexual abuse and have more of a psychological component to them. The Mexican drug war torture-killings are primarily physical torture based and short term in duration. Torture lasting for minutes might take place on the side of a deserted road or desolate spot. It would involve knee-capping the victim or shooting the individual with non-fatal wounds in various parts of the body prior to administering a fatal wound. Knives, wires, and farm or industrial tools can also be utilized to inflict non-fatal wounds, such as finger dismemberment, to elicit maximum suffering and could be utilized out in the open or in a work space or safe house, which would allow for the luxury of longer torture sessions.

Other torture methods and techniques can also be utilized including acid, fire, electricity, water, suffocation, excrement, and animals. In a February 2009 incident, retired general Mauro Enrique Tello Quiñonez was kidnapped along with his aide and driver in or near Cancun. The retired general had just been hired to set up a 100-man special anti-drug unit for the Cancun mayor which was a combination SWAT (Special Weapons and Tactics) team and intelligence unit composed of former military officers and federal agents.[8] Concerning the torture inflicted:

> 'The general was the most mistreated,' Rodriquez [Quintana Roo state prosecutor] said at a Tuesday night news conference monitored by El Universal newspaper. 'He had burns on his skin and bones in his hands and wrists were broken.' An autopsy revealed Tello also suffered broken knees and was shot 11 times, Mexico City's Excelsior newspaper said.[9]

Other drug war victims are now sometimes being found fully dismembered or partially dissolved in vats of acid and industrial chemicals. Two dismembered bodies were found in Rosarito Beach in December 2008, one outside of a small church, and partially dissolved bodies in barrels were found earlier in Tijuana in front of a seafood restaurant.[10] If these victims were dismembered or dissolved while still alive is unknown, but other documented incidents confirm that targeted individuals have been burned to death, thrown alive into containers containing acid (known as making 'guisado' or stew), and dismembered and fed to lions kept on ranches belonging to narcotraffickers.[11]

Across the border in the United States, rates of narco-violence and torture are much lower, and coverage is still somewhat of a rarity during nightly news broadcasts. Even so, torture is known to have been conducted there by Mexican drug traffickers, their enforcers, and affiliated and freelance kidnapping and human trafficking gangs. Drug distribution sub-contractors such as the Mexican Mafia and their Sureño foot soldiers, including the Avenues gang (Los Angeles based) and Mara Salvatrucha (MS-13) spread throughout the United States, have also utilized torture. A fair estimate is that some dozens of torture-killings are currently taking place on a yearly basis and far more – well into the hundreds – if 'torture-intimidation' for street and prison tax collection (extortion) and kidnapping purposes is considered. A few illustrative accounts of cartel and gang incidents of torture taking place in the United States are as follows:

- '"Brenda Paz [FBI informant] was pregnant, lonely and she missed her family – MS-13," Walutes said... "Oscar Garcia-Orellana put a rope around her throat and held her, while the other two stabbed and stabbed and stabbed," Walutes said.' (Northern Virginia, 2003)[12]
- 'All of the victims were robbed, and Aeriel and the group's other female, Iofemi Hightower, were sexually molested and cut with machetes and

knives, according to a lawsuit recently filed against the city school system and the alleged [MS-13] killers.' (Newark, 2007)[13]

- 'Investigators said the suspects used terrorist tactics of simulated drowning techniques (water boarding) as well as pliers applied to the male victim's genitals to learn where and when millions in cash and drug shipments were being made.' (US East Coast, 2008)[14]
- '... She was eventually released unharmed. So was another man, but only after being tortured for three days by smugglers. His wife had to listen to his screams over the phone – as well as field $100,000 for ransom. "They tried to take out the eyes and the ears and the finger, also" she said.' (Phoenix, 2008)[15]

For actual Mexican Mafia killings in prison, torture is rarely used because of a lack of time. Stabbings are quickly done with shanks (sharpened pieces of metal or plastic) which prisoners keep secreted in their rectums prior to use. On the streets, Sureños gang members traditionally rely upon small arms to kill other gang members and competitors with a hail of bullets or by means of execution-style slayings. However, both groups have used torture and continue to engage in such practices, although not currently anywhere near to the extent seen in Mexico or by cartel operatives now operating north of the border.

### Beheadings[16]

Beheadings first surfaced in Mexico in early to mid 2006. Before then Mexico had had no real history of beheadings. But now beheadings there have grown to be commonplace in several areas contested by rival cartels, including very near the US border where drug trafficking corridors or *plazas* exist. Beheading victims first included rival cartel members, police officers, and lawyers but quickly expanded to include journalists and eventually Mexican military troops. The purpose for most of the beheadings is business – a cartel protecting or furthering its interests. But since gangs or enforcers carrying out beheadings for the cartels are not homogeneous,[17] their reasons to behead can vary. Two of four beheadings which have occurred in the US were characterized by gang business – independent of, but potentially bad for, the cartel-related drug trafficking business from Mexico to the US. Furthermore, the weapons enforcers use to behead are typically common to the Latin American region and differ from those used for concurrent beheadings in the Middle East.

The earliest beheadings took place predominantly in southern Mexico, in Acapulco and Guerrero, with the exception of some incidents in the north, in Rosarito Beach and Tijuana, which began in mid 2006. In 2007, beheading incidents remained in the south but expanded to the Mexican Gulf coast, in areas contested by rival cartels. Beheadings became the most widespread in 2008 when their incidence migrated north through central Mexico as well as into areas on the west coast and near the US border, where several beheadings occurred in Ciudad Juárez. One of the first mass beheadings of modern times also occurred in 2008, on the Yucatán peninsula. Through mid 2009, cartel-related beheadings have continued throughout Mexico but have been occurring most frequently on or near the US–Mexican border. Additionally, at least one Mexican cartel-related beheading has occurred in Guatemala, where Mexican cartels have been setting up new operations, safely away from disruption by Mexican government forces. Overall, in a relatively short four-year period the occurrence of beheadings in Mexico has spread, with a troubling increase in the number occurring on the US–Mexican border (Table 1). A geospatial analysis was conducted on yearly combined occurrences of beheadings in Mexico from 2006 to mid-July 2009 using geocoordinates of towns where the beheadings took place. Initial findings were that over the three and a half year period the average yearly latitude numbers have increased (northwards) and the average shortest distances from incidents to the US/Mexico border have decreased, the overall outcome being that of an apparent northward trending of beheadings.[18]

Out of roughly 5600 killed in Mexico in 2008, beheadings accounted for 186 (approximately 3%) – a significant number when considering the potentially widespread psychological impact of each beheading as well as the value that impact has to the cartels. Cartels' strategic goals are both economic and political, but on a more tactical level their objective is the immediate and long-term control of territory, including the plazas by which drugs are making their way into the United States. To accomplish both their strategic and tactical objectives, cartels must keep police and soldiers at bay, out-terrorize rival cartels, silence reporters and eyewitnesses, keep lawyers from prosecuting and prevent investigators from investigating. Beheadings are one of the most effective means by which the cartels accomplish these objectives: '... [cartels] use the level of violence necessary to protect their markets and control their competition'.[19]

In January 2009 the Chief of Police of the Mexican municipality of Praxedis G. Guerrero was kidnapped along with five of his men. The Chief of Police was soon after beheaded. As a result, mass resignations ensued from the police forces of both Praxedis G. Guerrero and the neighboring municipality of Guadalupe, leaving these Texas-bordering towns without functioning police forces.

To carry out beheadings, cartels often use enforcers. Many of these hired enforcers are from Los Zetas, Los Kaibiles, Gente Nueva (*New People,* known to rival Los Zetas), Mata Zetas (*Anti Zetas*),[20] MS-13, and other mara gangs. Members of many of these groups have significant histories of violence and brutality; some even have military training. Los Zetas and Los Kaibiles have official nation-state military training, which includes US and Guatemalan Special Forces training. The violent tendencies of MS-13 members are derived from their gang and societal experiences as well as their need to survive government suppression in both the US and Central America. With the significant history beheadings have in both Central and South America, enforcers hired from these regions make ideal agents to carry out the dirty work of the Mexican cartels.[21] Enforcers receive significant pay, likely an incentive which will only perpetuate

Table 1. Beheadings by cartels, gangs and enforcers in Mexico[i]

| Date | Beheading | Organization | Location | Remarks |
|---|---|---|---|---|
| 20-Apr-06 | Two police officers beheaded | Unknown | Acapulco | The officers' heads were stuck on metal poles in front of a government building mere blocks from an Acapulco tourist strip. A note nearby read: 'So that you learn to respect.' |
| 8-May-06 | Lawyer beheaded | Possibly Millenium cartel | Aguaje, Michoacan | The lawyer was defending an alleged member of an independent drug cartel led by Armando Sanchez Arreguin, AKA *The Grandfather*. The head was hung from an archway that served as one of the entrances to Aguaje. A homemade *Welcome* sign was affixed nearby. |
| 21-Jun-06 | Beheaded bodies of three Baja police officers and one civilian found | Unknown cartel | Rosarito Beach | The heads were found hours later in Tijuana. The civilian was a Mexican American resident of Arizona. Witnesses claimed that some 100 persons wearing Mexican AFI uniforms kidnapped and killed the individuals. |
| 24-Jun-06 29-Jun-06 | One police officer beheaded Man's head found on City Hall steps | Unknown gang Possibly Los Zetas | Guerrero Acapulco | Three additional police officers were found shot. A handwritten note, signed with the letter Z was left. The discovery came one day after a beheaded body, with the letter Z carved into the chest, was found outside the residence of a city employee. |
| 30-Jun-06 | Two heads found | Possibly Los Zetas | Acapulco | The heads were placed in front of a government office, with a note signed with the letter Z. 'One more message, dirtbags, so that you learn to respect.' One of the heads had the eyes and mouth taped shut, while the other had one eye covered. |
| 21-Jun-06 | Three police officers and a civilian found beheaded | Arellano Felix | Tijuana | Authorities alleged that Arellano Felix ordered the beheadings while in prison. |

(*continues*)

Table 1 – *continued*

| Date | Beheading | Organization | Location | Remarks |
| --- | --- | --- | --- | --- |
| 10-Jul-06 | At least five heads left beside a cross | Unknown | Tepalcatapec | Killers reportedly avenging the death of a drug smuggler left heads beside a black metal cross which had been erected at the location of his death. Each head was left with a threatening message. |
| 18-Aug-06 | Milenio Cartel member beheaded | La Familia | Uruapan, Michoacan | Notes left. |
| 4-Sep-06 | Cheese-maker beheaded | Los Zetas | Apatzingan, Michoacan | The man was a relative of *The Grandfather* and was beheaded for revenge; four more beheadings followed. A note left with the cheese-maker warned: 'One by one you go falling. Greetings. La Familia sends its regards.' |
| 21-Sep-06 | Five severed heads dumped onto a nightclub dance floor | La Familia | Uruapan, Michoacan | Armed men with faces covered came into a dance hall and shot into the air. They dumped five heads from a sack they were carrying and left a message written on cardboard: 'The Family doesn't kill for money. It doesn't kill women. It doesn't kill innocent people, only those who deserve to die. Know that this is divine justice.' |
| 16-Mar-07 | Human head found outside state security office | Unknown | Villahermosa, Tabasco | Tabasco at the time was a relatively new target of traffickers. |
| 30-Mar-07 | Video showing the beheading of a cartel hit man | Gente Nueva | YouTube video | *Do something for your country, kill a Zeta!* Read a written message opening the 5-minute video. A man in his underwear was shown tied to a chair, with a Z written on his chest in marker and the message *Welcome, kill women and children...* The video showed the man being interrogated, punched several times, then beheaded with a cord tied to metal rods and twisted.[ii] The footage ends with 'Lazcano, you are next.' |

(*continues*)

| Date | Event | Location | Perpetrator | Notes |
|---|---|---|---|---|
| 3-May-07 | Mutilated, beheaded body found outside of a military base | Tijuana, at the US border | Unknown | |
| 26-May-07 | The severed head of a town councilman was dumped outside offices of a newspaper | Villahermosa, Tabasco | Unknown | The newspaper's publishers said that this was an attempt to intimidate reporters. Reportedly, the head was wrapped in newspaper inside a cooler and left by a man who stepped out of a sports utility vehicle. |
| 12-May-07 | A severed head was deposited at an army base | Veracruz | Gulf cartel, Zeta-10's, or *Gente Nueva* | The incident occurred a day after President Calderon's government announced it would send troops to the Gulf Coast state. A note signed by *Z-40* was left with the head: 'We'll keep on going when the federal forces get here.' |
| 17-Sep-07 | Head found on a road | Puenta Campuza bus stop | Unknown | The victim was likely a member of Preventative Police. |
| 24-Sep-07 | Beheaded and decomposed body of kidnapped police officer found | San Isidro, Lerdo, Durango | Unknown | Following the kidnapping, two other police officers failed to report to work. |
| 8-Oct-07 | Remains of three beheaded men found | Outside of Acapulco | Unknown | The bodies had been set ablaze and left near a highway. |
| 15-Dec-07 | Four beheaded bodies and one mutilated bodyfound | Mexico City (2) and Tlanhepantla (2) | Sinaloa | The beheadings were likely carried out to avenge a half-ton cocaine seizure at the airport. One head had an index finger stuffed in its mouth, another had a finger in its ear. |
| 7-Jan-08 | One head found | San Simon de la Laguna, Donato Guerra | Unknown | The victim's headless body was found earlier in a shallow grave. The head was found approximately one kilometer away on Highway 18. |
| 23-May-08 | Four heads in ice chests dumped on a highway | Durango city | Unknown drug-trafficking hit men | |
| 23-May-08 | Five bodes (two beheaded) found in an empty lot | Ciudad Juarez | Unknown rival to Sinaloa cartel | A co-located message read: 'This is what happens to stupid traitors who make the mistake of siding with El Chapo Guzman.' |

*(continues)*

Table 1 – *continued*

| Date | Beheading | Organization | Location | Remarks |
|---|---|---|---|---|
| 7-Jun-08 | Male head found | Unknown | Villahermosa, Tabasco | The head was left in front of the El Correo de Tabasco newspaper offices, while the headless body was found in an area ranch. Both sets of remains had messages that threatened informants. |
| 3-Jul-08 | Four beheaded bodies found on a street | Unknown rival to Sinaloa cartel | Culiacan, Sinaloa | |
| 4-Jul-08 | Three beheaded bodies found with a dead snake | Possibly Sinaloa | Culiacan, Sinaloa | The event was possibly related to the Beltran Leyva/Sinaloa rivalry. |
| 31-Jul-08 | Beheaded body found | Unknown rival to Sinaloa cartel | Chihuahua, Chihuahua | The body was accompanied by a message directed at El Chapo Guzman. |
| 3-Aug-08 | Two beheaded bodies found | Unknown | Vicente Guerrero, Durango | |
| 28-Aug-08 | 11 headless bodies with signs of torture found | Gulf Cartel and/or Los Zetas | Merida (a colonial city in Yucatan) | The bodies had been handcuffed, beaten, marked with star signs and the letter Z. The bodies also had tattoos, mainly of the *Death Saint*. Previously Yucatan had experienced only scattered violence, not violent rival cartel fighting. The following day, police arrested three suspects with a bloody hatchet. According to the press, police suspected that the heads were burned in a ritual; several scorched spots were discovered in a nearby clearing, and an altar to Santa Muerte was found in the home of two of the suspects. |
| 28-Aug-08 | Beheaded body found | Unknown | Small town east of Merida | The body showed signs of torture. During a seven day period ending 29 August 2008, more than 130 people died violently throughout Mexico and headless bodies turned up in four states. |

*(continues)*

| Date | Event | Perpetrator | Location | Details |
|---|---|---|---|---|
| 30-Aug-08 | Four beheaded bodies found | Rival, possible faction of Arellano Felix | Tijuana | The event was seemingly linked to control of the drug corridor into San Diego. One of the bodies had its head placed on the upper back. The other three were found with the heads placed at the feet, at an illegal dump. |
| 25-Sep-08 | Beheaded bodies of three men found | Unknown | El Huahote, Sinaloa | The bodies were found on a road with hands bound; the heads were found in sacks nearby. |
| 30-Sep-08 | Headless body found | Unknown | Ciudad Juarez | The head was found nearby in a black bag. |
| 4-Oct-08 | Two beheaded bodies found on a road | Unknown | Tijuana | The heads were found in black plastic bags nearby. |
| 17-Oct-08 | Four beheaded soldiers found | Unknown | Nuevo Leon | |
| 19-Oct-08 | Three beheaded soldiers found | Unknown | Monterrey, Nuevo Leon | |
| 1-Nov-08 | A man and woman found beheaded on a beach | Unknown | Tijuana | The heads were found in plastic bags; a message believed to be from a cartel was found besides them. |
| 5-Nov-08 | Two beheaded males discovered | Rival to Arellano Felix | Tijuana | The discovery was near the Otay Mesa border crossing with the US. The bodies were inside large plastic barrels, their heads placed on the lids. A handwritten message was left, signed *la mana*. |
| 7-Nov-08 | Beheaded, handcuffed man found hanging from an overpass | Unknown | Ciudad Juarez | The victim's head was found in a bag in a nearby plaza. |
| 15-Nov-08 | Man's head found wrapped in duct tape | Unknown | Tijuana | |
| 23-Nov-08 | Three bodies (two beheaded) found | Unknown | Tijuana | The bodies were dumped on baseball fields. |
| 30-Nov-08 | Nine adults beheaded | Unknown | Tijuana | The beheadings included two police officers whose badges were stuffed into their mouths. |
| 2-Dec-08 | Man found beheaded | Unknown cartel or enforcers | Iguala, south of Mexico City | The man had been in jail for killing three police officers, when armed men possibly impersonating agents from Mexico's Federal Investigative Agency broke into the jail and took him. A message left by his head was signed *The People's Avenger*. |

*(continues)*

Table 1 – *continued*

| Date | Beheading | Organization | Location | Remarks |
|---|---|---|---|---|
| 7-Dec-08 | Two headless corpses found | Unknown | Chilpancingo, Guerrero | A note read: 'Soldiers who are supposedly fighting crime, and they turn out to be kidnappers. This is going to happen to you.' |
| 9-Dec-08 | Mexican soldier decapitated | Possibly Beltran Leyva | Chilpancingo, Guerrero | Sergeant Carlos Alberto Navarrete Moreno's head was deposited in a bucket on the monument to the Flags, with the message: 'According to the soldiers, they are combating organized crime. They are kidnappers. This is going to happen to them because they're whores.' |
| 21-Dec-08 | Seven Mexican soldiers and one lawyer beheaded. | Possibly Beltran Leyva | Chilpancingo, Guerrero | The soldiers were between 21 and 38 years of age, assigned to the 35th Military Zone based in Chilpancingo. They were off-duty, and were intercepted at night in different areas of the city by one or more armed commandos – some intercepts occurred in front of several witnesses. Residents found the heads on a busy city street before dawn; hours later the bodies were found several kilometers away, according to police. Some showed signs of torture. Forensics showed that they had been beheaded while still alive, and that a giggy saw had been the beheading weapon. |
| 21-Dec-08 | Three beheaded bodies found | Unknown | Village outside of Chilpancingo, Guerrero | |
| ~Nov 08 | Head discovered in an ice chest | Gulf Cartel | Port city of Lazaro Cardenas, Guerrero | Retaliation against La Familia |

(*continues*)

| Date | Event | Attribution | Location | Details |
| --- | --- | --- | --- | --- |
| 17-Jan-09 | The head of a 62-yr old police chief found in an ice chest outside the police station | Sinaloa Cartel | Praxedis G. Guerrero, Chihuahua | Commander Martin Castro had been on the job only five days; he was abducted along with five other police officers. Following his beheading, mass police resignations occurred in two towns. |
| 17-Jan-09 | Three heads found in an ice box | Unknown | Ciudad Juarez | Additionally, a headless body was found in a dirty canal a few miles away, which may have belonged to one of six kidnapped policemen. |
| 9-Feb-09 | Beheaded man found | Unknown | Manzanillo, Colima | The body was identified as that of a known drug dealer. |
| 10-Feb-09 | Two heads in coolers found inside a car | Unknown | Tepotzotlan (outside Mexico City) | The heads were accompanied by a message threatening the municipal police chief. |
| 26-Feb-09 | Headless body found | Unknown | Manzanillo, Guerrero | Police found the body while on patrol in a neighborhood. A narco message had been placed next to the body. |
| 7-Mar-09 | Three beheaded men found by joggers | Unknown organized crime hit | Tijuana | One of the men was a US citizen and former Chula Vista, CA resident recently released from prison. The three bodies were missing their hands, and one its feet. A taunting narco message was co-located. |
| 10-Mar-09 | Five severed heads found | Unknown | Ixtlahuacan del Rio, Guadalajara, Jalisco | The heads – of males between the ages of 30 and 50, were found in five ice coolers left by the roadside. Each had their eyes taped shut. The tops of the ice chests were inscribed with messages, such as: 'Like these, I am going to finish everyone, and I'm going after you, Goyo.' Found by police. |
| 7-May-09 | One of two male bodies found was beheaded | Unknown | Tijuana | |
| 5-Jun-09 | Woman's beheaded body found | Unknown | Acapulco | The body was naked; police said that they were unable to identify her or establish a motive. |

*(continues)*

Table 1 – *continued*

| Date | Beheading | Organization | Location | Remarks |
|------|-----------|--------------|----------|---------|
| 5-Jun-09 | Two male heads found | Unknown | Tijuana | A message from one cartel to another gang was found, but officials would not comment on the contents. |
| 30-Jun-09 | Severed head found | Unknown | Apatzingan, Michoacan | |
| 1-Jul-09 | Police found beheaded body and severed head miles apart | Unknown | Veracruz state | |
| 1 Jul 09 | Residents found a man's beheaded body | Unknown | Boca del Rio, Veracruz | The body had its hands and feet bound and showed signs of torture. Police refused to make public a note from the killers attached to the body. Authorities found a head in a nearby city. |
| 4-Jul-09 | Severed head tossed into the street | Possibly Zetas or Mata Zetas | Boca del Rio, Veracruz | Mid-term elections were the next day. |
| 5-Jul-09 | Two human heads found | La Familia | Tetepantla | La Familia left a message claiming the two beheadings. |
| 7-Jul-09 | Five people beheaded | Hitmen wearing AFI uniforms | Coahuayutla, Guererro | The hitmen ambushed two pickups, murdering eleven people, five of which were beheaded. |
| 20-Jul-09 | Man shot and beheaded | Unknown | Cacahoatan, Chiapas | Residents in the area stated that the man had been involved in robbing houses in the area and was most likely a member of a criminal gang. Given this, police believe that the incident could have been related to a settling of scores. |

[i] From un-posted database: *Beheadings by Cartels, Gangs and Enforcers in Mexico*, derived from open sources.
[ii] The tool used was possibly a garrote, which is more of a strangulation device than a beheading tool; but it was twisted until the head fell off.

the occurrence of beheadings. Wealthy Mexican cartels and their violence-loving enforcers make a perfect marriage.

It is thought that most beheadings in Mexico are performed after the victim is already dead. But more recent cases show otherwise: in one of the largest modern-day mass beheadings, which took place in Yucatán, investigators determined that five of the twelve victims were alive when beheaded. Torture was also evident at this event. Police suspected the heads were burned in a ritual, one

Table 2.    Beheadings in the US connected to Mexican crime or Mara gangs[i]

| Date | Beheading | Organization | Location | Remarks |
|---|---|---|---|---|
| Fall-2001 | Male nearly beheaded [ii] | MS-13 | Alexandria, VA | A high-ranking clique leader, along with other MS-13 members, lured, stabbed and attempted to behead a suspected rival gang member using a dull steak knife. |
| 20-May-05 | Female hacked to death | MS-13 | Alexandria, VA | MS-13 members killed a pregnant teen who had returned to the gang after becoming a federal informant. She was discovered on the Shenandoah river; she had been stabbed 13 times and her head had been nearly cut off. |
| 24-Sep-07 | Headless male body found in a Louisiana river | Possible Mexican gang members | Atchafalaya River, St Marin, Louisiana | The victim had been shot and beheaded before being dumped in the river. All four suspects and the victim were Mexican nationals. Two of the suspects had tattoos said to be connected with Mexican gangs; however, the gang and/or cartel significance is unknown. |
| 30-Jun-08 | Young girl raped and beheaded | Mexican traffickers | Florida panhandle | A little girl, after resisting rape, was brought to Florida from Mexico and made an example of by being beheaded in front of other girls, who were being held to be raped repeatedly. Her body was left in a room with them for several hours. |

[i]From un-posted database: *Beheadings in the US with Possible Gang/Cartel Connections*, derived from open sources.
[ii]See Samuel Logan. *This is for the Mara Salvatrucha*. Hyperion Books, 2009, 51–56.

possibly associated with the death saint, Santa Muerte, which would mark an unusual deviation from both typical beheadings as well as death-saint worship.

Weapons used in beheadings are not often discussed, but beheadings carried out on behalf of the Mexican cartels are typically done with machetes and knives. In the Yucatán mass beheadings, suspects were captured with a bloody hatchet. In Otay Mesa, an expected beheading booby trap was discovered where US border agents patrol. A wire was found stretched across a road that the agents took in their all-terrain vehicles; the height of the wire was about neck level. Los Kaibiles cartel enforcers who are trained in hand-to-hand combat with large bowie knives are rumored to be behind a number of beheadings in Western Mexico some of which were identified as having been done by bowie knives. Another reported Kaibil specialty is decapitation by razor-sharp bayonet.[22]

Occurrences of cartel-related beheadings have spread northward across Mexico. They have also occurred in the US (Table 2). Four beheadings each linked to Mexican crime or mara gang activity took place in Virginia, Louisiana, and the Florida panhandle. Several factors make the potential spread, or occurrence, of cartel-related beheadings in the US seem less predictable than in Mexico. None of the US states where beheadings occurred border Mexico, and two of the beheadings pre-date all of those in the recent spate of beheadings in Mexico and were related to MS-13 gang business, not cartels. These early issues suggest that beheadings in the US may not take such an expected course as they did across Mexico. While the locations of future beheading in the US may be random, the victims are likely to be US citizens or Mexican nationals whose profession or function mirror those across the border. That is, as in Mexico, US beheading victims are likely to be those who get in the way of the cartels furthering their own interests; victims may be anyone from cartel affiliates to journalists. In December 2008, US citizen Felix Batista, an anti-kidnapping expert and US security consultant, was kidnapped (and possibly murdered) by Los Zetas in Saltillo, Coahuila, Mexico. It was thought Batista's captors may have mistakenly believed him to be a law enforcement officer because it was reported that they intended to ship his decapitated head back to the US as a 'message' to US law enforcement.[23] No evidence exists that Batista's head was shipped anywhere, nor was he ever found, but Batista's disappearance may be a precursor to more brazen, violent acts by cartels against US citizens and on US soil.

**Narcocultos**

The generally accepted definition of a 'cult' includes reference to a group of individuals whose beliefs and/or practices are unorthodox or extreme in nature, often led by a charismatic leader. Since the late 1980s, a number of cult-like belief systems have become closely associated with specific Mexican drug cartels and, in turn, with their criminal activities. The occurrences of torture and beheadings tied to these cartels, both in Mexico and more recently across the border into the United States, beg the question of the context in which they are being conducted. Most cases of torture or beheading are regarded as primarily secular in nature – a terrorist tactic tied to economic or political gain. In an even more macabre twist, however, certain instances have been seen as intertwined with a group's belief system, performed in ritual fashion to fulfill religious or spiritual demands. A continuum of these 'cult–cartel' relationships will be examined briefly and their potential links to cartel violence discussed.

Mexico has no official national religion but remains predominantly Catholic – approximately 88% according to the country's 2000 census figures[24] – despite inroads by evangelical Christian and other religious traditions. The Catholicism practiced in Mexico varies widely, from the strict theology of the conservative Catholic hierarchy to folk religious practices that incorporate traditional beliefs into the structure of the Catholic faith.[25] The latter, as perceived by the normal believer, is said to be:

> … a system in which the divine names and figures still have the power to alter fate, where life's ills can be resolved by a set of prayers, and cosmic symbolism can use lower things to move the things above them.[26]

Pleading to saints for their intercession with God on one's behalf is thus a common practice. Within the Catholic tradition, there are a number of sanctioned saints to whom one might pray in desperate situations. Saint Jude Thaddeus, aka San Judas Tadeo, is one of these 'saints-of-last-resort' and might be petitioned, for example, by those struggling with drug or alcohol addiction. While shrines to this saint have been found associated with marijuana growers,[27] pleas for protection for one's criminal venture, while likely not condoned by the Church, nonetheless still take place within otherwise mainstream Catholic religious practice. It is only a step further, however, for the disenfranchised to create their own unsanctioned 'saints' to address needs found lacking a proponent within mainstream traditions. While by no means their only worshippers, and indeed

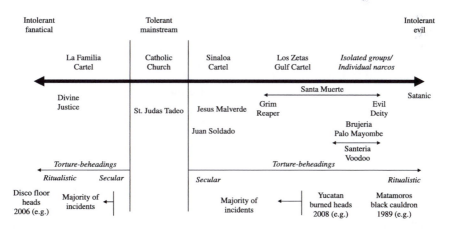

Figure 1.    Narcos and narcocultos in Mexico.

Figure 2.   Photo of the back of Gabriel Cardona with the image of 'Santa Muerte' tattooed on it. Cardona was a member of a 3 person sleeper hit man cell composed of US teenagers which operated in 2005–2006 and was based in Laredo, TX. The cell received 6-months of military-like training and was on retainer and contracted to the Zetas. Cardona is now serving a long prison sentence.
Source:    Laredo Police Department Photo.

likely constituting a minority of the total, it is precisely these unorthodox saints to whom narcotraffickers are drawn. As a noted scholar of the cultural life of Mexico puts it:.

> ... They learn to kill, and in the emptiness and absence of meaning that follows a murder, they look desperately for redemption and for grounding. They find it in consumer goods – narco jeans, narcotennis shoes, narcocars – and in the new religions, the narcocultos.[28]

It has been pointed out that the word 'culto', while a cognate to 'cult', does not in the Spanish translation carry the negative connotations of being a 'strictly controlled group' but rather to the 'rituals and practices associated with religious worship' and may, in fact, have no formalized membership at all.[29] The continuum presented here takes mainstream folk Catholicism as practiced in Mexico as its 'norm' and relates where those belief systems that have been identified as 'narcocultos' fall in relation to its doctrines (Figure 1).

From an anthropological perspective, these narcocultos are representative to some extent of a deeper and underlying tradition of embracing death which permeates Mexican society. This tradition has its origins not only with the indigenous pre-Columbian peoples of Mexico but also with the later Spaniards who conquered these lands of the New World. The manifestation of this tradition in the local Indian tribal groupings took place with the ritual human sacrifices conducted by the Aztecs. These sacrifices were meant to ensure good harvests by appeasing the Aztec deities with the cutting out of victims' hearts atop stone pyramids in elaborate ceremonies. In turn, the Spanish contribution to this Mexican tradition, initially derived from the conquistadors and the Inquisition, was to have brought plunder, conquest, and Christianity to the local natives at the point of a sword. Torture, death, and widespread depopulation were all byproducts of the empires initially carved out by the Spanish conquistadors of the sixteenth century. The subsequent melding of Indian and Spanish bloodlines, the overlay of Catholicism upon indigenous religious beliefs, and the passage of centuries of time in Mexico has resulted in a far more benign perspective on and relationship to death – one that is culturally unique:

> ... an intimacy with death abhorred by Anglo-Saxon cultures is ingrained in the Mexican psyche, according to Octavio Paz, the Nobel-prize winning Mexican writer. 'The word death is not pronounced in New York, in Paris, in London, because it burns the lips' declared Paz in his prescient essay on Mexico, *The Labyrinth of Solitude*. He explained: 'The Mexican by contrast is familiar with death, jokes about it, caresses it, sleeps with it, celebrates it; it is one of his favorite toys and his most steadfast love.'[30]

This cultural context explains how a martyred bandit and a death saint can come to be widely accepted objects of worship by those seeking ends not so unlike those one might pray for in the Catholic Church. The drug cartels, however, have co-opted this cultural perspective and twisted it in a way that allows unspeakable things to be undertaken with a sense of 'noble' intent. In Figure 1, it is understood that certainly not all who worship Jesus Malverde and/or Santa Muerte fall into the latter category. It is, however, the narcoculto forms of these traditions that are the subject of concern in this work.

### *Jesus Malverde*

Probably the earliest variant of mainstream religious tradition in Mexico to be recognized as associated with narcotraffickers by law enforcement officials in Mexico and the United States is the infamous 'patron saint of drug traffickers', Jesus Malverde, also referred to as 'the Angel of the Poor', 'the Generous Bandit', and most commonly, 'The Mexican Robin Hood'. Malverde, along with Juan Soldado 'the patron saint of illegal immigrants' and a number of others, belongs to the category of 'unofficial folk saints not recognized by the Roman Catholic Church' but whose status as 'underdogs with checkered pasts who battled the system or were failed by it' has given them popular acclaim.[31] In the case of Jesus Malverde, there is no clear evidence that he, in fact, ever existed and the likeness upon which his icons are based is often described as resembling the 1940s' Mexican matinee idol, Pedro Infante. Still, as legend has it, it was around the turn of the twentieth century when Malverde (Spanish for 'Bad-green'):

> ... rode through the hills near the city of Culiacán in Sinaloa wearing green clothing to blend into his environment, committing banditry, and distributing the

proceeds of his crimes to the area's impoverished inhabitants... [continuing]...
until 1909 when Mexican law enforcement officials captured and executed him.[32]

That he was a native son of Sinaloa probably explains why he has a strong
following among members of the Sinaloa Cartel (and those with which they have
strong ties) and among illegal immigrants to the US from that region. It is in
Culiacán, across the street from the government building that supposedly sits on
his grave, that the first large shrine to Jesus Malverde was built in the 1970s, and
it was during that period that the first reports of his image on drug loads were
noted. Links with infamous narcotraffickers include such Sinaloa-born figures
as Rafael Caro Quintero (Sonora Cartel) and Amado Carrillo Fuentes
(Juárez Cartel). It is more recently claimed that the street is shut down when
the head of the Sinaloa Cartel, Joaquin 'El Chapo' Guzman, or his associates
come to pray there, in order to allow them peace.[33] Others argue that this is
overplayed and that those narcos who do visit the shrine are only 'low-level
functionaries primarily involved in smuggling small quantities of contraband'.[34]
While a number of small shrines exist in people's homes and all along the drug
routes, particularly in border areas, it wasn't until 2006 that the first large public
shrine to Malverde was built – in Mexico City. These shrines, notably, often also
include statues or pictures of Jesus Christ or of officially recognized Catholic
saints. It is said to be common for Malverde believers to ask his help by saying
'ay 'danos, Chuy' (a nickname for the name Jesus) when crossing the border with
a drug load.[35] Drug traffickers pray to the saint for protection:

> ... before, during, and after their drug trafficking activities. To reinforce their
> beliefs, the traffickers often carried various items depicting Malverde's image
> hoping this paraphernalia would protect them further.[36]

To that end, there is a plethora of Malverde merchandise ranging from the
usual prayer candles, cards, statues, amulets, and scapulars to colognes and
aerosols and even Malverde beer, bottled in Jalisco. The wearing of Malverde
icons, or having his image on one's vehicle or drug loads, is akin to having a
lucky rabbit's foot – and is claimed by some to make drug loads invisible. These
images are so associated with drug trafficking in the United States that the
presence of such paraphernalia is a red flag to law enforcement officers.
In Bakersfield, California, for example, some 80% of Mexican nationals involved
in the drug trade in 2006 were said to possess a likeness of Malverde.[37] In a
landmark ruling, a Malverde icon has been upheld by an appellate court as a legal
basis for developing probable cause.[38]

Malverdian worship is relatively unstructured and based on individual
petitions along with the customary offering or pledging of good deeds in order
to receive the saint's blessing. Creehan describes how, at the Culiacán shrine,
the extent of structured worship is the tradition of taking a pebble (ostensibly
from his original gravesite) and returning it when the request is granted
although there is a 'true prayer' sheet available, there or online. He further
notes that it is also typical to make these 'intercessions' to Malverde in tandem

with ones to another saint recognized by the Catholic Church.[39] Although Sinaloa is home to perhaps the highest number of drug trafficking related deaths each year, there is no evidence of torture or human sacrifice having been made in the name of Jesus Malverde, either in terms of public acknowledgment of those ends or by virtue of directly occurring at the site of a Malverde altar as has been the case with other groups, but rather these events appear solely secular in nature.

### *Santa Muerte*

The group found next along the continuum in Figure 1 includes those embracing La Santa Muerte or Saint Death. If Malverde is said by Guillermoprieto to be 'deeply Mexican . . . from his legend . . . to his effigy', the skeletal appearance of Santa Muerte is seen as largely unrelated to the recognizable skeleton figures common to the Mexican Day of the Dead and rather as stemming from something decidedly more Old World.[40] Freese explains that, '[t]he Santa Muerte cult could be best described as a set of ritual practices offered on behalf of a supernatural personification of death . . . she is comparable in theology to supernatural beings or archangels.'[41] Without denying the syncretism that takes place in religions over time, Holman – who has studied the worship of Santa Muerte at length – has determined that her roots come primarily from the Angel of Death found in early European Judaism and Christianity, possibly dating back to the era of Bronze Age Greece, and that any ties to early Aztec roots are 'both distant and subliminal at best'. On the other hand, while her worship in Mexico has a long history, in its most recent incarnation as a product of its popularization beginning in the late 1980s and early 1990s stemming from links to narcotraffickers, he finds that she has been removed from her place as a fixture of Catholic based thinking with the role of 'Grim Reaper' who 'takes one to the place where the Souls of the Dead must go' and instead has been recast as a new age Goddess figure – the Bad-girl counterpart to the Virgin of Guadalupe.[42] Thus believers in La Santa Muerte fall along a sub-continuum between those who look to her for extra help and protection, yet consider themselves to still be good Catholics, all the way to those who consider her to be a deity unto herself. It is the latter group that should be cause for concern.

As with followers of Malverde and the 'saints of last resort', those who petition Santa Muerte are individuals who find themselves in extreme circumstances. Statues of the death saint portray her as a robed skeleton who carries a scythe and an hourglass or a set of scales, signifying justice for those who cannot expect their version of it any other way. It is noted that:

> . . . the biggest draw to the cult of Santa Muerte . . . [is that] . . . one can pray for vengeance . . . more than half of the prayers are directed at requesting something bad for another person . . .[43]

Additionally:

> At a time when death by beheading is not uncommon, narcos turn to Santa Muerte to implore protection and 'a good death'.[44]

While the worship of Santa Muerte is not formalized in the American sense of a 'cult', it nonetheless has far more ritualized aspects than the intercessions and offerings made to Jesus Malverde. Devotees of Santa Muerte must follow very detailed rituals, including specific prayers and color-coded candles, in order to receive the desired outcome. Associated offerings and gifts thanking the saint must also be appropriate as it is said that she is very jealous and will curse those who do not pay the right tribute. It is no wonder then that a number of incidences of torture and beheadings have been linked to Santa Muerte worship. Documented examples can be cited:

- On May 13, 2005, a car chase between unknown assailants from a rival drug trafficking group and members of the gang, Los Sapos, in the Tepitos neighborhood of Mexico City ended in a shootout at the Santa Muerte chapel, resulting in the brain death of one of its members. The victims were thought to have been seeking her protection.[45]
- In Tijuana, Mexico, 2006, four drug smugglers turned on one of their partners who they believed to have stolen money from them. 'This subject gets a saw and cuts off his leg, cuts off another leg, cuts off his arm. He's dead and then this girl gets the cutting saw and cuts off his head and offers it to Santa Muerte.'[46]
- Murdered victims of the notorious Mexican Gulf Cartel were left at a public shrine to Santa Muerte in Monterrey, Mexico on 11 May 2007.[47]
- In 2007, gunmen from the powerful Gulf Cartel handcuffed three men and shot them dead at a Santa Muerte altar in Nuevo Loredo, leaving lit candles, flowers, and a taunting message for rivals.[48]
- In southeastern Yucatán Peninsula, 12 headless bodies of local drug dealers were dumped into two ranches in August 2008. Five were decapitated while alive but the rest had been dismembered after first having been strangled or beaten to death. The suspects were alleged to have been members of the Zetas. Police also claim the killings may have had a ritual dimension after searching the suspects' houses and finding altars to the death saint.[49] It is believed that the presence of burned spots in a nearby clearing indicate that the heads were ritually offered to Santa Muerte.
- In Juárez, in 2008, decapitated and stacked bodies were found five separate times with the ritualized nature casting suspicions it might be related to Santa Muerte worship.[50]

These findings are of particular concern when it is recognized that the popularity of Santa Muerte worship continues to grow both in Mexico and across the US border. According to the official 'high priest' of the cult, Monsignor David Romo

Guillén, believers in Mexico number 5 million (up from a figure of 1 million in 2005) and are said to include a wide range of individuals from police and politicians to kidnappers and gangsters who ask for protection before setting out on hits.[51] Mexico City, especially the rough Tepito neighborhood, has the largest reported concentration of shrines and altars to the death saint. One of the main breeding grounds for her worship among narcotraffickers is located in the Reclusorio Norte prison in Mexico City where guards are increasingly alarmed by the proliferation of Santa Muerte altars in inmate cells.[52] Approximately 40% of those in Mexico's jails are devotees, with inmates exhibiting tattoos, amulets, and charms with the saint's likeness.[53]

Narcoshrines to the death saint understandably follow the drug routes across the border into the United States. US law enforcement officials have found a proliferation of these shrines in Arizona, Florida, Tennessee, and Texas. Such shrines have been associated with criminal activity including human and drug trafficking:

- In 2006 in Laredo, Texas, sheriff's deputies report finding a Santa Muerte altar in a stash house upon which pictures of a Mexican military unit lay in a bowl of blood, sprinkled with herbs and roots.[54]
- Seven murders over a one-year period in Laredo, Texas in 2005 led to the arrest of two US teens – homegrown assassins recruited into Los Zetas to carry out hits for the Mexican Gulf Cartel. Both sported tattoos of 'Santa Muerte'.[55]
- Small altars are becoming a common scene at stash houses in South Texas. 'People begin with incense, candles, to indescribable things, like obtaining items from a cemetery, human remains to accomplish what you want,' a 2008 source said.[56]
- In March 2009, La Joya officers found 10 illegal immigrants packed into an SUV covered with decals of Santa Muerte... An anthropologist at UT-Brownsville says worship of the saint came to the valley around about a decade ago and 'In the last five years, it's spread like wildfire.'[57]
- In Charlotte, NC, a man was sentenced in April 2009 to 24 years in prison for sex trafficking. One of his victims reported being taken to a Santa Muerte shrine and threatened with her wrath if the woman tried to escape or report him.[58]
- At Webb County Jail, South Texas, 2009, inmates arrested on drug trafficking charges pray for help to Santa Muerte at an altar that the Director let them set up.[59]

In Mexico, the logical next step in the drug war has been a concerted effort to crack down on public 'narcoshrines' along with the narcocorridos glorifying drug traffickers. In March 2009, the Mexican army oversaw the destruction of over 30 such shrines near Nuevo Loredo and nearly a dozen more near Tijuana and Rosarito Beach. It appears that this act has 'begun to galvanize devotion to Santa Muerte into a formal religious institution' under the de facto leader of the movement, Romo Guillén, who led protests in Mexico City. What concerns Mexican government and Catholic Church officials is that Romo Guillén has called for a 'Holy War' against them, leading some to call him a terrorist, comparable to the Taliban and Al Qaeda.[60] Probably a question of bigger concern for the purposes of this work is to what extent the violence currently associated with the worship of Santa Muerte by narcos is undertaken with the intent of offering up human sacrifice to gain favor for that individual or his group versus whether the offering was made as a target of opportunity after a killing that would have taken place in similar fashion anyway.

### *Occult/satanic religions*

At the extreme right of the continuum presented earlier is listed the category of true 'occult' groups and those espousing 'Satanism'. In 1989, American college student Mark Kilroy was brutally murdered and dismembered, along with 14 other people, by a narcotrafficking group in Matamoros, Mexico. The members of the group espoused a combination of occult beliefs but primarily an extreme form of Palo Mayombe, which required human sacrifice to ensure the protection of its practitioners, and Kilroy's brain was found in their ritual black cauldron or nganga. It has since been observed that photos of the crime scene reveal a statue of Santa Muerte among the collection of the group's ritualistic tools.[61] At their extreme, then, some worshippers of Santa Muerte may fall into this category. Statues of the saint are primarily clothed in one of three colors that correspond to intent: white (neutral), red (love/binding rituals), and black (harm to others/death). Brujos and brujas (practitioners of witchcraft) make a pact with the black-robed Santa Muerte in order to use the black magic associated with the latter to cast spells which cause harm.[62] Freese says that one reason her worshippers find her so welcoming is because 'she does not distinguish between good and evil practitioners.' He writes that, in 2005, a Milenio journalist interviewed an inmate of the Tapachula (Chiapas) State Prison and leader of the Mara Salvatrucha or MS-13 gang about the group's connections to Santa Muerte and/or Satanism. Though denying such a connection, tattoos on his back revealed references to MS-13, the words 'Satanic Member', and a skeletal hand of death. Statements made by the prisoner implied that other gang members shared these beliefs.[63] This incident is the only documented evidence of a blending of actual Satanism and Santa Muerte worship among a drug trafficking group.

In the Matamoros case, members referred to the religion of the group as 'voodoo'. Whether termed Palo Mayombe, Santeria, or Voodoo, modern religious scholars deny that any of these require human sacrifice and say media characterizations are unjust. Some individuals working in US law enforcement, however, argue that in their experience Mexican immigrant criminals in general have been found to practice any number of variant forms of the Afro-Cuban religions and that these have been linked to drug-related homicides. It was quite common in South Dallas when investigating these groups to find:

> ... little altars where they would have little army men, except they were policemen you could buy at the five-and-dime store. And you would find them in there burning. You'd find little police cars burning ... It was all kind of mumbo-jumbo.[64]

Reports suggest that the Zetas are linked to Satanic rituals and may also be involved in acts of 'narco-Satanism' where, after burning a victim, they engage in a ritual called 'smoking death'[65] in which:

> ... they place a victim's ashes in a pipe and mix it with cocaine ... [and] say aloud to the corpse: 'You are still here, you have not gone away; you are part of us and will always watch over us.'

Much of what is practiced by drug-trafficking groups in the name of punishment or revenge, whether the torture of rivals, the beheading of police officers, or leaving burning plastic police cars or bloody pictures of the Mexican Army on a sacrificial altar, begs the definition of 'evil'. An article in the *FBI Law Enforcement Bulletin* on spirituality and law enforcement employs this definition from T.L. Depue:

> In many contexts, evil can be defined as a destructive, poisonous form of spirituality with outward expressions that degrade, dispirit, disintegrate, dehumanize, and destroy human beings, as well as the set of ideas, dignity, freedoms, networks, property, capital, and activities engulfing the constructive social institutions that people depend on for survival.

The article cautions that, while law enforcement personnel are sworn to protect citizens from this evil, the constant contact with evil is corrosive and cumulative and, ultimately, can prove deadly.[66]

### La Familia

In returning to the continuum in Figure 1, one narcotrafficking group, La Familia Michoacana, is found to lie further to the left on the spectrum from mainstream to pure occult/Satanic due to its position as espousing an overtly conservative form of Christian evangelical belief system. Reynolds has succinctly described La Familia as:

> ... a faith-based right-wing populist socialist movement emanating from and orchestrated by an organization that just happens to be a well-armed, well-financed violent criminal enterprise.[67]

The group emerged into the spotlight only a few years ago when, in September 2006, it left five heads and its cardboard calling card with the message that the act was 'divine justice'. The men were apparently alive when their heads were hacked off with bowie knives.[68] This group perhaps stands out as the closest in form to a true 'cult' in that it not only espouses fringe beliefs, strictly enforced, but it additionally lies under the control of a charismatic, or strongly authoritarian, leader. The moral leadership of the group centers around Nazario Moreno

Gonzales, aka 'El Mas Loco' or 'The Craziest One'. Moreno Gonzales reportedly requires recruits to read his own religious work – based on the Bible and writings by Christian author and former Focus on the Family senior fellow John Eldredge – and to attend prayer meetings. La Familia's moral code of conduct also includes a ban on alcohol or drug use and the group often recruits members from local rehab clinics. Notably, news reports in September 2009 highlighted two massacres occurring at rehab facilities in Ciudad Juárez that month, with the suspects being members of the Sinaloa Cartel – La Familia's biggest rival.

It is believed that La Familia was founded on providing vigilante justice to Michoacan, which happens to be Mexican President Felipe Calderón's home state, as the pressures of methamphetamine trafficking brought increased drug use and criminal activity to the region. It joined forces early on with the Gulf Cartel, and their enforcers the Zetas, but by 2006 sought dominance over operations in Michoacan and has expanded into the states of Guerrero, Queretaro, and Mexico even as it continues to battle its former allies.[69] Now considered one of Mexico's five largest drug trafficking organizations, reports indicate that beyond trading in cocaine, marijuana, and methamphetamine, the group has further diversified into kidnapping, armed robbery, and counterfeiting.[70] On 15 April 2009, the Obama administration added La Familia to its kingpin list.

The group is a study in contrasts. On the one hand, they are seen as going beyond the usual 'money-only' interests of drug cartels to seek social and political standing. The group is known to have financed dozens of local politicians; built schools; supported churches and drug rehab centers; provided gifts to the poor and to children; and, most recently, offered consumer loans.[71] These have helped to secure its position as protector of the community. On the other hand, La Familia has emerged as a group ruthless in its use of 'righteous' violence against its enemies with a cartel spokesman quoted as saying 'If the mistake is grave, they are tortured. If there is a loss of trust and treachery, they must die.'[72] A STRATFOR memo believes this disconnect between its so-called principles and the violence of its crimes is representative of the fact that it puts forth propaganda and rhetoric rather than a true ideology and may be indicative of factional splits. The memo questions whether La Familia actually differs from other groups in money motivation or whether it merely uses these tenets to make the organization more mysterious and attractive to recruits.[73] Raul Benitez, an expert on drug trafficking organizations, contends that:

> La Familia uses religion as a way of forcing cohesion among its members. They are building a new kind of disciplined army that we have never seen here before. It makes them more dangerous.[74]

This cohesion is further secured through rigorous, military-style training. US anti-drug experts say 'members of La Familia must complete a three-to-six month training camp in Michoacan run by former Mexican and Guatemalan elite soldiers.'[75] This may prove important as others have found fragmentation within the group has resulted in divisions between:

- Los Historicos – linked to Los Zetas;
- Los Extorsionistas – businessmen and growers who extort money from others;
- Los Cobradores de Duedas – debt collectors who traffic in meth and ally with the Milenio and Sinaloa cartels; and
- An offshoot group trafficking in pirated films and DVDs.[76]

The group is said to have between 4000 and 9000 members. It has not only expanded operations in Mexico outside Michoacan but seeks to dominate the distribution route to the US border. To this end, La Familia has established drug-running operations in 20 to 30 cities across the US, including Los Angeles.[77] The potential for violence by this group has not abated. The group likes to take credit for its enforcement of divine justice in notes left at the scene, and decapitations are a common method of enforcement. In July 2009, in response to the detainment of one of its top leaders, La Familia killed 12 off-duty federal police officers and piled their bodies on the side of the road. Four more officers were killed the following week in a round of violence dubbed 'the TET offensive of the drug war'.[78] In a follow-up call to a news show, Servando Gomez, a La Familia leader, maintained the moral high ground, stating 'Our fight is with the federal police because they are attacking our families... what we want is peace and tranquility.' This is in contrast to a statement from a supporter called the Messenger that 'Nobody is saved from divine justice and they cannot imagine the pain and suffering they will go through'.[79] Facundo Rosas, recently appointed as Mexico's Federal Police Commissioner, warns of:

> An 'explosive mixture' of religion and criminal activity... [wherein] religious elements are used by criminals as a way of seeking divine or supernatural protection that will intercede with God on their behalf, and thereby expiate their sins... [in this way]... criminal organizations in Mexico are following the pattern that has been used by armed groups with political or ideological goals such as those in the Middle East.[80]

George Grayson goes so far, somewhat controversially, as to imply that La Familia's leaders may have ties to the New Jerusalem movement in Mexico.[81] This long surviving traditionalist Catholic colony in the western Michoacan hills is described as the 'biggest apocalyptic colony in the world' and 'bigger than the Branch Davidian settlement at Waco, Texas or Jonestown in Guyana'.[82] While any such link is tenuous at best, it gives pause when combined with the fact that it was likely La Familia that was responsible for the public bombing on 15 September 2008 – Mexican Independence Day – that killed eight innocent people.[83]

## Trends and projections

Incidents of torture tied to the Mexican cartels and their affiliates both in Mexico and in the United States show no sign of abating in the future. Torture will continue to be used for intimidation purposes at the street level against those being extorted and taxed and who owe money to drug traffickers. It will also continue to be used against rival groups and those inside the cartels and affiliated organizations who do not follow the rules and dictates of the cartel leaders and gang shot callers. The use of torture against Mexican law enforcement, military, political, and other officials and those reporters and citizens who interfere with cartel business will also continue. Torture directed at US officials and agents is expected to remain almost non-existent north of the border for the foreseeable future. Still, US governmental representatives face the constant danger of being kidnapped and tortured while carrying on their duties inside of Mexico.

Beheadings are a recent phenomenon of the drug wars, and their future trajectory is still not fully understood. Between 2006 and 2009, the course of the occurrences of Mexican beheadings moved in a predominantly northward pattern across Mexico, stopping for the most part just short of the US border. Within Mexico, the occurrence of beheadings moved with the overlapping expansion of claimed territories by rival cartels. However, cartel activity and the spread of beheadings in Mexico do not lend a good example or make predictable the same in the US. Mexican cartel and mara gang activity is already widespread there. Violence related to both regularly occurs at and across the US–Mexican border as well as sporadically throughout the US. Evidence of Mexican crime- or mara gang-related beheadings has emerged randomly in Virginia, Florida, and Louisiana. These first beheadings, the strength of US law enforcement infrastructure, and the more clandestine nature of cartel and gang activity in the US begs the questions: how truly deep is the Mexican cartel infiltration over the border and will cartel-related beheadings become commonplace there as well?

As noted, a subset of the overall instances of torture and beheadings by cartels in Mexico has been also linked to religious or spiritual practices that have been designated 'narcocultos'. Not all of the narcocults have exhibited a need or desire for human sacrifice. In the case of followers of Jesus Malverde, for example, there is no documented evidence to date of such a link. In the case of those embracing Santa Muerte, we find troubling evidence that, while still seen as anomalous in its occurrence, there have been enough cases with a concrete link between torture and beheading and her worship as to give pause to what the future portends. Some have implied that – given the current merchandising of her likeness on everything from candles to T-shirts and bumper stickers – a belief in Santa Muerte is 'trendy' and, as seemed to happen between narcos and Malverde, her popularity will ultimately wane. Others contrarily see the current increase in the number of her worshippers, particularly as she has been taken out of the confines of Catholicism and raised to 'goddess' status, as a sign that there has been a real cultural shift in Mexico to a 'narcocultura'. If the latter is the case, and society's social structures and institutions are becoming increasing corrupted by drug cartels and the drug culture, the consequent need to believe in an accepting form of supernatural protection and to have the moral high ground by those engaging in drug-related activities would seem to go hand in hand with a real risk of increasing violence in her name. In the case of La Familia, a bigger issue may also be at stake. In this group, not only do we find a willingness time and time again to blatantly label heinous acts of torture and beheading as 'divine justice', but we see a concerted effort to indoctrinate those belonging to the cartel in this belief. This is also a group that has been implicated in an act of domestic terrorism within its own country. If this cartel, which has gained amazing ground in a very short time, should continue to expand, the implication is that the US will find itself with a narco terrorist organization with an organized fanatical religious component sitting on its very border. This is certainly of great concern.

**Notes**

1. While Mexican law enforcement, military, and vigilante groups have also engaged in torture on behalf of their government and local communities against the drug cartels such incidents are not the focus of this essay.
2. KPBS, 'Border Battle: Bringing Home the Drug War, Glossary'.
3. Roig-Franzia, 'Mexican Drug Cartels Leave a Bloody Trail on YouTube', A01.
4. Quinones, 'State of War'.
5. Grillo, 'Behind Mexico's Wave of Beheadings'.
6. US Department of Justice, Drug Enforcement Agency, 'Biographies of DEA Agents and Employees Killed in Action: Enrique S. Camarena' and Lake, 'Who killed Kiki Camarena'.
7. Lake, 'Who killed Kiki Camarena'.
8. Booth, 'Warrior in Drug Fight Soon Becomes a Victim', A01.
9. Cnn.com, 'Mexico drug fighter killed after less than a day on job'.
10. Marosi, 'Mexico Under Siege: Violence unabated in Tijuana', and Quinones, 'State of War'.
11. Gomez, 'Local ICE agent taking border experience to Washington', and Fleming, *Drug Wars: Silver or Lead.*
12. Barakat, 'Lawyer Admits Client's Guilt in MS-13 Killing of Pregnant Teen'.
13. Kleinknecht, '"Strong gang component" revealed in Newark schoolyard slayings'.
14. Webster, 'Mexican Drug cartels terror reaches deep into the US'.
15. Keteyian, 'Drug Cartels Flex Muscle in Southwest'.
16. Sources used as background for this section are Grillo, 'Behind Mexico's Wave of Beheadings', STRATFOR, 'Beheadings in Mexico: The Foreign Element in Mexico's Drug Wars', and STRATFOR, 'Kaibiles: The New Lethal Force in the Mexican Drug Wars'.
17. Manwaring, 'A Contemporary Challenge To State Sovereignty'.
18. The study was conducted by Joel K. Myhre, Principle Consultant for Nordic Geospatial Consultants based on open source data set provided by Lisa Campbell, July 2009: 2006 – Avg Latitude = 22.197844, Avg Dist in Miles to US Border = 425; 2007 – Avg. Latitude = 19.869287, Avg Dist in Miles to US Border = 491; 2008 – Avg. Latitude = 25.359474, Avg. Dist in Miles to US Border = 302; 2009 – Avg. Latitude = 25.414780, Avg. Dist in Miles to US Border = 274.
19. Manwaring, 'A Contemporary Challenge To State Sovereignty', 5.
20. It is not yet known who the *Mata Zetas* (aka *Matando Zetas*) are or who they work for. They first surfaced on YouTube with a reported beheading video. The video, which had several similarities to Islamic beheading videos in Iraq, portrayed four heavily armed men, dressed in black and with black hoods, interrogating two Los Zetas members, at least one of whom was later found to have been beheaded.

21. Campbell, 'The Use of Beheadings by Fundamentalist Islam', 263–71. There were several mass beheading incidents in Iraq in the 2004–06 timeframe, including one with up to 30 heads found in a single spot.
22. Canby, 'Getting Away With Murder'.
23. Marizco, 'The Case of Felix Batista Resurfaces'.
24. Association of Religious Data Archives web site, 'Mexico 2008, subheading: Religious Demography'.
25. Merrill and Miró, eds., 'Religion', *Mexico: A Country Study*. It is interesting to note that Mexico's modern Catholicism is practiced in some areas with a direct nod to ancient Mayan religion, including animal sacrifice as part of religious practice. See Schlein, 'Chiapas, Mexico Offers Ancient, Modern Religion Mix'.
26. Vazquez, 'Reditus: A Chronicle of Aesthetic Christianity'.
27. Burke, 'The Public Land's Biggest Crop'.
28. Guillermoprieto, 'The Narcovirus', 3–6.
29. Freese, 'The Death Cult of the Drug Lords'.
30. Davies, 'Santa Muerte: the Mexican Death Cult'.
31. Watson, 'Residents along U.S.-Mexican Border find strength in local folk saints'.
32. Botsch, 'Jesus Malverde's significance to Mexican drug traffickers'.
33. Guillermoprieto, 'The Narcovirus', 3–6.
34. Creechan and Garcia, 'Without God or Law', 12.
35. Holman, 'Jesus Malverde and Nino Fidencio'.
36. Botsch, 'Jesus Malverde's significance to Mexican drug traffickers'.
37. Butler, 'Jesus Malverde: The Narco Saint'.
38. Davis, 'Jesus Malverde Legend Continues'.
39. Creechan and Garcia, 'Without God or Law', 9–13.
40. Guillermoprieto, 'The Narcovirus', 3–6.
41. Freese, 'The Death Cult of the Drug Lords', 3. In the text we refer to Santa Muerte or the death saint but Freese has a comprehensive list of alternate or nicknames for the saint – a further sign, he says, of how attached to her that her followers are – including Santisima Muerte (Most Holy Death), Sagrada Muerte (Sacred Death), Querida Muerte (Beloved Death), Poderosa Senora (Powerful Lady), La Comadre (The Co-Mother), La Madrina (The Godmother), La Hermana (The Sister), Santa Marta (Saint Martha), Martita (Little Martha), La Santa Nina Blanca (The Holy White Girl), La Bonita (The Pretty Girl), La Flaca or Flaquita (The Skinny Girl), and Negrita (Little Black Girl).
42. Holman, *The Santisima Muerte: A Mexican Folk Saint*.
43. Ortega-Trillo, 'The Cult of Santa Muerte in Tijuana'.
44. Davies, 'Santa Muerte: the Mexican Death Cult'.
45. Freese, 'The Death Cult of the Drug Lords', 11.
46. Swann, 'The Dark Religion of the Santa Muerte'.
47. Kail, 'Santisima Muerte: Patron saint of security threat groups'.
48. Reuters, 'Mexico's "Saint Death" cult says it is drug war victim'.
49. Grillo, 'Behind Mexico's Wave of Beheadings'.
50. Swann, 'The Dark Religion of the Santa Muerte'.
51. Reuters, 'Mexico's 'Saint Death' cult says it is drug war victim'.
52. Ortega-Trillo, 'The Cult of Santa Muerte in Tijuana'.
53. Davies, 'Santa Muerte: the Mexican Death Cult', and Kail, 'Santisima Muerte: Patron saint of security threat groups'.
54. Carter, 'Links between illegal immigrants, terrorism, drug trade worry US officials'.
55. Lavandera, 'Police: U.S. teens were hit men for Mexican cartel'.
56. Castillo, 'Action 4 Investigates: La Santa Muerte'.
57. Ripley, 'La Santisima Muerte: Inside the Death Cult'.

58. Wright and Ordones, 'Man gets 24 years for running sex ring'.
59. Swann, 'The Dark Religion of the Santa Muerte'.
60. Laycock, 'Mexico's War on Saint Death', and Carroll, 'We Pray for Hope and Courage'.
61. Kail, 'Crime Scenes and Folk Saint: The Cult of Santa Muerte'.
62. Holman, *The Santisima Muerte: A Mexican Folk Saint*, in endnote mention shrine to black Christ visited by assassins.
63. Freese, 'The Death Cult of the Drug Lords', 13–14.
64. Schultze, 'Bad Mojo: Evil spirits walk in the criminal world'.
65. Brayton, 'El Taliban Invades America: Zetas at the Alpha Beta'.
66. Feemster, 'Spirituality: The DNA of Law Enforcement Practice', 12–13.
67. Reynolds, 'From the Focus on the Family to Familia Michoacan'.
68. Grayson, 'E-Notes: La Familia: Another Deadly Mexican Syndicate'.
69. Wilkinson, 'Mexico drug traffickers corrupt politics'.
70. Tuckman, 'Teetotal Mexican drugs cartel claims divine right to push narcotics'.
71. For more, see Ibid., Rodriguez, 'Michoacan Drug Cartel Offers Bank Services', and Reuters, 'Cult-like gang gains power in Mexico drugs war'.
72. Grillo, 'Drug-Dealing for Jesus: Mexico's Evangelical Narcos'.
73. STRATFOR, 'Ideology of Criminal Groups in Mexico'.
74. Tuckman, 'Teetotal Mexican drugs cartel claims divine right to push narcotics'.
75. Reuters, 'Cult-like gang gains power in Mexico drugs war'.
76. Grayson, 'E-Notes: La Familia: Another Deadly Mexican Syndicate'.
77. Wilkinson, 'Mexico drug traffickers corrupt politics'.
78. Grillo, 'Drug-Dealing for Jesus: Mexico's Evangelical Narcos'.
79. Ibid.
80. Gomez, 'The Use of Religion in the World of Organized Crime'.
81. Grayson, 'E-Notes: La Familia: Another Deadly Mexican Syndicate'.
82. Hawley, 'Government, leader deaths reshape apocalyptic sect in Mexico'.
83. Economist Staff, 'Mexico's drug Gangs: Taking on the unholy family'.

## Bibliography

Association of Religious Data Archives web site. 'Mexico 2008, Subheading: Religious Demography'. n.d., http://www.thearda.com/internationalData/countries/Country_149_2.asp (Accessed 18 September 2009).

Barakat, Matthew. 'Lawyer Admits Client's Guilt in MS-13 Killing of Pregnant Teen'. *Wtopnews.com* (12 April 2005), http://www.wtopnews.com/?sid=502844&nid=25.

Booth, William. 'Warrior in Drug Fight Soon Becomes a Victim'. *The Washington Post* (9 February 2009), A01

Botsch, Robert J. 'Jesus Malverde's Significance to Mexican Drug Traffickers'. *FBI Law Enforcement Bulletin* (August 2008), http://www.fbi.gov/publications/leb/2008/august2008/august2008l3b.htm.

Brayton, Colin. 'El Taliban Invades America: Zetas at the Alpha Beta?'. *cbrayton.wordpress.com* (3 March 2008), http://www.cbrayton.wordpress.com/2008/03/03/el-taliban-invades-america-zetas-at-the-alpha-beta/.

Burke, Adam. 'The Public Land's Biggest Crop'. *High Country News* (31 October 2005), http://www.hcn.org/issues/309/15867.

Butler, Allen. 'Jesus Malverde: The Narco Saint'. *Associated Content* (8 June 2006), http://www.associatedcontent.com/article/36310/jesus_malverde_the_narco_saint.html.

Campbell, Lisa J. 'The Use of Beheadings by Fundamentalist Islam'. In *Criminal-States and Criminal-Soldiers*, edited by Robert J. Bunker. London: Routledge, 2008, 263–71.

Canby, Peter. 'Getting Away with Murder'. *The Nation* (13 September 2007), http://www. thenation.com/doc/20071001/canby.

Carroll, Felix. 'We Pray for Hope and Courage: Mexican Border Violence Sparks Call for Conversion through The Divine Mercy'. *thedivinemercy.org* (13 April 2009), http:// www.thedivinemercy.org/news/story.php?NID=3594.

Carter, Sara A. 'Links between Illegal Immigrants, Terrorism, Drug Trade Worry US Officials'. *DailyBulletin.com* (28 December 2006), http://www.dailybulletin.com/ news/ci_4917114.

Castillo, Victor. 'Action 4 Investigates: La Santa Muerte'. *ValleyCentral.com* (30 October 2008), http://www.valleycentral.com/news/story.aspx?id=214857.

*Cnn.com.* 'Mexico Drug Fighter Killed after Less than a Day on Job'. Updated 2:06 p.m. EST, Wednesday, 4 February 2009, http://www.cnn.com/2009/WORLD/americas/02/ 04/mexico.general/.

Creechan, James H. and Jorge de la Herran Garcia. 'Without God or Law: Narcoculture and belief in Jesus Malverde'. *Religious Studies and Theology* 24, no. 2 (2005): 5–57.

Davies, Twiston. 'Santa Muerte: The Mexican Death Cult'. *TimesOnline* (3 April 2009), http://www.timesonline.co.uk/tol/comment/faith/article6023064.ece.

Davis, Matt. 'Jesus Malverde Legend Continues'. *Portland Mercury* (28 May 2009), http:// blogtown.portlandmercury.com/BlogtownPDX/archives/2009/05/28/jesus-malverde-legend-continues.

Economist Staff. 'Mexico's Drug Gangs: Taking on the Unholy Family'. *Economist.com* (23 July 2009), http://www.economist.com/world/americas/displaystory.cfm? story_id=14091538.

Feemster, Samuel. 'Spirituality: The DNA of Law Enforcement Practice'. *FBI Law Enforcement Bulletin* (November 2007).

Fleming, Jr., Gary A., dir. *Drug Wars: Silver or Lead.* DVD, 2008, 83 mins, http://www. drugwarsthemovie.com.

Freese, Kevin. 'The Death Cult of the Drug Lords: Mexico's Patron Saint of Crime, Criminals, and the Dispossessed'. *Foreign Military Studies Office Report,* n.d., http:// fmso.leavenworth.army.mil/documents/Santa-Muerte/santa-muerte.htm.

Gomez, Francisco. 'The Use of Religion in the World of Organized Crime'. *El Universal* (23 June 2009), translated by Sylvia Longmire, in her border violence and analysis blog, http://borderviolenceanalysis.typepad.com/mexicos_drug_war/2009/07/the-use-of-religion-in-the-world-of-organized-crime.html.

Gomez, Ray. 'Local ICE Agent Taking Border Experience to Washington'. *Pro8news.com* (4 December 2008), http://www.pro8news.com/news/local/35572244.html.

Grayson, George W. 'E-Notes: La Familia: Another Deadly Mexican Syndicate'. Foreign Policy Research Institute (FPRI), February 2009, http://www.fpri.org/enotes/200901. grayson.lafamilia.html.

Grillo, Ioan. 'Behind Mexico's Wave of Beheadings'. *Time* (Monday, 8 September 2008), http://www.time.com/time/world/article/0,8599,1839576,00.html.

Grillo, Ioan. 'Drug-Dealing for Jesus: Mexico's Evangelical Narcos'. *Time* (Sunday, 19 July 2009), http://www.time.com/time/world/article/0,8599,1911556,00.html.

Guillermoprieto, Alma. 'The Narcovirus', US–Mexico Futures Forum based on a lecture given 18 March 2009. *Berkeley Review of Latin American Studies* (Spring 2009): 3–6, http://74.125.155.132/search?q=cache:5MWBZSBGht4J:clas.berkeley.edu/ Publications/newsletters/Spring2009/pdf/BRLAS-Spring2009full.pdf+berkeley+ review+of+latin+american+studies+Spring + 2009&cd=1&hl=en&ct=clnk& gl=us.

Hawley, Chris. 'Government, Leader Deaths Reshape Apocalyptic Sect in Mexico'. *ArizonaRepublic.com* (20 November 2008), http://www.azcentral.com/ arizonarepublic/news/articles/2008/11/20/20081120 newjerusalem1120.html.

Holman, E. Bryant. 'Jesus Malverde and Nino Fidencio'. The Lucky Mojo Esoteric Archive (7 July 2002), http://www.luckymojo.com/esoteric/occultism/magic/folk/latinamerican/ebh200207_malverde_fidenci.html.

Holman, E. Bryant. *The Santisima Muerte: A Mexican Folk Saint, lulu.com*, ID 1185571, 2007.

Kail, Tony. 'Crime Scenes and Folk Saint: The Cult of Santa Muerte'. Forensic Theology Resource Center, 2006, http://www.cultcrime.org/santamuerte.html.

Kail, Tony. 'Santisima Muerte: Patron Saint of Security Threat Groups'. 4 July 2007, http://www.corrections.com/news/article?articleid=16090.

Keteyian, Armen. 'Drug Cartels Flex Muscle in Southwest'. *CBS News Phoenix* (12 November 2008), http://www.cbsnews.com/stories/2008/11/12/cbsnews_investigates/main4597299.shtml.

Kleinknecht, William. '"Strong gang component" revealed in Newark Schoolyard Slayings'. *The Star–Ledger* (15 September 2008), http://www.nj.com/news/index.ssf/2008/09/an_essex_county_grand_jury.html.

KPBS. 'Border Battle: Bringing Home the Drug War, Glossary'. n.d., http://www.kpbs.org/special-reports/border-battle/ (Accessed 22 September 2009).

Lake, George Byram. 'Who killed Kiki Camarena'. *National Review* (29 August 1986), http://findarticles.com/p/articles/mi_m1282/is_v38/ai_4328780.

Lavandera, Ed. 'Police: U.S. Teens Were Hit Men for Mexican Cartel'. *CNN.com* (13 March 2009), http://edition.cnn.com/2009/CRIME/03/12/cartel.teens/.

Laycock, Joseph. 'Mexico's War on Saint Death'. *religion dispatches.org* (6 May 2009), http://www.religiondispatches.org/archive/international/1428.

Logan, Samuel. *This is for the Mara Salvatrucha*. New York: Hyperion, 2009.

Manwaring, Max G. 'A Contemporary Challenge to State Sovereignty: Gangs and Other Illicit Transnational Criminal Organizations in Central America, El Salvador, Mexico, Jamaica, And Brazil'. Carlisle, PA: Strategic Studies Institute, December 2007, http://www.Strategic Studies Institute.army.mi1/.

Marizco, Michel. 'The Case of Felix Batista Resurfaces'. *Border Reporter* (15 May 2009), http://borderreporter.com/?p=1963.

Marosi, Richard. 'Mexico Under Siege: Violence Unabated in Tijuana'. *Los Angeles Times* (Tuesday, 2 December 2008), http://articles.latimes.com/2008/dec/02/world/fg-tijuana2.

Merrill, Tim L. and Ramón Miró, eds. 'Religion'. In *Mexico. Country Study*. Washington, DC: GPO for the Library of Congress, 1996, http://countrystudies.us/mexico/61.htm.

Ortega-Trillo, Alfredo. 'The Cult of Santa Muerte in Tijuana'. *San Diego News Notes* (June 2006), http://www.sdnewsnotes.com/ed/articles/2006/0606ao.htm.

Quinones, Sam. 'State of War'. *Foreign Policy*, March–April 2009, http://www.foreignpolicy.com/story/cms.php?story_id=4684.

Reynolds, Joseph Michael. 'From the Focus on the Family to Familia Michoacan'. Julydogs Blog, *talk2action.org* (8 June 2009), http://www.talk2action.org/story/2009/6/8/162951/0094.

Reuters. 'Mexico's "Saint Death" Cult Says it is Drug War Victim'. *Reuters.com* (10 April 2009), http://www.reuters.com/article/latestCrisis/idUSN10330660.

Reuters. 'Cult-like Gang Gains Power in Mexico Drugs War'. *Reuters.com* (22 July 2009), http://www.reuters.com/articlePrint?articleid=USN22401501.

Ripley, Will. 'La Santisima Muerte: Inside the Death Cult'. *KRGV News Texas* (7 May 2009), http://www.rickross.com/reference/santa_muerte/santa_muerte1.html.

Rodriguez, Carlos Manuel. 'Michoacan Drug Cartel Offers Bank Services'. *Bloomberg* (15 September 2009), http://mexicoinstitute.wordpress.com/2009/09/15/michoacan-drug-cartel-offers-bank-services-ovaciones-reports/.

178    *P.L. Bunker* et al.

Roig-Franzia, Manuel. 'Mexican Drug Cartels Leave a Bloody Trail on YouTube'. *The Washington Post* (Monday, 9 April 2007), A01.

Schlein, Lisa. 'Chiapas, Mexico Offers Ancient, Modern Religion Mix'. *Voice of America News* (3 August 2009), http://www.voanews.com/english/archive/2009-08/2009-08-03-voa12.cfm.

Schultze, Jim. 'Bad Mojo: Evil Spirits Walk in the Criminal World'. *DallasObserver.com* (27 February 2007), http://www.dallasobserver.com/content/printVersion/420486.

*STRATFOR*. 'Beheadings in Mexico: The Foreign Element in Mexico's Drug Wars'. 13 May 2006, http://www.stratfor.com.

*STRATFOR*. 'Kaibiles: The New Lethal Force in the Mexican Drug Wars'. 25 May 2006, http://www.stratfor.com/kaibiles_new_lethal_force_mexican_drug_wars.

*STRATFOR*. 'Ideology of Criminal Groups in Mexico'. *Mexico Security Memo* (27 April 2009), http://www.stratfor.com/analysis/20090427_mexico_security_memo_april_27_2009.

Swann, Ben. 'The Dark Religion of the Santa Muerte'. KTSM News Channel 9 (26 March 2009), http://www.ktsm.com/news/only-9-the-dark-religion-santa-muerte.

Tuckman, Jo. 'Teetotal Mexican drugs cartel claims divine right to push narcotics'. guardian.co.uk (5 July 2009), http://www.guardian.co.uk/world/2009/jul/05/la-familia-mexico-drug-cartel.

US Department of Justice, Drug Enforcement Agency. 'Biographies of DEA Agents and Employees Killed in Action: Enrique S. Camarena', http://www.usdoj.gov/dea/agency/10bios.htm (Accessed 19 February 2009).

Vazquez, Arturo. 'Reditus: A Chronicle of Aesthetic Christianity'. 22 January 2009, http://arturovasquez.wordpress.com/2009/01/22/la-santisima-muerte-a-mexican-folk-saint/.

Watson, Julie. 'Residents along U.S.–Mexican Border find Strength in Local Folk Saints'. *The Miami Herald* (16 December 2001), http://www.latinamericanstudies.org/religion/juan-soldado.htm.

Webster, Michael. 'Mexican Drug Cartels Terror Reaches Deep into the US'. *American Chronicle* (5 June 2008), http://www.americanchronicle.com/articles/view/64138.

Wilkinson, Tracy. 'Mexico Drug Traffickers Corrupt politics'. *latimes.com* (31 May 2009), http://www.latimes.com/news/nationworld/world/la-fg-michoacan-drugs31-2009may31,0,7938043,print.story.

Wright, Gary L., and Franco Ordones. 'Man Gets 24 Years for Running Sex Ring'. *Charlotte Observer* (8 April 2009), http://www.triadladderofhope.org/CharlotteNews.html.

# Counter-supply and counter-violence approaches to narcotics trafficking

John P. Sullivan

*Center for Advanced Studies on Terrorism (CAST), Los Angeles, CA, USA*

Narcotics and the drug trade contribute to a range of social ills. Among these are social instability, violence, corruption, and a weakening of the state. A range of criminal enterprises, including transnational gangs and drug cartels are engaged in the global trade in illicit drugs. This essay looks at measures to stem this trade through interventions directed against the drug supply and efforts to limit the violence that results from the drug trade. As such it looks at 'counter-supply' and 'counter-violence' approaches. While it emphasizes the impact on the Western Hemisphere – the United States and Latin America – it has international implications for global and national security, intelligence, and law enforcement.

The global drug trade has significant destabilizing effects on society, nations, communities, crime, and policy. For the United States, illegal drugs are a '$60 billion-dollar-per-year industry patronized by at least 16 million Americans'.[1] Attempts to come to grips with the global drug trade have been fraught with frustration, political and policy stalemates, and growing violence and instability.

A range of policy approaches have been embraced to control the supply of drugs. The majority are enforcement oriented. These include prohibition of possession and 'supply-side' approaches designed to make obtaining illegal drugs more difficult. From an enforcement perspective, interventions against drug supply include activities conducted by the police, customs, and military services to reduce drug supply. These strategies involve stemming production, as well as the wholesale and retail drug trade, and range from crop eradication, reduction and alternative development, interdiction of drugs in transit including counter-trafficking and 'counter-smuggling', and disrupting street markets.

Over the past 15 years, these approaches have had dramatic impacts, but they 'have not, however led to substantial decreases in the severity of America's drug related problems'.[2] Thus we face a policy conundrum. At best, the drug trade will decrease or continue at present levels and policy struggles will continue; at worst, the drug trade and its attendant violence will continue to spiral out of control, and states will be challenged by the impact of increasingly powerful transnational criminal enterprises.

This essay will examine both counter-supply and counter-violence measures to reduce the impact of narcotics trafficking and transnational criminal organizations. First, it will briefly look at the current situation, providing insight into the current threat, criminal players, and their destabilizing impacts. Next, the essay will examine counter-narcotics (counter-supply) policy approaches, assess their results and effectiveness, and briefly discuss counter-violence efforts. Finally, it will explore emerging potentials and conclude with comments on future approaches.

## Current situation

Violence and drug trafficking are an intersecting problem. Drug profits fuel corruption and violent conflict. They introduce and reinforce existing conflicts and social fissures, empower gangs and criminal enterprise, and contribute to an erosion of state authority and legitimacy. As a case in point, South America's Andean region produces the world's cocaine supply. Most of this cocaine originates in Colombia, Bolivia, and Peru. Some 1,000 tons of cocaine are produced annually, 'most of which are shipped to 10 million consumers in the United States and Europe'. [3] A breakdown of these shipments moving to markets in North America is 450 tons or 44% of production in 2007[4] and in Europe is 250 tons or 25% of production.[5] Currently, some 90% of this cocaine is being shipped via the Mexico–Central American corridor.[6] Recently, an increasing amount of this product is being transshipped to Europe via West Africa.

The broad impact of narcotics trafficking in the Americas has been significant. According to the United Nations Office on Drugs and Crime (UNODC) this includes:[7]

- An impact on other forms of crime – violent crime in particular. In extreme cases, it can even fuel insurgency – as in Colombia.
- Drug violence contributes to Latin America and the Caribbean having the highest rates of criminal violence in the world.
- The drug trade is accompanied by illicit firearms and violence and interacts negatively with street gangs.
- Money laundering and corruption linked with drug trafficking undermine the economy and governance.

Drug trafficking in Central America and Mexico is closely linked to a range of criminal enterprises. Increasingly, Mexican drug trafficking organizations (popularly called cartels) are poly-drug enterprises. They also engage in human trafficking, CD and video piracy, kidnapping, money laundering, and other activities including the theft of petroleum products for 'black market' resale. Central American nations are currently being used as staging areas for moving drugs to points north. While traditionally transit countries, many Central American states are also seeing an increase in internal drug consumption. Trafficker interactions with local gangs or *maras* are also having a negative impact on local conditions. For example, the Gulf Cartel is reported to be recruiting *Mara Salvatrucha* (MS-13) members from El Salvador to serve as enforcers (or *sicarios*).[8]

Ivan Briscoe, a researcher at Madrid's FRIDE, observes that the unabated illicit narco-trade in Mexico and Central America is transforming simple criminal enterprises into new dangerous actors. This transformation accompanies the economic optimization of smuggling networks achieved through the creation of 'stateless territories (Colombia) or mafia-dominated municipalities (Guatemala, Mexico), both firmly linked to wider international economic circuits'.[9] Briscoe concludes that these criminal non-state actors have established 'novel, extra-legal and sectarian control over trading zones and trafficking channels, creating in the process new forms of non-state authority and new models of citizenship'.[10] He adds, 'Armed militia, gangs, warlords, Mafia rings and youth fighters are synonymous with this process in different contexts.'[11]

Mexico is severely impacted by drug violence. Cartel violence has killed over 5000 persons by September of this year (2009), nearing the annual death toll of approximately 5800 for 2008.[12] Mexican cartels are rapidly becoming dominant players in the global drug trade. As a recent Associated Press report recounts: 'Mexican drug traffickers are branching out as never before – spreading their tentacles into 47 nations, including the US, Guatemala and even Colombia, long the heart of the drug trade in Latin America.'[13] The Mexican cartels are simply 'following the money'. In doing so, they are adapting and morphing into new forms to stay in business and fend off state enforcement efforts. Prior to Mexico's heightened crackdown on cartels in 2006, Mexico was dominated by four main cartels. Now, after three years of brutal combat against the state and each other, 'new armed groups are springing up as the heightened attention has forced new cartels to splinter and evolve'.[14]

*La Familia Michoacána*, also known as *La Familia*, is a notable example of the new breed of cartel evolving. *La Familia* started, seemingly as vigilantes, in the 1980s with the stated purpose of bringing order to Michoacán, emphasizing help and protection for the poor. 'Since then, La Familia has capitalized on its reputation, building its myth, power and reach to transition into a criminal gang itself. While doing so, it has become a powerful regional polydrug organization with its fingers in methamphetamine, marijuana and cocaine trafficking; kidnapping for ransom; and pirated CDs and DVDs – not to mention co-opting politicians and seizing political control and influence.'[15]

Banditry and violence are *La Familia's* staple. They carefully craft the myth of being vigilantes standing up to interlopers and the corrupt state while using beheadings as 'messages' to demonstrate their potency. *Narcomantas*, Internet pages, banners, and ads in local newspapers help solidify control, while intricate networks of patronage, coercion, and corruption reinforce the impact of their symbolic violence. *La Familia's* paramilitary and political tactics are in large measure designed to 'force the Mexican government to cease its crackdown and let the cartels influence the political arena so they can move their drugs in peace'.

*La Familia's* July counterattacks in Michoacán signal a new phase in Mexico's 'criminal insurgency'.[16] In this sequence, *La Familia* initiated coordinated attacks against 10 cities. At least 19 police and soldiers were killed in *La Familia's* counterattack. 'The cartel's actions included six near-simultaneous assaults of federal police stations; a pair of cartel commando raids by nearly 50 gunmen armed with assault rifles and grenades signaled the gang's resolve. This action was followed by the torture and assassination of 12 off-duty police intelligence agents.'[17]

In a novel adaptation of high intensity endemic criminal violence, the Mexican cartels are engaged in serious insurgent-like campaigns. As Sullivan and Elkus noted while commenting on *La Familia*, 'Armed with military infantry weapons, their gunmen use complex small-unit tactics that differ from the usual "pray and spray" methods beloved by criminals. Cartels run training camps for assassins on the border. They attempt to agitate the populace against the Mexican military through political subversion. And they control towns and neighborhoods that the military tries to retake through force.'[18]

Essentially, some of Mexico's cartels are evolving distinct political aims. La Familia is potentially the beta version of this model: 'Using social services and infrastructure protection as levers in rural areas and small towns, they are building a social base. In urban areas, they are funding political patron–client relationships to extend their reach. Reinforced by corruption, propaganda, political marches and demonstrations, as well as social media such as "narcocorridos," such activity helps to shape the future conflict.'[19] These daunting potentials will be discussed in greater length in the upcoming section on Emerging Potentials.

### Counter-narcotics approaches: counter-supply and counter-violence

Stemming the tide of narcotics violence and containing global narcotics trade is a complicated yet vital need. While a range of approaches are possible, this essay will focus on two: counter-supply and counter-violence. Essentially, this essay will make the case that the two need to be synchronized for maximum benefit. The essay will also assert that a comprehensive reassessment of counter-narcotics policy approaches is needed.

The International Crisis Group has completed a major two-part assessment of the Latin American Drug situation. In their first part of the report (*Latin American Drugs I: Losing the Fight*), they assess:

> Despite the expenditure of great effort and resources, the counter-drug policies of the U.S., the European Union (EU) and its member states and Latin American governments have proved ineffective and, in part, counterproductive, severely

jeopardising democracy and stability in Latin America. The international community must rigorously assess its errors and adopt new approaches, starting with reduced reliance on the measures of aerial spraying and military-type forced eradication on the supply side and greater priority for alternative development and effective law enforcement that expands the positive presence of the state.[20]

A paucity of international cooperation and coordination – especially a lack of synchronized policy and action between the US and Europe, as well as among the US, Europe and Latin America – has benefited transnational drug networks. The result has allowed the narco-organizations to expand their reach and power. Again, the International Crisis Group characterizes the situation:

> Well-armed, well-financed transnational trafficking and criminal networks are flourishing on both sides of the Atlantic and extending their tentacles into West Africa, now an important way station on the cocaine route to Europe. They undermine state institutions, threaten democratic processes, fuel armed and social conflicts in the countryside and foment insecurity and violence in the large cities across the Americas and Europe. In Colombia, armed groups derive large incomes from drug trafficking, enabling them to keep up the decades-long civil conflict. Across South and Central America, Mexico and the Caribbean, traffickers partner with political instability. [21]

In short, the policies of the past few decades are not effectively countering the current and emerging situation. The International Crisis Group concludes that traditional, counter-supply, drug control efforts have failed to stem the flow of cocaine from the Andean source countries of Colombia, Bolivia, and Peru to the US and Europe. As a result, cocaine availability and demand have remained stable in the US and are on the rise in Europe and Latin American 'transit' countries. This legacy of insufficient policy is causing significant collateral damage in Latin America and demands a collaborative policy reassessment and a new balance between enforcement and alternative development to curb supply. The absence of collaborative discourse and counter-drug coordination on both sides of the Atlantic has hobbled the efforts of counter-drug authorities on three continents and has allowed transnational drug organizations in the same three continents (and beyond) to adapt and enhance their exploitation of the lucrative global appetite for drugs.[22]

In order to better understand the situation, it is useful to look at the progress of global counter-drug efforts over the past decade. RAND Europe conducted a review of the situation for the European Commission; the resulting 2009 report, provided 'no evidence that the global drug problem was reduced during the . . . period from 1998 to 2007'.[23] Indeed, the report found that while 'Interventions against production can affect where drugs are produced, such as changing the location of coca growing within the Andean region . . . there is a lack of evidence that controls can reduce total global production. The same applies to trafficking.'[24] In addition, the report found that enforcement of drug prohibitions has caused substantial unintended harms'.[25]

Notable observations on efforts to control drug production and distribution from the RAND Europe study may help inform future directions for enforcement. These observations shed light on the organization, participation in, and response to enforcement and control efforts experienced in drug markets; they include:

- 'The cost of production, as opposed to distribution, is a trivial share of the final price in Western countries, roughly one to two percent. That statement holds true even if one adds the cost of refining.'[26]
- 'The vast majority of costs are accounted for by domestic distribution in the consumer country. Smuggling, which is the principal transnational activity, accounts for a modest share but much more than production and refining in the source country.'[27]
- 'Most of the domestic distribution revenues go to the lowest levels of the distribution system.'[28]

The RAND Europe report notes that drug enforcement takes many forms, on the counter-supply side these include several targeted activities: production, smuggling, high level trafficking (i.e. wholesale), and retailing.[29] Specific programs can – and are – tied to these targets. For example, counter-production efforts include crop eradication, providing producers alternative livelihoods, and enforcement directed against manufacturers and grower. Counter-smuggling efforts involve interdiction, efforts to stem wholesale or high level trafficking operations rely upon investigation, prosecution, and incarceration, and counter-retail operations focus on arrest and confiscation. Not unsurprisingly, the report found that 'Most drug enforcement efforts in any country are aimed at the retail market, either at the seller or the user. That is in part because most participants in the trade operate at that level.'[30] It is also likely that this occurs because most policing efforts and funds are allocated to local levels, hence more enforcement volume can and does occur at this point in the distribution chain.

### Assessing counter-supply approaches

Counter-drug policies have attempted to reduce supply through a mix of crop eradication, interdiction, alternative development, and law enforcement. The mix employed by the US and European Union, as well as South American states has varied and the results have been less than desired. Despite significant attention, the US market has remained relatively stable and consumption is growing in Europe, Argentina, Brazil, Chile, and Mexico. In addition, traffickers are agile, exploiting weaknesses in counter-drug coordination and cooperation, and resilient, shifting their operations to new regions when enforcement blocks their activities.[31] In addition, the expansion of transnational criminal networks and drug use across Latin America is exerting great pressure on democratic institutions and stability in several Latin American states.[32]

US counter-supply measures, including law enforcement, and crop eradication, have been heavily weighted in the balance between supply- and demand-side approaches since President Richard Nixon declared a 'war on drugs' in 1971.[33] This is true both domestically and abroad. In the domestic sphere, federal, state and local law enforcement devote a great deal of effort to drug enforcement. Increasingly, this is merged with counter-gang enforcement to stem violence in communities. US policy for source and transit countries is focused on stopping production, transport, and trafficking through crop eradication, interdiction, law enforcement, and alternative development. For Latin America, these supply-side efforts focus largely on the first three stages of supply: cultivation, processing, and transit and cost over $1 billion a year.[34]

European supply reduction efforts are largely focused on 'tracking down, dismantling and prosecuting shipment and distribution rings on the continent'.[35] Combating organized crime has led to the establishment of Europol (The European Police Office) and a €600 million funding for drug intelligence analysis and investigative case support for 2007–13.[36] Much EU counter-supply activity is concentrated on interdiction in European littoral waters. This emphasis led several European states – Italy, Spain, Portugal, France, the UK, Netherlands, and Ireland – to establish a 'Maritime Analysis and Operational Centre on Narcotics (MAOC-N) in Lisbon to coordinate intelligence and interdiction operations.[37] In addition to European efforts, several EU states cooperate with US and Latin American law enforcement authorities through drug liaison officers operating from their embassies. The EU favors alternative development (i.e. encouraging farmers to raise crops other than narcotics) over forced eradication efforts.

In the Andean region we see a mix of counter-supply approaches. Colombia ties its drug strategy to its Domestic Security Policy (DSP) and seeks to rebuild security in conflict zones where illegal armed groups use drug trafficking to support their operations. Colombia receives fiscal and operational support from the US and uses both military and law enforcement approaches. A large segment of Colombia's activities revolve around crop eradication (aerial spraying and manual removal) and strengthening rule of law institutions. Finally, Colombia seeks to disrupt the finances of trafficking organizations and illegal armed groups.[38] Bolivia places its emphasis on consensual eradication, while Peru employs both consensual and forced or 'programmed' eradication.[39]

Mexico has embraced a full-scale assault on drug trafficking organizations. The Mexican approach is heavily weighted on military interdiction and counter-cartel enforcement. The military option is largely due to pervasive corruption within Mexico's police – especially state and municipal police.[40] Throughout Latin America one sees drug trafficking and transnational organized crime eroding the rule of law, security, and stability.

The situation in Mexico is a dire warning to the entire Western Hemisphere. In varying degrees, throughout the region, trafficking organizations have increased their reach, infiltrated courts, and corrupted and co-opted public officials to sustain their illicit trade. Decades of sustained counter-supply effort have not reduced supply; rather democracy and state institutions have been weakened. In short, the drug trade is a conflict generator threatening regional stability:

> Colombia's decades-old armed conflict is clearly fuelled by drug trafficking. In Mexico, Venezuela and Haiti, criminal organizations are shaping to their advantage the institutional and political setting in which they operate or exploiting institutional fragility.[41]

In Colombia, this means insurgent groups (like the FARC) control large segments of drug production including growing crops and initial production; in Peru, remnants of the Shining Path provide security to drug producers; and in Venezuela, Argentina, and Brazil, turf wars between criminal street gangs over drug distribution are catalysts for extreme urban violence.[42]

### Unintended consequences of counter-supply efforts

A major finding of the RAND Europe report is an identification of a distinctive side effect of drug policy and enforcement: 'unintended consequences'.[43] Many of these are negative consequences of enforcement. At the macro-level, unintended consequences include an erosion of political stability in some fragile states. This has certainly been the case in Colombia and is now occurring in Mexico, Guatemala, and increasingly in other parts of Central America. The report notes 'Colombia's political stability has been affected over a long period of time by the intense efforts to control coca production, which have given a lucrative role to the rebel movement, the FARC, in protecting coca farmers from the government.'[44]

The situation in Mexico certainly shows that enhanced enforcement can cause drug enterprises to splinter, mutate, and seek new alliances. In Mexico, when faced with a crackdown, the cartels chose to battle each other and the government to maintain a stake in the game. A high level of violence, impunity, and a criminal insurgency were thus an unintended side effect. Other unintended consequences include environmental damage from spraying counter-crop pesticides and the 'balloon effect' or ability of drug producers and traffickers to shift operations to a new venue due to enforcement pressures. This could involve selecting new production areas, new trafficking routes, and operations in entirely new markets.[45]

When applied to production and trafficking controls, shifting the criminal area of operation is the essence of the 'balloon effect'. While it is clear intense enforcement action can suppress where drugs are produced and the corridors they travel, it is less clear that intervention has an effect on total production output.[46] Examples include the observation that intense control efforts in Peru may have shifted production to Colombia[47] and that the rise of new trafficking routes from South America to Europe via West Africa are having a severe impact on Guinea-Bissau and to a lesser degree Ghana.[48]

The taxonomy of key unintended counter-supply consequences includes: *geographic displacement* or shifting operations, *inaccurate crop spraying, expansion of production areas, and corruption as the result of intensified interaction.*[49] For example, geographic displacement as the result of targeted geographic enforcement could lead to a shift in production areas, a change of trafficking routes, or a change in drug or product. Increased corruption could also result. Inaccurate spraying of pesticides in crop eradication efforts could wipe out legitimate crops, cause economic loss and environmental damage to legitimate farmers, and potentially stimulate support for narco-insurgents and gangs. Eradication efforts could force the opening of new areas for crop cultivation, spreading the reach of cartels and gangsters, while causing environmental damage. Eradication efforts have also helped enhance the standing of guerrilla movements engaged in trafficking. Guerrillas or insurgents derive political and military advantages trough their control of drug production and trade. Among these advantages are increased capabilities (derived from financial gain), freedom of action, and most importantly political legitimacy. Specifically, enhanced legitimacy is an unintended consequence of eradication efforts. According to Felbab-Brown, 'Efforts to eradicate crops will have the unintended consequences of strengthening the alliances between the guerrillas and the peasants and the guerrillas and the drug-traffickers while hampering intelligence gathering and the government's overall strategy for defeating the guerrillas and establishing firm control over the post-conflict territory.'[50] Felbab-Brown suggested that interdiction at national borders and at sea, as well as seizing the profits by countering money laundering, would minimize the enhancing guerrilla legitimacy.[51]

Finally, intensified interdiction due to seizing a higher percentage of drug products may lead to increased corruption or direct attacks on the police and state to inhibit enforcement efforts.

### Assessing and improving effectiveness

Indicators of effectiveness (or the lack thereof) of counter-supply efforts are problematic at best. Caulkins et al. suggest that they can be found in metrics associated with drug supply pipelines and markets. In their assessment, they assert that, while the amount of drugs seized is too gross an indicator to be meaningful, measures of price and street-level availability are more valuable. In short, increased prices should make drug use less attractive. Unfortunately, their research found that the 'price record suggests that supply control efforts have failed to much reduce the use of any established drug'.[52]

This situation does not mean that enforcement is without utility. Rather, it suggests that the balance between enforcement and other strategies could be improved. This includes fine-tuning not only the balance between counter-supply and counter-demand strategies, but also the balance between various drug enforcement approaches and counter-drug and counter-violence (or counter-gang) efforts. Caulkins et al. remind us that enforcement itself covers a diverse range of activities, directed at different stages of the drug production 'pipeline'.

These include source country control, interdiction during transport, and domestic enforcement in the consumer nation.[53]

Source country control includes financial, technical, intelligence, and equipment aid to support source country enforcement. Interdiction en route includes law enforcement, customs, coast guard, naval and military support to tracking and interdiction of drug shipments limiting the movement of drugs. Domestic enforcement includes the seizure of drugs, and assets of drug traffickers and criminal enterprises, as well as arrest and prosecution of drug gangsters. All of these efforts can create temporary disruption of drug supply networks, and reduce the severity of consequences (such as reducing violence or the reach of a criminal enterprise) even if the overall drug trade continues. Finally, enforcement can 'tax' the supply chain imposing additional cost to the traffickers. Of course, these are adjusted for over the long-term. Caulkins et al. found that conventional enforcement was the most cost effective measure, followed by interdiction. Source country control has been the least cost effective enforcement measure.[54]

### Counter-violence activities

Counter-violence efforts are an essential element of containing the violence that accompanies the drug trade. Gangs and organized crime organizations (i.e. drug trafficking organizations and drug cartels) utilize violence to secure their market niche, protect their shipments, protect their turf, or the lucrative *plazas* for transshipping product, to ward off competitors, and sustain their power. Increasingly, as dramatically seen in Mexico, they use violence to counter drug enforcement efforts.

Typical counter-violence efforts include targeted enforcement of violent criminal gangs. This is largely a reactive affair. Once the gang or cartel utilizes violence (i.e. drive-by shootings, assassinations, and a wide-range of attacks), the police respond with investigations to identify and arrest the attackers, saturation patrols in high violence areas, and by enforcing a wide-range of criminal statutes in areas frequented by gangs and traffickers. More detailed gang enforcement strategies include gathering intelligence on gang members and their organizations, enforcing warrants that have been issued against traffickers and gang members for past crimes, and the development of conspiracy and racketeering cases against the gangsters.[55]

A newer approach to countering gang violence is the use of civil gang injunctions to disrupt a gang's control and hold over a fearful and victimized community. Civil gang injunctions originated in Los Angeles. Essentially, they employ a civil court order that prohibits a gang and its members from conducting certain specified activities in a designated geographic area or neighborhood known as a 'safety zone'. The court order declares the gang and its criminal activities a public nuisance. The targeted gang members must be shown to be members of the gang and be given notice of the injunction. If the gang member violates the terms of the injunction they can be prosecuted for violating the court order. Proven violations are misdemeanors punishable by a fine and up to a six-month jail term. Typical prohibited activities are:

- associating with other known gang members;
- use of gang signs and colors;
- use, possession, sales, and transportation of drugs;
- use or possession of alcohol;
- use or possession of dangerous or deadly weapons;
- graffiti and vandalism; and
- intimidating, threatening or harassing people.

As of June 2009, the City of Los Angeles had 42 active injunctions covering 67 gangs (that is less than 17% of that city's 400 known gangs).[56] Gang injunctions have been controversial. Many feel they violate rights to free association, may not be effective in reducing crime, or may shift gang crime and activity to another location (i.e. spillover). While few studies have empirically measured the effectiveness of gang injunctions, data reviewed by Grogger suggests that civil gang injunctions in Los Angeles have reduced violent crimes (mainly assaults) in the areas he studied.[57] More research is needed to validate this finding and measure the impact on civil liberties and of spillover to other communities.

Other initiatives to counter violence are efforts at gang diversion, employment programs, and efforts to build community stability and resilience. In the long term, these are likely to be the most effective means of limiting narco-gang violence in a community. One notable example of such programs is 'Homeboy Industries' founded by Father Greg Boyle, S.J. in Los Angeles. Homeboy Industries provides jobs to male and female gang members to foster their transition away from gang life. Examples of its activities include the 'Homeboy Bakery' and 'Homegirl Café'.[58] In any event, to be effective enforcement, activities must reinforce police legitimacy and be strongly grounded in community support. Without strong community involvement and support – i.e. community policing – counter-violence efforts will likely lose effectiveness in the long term.

### Emerging potentials

The systemic failure of counter-supply efforts, as well as the failure of counter-drug policy in general has contributed to the continued stability (and in many cases growth) of the global illicit drug industry. In the worst cases – for example, in Mexico and now other parts of Central America, South America, and West Africa – drug cartels are a significant threat to the stability of the states they are operating within. As Sullivan and Elkus have argued, Mexico is currently facing a significant threat to its internal security from drug cartels and gangs. These powerful and violent groups are waging a sustained assault on the Mexican state and each other to control the lucrative drug trade, its *plazas*, and production zones.[59]

Mexican cartels have employed psychological operations, fomented anti-government protests, attacked both police and military in infantry-style assaults, assassinated political officials, journalists, beheaded and maimed their victims, to amplify the strategic impact of their attacks, and co-opted and corrupted the military, police and political officials at all levels of government. The result is extreme brigandage, and a set of interlocking 'criminal insurgencies' culminating in virtual civil war.[60] As a consequence, some Mexican cartels, like *La Familia*, have embraced high order violence, religious and cult symbols, and political action to assert their control over the mega-turf they seek to dominate. They also seek community legitimacy cultivating a folk perception that they are social protectors – i.e. they seek to be seen as 'social bandits'.[61]

In addition to challenging the Mexican state, Mexican cartels have spread their operations throughout Central America, into South America, and across the Atlantic to West Africa.[62] Not only have the cartels destabilized entire segments of states with high intensity crime and violence, they have embraced new criminal enterprises (human trafficking, pirated goods, extortion, etc.) and as a consequence developed criminal enclaves of 'dual sovereignty' or 'parallel states' policed by their own enforcer gangs – like the *Zetas* – within their areas of operations. This is effectively a new security dynamic. As Manwaring aptly notes:

> In Mexico, that new dynamic involves the migration of traditional hard power national security and sovereignty threats from traditional state and nonstate adversaries to hard- and soft-power threats from small, nontraditional, private nonstate military organizations.[63]

Essentially, the failure of global drug policy has fostered the development of non-state criminal challengers or 'criminal soldiers' that threaten state institutions and have an eroding impact on sovereignty. 'Criminal soldiers' come in a variety of shapes and sizes. They may be street gang members, insurgents, warlords, or cartel and mafia members. In any guise, they challenge the traditional state monopoly on violence and political control. 'They may co-exist within stable sates, dominate ungovernable, "lawless zones," slums, or "no-go" zones, or be the *de facto* rulers of criminal enclaves or free-states.'[64]

A shift in power is the key 'unintended consequence' of failed drug policy. As Ivan Briscoe has observed, drugs provide unseen sources of power:

> ...the criminalized drug economies are silting into durable structures, uniting public allegiance, political and official allies, money and reliable armed units so as to feed growing demand. They are quasi-states, in fact straddling law and crime much like the policemen-anarchists in Chesterton's *The Man who Was Thursday*.[65]

This shift over power to non-state criminal actors at levels ranging from neighborhoods, to entire villages, segments of cities, wide swaths of Mexico's states, frontier and peripheral areas in Central America, and virtual narco-states like Guinea-Bissau in West Africa are significant concerns. These criminal enclaves or virtual 'statelets' are increasingly networked and a potentially escalating global security challenge.

**Conclusion: future approaches**

Stabilizing the global illicit drug and transnational organized crime threat is increasingly important to global stability and the national security of several states in the Americas and Africa. The threat is particularly acute in Mexico and increasingly in Central America. Finding a new way to limit both the 'harm of drugs' and the 'harm of drug enforcement' will require concerted efforts from multiple political levels: community, national, regional, hemispheric, and global. Police and law enforcement are essential to the enforcement of existing law and limiting violence – this insight drawn from counterterrorism enforcement has value in a counter-drug context. Indeed, 'crime control at local levels, linked into a distributed global network and supported by intelligence, economic, military, and civil society action can limit and ameliorate the threat posed by gangs, criminals, and terrorists acting both locally and globally'.[66]

Future counter-supply and counter-violence enforcement strategies must be synchronized and harmonized. All too often, increased drug enforcement and crackdowns trigger gang warfare and violent blowback. Community interaction, investigative initiatives, intelligence, and enforcement must be calibrated to minimize violent outbreaks and degrade gang and cartel operational effectiveness. This will require multilateral government, police, intelligence, and civil society action against what are essentially 'global criminals'.

Transnational and 'cross-border' policing will require enhanced cooperation, the 'co-production of intelligence' and new policy coordination frameworks. This will require participation and action from the United Nations (especially the UNDOC), Interpol, the European Union – and EU institutions like Europol and Eurojust, and efforts throughout the Americas and Africa. Essentially this is now a global problem with a triple front line (the Americas, Europe, and Africa). Among the new policy approaches to consider are: refocusing supply reduction efforts to emphasize close to user nation interdiction to increase costs to traffickers; emphasizing anti-money laundering approaches to diminish cartel fiscal returns; and establishing stronger interoperation and cooperation among global police and intelligence agencies.

All of these efforts need to emphasize dismantling drug trafficking entities, not only interdiction and eradication of drugs and drug crops. These need to be augmented by alternative development and community and economic stabilization in production and transit areas to deny the opportunity for drug organizations to re-emerge. The development of effective and corruption free rule of law institutions (police, judiciary, corrections), as well as corruption free military and government security agencies that respect the rule of law and human rights law is a necessary prerequisite for any effective counter-supply and counter-violence effort.

All of these efforts require multilateral, and indeed networked collaborative structures. These include informal and formal initiatives, amounting to 'global metropolitan policing'.[67] Examples of such networked collaboration include the deployment of New York Police Department detectives as liaisons to police agencies worldwide and the development of the joint US–Salvadoran Transnational Anti-Gang (TAG) initiative.[68] Similar efforts include police advisors to conflict-ridden zones such as areas plagued with high intensity gang activity crime.

Finally, it is important to emphasize that these initiatives must include not only national agencies, but also constituent state and local (municipal) police and government agencies, in all branches of government, cooperating with civil society and humanitarian non-governmental agencies to foster resilient and stable communities. Enforcement is still vital, but police must take the front lines. The military can provide the conditions for the security necessary to rebuild stability, but transition to post-conflict policing is essential. This may require the development of gendarmerie/formed police units to absorb the high intensity violence seen in some segments of the current 'drug war' (notably in Mexico and Guatemala).

**Notes**

1. This amount is in the upper range of illicit narcotic industry estimates. See Caulkins et al, *How goes the 'War on Drugs'?*, 1.
2. Ibid.
3. Maertens and de Andrés, 'David against Goliath', 1.
4. Ibid., 2.
5. Ibid.
6. Ibid.
7. United Nations Office on Drugs and Crime (UNDOC), *The Threat of Narco-Trafficking in the Americas.*
8. Ibid., 4.
9. Briscoe, 'Trouble on the borders', 5.
10. Ibid., 6.
11. Ibid.
12. Althaus, 'Gang killings in Mexico top 5,000 for the year'.
13. Llorca and Bajak. 'AP IMPACT'.
14. Hawley, 'Bold new cartels emerging in Mexico'.
15. Logan and Sullivan. 'Mexico's "Divine Justice"'.
16. See Sullivan and Elkus, 'State of Siege' and 'Plazas for Profit'.
17. Sullivan and Elkus. 'Mexican Crime Families'.
18. Ibid.
19. Ibid.
20. International Crisis Group. *Latin American Drugs I: Losing the Fight.*
21. Ibid., Executive Summary.
22. Ibid.
23. Reuter et al. *Assessing Changes in Global Drug Problems*, 1998–2007, xi.
24. Ibid., xii.
25. Ibid.
26. Ibid., 5.
27. Ibid.
28. Ibid.
29. Ibid., 30.
30. Ibid., 32.
31. International Crisis Group. *Latin American Drugs II*, 1.

32.  Ibid.
33.  Ibid., 2.
34.  Ibid., 2–3.
35.  Ibid., 9.
36.  Ibid.
37.  Ibid., 11.
38.  Ibid., 16–18.
39.  Ibid., 19–21.
40.  Ibid., 28.
41.  Ibid., 35–6.
42.  Ibid., 37–8.
43.  Reuter et al., *Assessing Changes in Global Drug Problems*, 46–8.
44.  Ibid., 47.
45.  Ibid.
46.  Ibid., 51.
47.  Ibid.
48.  Ibid., 52.
49.  Ibid., 48.
50.  Felbab-Brown, 'Drugs and Conflict'.
51.  Ibid.
52.  Caulkins et al., *How goes the 'War on Drugs'?*, 7.
53.  Ibid., 19.
54.  Ibid., 20–1.
55.  Examples of such efforts in the US are employment of California's Street Terrorism Enforcement and Prevention Act/California Penal Code § 186.22 and Federal Racketeer Influenced and Corrupt Organizations Act/Title 18, Chapter 96 prosecutions.
56.  For additional information on gang injunctions in Los Angeles, see the Los Angeles City Attorney's website at http://www.lacity.org/atty/.
57.  Grogger, 'The Effects of Civil Gangs Injunctions'.
58.  See http://www.homeboy-industries.org/ for information on this valuable program.
59.  The Mexican government has deployed some 50,000 soldiers across the country to confront the cartels, whose fierce drug wars have claimed over 14,000 lives since 2006. See Sullivan and Elkus, 'State of Siege' and 'Plazas for Profit'.
60.  Sullivan, 'Criminal Netwarriors in Mexico's Drug Wars'.
61.  See Logan and Sullivan, 'Mexico's "Divine Justice"'.
62.  See Logan and Sullivan, 'Costa Rica, Panama in the Crossfire'; and Cockayne and Williams, 'The Invisible Tide'.
63.  Manwaring, *A 'New' Dynamic*, 1.
64.  Sullivan and Weston, 'Afterword: Law Enforcement Response Strategies for Criminal-states', 616.
65.  Briscoe, 'Lockdown in Vienna'.
66.  Sullivan and Weston, 'Afterword: Law Enforcement Response Strategies for Criminal-states', 620.
67.  Sullivan and Wirtz, 'Global Metropolitan Policing'.
68.  See Sullivan and Wirtz, 'Global Metropolitan Policing'; and Sullivan, 'Forging Improved Government Agency Cooperation to Combat Violence'.

## Bibliography

Althaus, Dudley. 'Gang killings in Mexico top 5,000 for the year'. *Houston Chronicle* (13 September 2009).

Briscoe, Ivan. 'Trouble on the Borders: Latin America's New Conflict Zones'. Madrid: FRIDE, Fundación para las Relaciones Internacionales y el Diálogo Exterior, Comment, July 2008.

Briscoe, Ivan. 'Lockdown in Vienna: The UN's Drug Summit'. *openDemocray* (23 March 2009), http://www.opendemocracy.net/article/lockdown-in-vienna-the-un-s--drug-summit

Caulkins, Jonathan P., Peter Reuter, Martin Y. Iguchi and James Chiesa. *How Goes the 'War on Drugs'? An Assessment of U.S. Drug Problems and Policy.* Santa Monica, CA: RAND, Drug Policy Research Center, 2005.

Cockayne, James, and Phil Williams. *The Invisible Tide: Towards an International Strategy to Deal with Drug Trafficking Through West Africa.* New York: International Peace Institute, October 2009.

Felbab-Brown, Vanda. 'Drugs and Conflict: Lessons from Asia and Latin America'. Paper presented at the annual meeting of the International Studies Association, Honolulu, Hawaii, 5 March 2005, http://www.allacademic.com/meta/p71256_index.html.

Grogger, Jeffrey. 'The Effects of Civil Gang Injunctions on Reported Violent Crime: Evidence from Los Angeles County'. *Journal of Law and Economics* 45 (April 2002): 69–89.

Hawley, Chris. 'Bold New Cartels Emerging in Mexico'. *Arizona Republic* (30 August 2009), http://www.azcentral.com/news/articles/2009/08/30/20090830lafamilia.html.

International Crisis Group. *Latin American Drugs I: Losing the Fight.* Latin America Report no. 25, 14 March 2008, http://www.crisisgroup.org/home/index.cfm?l=1&id=5327.

International Crisis Group, *Latin American Drugs II: Improving Policy and Reducing Harm.* Latin America Report no. 26, 14 March 2008, http://www.crisisgroup.org/home/index.cfm?id=5328&l=1.

Llorca, Juan Carlos, and Frank Bajak. 'AP IMPACT: Mexican Drug Cartels Expand Abroad'. *San Diego Union-Tribune* (21 July 2009), http://www3.signonsandiego.com/stories/2009/jul/21/lt-drug-war-beyond-mexico-072109/.

Logan, Samuel, and John P. Sullivan. 'Mexico's "Divine Justice"'. *ISN Security Watch* (17 August 2009), http://www.isn.ethz.ch/isn/Current-Affairs/Security-Watch/Detail/?lng=en&id=104677.

Logan, Samuel, and John P. Sullivan. 'Costa Rica, Panama in the Crossfire'. *ISN Security Watch* (7 October 2009), http://www.isn.ethz.ch/isn/Current-Affairs/SecurityWatch/Detail/?ots591=4888CAA0-B3DB-1461-98B9-E20E7B9C13D4&lng=en&id=106768.

Maertens, Francis, and Amado Philip de Andrés. 'David against Goliath: Can Mexico, Central America and the Caribbean Effectively Fight Drug Trafficking, Organized Crime and Terrorism?'. Madrid: FRIDE, Comment, February 2009.

Manwaring, Max, G. *A 'New' Dynamic in the Western Hemisphere Security Environment: The Mexican Zetas and other Private Armies.* Carlisle Barracks: Strategic Studies Institute, US Army War College, September 2009.

Reuter, Peter H., Franz Trautmann, Rosalie Liccardo Pacula, Beau Kilmer, Andre Gageldonk and Daan van der Gouwe. *Assessing Changes in Global Drug Problems.* Cambridge and Santa Monica: RAND Europe, 2009.

Sullivan, John P. 'Forging Improved Government Agency Cooperation to Combat Violence'. *National Strategy Forum Review* 4, no. 4 (Fall 2008): 24–9.

Sullivan, John P. 'Criminal Netwarriors in Mexico's Drug Wars'. *Groupintel* (22 December 2008), http://www.groupintel.com/2008/12/22/criminal-netwarriors-in-mexico's-drug-wars/.

Sullivan, John P. and Adam Elkus. 'State of Siege: Mexico's Criminal Insurgency'. *Small Wars Journal* (19 August 2008), http://smallwarsjournal.com/blog/journal/docs-temp/84-sullivan.pdf.

Sullivan, John P., and Adam Elkus. 'Plazas for Profit: Mexico's Criminal Insurgency'. *Small Wars Journal* (26 April 2009), http://smallwarsjournal.com/blog/journal/docs-temp/232-sullivan.pdf,

Sullivan, John P., and Adam Elkus. 'Mexican Crime Families: Political Aims and Social Plans'. *Mexidata* (27 July 2009), http://mexidata.info/id2344.html

Sullivan, John P. and Keith Weston. 'Afterword: Law Enforcement Response Strategies for Criminal-states and Criminal Soldiers'. *Global Crime* 7, nos. 3–4 (August–November 2006): 615–28.

Sullivan, John P., and James J. Wirtz. 'Global Metropolitan Policing: An Emerging Trend in Intelligence Sharing'. *Homeland Security Affairs* 5, no. 2 (May 2009), http://www.hsaj.org/?article=5.2.4.

United Nations Office on Drugs and Crime (UNDOC). *The Threat of Narco-Trafficking in the Americas*. Studies and Threat Analysis Section, October 2008, http://www.unodc.org/documents/data-and-analysis/Studies/OAS_Study_2008.pdf.

# Counter-demand approaches to narcotics trafficking

Robert J. Bunker[a] and Matt Begert[b*]

[a]Counter-OPFOR Corporation, Claremont, CA, USA; [b]National Law Enforcement and Corrections Technology Center (NLECTC) – West, El Segundo, CA, USA

The illegal narcotics demand in the US is discussed in relation to the products supplied by the Mexican cartels. This is then contrasted with major legal commodities with addictive properties consumed in the US. Overlaps of use are also noted. Traditional, right of center, and left of center counter-demand approaches to narcotics trafficking are also surveyed. All of these approaches represent no-win scenarios for the US with its 'troubled population' of addicted users. Final analysis suggests that a blended counter-demand strategy should be explored based on extinguishing demand, coercing the users, and, to some extent, fulfilling user demand by the provision of prescription narcotics to 'special status' addicts and by means of limited decriminalization of personal marijuana use. Such a suggested strategy would have its own negative elements and should be considered less of a bad choice than the other, even worse, US counter-demand policy options that exist.

This essay is first and foremost about the minority of individuals in the US who comprise a 'troubled population' who are willing to break the law in their demand for and use of illegal narcotics due to their powerful addictions to such substances. It covers the illegal narcotics demand in the US in relationship to the products supplied by the Mexican cartels and then contrasts this with major legal commodities with addictive properties consumed in the US. Overlaps of use will also be noted. Traditional, right of center, and left of center counter-demand approaches to narcotics trafficking will then be surveyed.

A final analysis will then be provided that suggests a blended counter-demand strategy should be explored based on problem targeting derived from extinguishing demand, coercing the users, and, to some extent, fulfilling user

---

*The views expressed here do not represent those of the National Institute of Justice (NIJ), The Aerospace Corporation, US Air Force, the Department of Defense, or the US Government.

demand by the provision of prescription narcotics to 'special status' addicts and by means of limited decriminalization of personal marijuana use. While such a suggested strategy would have its own negative elements it should be considered less of a bad choice than the other, even worse, US counter-demand policy options that exist.

### Illegal narcotics demand in the US

The sustained demand for illegal narcotics by a minority of individuals in the United States is universally recognized as the dominant market from which the Mexican drug cartels and their associates are profiting. That market is presently in the $14 billion yearly range and represents a significant proportion of Mexican cartel, Sureños gangs, and mercenary economies, amounting to approximately $20 billion per year.[1] Secondary narcotics markets have now also been aggressively developed in Mexico and Central America and, in addition, large market inroads have been made into South America and Europe. While consumers may enjoy the effects – such as feelings of euphoria – the illicit narcotics provide, in all cases sustained demand for them is ultimately derived from individual consumers who are psychologically and/or physiologically addicted to the narcotics they utilize. The four major illegal narcotics supplied by the Mexican cartels, the active chemical involved, user effect, their natural or synthetic origins, and their estimated monetary value is portrayed in Table 1.

These narcotic substances – marijuana (a hallucinogen and a depressant), cocaine (a stimulant), methamphetamine (a stimulant), and heroin (a depressant) – each contain a different active chemical which forms the basis of the consumer's addiction (see Table 1). Results from the *2007 National Survey on Drug Use and Health: National Findings* (NSDUH) estimate (based on past month use) that 14.4 million individuals aged 12 and older used marijuana (and hashish), 2 million used cocaine (and crack), 0.529 million used methamphetamine, and 0.153 million used heroin. The estimate for all forms of narcotics use was 19.8 million.[2] This suggests that the Mexican drug cartels potential market of 17 million users is 85.8% of the domestic illegal US drug market or about 6.86% of all persons aged 12 or over.[3]

Illegal narcotics supplied by the Mexican cartels to US consumers can be better placed in context when compared to major legal commodities with addictive properties consumed in the US. These commodities represent a $320 billion a year industry and are compared in similar fashion to illegal narcotics (See Table 2). Some debate exists concerning whether this is even close to being to an 'apples to apples' comparison since these commodities do not offer the immediate addictive effects of narcotics such as methamphetamine or cocaine in its synthetically altered form, crack. On the other hand, some of these illegal narcotics have long histories of legitimate consumption. In the case of cocaine, it was used in nineteenth-century tonics and remedies, including the Coca-Cola

Table 1. Illegal narcotics supplied by Mexican narcotics traffickers to US consumers.

| Narcotic substance | Active chemical[a] | User effect[a] | Origins[a] | Monetary value (2008)[b] |
|---|---|---|---|---|
| Marijuana | THC; delta-9-tetrahydrocannabinol | Hallucinogenic & depressant | Natural | $8.5 billion |
| Cocaine (Crack) | Cocaine Hydrochloride; benzoylmethylecgonine | Stimulant | Natural (Semi-Synthetic) | $3.9 billion |
| Methamphetamine | *Same as the narcotic;* N-methyl-1-phenyl-propan-2-amine or d-alpha-dimethylphenethylamine | Stimulant | Synthetic | $1.0 billion |
| Heroin | Diacetylmorphine | Depressant | Natural | $0.4 billion |

[a] The Partnership for a Drug-Free America (*drugfree.org*), National Institute on Drug Abuse (NIDA); Drug Enforcement Administration (DEA) and other open source information.
[b] Stevenson, 'Marijuana Big Earner for Mexico Gangs'. Figures from US drug czar John Walters. Heroin value estimated by subtracting other major narcotics from total estimate.

Table 2.    Major legal commodities with addictive properties consumed in the US.

| Commodity | Active chemical | User effect | Origins | Monetary value (year) |
|---|---|---|---|---|
| Spirits, wine, beer | Alcohol | Depressant | Natural | $115.9 billion (2003)[a] |
| Tobacco products | Nicotine | Stimulate | Natural | $93.1 billion (2007)[b] |
| Coffee, tea, soft & energy drinks, chocolate & cocoa | Caffeine | Stimulate | Natural | + $110.0 billion (Current)[c] |

[a] Economic Research Service of the United States Department of Agriculture.
[b] *Marktanalyse – Tobacco – North America (NAFTA) Industry Guide*. 2/2009, http://www.marktforschung.de.
[c] Derived from industry reports. The US coffee market is at about $18 billion, US tea sales are at about $7 billion, the US soft drink industry is at about $ 88 billion, including non-caffeinated drinks, and chocolate sales are about $17 billion.

beverage, prior to its later criminalization in 1914 via the Harrison Narcotics Tax Act.

Still, the main basis of demand for these commodities as with the narcotic substances is their pleasurable and ultimately addictive qualities. Caffeine (a mild stimulant) is socially acceptable in its use. It can cause medical detriment, such as contributing to miscarriage, in addition to promoting some medical benefits, such as limiting Alzheimer's effects, though it also has issues of causing hyperactivity from overuse and headaches during detoxification. Alcohol (a depressant) is also socially acceptable in its use by those who have come of legal age. Increasingly, however, society is now far less tolerant of alcohol abuse, having enacted severe drunk driving (DUI; *driving under the influence*) penalties. Further, heavy long-term alcohol use causes liver disease and other health ailments. Views on its consumption have ranged dramatically over time in American society, with the US government deeming any form of alcohol use criminal, during the 1919–33 Prohibition era. Nicotine (stimulant) products now exist in a gray zone of use/acceptability and are also meant only for adult consumers. Modern US society increasingly looks down on nicotine product use, due to its link with cancer as well as second hand smoke concerns. Both nicotine and alcohol-based commodities are banned by the federal government to those who are not generally considered to have reached semi-adulthood (18) or full adulthood (21), respectively, because of these serious potential side effects. Further, a number of states have increased the minimum age of nicotine product consumption to 19. While commodities with caffeine in them are in use by practically the entire US population, somewhere in the 98th or 99th percentile, alcohol and tobacco product consumers are a much lower percentage:

> Slightly more than half of Americans aged 12 or older reported being current drinkers of alcohol in the 2007 survey (51.1 percent). This translates to an estimated 126.8 million people.

In 2007, an estimated 70.9 million Americans aged 12 or older were current (past month) users of a tobacco product. This represents 28.6 percent of the population in that age range.[4]

Of interest is the correlation of consumer use levels between (a) alcohol and nicotine and (b) between alcohol and nicotine and illegal narcotics. This relationship can be viewed in passages from the 2007 NSDUH:

> Alcohol consumption levels also were associated with tobacco use. Among heavy alcohol users aged 12 or older, 58.1 percent smoked cigarettes in the past month, while only 19.0 percent of non-binge current drinkers and 16.4 percent of persons who did not drink alcohol in the past month were current smokers. Smokeless tobacco use and cigar use also were more prevalent among heavy drinkers (12.3 and 17.5 percent, respectively) than among non-binge drinkers (2.0 and 4.3 percent) and nondrinkers (1.9 and 2.2 percent).

> The level of alcohol use was associated with illicit drug use in 2007. Among the 17.0 million heavy drinkers aged 12 or older, 31.3 percent were current illicit drug users. Persons who were not current alcohol users were less likely to have used illicit drugs in the past month (3.4 percent).

> Use of illicit drugs and alcohol was more common among current cigarette smokers than among nonsmokers in 2007, as in 2002 through 2006. Among persons aged 12 or older, 20.1 percent of past month cigarette smokers reported current use of an illicit drug compared with 4.1 percent of persons who were not current cigarette smokers.[5]

This is reminiscent of the old gateway drug arguments – still highly controversial – where users would begin with marijuana and then move into harder forms of narcotics. In this case, however, these two major commodities with addictive properties, alcohol and nicotine products, would be substituted for marijuana in terms of lead in to stronger drugs. It would seem that many of the same minority of individuals who consume the bulk of illegal narcotics in the US are also generally those who are heavy users of addictive commodities containing alcohol and nicotine. This suggests that this is the consumer target set for which counter-demand approaches to narcotics trafficking should focus and implies that the legality of a consumable is not fully the main factor of choice of use. Rather, the pleasurable effects and underlying addictive qualities are what get the consumer hooked on a product in the first place.

If it is accepted that this is the case, the problem at hand is how then the US government and its society at large can convince, or if need be ultimately force, a 'troubled population' with a willingness to break the law, into changing their demand behavior for illegal narcotics. This population very well believes that they have individual needs that supercede the legal basis of the state and the collective needs of society. From the perspective of traditional society, the actions of this group of individuals may appear immature and hedonistic but, nonetheless, they correlate with powerful psychological and/or physiological addictions to illegal narcotics. This also suggests that part of this troubled population may never be convinced or forced to stop wanting to use illegal narcotics. With this in mind, the strategies and approaches that can be utilized for counter-demand purposes will now be summarized.

## Traditional approaches

The United States government established its traditional drug strategy by declaring a 'war' on drugs in 1970, with the intent to eliminate illicit drug use in society. The initial strategy was to target production, distribution, and trafficking of drugs from the countries of origin or countries that facilitated shipment. In 1988, that strategy was expanded to target illicit drug users, by holding them accountable and punishable for sustaining demand.

The War on Drugs has had consistent base assumptions to eliminate drug abuse as a social problem because of its threat to societal stability and to national security. The strategy has been to focus on production and distribution of illicit substances, with a primary effort external to the US borders. The targets of this effort have been agriculture, processing labs, distribution networks, transshipment countries, and ports of entry. The outside-the-borders effort has enabled the use of national military power and diplomatic statecraft to engage other nations' governments to assist in supply depletion efforts. Trafficking (distribution to users) had been the main focus of internal law enforcement regulation until 1988, when new policy broadened the strategy to include 'user accountability' as part of the overall effort.

User accountability created incentives and punishments for the elimination of user purchase, possession, and use. The strategy has also included government monitoring of popular media and the denial of government benefits to citizens and US persons for certain violations. The user strategy was implemented after criticism, notably by economists, for not addressing both the supply side and the demand side of the illegal market. The federal government policy was that social disruption from illicit drug use was sufficient to justify the monitoring of popular media and the denial of government benefits to citizens for certain violations in order to shape and monitor behavior.[6]

History of recreational psychoactive drug use in America can be traced to the import and use of opium by Chinese immigrants in California in 1848–49. Opium history in American society is an exemplar of the evolution of drug attitudes in the society. Opium dens were popular and well-known because they sprang up in big cities and, in particular, Hollywood (actor Error Flynn was a frequent user). Addicts were first considered inevitable collateral damage, like drunks and gambling addicts. Social attitude was laissez-faire until concern over addiction led to the passage of the Harrison Act in 1914. Its purpose was to regulate the import and distribution of drugs. This led to concern. Most initial prosecutions involved distribution by physicians, not traffickers. Not long after, addicts were perceived not as unfortunates, but as criminals, as concern heightened about drug dangers. With illegality came a black market and overstated social ills such as rampant violent crime, illicit sex, and health devastation.[7]

Concern over the negative effects of these substances waxed and waned between 1914 and 1960. Worries of morphine addiction of World War I veterans surfaced, but Prohibition captured much of the national attention, created a vibrant black market for alcohol, and became the focus of policy and law enforcement. International concern created a Permanent Central Opium Control Board under the League of Nations, with some record of successful cooperation and international regulation between 1920 and 1930.[8] The only success that seems to be recorded for supply reduction was during World War II, when the supply of morphine dwindled because of war demands. The number of addicts in America dropped from 200,000 to between 20,000 and 40,000.[9] The American societal attitude remained diverse: cocaine was a popular additive to a hard liquor cocktail for some; addictive personalities were considered at risk of becoming hooked; and the psychiatric/medical community did not have a unified opinion on the utility of psychoactive drugs for patients.

By the 1960s, drugs were labeled as a threat to American values. Influential events included exposure of American servicemen in Vietnam to the Golden Triangle drug market, as well as the popularity of marijuana among American college students, the production of the more pure crack cocaine, and the associated profitability of the black market for this drug demand. In 1973, heroin was identified as one of the biggest consumer import products in the United States.[10]

Laws for possession of any amount of marijuana became harsher in the 1960s in reaction to the fear of declining social responsibility. President Johnson (1963–69), observing these changes, declared the situation '... a serious national threat'.[11] This set the stage for President Nixon to label illicit drugs 'Public Enemy Number One', and to formally declare 'a War on Drugs' in 1970. Each president has re-declared war on drugs until the Obama administration. In 1988, President Reagan augmented both the policy and the strategy with the passage of the Anti-Drug Abuse Act. It is described by the Drug Enforcement Administration as follows:

> Congress passed the Anti-Drug Abuse Act of 1988, P.L. 100–690. Two sections of this Act represent the US Government's attempt to reduce drug abuse by dealing not just with the person who sells the illegal drug, but also with the person who buys it. The first new section is titled, 'User accountability' and is codified in 21 U.S.C. section 862 and various sections of Title 42, U.S.C. The second involves 'personal use amounts' of illegal drugs, and is codified in 21 USC, section 844a.[12]

The Reagan administration expanded the international hunt for growers, producers, distributors, and international traffickers using extradition arrangements and direct military action. The 1988 law mandates outreach programs such as the Drug Abuse Resistance Education (DARE) program in elementary school, an anti-drug advertising campaign in various popular media to shape behavior, and the establishment of Drug Courts which give abusers, under certain conditions, the opportunity to avoid a criminal record by choosing to modify their drug abuse behavior and demonstrate compliance over a period of years. In contrast, repeat offenders who will not change drug abuse behavior can, under this law, be denied all federal benefits.[13] This law also created the White House Office of Drug Control Policy to provide oversight on the domestic and international anti-drug efforts. Scientific study and evaluation of drugs, drug abuse, addiction, and associated research is the responsibility of the National Institute on Drug Abuse (NIDA).

The overarching strategy between 1988 and 2009 has been in support of a policy that targets both the supply and demand side of the market. National military power, federal law enforcement, and diplomatic power is used internationally to stem the supply side. Counter-demand strategy includes stopping the demand before it begins with youth deterrence campaigns and popular media messages (e.g. the DARE program and an advertising campaign), behavior modification incentives, deterrents and behavior monitoring (rehabilitation and drug courts), and use deterrence based either on economic sanction and benefit denial, incarceration, or both.

The Obama administration strategy differs. The President's National Drug Control Strategy of January 2009 deletes the reference to the War on Drugs[14] and describes the way forward as a balance among efforts to stop initiation, efforts to heal users, and disrupting the illegal drug market.[15] Speaking in Mexico on 27 July 2009, Gil Kerlikowski, the director of the Office of White House Drug Control Policy said that the strategy focuses on reducing drug use, supporting domestic law enforcement work against drug trafficking, and coordinating with other countries that either produce or assist in the distribution of drugs intended for transport to the United States.[16]

The cost-benefit analysis of this long war is difficult to assess. The Office of National Drug Control Policy report of 2009 indicates significant reduction in initiation of drug use by youth, reduction in positive drug tests in the workforce, and claims the lowest levels of drug abuse in the US workforce since 1988. The report consistently indicates the need to continue and intensify the effort to reach a tipping point of demand reduction. The base addicted population remains at 7–8%. One in four youths aged 12–17 reporting use of marijuana display characteristics of addiction.[17] If the tipping point of demand reduction is contingent on reducing the percentage of the addicted population, and one in four is at risk of addiction, then achieving the lower percentage addiction rate to break the demand curve may be difficult.

The problem of addiction and abuse is often seen, internationally, as an American problem. Devolving the problem of illicit drug use, while a benefit to the United States, can be viewed as a cost to cooperating countries. Certainly it is a cost to the Mexican drug cartels and the network of distribution and trafficking. The United States is criticized for wanting the benefit of drug demand reduction at the expense of cooperating countries, such as Mexico, which is left to deal with cartel violence and backlash. The American benefit of demand reduction will, at some point, translate to Mexican cartel cost. The expected outcome of that reversal will be, at least, an increase in violence.

**Right of center approaches**

Public policy strategies often move to the right of center in reaction to perception of clear and present danger to the society. Threats that accumulate slowly, over time, do not produce a dramatic change in public policy until there is a crisis or a culminating point. Sudden threatening events, by contrast, may produce a quick, reactionary public policy shift. The threat of illicit drugs is an example of the former; September 11, 2001 is an example of the latter.

When the drug problem is perceived as this clear and present danger, a public policy shift to the far right would be a consideration. The situation might look like this: A magnitude of change in illicit drug counter-demand strategy and policy implementation is needed immediately because American society is threatened by the entire network of cartels, traffickers, transshipment countries, and the situation at the border. Using the War on Drugs as a legacy for counter-supply strategy, new policy, law, and technology must be applied to counter the demand by the core addict population and the illicit drug affinity population.

At this point 40 years after the War on Drugs began, these are the right-of-center perceptions and assumptions:

- Illegal narcotics use is unacceptable and anathema to American values.
- The War began with a counter-supply strategy in 1970 and in 1988 changed policy to also counter demand. In spite of these efforts, addiction has remained at 7–8% of the population, with no indication of reduction.
- There will be no reduction in drug use if left-of-center counter-demand strategies are implemented.
- The effort to eradicate the demand must use technology to achieve the goals quickly and efficiently.

The goal of a hypothetical right-of-center strategy would be to create and implement a counter-demand strategy to complement an improved and intensified counter-supply strategy. The counter-supply strategy has been in place and has been refined since the declaration of the War on Drugs in 1970.[18] From this legacy, the strategy would evolve to balance the effort applied to both counter-demand and counter-supply. The counter-demand strategy was intensified in 1988, but has not produced the desired result. A substantive result of this increased effort is the reduction of the addicted population. The addicted population has been perpetually 7–8%. The aim is to reduce the percentage to a tipping point (unknown percentage). At that point, the social problem would be negligible or disappear. The counter-demand strategy would target behavior and use. Behavior, defined as an individual choice, can be influenced or restricted. Use can vary from experimentation to addiction. The policy would be to eliminate use completely. There are various ways to compel appropriate behavior and restrict use.

The media campaign to counter drugs by TV advertisement, influencing the scriptwriting of popular TV shows, and video messages on YouTube[19] would be transformed into an information operations and psychological operations campaign. Information operations would address this as a national problem, shaping the popular opinion and specifically negating the left-of-center strategies, groups, and opinions aggressively, appealing to emotion and fear as well as civic duty. Psychological operations would be used to stop initiation or reverse experimentation in the non-addicted population. Information operations and psychological operations would be intended to shape behavior and modify behavior. The addicted population would probably be immune to these overt messages and warnings. Ideally, the population considering drug experimentation/use would evaluate these public messages that would appeal to fear, urgency, immediate danger, and citizen duty, among other concepts. The objective would be to compel the population to decide against drug use and have them think that they came to that conclusion on their own. Furthermore, the affinity population must be persuaded or compelled to alienate the addicted population, creating a degree of separation to minimize, association, communication, and crossover. To do so, information and psychological operations must portray addicts as criminals that are a social stigma to be avoided at all cost. As addicts become more isolated, they become more vulnerable to rehabilitation.

For the percentage of the drug affinity population that does not respond to behavior shaping or modification with information and psychological operations, the follow-on escalation is deterrence by threat of economic sanction, incarceration, or both. Next is behavior monitoring. The current system of drug courts is an example where offenders have a choice to make a behavior change in return for a clean reputation, but are monitored for several years to ensure compliance.[20] This concept can be further developed, made more efficient, and organized around harsher penalties for minor infractions. The combination of harsher penalties with the possibility of an expunged record would appeal to a significant portion of the population because of the increased intensity of information operations. Current policies such as drug-free workplaces, required for federal government funding, and drug-free zones such as public housing are soft examples of what would be done to augment this effort.

When deterrence fails, offenders would be subjected to the threats of economic sanction and incarceration. For maximum effect, the psychological and information operations would play here as well, emphasizing the individual's contribution to weakening society and associating it with national security degradation. After the appropriate punishment, behavior monitoring would be mandatory. Technology can be developed or modified to track and record post-incarceration activity and detect any illicit drug use. Current law denies any federal benefits to drug offenders for certain violations.[21] This would be expanded.

Some offenders would not be persuaded to change behavior and would not comply with soft rehabilitation. Through an appropriate but swift legal process, these offenders would be labeled addicts.[22] This would be a crossover point, and the rules would change. Addicts would be subjected to different treatment under law. The addict would be incarcerated and directed to a mandated rehabilitation/course of therapy under supervision. The rehabilitation would have a time limit after which the addict would be evaluated for suitability and chance of success in rehabilitation. In the most severe of cases, those in which rehabilitation is clearly not possible, the addict if the policy is taken to its logical extreme, may be put to death (*Note – putting addicts to death is realistically not a viable US policy option*). The justification is the long-term inability of any current policy so far to reduce the percentage of addicts in the population. These instances can be used as examples of the consequences of inappropriate choice and lack of will. The situation and circumstances can be recorded and used in psychological operations against other addicts, as well as in information operations to the public.

This rehabilitation must include methods and technology that are as scientifically advanced as possible, and this course of therapy must be unrelenting in its goal to rehabilitate the addict. Constant monitoring using technology that detects drug ingestion would be mandatory, as would substances that are ingested or injected to react with any drugs to make the addict sick, or cause death, as an incentive to succeed. These draconian measures would be justified because of the failure to eradicate illicit drug use and the necessity for the survival of a capable American society. Continued research and development for technology to assist in this effort should be considered a funded responsibility of the National Institute on Drug Abuse.

The benefit of this course of action would be a drug-free society. America first formally acknowledged the need to regulate psychoactive drugs in 1914 with passage of the Harrison Act[23] and has had to deal with the influence of these substances since. Causes and conditions such as the development of crack cocaine, the exposure of the US military in Vietnam to the Golden Triangle, college student affinity for marijuana in the 1960s, and a drug culture that had emerged during that time of social change have created a thriving black market industry that should not exist. Fast and dramatic action would produce positive results that would encourage the perpetuation of this policy until the addict population reaches the tipping point and addiction/abuse is extinguished. It is important that this be swift, because it is challenging, and quick results would help maintain the political will. Once established, however, the nation would have defeated the addiction problem and there would be a mechanism in place to minimize the danger of an influential addicted population arising again.

This effort would be costly, requiring resources, management, and coordination of the appropriate agencies to establish or modify facilities, train personnel and orient the judicial system to support quick implementation and continued operation. There would be a cost due to public reaction. Human rights groups, civil liberties groups, and advocates of the use of illicit drugs for medical purposes, to identify a few, would push back at the absolutist character of the program. Additionally, this would create a police state atmosphere, with significant possibility of hostile reaction from the public at large. Psychological and information operations would then have a component to address this inevitability.

There would be a cost to confront the reaction of the drug cartels and the distribution network that would inevitably consider this a threat to business prosperity and profit. Inevitably, the level of violence would increase as the drug support network resources are threatened and reduced. The cartel reaction would be unencumbered by the rule of law, so countering this threat would require increased law enforcement involvement and protection. The threat of further cartel violence is by no means considered a deterrent to governmental decision making; rather it is a second order effect that must be simply taken into planning consideration.

A historical study of government programs describes three things that must exist if it is to be sustained. The effort must be politically sustainable, in other words, the public must support it through the mechanism of the republic, it must be operationally supportable, meaning that it must have the resources, facilities, and methods to actually function, and it must demonstrate that it produces public value, meaning there must be a concrete benefit derived from using the energy and resources for the effort.[24] In the case of a right-of-center counter-demand drug policy, the risk is at least twofold. It must produce a measurable result in a short amount of time to sustain the political will for a draconian police-state and it must be prepared to handle the differing backlash from the public and from Mexican drug cartel networks. Finally, the reduction/elimination of the addict population must be determined to be of ultimate public value.

### Left of center approaches

The other end of the political spectrum views the use of some or all forms of illegal narcotics as less of a threat to American society than US governmental attempts to eliminate said narcotics use. Some holders of this view also see some illegal narcotics as either harmless or potentially even beneficial as in the case of marijuana. These political views run the gamut from use of selective illegal narcotics for medical purposes only through decriminalization of product use to legalization (or re-legalization) of one or more forms of illegal narcotics. As a view supports more and more encompassing forms of illegal narcotics use, their supporters quickly drop off in numbers with those supporting pro-legalization of all forms of illegal narcotics representing a very small minority of individuals. More extreme proponents of these views also see the War on Drugs as more of a war on marginalized socio-economic groups within society, the poor and minorities, than anything else and begin at some point to adhere to governmental conspiracy theories.

Some of the basic left of center assumptions held are that counter-distribution approaches to narcotics trafficking will always fail because of domestic user demand; it is preferable to fulfill demand, partially or fully, than continue with the undesirable outcomes of traditional (status quo) or the specter of even more right of center counter-demand strategies; by partially or fully fulfilling user demand, the economic back of the threat groups (cartels, gangs, and mercenaries) will be broken and the threat will diminish; and satisfying user demands will result in new governmental revenues and potentially safer narcotic use experiences for the consumers.

Calls for decriminalization are not as far fetched as they may sound. Decriminalization of one or more types of illegal narcotics has been in effect for some time now in Holland (1976; marijuana, hashish, and hash oil for personal use) and in Portugal (2001; all drugs for personal use).[25] Domestic proponents cite *The National Commission on Marihuana* [sic] *and Drug Abuse* report written in 1972 that advocated that possession of marijuana for personal use be decriminalized. About a dozen US states have decriminalized such possession, which is still a criminal offense under federal law. California is an interesting case with its medical marijuana use laws and the fact with its severe budget crisis attempts at taxing medical marijuana, like any other legitimate commodity, are currently being discussed in that state. While calls for outright legalization are always being made by some vocal proponents, no such legislation is being considered domestically or overseas by any governmental bodies, although marijuana legalization ballots have been attempted and defeated in California (1972), Oregon (1986), Alaska (2000), and Nevada (2002).[26]

From a cost-benefit analysis, the left of center approaches draw on arguments that include how much the War on Drugs is costing the country economically, the large increase in jail and prison population since the enactment of the 1988 Anti-Drug Abuse Act, and the international ill will it has created between the US and illegal narcotics production and transit countries. Direct federal drug war costs are currently $14.1 billion per year (FY 2009 Presidential request) according to the Office of National Drug Control Policy.[27] If costs of police narcotics task forces, creating and maintaining prison and jail infrastructure for drug offenders, hiring correctional personnel, engaging in prosecution and defense (public defenders), and follow-on parolee officers are calculated, these figures are easily doubled. While this conservative $28 billion dollar figure is much lower than estimates published in *The Economist,* which states that the US spends $40 billion[28] a year on the drug war (and is line with some other analyses) it conveys the point that substantial sums of money are in play. Thus, sustained drug war costs over the course of decades are well into the hundreds of billions of dollars and at some point will eventually surpass the trillion-dollar mark.

Prison population increase arguments in support of left of center approaches highlight the fact that:

- Drug offenders, up 37%, represented the largest source of jail population growth between 1996 and 2002.
- More than two-thirds of the growth in inmates held in local jails for drug law violations was due to an increase in persons charged with drug trafficking.

- In 2000, an estimated 57% of Federal inmates and 21% of State inmates were serving a sentence for a drug offense ...
- [B]etween 1990 to 2000 .... drug offenders accounted for 59% of the growth in Federal prisons.[29]

This is representative of US policies that have resulted in it having more individuals incarcerated than any other country in the world. According to US Department of Justice's Bureau of Justice Statistics, 'at year end 2007, the total incarcerated population reached 2,413,112 inmates' for all US territories and possessions.[30] Based on an analysis derived from this data, the underlying report, and their own statistics, Stopthedrugwar.org states that:

> Drug offenders made up 19.5% of all people doing time in the states, or roughly 400,000 people. In the federal system, drug offenders account for well over half of the 200,000 prisoners (those numbers are not included in this report), bringing the total number of people sacrificed at the altar of the drug war to more than half a million.[31]

Concerning international ill will stemming from the War on Drugs, the recent report by the Latin American Commission on Drugs and Democracy, entitled *Drugs and Democracy: Toward a Paradigm Shift,* is an indictment of US policies by a number of former Latin American political officials and other respected commission members. The timing of this report is interesting because a revaluation of Latin American drug policies towards decriminalization of personal use of one or more illegal narcotics are now taking place in a number of countries including Mexico (2009; personal marijuana, LSD, cocaine, methamphetamine, and heroin use decriminalized), Argentina (2009; personal marijuana use decriminalized), Brazil (in debate) and Ecuador (in debate).[32]

To be fair, counter-viewpoints to all of these arguments can and have been made by the US government and its agents in what has become a visceral debate over the merits and pitfalls of present and future national narcotics policy. One of these rebuttals concerning illegal narcotics use can be found in a balanced and well-reasoned *Police Chief* magazine article written in 2005 though numerous counter-rebuttals, many of which are articulate, can be found in pro-drug websites and publications such as the *Mother Jones* feature, 'Totally Wasted', written in 2009.[33]

## A blended strategy and the future

The intriguing aspect of a troubled population's demand for illegal narcotics vis-à-vis the needs of the American state is in differing interpretations of an individual's right to 'life, liberty, and the pursuit of happiness' with an emphasis on what pursuits of happiness are, and are not, allowed because they may threaten an individual, society itself, and its underlying values and principals. Traditional counter-demand approaches represent the status quo and must be considered the current baseline effort – one arguably, since the enactment of the 1988 Anti-Drug Abuse Act, which is very harsh in its approach to the sentencing of drug users. With the Obama administration now in office, a softening is already taking place but whether national drug policies will remain squarely in the traditional approach category or would even attempt to drawn upon some of the left of center approaches is unknown.

Right of center approaches, as characterized in their extreme, are truly chilling in their societal and governmental implications. They represent a true 'war' on drugs and overtly designate both illegal narcotics suppliers and users as enemies of the state. On the counter-demand side in order to get reductions in that 7–8% user population, more and more draconian measures are required to get that population down towards 0% because the law of diminishing returns is fully in effect. At some point, what remains is simply a group of troubled and non-compliant individuals with whom the continuum of deterrence, intimidation, monetary fine, and imprisonment simply does not work.

On the other hand, left of center approaches, come with their own problematic issues and domestic concerns. The most glaring is the high likelihood that the 7–8% of the user population would increase because either individual drug use is decriminalized across the board or in fact legalized. At some point, we are sending a message to US citizens that use of drugs now illegal is tolerated as a vice or even accepted as normal behavior. The enforcement of US laws becomes selective in its application across society and eventually traditional American values come into question when going down this path.

In the final analysis, the US due to circumstances, a troubled population of illegal narcotics users, and its past policies has for some time now found itself in a no-win situation. The traditional approach is simply not working with stabilized addiction rates and Mexican cartel violence beginning to creep over the US border, the right of center approach would turn the nation into a police-state (especially when combined with the implementation of overly zealous counter-terrorism and homeland security policies), and the left of center approach would likely result in a larger user population and a fundamental change in what many conceive are traditional American values.[34]

The best bet at this point is to attempt a blended counter-demand strategy. While it would be impossible to fully articulate what such a suggested strategy could or should look like, some initial impressions will be discussed. The focus of such a suggested strategy would be derived from three basic and understandable user demand targeting criteria. These targeting criteria and the various (blue-sky) elements that can be used to fulfill them are as follows:

- *Extinguish demand:* (a) *Behavior shaping*: educational and media campaigns to make sure the initial demand does not develop/preemption; (b) *Behavior modification*: counseling and treatment after user demand has emerged; and (c) *Advanced technology use*: Altering the user in some way (e.g. a vaccination) in order to render the narcotics ineffective by blocking or changing their effects.
- *Coerce the users:* (a) *Use deterrence*: threat of economic sanction, incarceration, and death; and (b) *Use punishment*: economic sanction,

incarceration, and death. Includes the use of small rewards and incentives for compliance.

- *Fulfill demand:* (a) *Product replacement*: substitution of another substance/item for the illegal narcotic – e.g. methadone for heroin; (b) *Illegal narcotic provision*: provide the illegal narcotic to the user; (c) *Non-enforcement of narcotics laws*: non-prosecution; (d) *Administrative offense*: decriminalization; and (e) *Make it a legitimate commodity*: legalization.

Some of the various approaches to achieve these targeting criteria are of course from a US governmental policy perspective totally unacceptable – such as complete legalization as a means to fulfill user demand or for that matter probably almost all forms of decriminalization. The killing of users as a form of punishment is also certainly viewed as an unacceptable governmental policy. Such a strategy itself would almost certainly pull more from attributes of the traditional approaches mentioned than that of the right of center or the left of center approaches. Still, some elements of both of these approaches may have some utility. From a political perspective, drawing concepts from the ends of the political continuum would likely please no one but the intent is to create a pragmatic and pro-US government strategy that would have some chance of actually succeeding. With this in mind, the best path ahead for a blended counter-demand strategy would focus upon a two-pronged approach. The first element is based on the creation of a new designation for hardcore users.[35] Something along the lines of an administrative 'special narcotics user status' would be enacted.[36] By so doing, the US government and the society that it represents would accept the fact that a grouping of troubled individuals exist, and short of a technological breakthrough such as illegal narcotics vaccinations, this small grouping will likely not be deterred or coerced in any way, shape, or form from its powerful addiction to illegal narcotics.

This is reminiscent of a medicalization or public health approach to user-demand with the caveat that the majority of such troubled individuals may just be deemed untreatable. From a societal perspective, they have been medically triaged and this methodology has been blended to some extent with a modified Drug Courts approach. This population set, once designated, would operate under a parolee type of mechanism and monitored with ankle bracelets or other forms of GPS location. They would no longer be incarcerated solely for their illegal narcotics use activities. Further, their status needs to be sufficiently stigmatized and burdened with the loss of societal privileges and economic benefits (such as public benefits and health care) that it would be undesirable for non-narcotic addicts to emulate their special status. From the other extreme, an individual cost-benefit analysis also has to be conducted that would make an addict accept their special status designation over that of being simply incarcerated in the prison or jail system. This is where enacting some harsher right of center penalties for those opting not to select the special status designation may be justified.

All special status individuals would be provided mandatory counseling and treatment to modify their user behavior in coordination with the controlled medical provision of illegal product replacement with other substances. These would be prescription narcotics such as methadone and other products administered under the care of a physician or a public health officer. Like it, or not, the provision of prescription narcotics needs also to be considered in some user addiction circumstances. This would be by far the most controversial aspect of the envisioned counter-demand strategy and would require a paradigm shift in drug war thinking. The US government, or its agents, would in some instances be required to fulfill addict product demand. This would mean that federal or corporate laboratories and facilities would be required to produce replacement products for addicts undergoing treatment and, potentially, even powerful substitute prescription narcotics to what would be considered unsalvageable addicts. Such unsalvageable addicts would be allowed their chemically induced 'pursuit of happiness' as long as they do no harm to others and maintain a limited societal cost footprint so traditional society is not burdened by their self-destructive lifestyle choices.[37] Definitions of harm to others would by necessity need to be extended to dependent children in their households who they would no longer be allowed to associate with or influence.

The second element to the blended counter-demand strategy would be an easing up of federal narcotics policy in regards to marijuana use. While marijuana use should in no way be condoned, in fact it should be overtly discouraged and stigmatized as is being done with alcohol and nicotine use, it should become decriminalized with regard to personal use. This would make it an administrative offense unless of course it is being used while operating a motor vehicle or acting in another unsafe or unlawful manner as is done relating to alcohol use. This policy is already in effect in California, Texas, and many other states.

The strategic concern expressed by the authors is that, as the US federal government starts to become more preoccupied by both emergent and divergent radical Islamic and Mexican cartel and gang related threats domestically, it may become even more centralized and draconian in some of its domestic security policies. The intent is to vent out some of the pressure that is building up in regards to US governmental policies concerning illegal narcotics use domestically. At some point federal governmental policies and US citizen perceptions may so diverge as to be directly at odds with one another. The Vietnam War is a perfect example of the potentials such divergence can bring to the streets of America. At a time when the US homeland is being increasingly threatened and its government may be forced to implement trade-offs between personal freedoms and collective security, it is strategically prudent to give ground in other areas and remove the 'criminal designation' from the over 14 million US citizens who use marijuana.[38]

The alternative to this strategy is continuing on with the current status quo policies and locking up addicts, and for that matter soft drug users, in jail or prison because of their illegal narcotics use and then while incarcerated be unable to stop them engaging in said illegal narcotics use because of the inability of the penal system to keep controlled substances out of such facilities in the first place.[39] The economic cost of incarcerating such drug users is no longer sustainable in an environment where the US is now being subjected to governmental budgetary constraints and mounting societal economic debt. The status quo has also resulted in the emergence of powerful drug cartels first in Colombia and now in Mexico. Even when powerful and early generation cartels are dismantled by governmental forces, as in the case of Colombia with the Medellín and Cali cartels, hundreds of small and more networked cartels arise to take their place because user demand in the US still exists.

As aforementioned with regard to US counter-demand approaches, every imaginable approach basically represents a no-win scenario. The question is which approach or strategy is less threatening to US society and its security than the others. Philosophically, illegal narcotics are not legitimized or decriminalized following such a special status designation. Rather special status addicts become administratively monitored by law enforcement and the judicial system and medicalized as part of a counseling and treatment regime being provided to these troubled individuals – though large numbers of these addicts are quite possibly incurable. The decriminalization of small amounts of marijuana for personal use on the other hand is more problematic. By doing so we are implying, and probably rightly so, that the addictive chemical THC is somewhat on par with alcohol and nicotine found in legal addictive commodities. This ends up being both a scientific and an ethical debate with no clear consensus between those taking differing viewpoints. What this policy does do, however, is vent out some societal tensions over federal narcotics policies and bring the US government closer in line with the American public's perceptions.

The collateral benefits of this two-pronged approach are that the Mexican drug cartels and their gang-facilitated street level distribution network would over time be economically imperiled as the bulk of the illegal narcotics users in the US are identified and brought under a parolee type of mechanism with treatment capabilities and, if need be, some sort of prescription drug user demand fulfillment capacity. As the US program stands up, harsher and harsher penalties for illegal narcotics distribution could in turn be conceivably enacted to help eliminate the hard drug illegal narcotics market. The decriminalization of marijuana policy is once again problematic because it does not further the elimination of all forms of illegal narcotics and does not support and could even to some extent be viewed as slightly at odds with the special user approach. At best, it would have to be considered a transitory policy that in the long term would either be required at some point to be revoked, with personal marijuana use once again criminalized, or further implemented towards its legalization as an addictive commodity for adult users. It is recognized by the authors that with marijuana (hashish) currently accounting for the largest percentage of Mexican drug cartel revenues, it is only full legalization of this product that is likely to break the economic backs of the cartels. However, this minimal decriminalization trial balloon with regard to personal marijuana use will, beyond its 'venting' value, allow the viewing of some of the potential second order societal effects to expanding this policy.

The blended counter-demand strategy takes a very different focus concerning the vast majority of individuals in American society. The emphasis is on extinguishing illegal narcotic demand before it emerges. This method focuses on behavior shaping techniques and draws upon the DARE, other programs currently in effect, and future programs. Those societal members who fall through the cracks should then be subjected to coercive governmental responses ranging from the threat of, and actual application of economic sanction to incarceration. The 'troubled individuals' who can be rehabilitated with the economic resources allocated are and those who fall further through the cracks and become hardcore addicts end up with the special status designation.

Ultimately, as a nation the US does not want to normalize or in any way condone illegal narcotics use because it challenges its traditional value system. On the other hand, a triage system should be implemented and those deemed too far gone should, rather than being locked away in a prison cell, be allowed to self-destruct within a monitored parolee-like program. As a side benefit, such a program as part of the larger proposed counter-demand US strategy would over time economically undermine the financial wealth and corruptive power of the Mexican drug cartels. This would represent a viable means of challenging the narco virus that has Mexico firmly in its grasp and increasingly is coming over the US border.

Of course, prior to the implementation of such an envisioned counter-demand strategy, a limited program should first be established with a specific sunset clause (termination date) enacted. Such a trial governmental counter-drug program would be attempted in a limited geographic area. Further, it would undergo the necessary program review and cost-benefit analysis prior to its inception and be under external and independent audit and review during the course of its limited existence. At such a point the envisioned blended counter-demand strategy would either be deemed to have public policy merit and be more broadly implemented or would fall short in its expectations, costs versus benefits, and impact and be considered an attempted, yet flawed, counter-drug program.

### Notes

1. See the section on The Illegal Economy of Mexican-US (Sureños) Gangs, Cartels, & Mercenaries in Bunker, 'Strategic Threat'. This is a very conservative estimate of yearly Mexican cartel and affiliate revenues with other estimates ranging from $40–60 billion.
2. Table G.5 – Types of Illicit Drug Use in the Past Month among Persons Aged 12 or Older: Numbers in Thousands, 2002–2007, in Substance Abuse and Mental Health Services Administration, Office of Applied Studies, *Results from the 2007 National Survey on Drug Use and Health: National Findings.*
3. Table G.6 – Types of Illicit Drug Use in the Past Month among Persons Aged 12 or Older: Percentages, 2002–2007, in Ibid.

4.  Section 3.1. Alcohol Use among Persons Aged 12 or Older and 4. Tobacco Use, in Ibid

5.  Section 2. Illicit Drug Use, Association with Cigarette and Alcohol Use, Section 3. Alcohol Use, Association with Illicit Drug and Tobacco Use, and Section 4. Tobacco Use, Association with Illicit Drug and Alcohol Use, in Ibid

6.  US Drug Enforcement Administration. 'Chapter 1 The Controlled Substances Act' subsection 'User Accountability'.

7.  Booth, *Opium: A History*, 193, 198.

8.  Ibid., 184.

9.  Ibid., 203.

10. Chepesiuk, *The Drug Wars*, xxiv.

11. Ibid.

12. US Drug Enforcement Administration, 'Chapter 1 The Controlled Substances Act'.

13. Ibid.

14. Fields, 'White House Czar Calls for End to "War on Drugs"'.

15. Office of National Drug Control Policy, *The President's National Drug Control Strategy*.

16. Meiners and Burton, 'The Role of the Mexican Military in the Cartel War'.

17. Office of National Drug Control Policy. *The President's National Drug Control Strategy*.

18. Chepesiuk, *The Drug Wars*, xxi.

19. *Wikipedia*, 'Office of Drug Control Policy'.

20. US Drug Enforcement Administration, 'Chapter 1 The Controlled Substances Act'.

21. Ibid.

22. Peele, *The Meaning of Addiction*, 1.

23. Chepesiuk, *The Drug Wars*, xxix.

24. Moore, *Creating Public Value*.

25. Amsterdam Information, 'Amsterdam Drugs'; and Greenwald, 'Drug Decriminalization in Portugal'.

26. Initiative & Referendum Institute at University of Southern California, 'Focus on Marijuana', 1.

27. Office of National Drug Control Policy, 'National Drug Control Strategy; FY 2009 Budget Summary'.

28. *The Economist*, 'Failed states and failed policies'.

29. US Department of Justice, Office of Justice Programs, Bureau of Justice Statistics. 'Criminal Offender Statistics'.

30. US Department of Justice, Office of Justice Programs, Bureau of Justice Statistics, 'Prisoners in 2007'.

31. *Drug War Chronicle*, 'Sentencing: US Jail and Prison Population Hits All-Time (Again) – 2.3 Million Behind Bars, Including More Than Half a Million Drug Offenders'.

32. For various language versions of this report, access http://www.drogasedemocracia. org/. Concerning the decriminalization trend in Latin America, see *Foreign Policy*, 'Passport: Argentina to decriminalize personal marijuana use'; and *Time*, 'Mexico: Decriminalizing Drugs', 13.

33. Hartnett, 'Drug Legalization: Why It Wouldn't Work in the United States'; and *Mother Jones*. 'Features: Totally Wasted' 28–53, 80.

34. Concern has also been expressed concerning the left of center approach and criminality. A possible unintended second order effect would be for the Mexican cartels and their associates to turn to other forms of crime in order to make up for their loss of billions of dollars of yearly revenues. This may be a moot point as this

trend has already taken place concerning human smuggling, kidnapping, theft, and other illegal activities in both Mexico and the US.

35. Debate exists if hardcore marijuana users should or should not also be given such a special status designation – for cocaine (& crack), methamphetamine, and heroin users most certainly.

36. This is envisioned as a modified extension of the drug courts program. For more on these courts see, Office of National Drug Control Policy, 'Drug Courts'.

37. The medical marijuana movement is another issue and, while in violation of federal law, the societal question is should cancer and AIDS patients (especially terminal ones) have access to this illegal narcotic? The potentials for abuse of such programs are, however, immense as have taken place in Los Angeles with the large numbers of sham dispensaries that have arisen.

38. Hierarchical structures, such as states, will under time of threat further centralize their activities. As the US begins to suffer domestic terrorist incidents it is expected that the federal government will follow this pattern. See Brafman and Beckstrom, *The Starfish and the Spider*; this centralizing under threat theme is evident throughout the work.

39. Jails and prisons are notorious for illegal contraband such as narcotics, and even cell phones, making its way into these facilities.

**Bibliography**

Amsterdam Information. 'Amsterdam Drugs'. n.d., http://www.amsterdam.info/drugs/ (accessed 7 September 2009).

Brafman, Ori and Rod. A Beckstrom. *The Starfish and the Spider*. New York: Penguin Group, 2006.

Booth, Martin. *Opium: A History*. New York: St Martin's Griffin Press, 1999.

Bunker, Robert J. 'Strategic Threat: Narcos and Narcotics Overview'. *Small Wars and Insurgencies* 21, no. 1 (2010): 8–29.

Chepesiuk, Ron. *The Drug Wars: An International Encyclopedia*, Santa Barbara, CA: ABC-CLIO, 1999.

*Drug War Chronicle*. 'Sentencing: US Jail and Prison Population Hits All-Time (Again) – 2.3 Million Behind Bars, Including More Than Half a Million Drug Offenders'. no.564, 12 December 2008, http://stopthedrugwar.org/chronicle/564/US_jail_prison_population_all_time_high_drug_offenders (accessed on 5 September 2009).

Economic Research Service of the United States Department of Agriculture website, n.d., http://www.ers.usda.gov/ (accessed repeatedly in August 2009).

*The Economist*. 'Failed States and Failed Policies: How to Stop the Drug Wars', 5 March 2009, http://www.economist.com/opinion/PrinterFriendly.cfm?story_id=13237193 (accessed 7 September 2009).

Fields, Gary. 'White House Czar Calls for End to "War on Drugs"', *The Wall Street Journal* (14 May 2009), http://online.wsj.com/article/SB124225891527617397.html.

*Foreign Policy*. 'Passport: Argentina to Decriminalize Personal Marijuana Use', 25 August 2009, http://blog.foreignpolicy.com/posts/2009/08/25/argentina_decriminalizes_personal_drug_use (accessed 5 September 2009).

Greenwald, Glen. 'Drug Decriminalization in Portugal: Lessons for Creating Fair and Successful Drug Policies', White Paper. Washington, DC: CATO Institute, 2 April 2009.

Hartnett, Edmund. 'Drug Legalization: Why it Wouldn't Work in the United States', *The Police Chief* 72, no. 3 (March 2005), http://policechiefmagazine.org/magazine/index.cfm?fuseaction=display_arch&article_id=533&issue_id=32005 (accessed 7 September 2009).

Initiative & Referendum Institute at University of Southern California. 'Focus on Marijuana', *Ballotwatch*, no. 2 (September 2004).

Latin American Commission on Drugs and Democracy. *Drugs and Democracy: Toward A Paradigm Shift*, Final Report, 2009, http://www.drogasedemocracia.org/English/ (accessed 17 September 2009).

Meiners, Stephen, and Fred Burton. 'The Role of the Mexican Military in the Cartel War'. *Global Security and Intelligence Report* (29 July 2009).

Moore, Mark H. *Creating Public Value: Strategic Management in Government, 1997*. Cambridge, MA: Harvard University Press, 1997.

*Mother Jones 'Features: Totally Wasted'*. *Mother Jones* Magazine, 34, no. 4 (July–August 2009): 28–53, 80.

Office of National Drug Control Policy. 'National Drug Control Strategy; FY 2009 Budget Summary'. February 2008, http://www.whitehousedrugpolicy.gov/publications/policy/09budget/ (accessed 7 September 2009).

Office of National Drug Control Policy. 'Drug Courts'. n.d., http://www.whitehousedrugpolicy.gov/enforce/DrugCourt.html (accessed 17 September 2009).

Office of National Drug Control Policy. *The President's National Drug Control Strategy*, Washington, DC, January 2009, http://www.whitehousedrugpolicy.gov/publications/policy/ndcs09/index.html (accessed 17 September 2009).

*The Partnership for a Drug-Free America website*. n.d., http://www.drugfree.org (Accessed repeatedly in August 2009).

Peele, Stanton. *The Meaning of Addiction: Compulsive Experience and its Interpretation*. San Franciso, CA: Jossey-Bass, 1998. See also http://www.peele.net/lib/moa.html.

Portal für Marktforschung, Studien, Beratung. *Marktanalyse – Tobacco – North America (NAFTA) Industry Guide*, February 2009, http://www.marktforschung.de.

Stevenson, Mark. 'Marijuana Big Earner for Mexico Gangs'. *USA Today* (21 February 2008).

Substance Abuse and Mental Health Services Administration, Office of Applied Studies. *Results from the 2007 National Survey on Drug Use and Health: National Findings*. NSDUH Series H-34, DHHS Publication No. SMA 08–4343 Rockville, MD: Government Printing Office, 2008.

*Time*. 'Mexico: Decriminalizing Drugs' (7 September 2009), 13.

US Department of Justice, Office of Justice Programs, Bureau of Justice Statistics. 'Criminal Offender Statistics'. Last updated 8 August 2007, http://www.ojp.usdoj.gov/bjs/crimoff.htm (accessed 5 September 2009).

US Department of Justice, Office of Justice Programs, Bureau of Justice Statistics. 'Prisoners in 2007', NCJ 224280 Washington, DC: Government Printing Office, December 2008.

US Drug Enforcement Administration. 'Chapter 1 The Controlled Substances Act', subsection 'User Accountability' n.d., http://www.usdoj.gov/dea/pubs/abuse/1-csa.htm (accessed 18 September 2009).

*Wikipedia*. 'Office of Drug Control Policy'. n.d., http://en.wikipedia.org/wiki/Office_of_National_Drug_Control_Policy (accessed 17 September 2009).

# Afterword: criminal violence in Mexico – a dissenting analysis

Paul Rexton Kan[a] and Phil Williams[b*]

[a]US Army War College, Carlisle Barracks, PA, USA; [b]Matthew B. Ridgway Center for International Security Studies, University of Pittsburgh, Pittsburgh, PA, USA

## Introduction

The prospects of drug-fueled violence leading to the significant impairment of the Mexican state, and trafficking organizations obtaining territorial and political control and even establishing a narco-state in Mexico are not difficult to imagine. Such scenarios are of grave concern to the United States. Nevertheless, it is important to assess correctly what is going on in Mexico. The US response to developments there should be driven by sound analysis rather than reflex responses to over-simplistic labels such as 'narco-terrorism' or to facile analogies with Colombia. Terms such as 'narco-terrorism' are politically appealing and certainly help to draw attention to a serious problem and keep it on what is a very crowded policy agenda in Washington. Perhaps it is not surprising, therefore, that they have become common. After a visit to Mexico in late 2008, for example, General Barry McAffrey (retired), former head of the Office of National Drug Control Policy, wrote that:

> A failure by the Mexican political system to curtail lawlessness and violence could result in a surge of millions of refugees crossing the US border to escape domestic misery of violence, failed economic policy, poverty, hunger, joblessness and the mindless cruelty and injustice of a criminal state. Mexico is not confronting dangerous criminality – it is fighting for survival against narco-terrorism.[1]

Such comments have given new urgency to claims that 'Mexico is becoming the next Colombia'.[2] Unfortunately, such labels and analogies have little analytic value. Indeed, they are highly pernicious, encouraging worst-case thinking about Mexico as a country on the verge of state failure. Such assessments take the extremely rare contingency of state failure and apply it to a country which has the 14th largest economy in the world, exhibits a cultural dynamism and social resilience that make it the envy of many other countries, and currently has a

---

* The views expressed here do not represent those of the US Army, Department of Defense, or the US Government.

government which has chosen to confront organized crime rather than rely on traditional patterns of collusion and corruption.

Some of this is understandable. Given the seriousness and complexity of drug trafficking-related violence in Mexico, the use of labels and analogies helps to reduce ambiguity and offers shortcuts in conceptualizing the problem. Nor is it uncommon: just as acts of interstate aggression between nation-states routinely prompt the Munich analogy, intensifying levels of drug-related violence prompt analogies to Colombia. But the appeal of labels and analogies can be overly seductive. Caution is needed. If labels and analogies are inappropriate, policy responses based on them will be distorted and ineffective. None of this is meant to downplay the severity of the challenge to Mexican – and by extension US – national security stemming from drug trafficking organizations and the violence they use. It is to argue, though that violence itself is not necessarily a clear indication that things are going badly. In South Vietnam, for example, a decrease in the levels or an absence of violence in villages was typically interpreted as an indicator of the success of US counter-insurgency strategy when, in fact, it meant the village had fallen under the influence of the Vietcong.[3] Claims by the Mexican government that the increase in violence is an indicator of success are at least as plausible as clams by critics that the growth of violence is an in indicator of the bankruptcy of Calderón's policy of confrontation.

Against this background, this afterword offers a dissenting voice from some of the main themes articulated in this volume. While many of the preceding analyses suggest that drug trafficking organizations in Mexico are increasingly evolving into military and insurgent type formations of the kind long evident in Colombia, the thesis here is that we are simply seeing brutal but not atypical competition among criminal organizations and some attacks on government forces in an attempt to maintain an operating space for the illicit drug business. We also argue that there are precedents in other countries for the surge of drug-related violence in Mexico, which began during the Fox Administration and intensified even more dramatically under Calderón. In many respects, the Mexican experience has broad parallels with organized crime in several other countries – even though the associated violence is greater in Mexico. If Mexico differs in significant respects from Colombia, it has often overlooked similarities with organized crime violence in Russia, Italy, and Albania. This mix of differences and similarities suggests that while Colombia offers very few lessons for Mexico, other countries have more relevant experiences and in some cases well-articulated responses. Accordingly, this analysis first examines differences with Colombia, where parallels are often overstated and then similarities with several other countries, where parallels are typically overlooked.

## Mexico and Colombia: differences matter

Comparisons of Mexico and Colombia are often imprecise: it is sometimes uncertain whether commentators are pointing to the Colombia of today or the

Colombia of the 1980s and 1990s; if the comparison is between the perpetrators of violence or the levels, targets, and objectives of the violence; or if drug trafficking penetration of the political system has reached similar levels in the two countries. Such issues, along with divergent patterns of US involvement in the two cases, suggest that the Colombia analogy is of limited utility when assessing the situation in Mexico. This is not to ignore the similar plagues of violence – murders, kidnappings, extortions, and assassinations are high in Mexico. Nor is it to ignore the extension of corruption into many recesses of the Mexican state. Moreover, the increased violence of the last several years and the emergence of vigilante groups are in some ways reminiscent of Colombia's experience. So too is the gruesome nature of drug-related violence in Mexico. In the Colombian case, however, much of the violence had more to do with ideological political divisions than with drugs. The period known as 'La Violencia' preceded the emergence of large powerful drug trafficking organizations but left a polarized country with a weak state suffering from more serious legitimacy deficits than does Mexico. Moreover, Colombia still continues to exhibit one of the highest homicide rates in the world and certainly in Latin America. Mexico, in contrast, remains in the middle tier of states in Latin America in terms of violence. Consequently, tactical similarities should not be confused with strategic congruency. The differences between the two cases are more revealing than the similarities.

Colombia exhibits far greater ideological division than does Mexico and in the last 50 or 60 years has had a much greater propensity for political violence. The Colombian state has faced multiple challenges and during the 1980s – when the Medellín and Cali trafficking organizations were very powerful – was heavily compromised by fighting leftist insurgent groups which were sometimes seen as more threatening than the traffickers. Not surprisingly, the government often turned a blind eye to right-wing paramilitaries who participated in the drug trade as a way to earn money to fight against leftist insurgent groups like the FARC and ELN. For their part, Escobar and other traffickers used nationalist rhetoric, painting extradition as an affront to Colombian sovereignty. They also funded paramilitary groups that went after guerrillas more aggressively than the Colombian military, thereby legitimizing themselves in the eyes of many Colombians.[4] Ironically, despite their conservatism, the traffickers were not beyond using the guerrillas for their own purposes, financing the M-19 operation against Colombia's Palace of Justice in 1985 as a cover for the destruction of extradition files in the court's archives.[5] In other instances, Cali traffickers led by the Orejuela brothers and Santacruz Londono worked with the right-wing paramilitaries to form Los Pepes, a group dedicated to the elimination of Pablo Escobar. Such ideological prisms are absent in Mexico. The Mexican state is not challenged by competing ideological insurgencies and paramilitary forces. Even the rise of the Zetas is not comparable to the rise of the AUC in Colombia. The Zetas are not a right-wing paramilitary organization involved in the drug trade as a means to fight against leftist insurgents; initially an enforcement group they are now a drug trafficking organization intent on earning large sums of money. For its part, La Familia in Michoacán, which combines vigilantism with quasi-religious expressions of mysticism, is very different from both the Colombian paramilitary groups and Los Pepes – and probably is more akin to Aum Shinrikyo in Japan than any group in Colombia.

Any comparison between contemporary Colombia and Mexico also falters. The main perpetrators of violence against the Colombian state are not the smaller and numerous *cartelitos*, but FARC which – along with demobilized paramilitaries – has become a major player in the drug business. Whether this has transformed the insurgency from an ideological revolutionary movement business into a drug trafficking organization seeking a continued veneer of legitimacy through ostensible adherence to its ideals is uncertain. Whatever the case, there is no comparable insurgent group in Mexico that is as dedicated to the drug trafficking business as FARC. The Zapatista (EZLN) insurgency of the mid-1990s did not appear to play any role in drug trafficking even though it was perfectly positioned in Chiapas to do so.

What is portrayed in much of this volume as low intensity conflict in Mexico – due to the levels and targets of violence – is more akin to what John Mueller calls 'high intensity crime'.[6] Although Mueller uses this term to describe some acts that occur during intrastate conflicts that distort the political objectives of some warring groups, the term works well to describe the Mexican trafficking organizations and their particular form of hyper-gangsterism and violence. Mexico is not suffering from an insurgency, criminal or otherwise. The purpose of the violence in Mexico is quite different. Insurgent groups use violence in the pursuit of political and ideological goals while drug trafficking organizations use violence in the pursuit of criminal goals surrounding profit-maximization and personal enrichment. While both types of violence challenge the authority, legitimacy, and capacity of the state, they do so for differing reasons that should not be conflated.

Other differences reinforce this. The production of coca and cocaine can be understood as Colombia's particular form of resource curse; Mexico, in contrast, suffers from a location curse lying between cocaine suppliers and the US market. Border cities such as Nuevo Laredo, Juárez, and Tijuana have a strategic location in the cocaine trade and consequently have witnessed intense fighting. Complicating matters, Mexico also supplies marijuana and methamphetamine to US users, creating an additional reason for competition. In addition, Mexico has developed a consumer market for drugs – and some of the violence in places like Acapulco reflects a struggle for control of local retail markets. In regional drug trafficking networks, Mexico is a unique hybrid acting simultaneously as a transit, source, *and* demand country. The long-standing cultural and economic ties between Mexico and US border communities also ensure that Mexican drug violence affects Americans in ways that Colombian violence could not.

The broad scope of the relationship and the shared border between Mexico and the United States portend more profound problems for the United States than were ever experienced in its relationship with Colombia. There is already a spillover effect of Mexican drug violence. Home invasions and kidnappings, particularly in the Phoenix area, are on the rise. In 2008, 368 abductions were reported in Phoenix, compared with 117 in 2000.[7] Traffickers and besieged law enforcement officials have moved their relatives to the US to escape the violence in Mexico but have nonetheless become targets. Moreover, since 2004, over 200 American citizens have been killed in Mexico, making the country the deadliest place for Americans after Iraq and Afghanistan.[8] The trafficking organizations also lure American teenagers to act as paid assassins in the US and Mexico.[9]

Finally the outlook and behavior of drug trafficking organizations in Mexico seem different from those in Colombia where the business was traditionally seen as an avenue for social mobility as well as economic success. Traffickers in Medellín and Cali sought to become members of the Colombian elite and established firm links to the 'upper world' where they supported numerous community initiatives, national policies, and political candidates, earning the loyalty and admiration of many citizens who benefited from their largesse. Mexican trafficking organizations 'are not known for providing large scale humanitarian services or making it a priority to win over the local population'.[10] Rather than making direct investments in the upper world of Mexican society to legitimize their public face, the traffickers appear content to use corruption for information and protection and revel in a narco-culture where songs, videos, and banners venerate their exploits[11] and youngsters seek to emulate their style.[12] Mexican drug trafficking organizations appear to be using counter-cultural messages to earn respect and adulation rather than seeking the co-optation of legitimate society.

If Mexican and Colombian experiences are very different, however, there are some similarities between Mexican organized crime and organized crime elsewhere which can be analytically revealing and offer a broader range of experiences and lessons than that normally available.

## Mexico in comparative perspective: similarities matter

Mexican organized crime in the first decade of the twenty-first century has many similarities to organized crime in Russia in the 1990s. The collapse of the Soviet Union and the Communist Party removed social and political control mechanisms which had had allowed elite exploitation of organized crime while keeping the level of violence under control. In effect, the weakness of the Russian state in the 1990s allowed organized crime to flourish, while the shift to a market economy offered unprecedented opportunities for criminal entrepreneurialism. The result was the rise of what was often characterized as 'the wild east'.[13] The loss of monopoly control by the PRI in Mexico had a less dramatic but somewhat similar effect. Drug traffickers in Mexico historically required the permission of governors along with the collusion of the military and police to operate.[14] During the 1990s, however, these traditional criminal-corruption networks began to break down as the PRI became weaker at the same time as the movement of Colombian cocaine through Mexico offered new opportunities – along with unprecedented wealth and power – for Mexican drug trafficking organizations.[15] When there is a shift in the balance of power within what Roy Godson termed the 'political-criminal nexus' the result is often a violent free-for-all as criminal organizations seize new opportunities, attempt to establish territorial dominance, and compete for a greater share of illicit markets.[16] Inevitably this process is accompanied by an increase in violence. In Russia, during the 1990s the violence often took the form of contract killings. The traditional vory-v-zakone were challenged by new more entrepreneurial criminals, competition erupted among ethnic groups (particular Slavic groups versus groups from the Caucasus), and competing organizations fight for dominance in particular sectors of the economy or over industrial facilities such as aluminum plants. Generally the criminal organizations targeted rivals, anyone who posed a threat (this ranged from reformist politicians to investigative journalists and honest policemen), and those who were obstacles to efforts to seize control of particular businesses ranging from banks to hotels and gasoline stations. Sometimes the groups did their own killings and sometimes they contracted out to specialists. Mexican drug trafficking organizations have behaved in a very similar way, and as noted above they struggle for control over strategic warehouses and routes providing easy access into the United States. They have also killed journalists, high-ranking and low level policemen, members of the military and members of rival groups. In this respect, criminal violence and contract killings in both countries were very instrumental and were simply a continuation (both protective and expansionist) of their illicit business by other means.

Russian organized crime during the 1990s and Mexican organized crime today have other similarities. For Russia the period was characterized by transition and turmoil. Violence became the norm both among and within criminal organizations: spheres of influence were disputed and the internal cohesion of many groups was limited, with fractures and splits resulting in killings of group members. Mexican drug trafficking organizations seem be going through a period of similar turbulence with intensified competition among organizations accompanied by internal fractures, defections, and shifts of alignment. In both cases government and law enforcement efforts might have contributed inadvertently to this increased volatility. Indeed, law enforcement and criminal competition sometimes interact in unexpected and pernicious ways. Law enforcement in Russia, for example, sometimes weakened particular criminal organizations making them attractive and vulnerable targets for attack by rival criminal groups. Something similar seems to have happened in Mexico where the government strategy of sequentially attacking particular criminal organizations has had the inadvertent consequence of encouraging increased violence. In this connection, Richard Friman has provided a compelling analysis of how law enforcement strategies of amputation, decapitation, and elimination create 'vacancy chains'.[17] The larger these vacancy chains and the greater the uncertainties about either the internal succession or external replacement, the greater the competition and the greater the level of violence. On some occasions, the weakening of one organization encourages a feeding frenzy by other groups as they seek to eliminate and replace that organization. The decapitation of the Arellano Felix Organization and the absence of a clear line of succession led to a struggle between rival factions in Tijuana, one of which is allied to the Sinaloa organizations led by Guzman.

Having highlighted the similarities between Russia and Mexico, it has to be acknowledged that there is a major difference which reflects the more personal nature of much of the killing in Mexico. It was often stated in Russia that contract killings were business rather than personal; in Mexico killings of members of rival organization often seem to be driven by personal antipathies rather than business considerations. The animosity between Chapo Guzman and the Arellano Felix family, for example, might have been sparked initially by business rivalry but it took on a very personal quality. The more recent split between Guzman and the Beltran-Leyvas became even more personal after one of the Beltran-Leyvas was arrested and Chapo Guzman's son was killed in retaliation. In this sense, drug-related violence in Mexico clearly is similar to that of Albanian clans which were as noted for their blood feuds as for their criminality. It also has parallels with violent feuds among 'Ndrangheta families in Calabria, which in 2007 led to the killing of six members of an 'Ndrangheta family in Duisberg Germany. Yet this is not new in Mexico. In a compelling analysis of lawlessness in the Sierra Madre, for example, one British journalist noted how in some small towns, machismo, family ties, and acts of violence often created a cycle of vengeance and reprisal that lasted for years and even decades and was difficult to stop.[18]

While most of the drug trafficking violence in Mexico is internecine warfare either among major organizations and associations or among local groups competing over burgeoning local retail markets, there is another strand (somewhere between five to 10% of the killings) which targets representatives of the state. In part, this can be seen as an attempt to increase the costs to the government of its confrontational stance towards Mexican drug trafficking organizations. Some of the killings are also retaliation for those who have interfered too successfully with the drug trafficking business. In effect, the violence is the cost the administrations of Fox and Calderón have had to pay for defecting from the tacit acquiescence which characterized successive PRI governments. This has some parallels with the Italian experience, when the Sicilian Mafia in the early 1990s attacked the Italian state in retaliation for a betrayal of the long-term exchange relationship with the Christian Democrats in which political protection was traded for electoral support. The maxi-trials and the actions of magistrates such as Falcone and Borsellino created a sense of grievance and a desire for revenge. This was manifested in the killings of these magistrates and a broader campaign of terror, targeting innocent civilians and some of Italy's historic monuments. For the most part, this kind of terror campaign has been absent in Mexico. The grenade explosions in Morelia in September 2008, which might have marked the beginning of such a campaign, evoked almost universal denials of responsibility and even condemnation from drug trafficking organizations. Although it could become more pronounced in the future, the attack on the state in Mexico, while significant, is not as blatant as that in Italy in the early 1990s.

To suggest that the Mexican experience of drug-related violence has similarities with other countries is not to deny that the intensity of the violence in Mexico surpasses that of most other countries. In part this can be understood by a trend towards professionalization and militarization of drug trafficking organizations as evident in the transformation of Los Zetas from an enforcement arm of the Gulf drug trafficking organization to a major trafficking organization in its own right. The claim by Sedena that one out of every three traffickers have military experience, along with anecdotal evidence about the involvement of former policemen, suggests that the rise of the Zetas is part of a broader trend.[19] Such a trend, however, is not unique to Mexico. In Russia after the collapse of the Soviet Union, a surplus of experts in violence contributed significantly to both the growth of organized crime and the growth of violence associated with organized crime. Similar dynamics were at work elsewhere in the former Soviet bloc as intelligence agencies and military contracted significantly. The disbanding of the Ba'athist Army in Iraq had a similar effect – although in that case the unemployed specialists in violence engaged in insurgency as well as organized crime. A key difference is that in Mexico the professionals in violence were not suddenly unemployed and left with a choice of organized crime or nothing; rather they defected from the state. Nevertheless, the overall infusion of violent entrepreneurs into the mix which brought an inevitable increase in violence has parallels elsewhere and is certainly not unprecedented. And unlike in Colombia, these entrepreneurs do not appear to have a political agenda beyond protecting their activities and profits.

Another development in Mexico has been an increased emphasis on what Sebastian Rotella termed 'the semiotics of murder'. Writing in the late 1990s Rotella argued that 'to the outside world, the drug wars were frenzied and murky. For the participants, the violence had very specific codes and objectives, a logic all its own. The gangsters perfected the art of using murders to send messages. The choice of the victim, the method and the location were often calculated to make a statement.'[20] The increase in decapitations and messages left on victims, as well as the posting of killings on the Internet are the latest refinements in this process. The messages have become more gruesome, more strident, and more frequent, but have a pedigree in Mexico that can be traced back well before Fox and Calderón. The use of violence for communications in the world of organized crime has also been evident in Russia, Sicily, and even the United States. Moreover, the use of high caliber weaponry and acid to dispose of bodies are characteristic not only in the Mexico of today but of Sicily in the 1980s and early 1990s.[21]

None of this is intended to deny that the scale of organized crime violence in Mexico is typically much higher than counterpart violence elsewhere. In one comparison of homicide rates in Campania, the home of the major Camorra organized crime clans, and several Mexican states, for example, it emerged that Sinaloa (the Mexican state with the highest murder rate) had 19.3 killings per 100,000 population compared to Campania's 1.6.[22] One of the key points, however, is that drug trafficking violence in Mexico is concentrated in several key cities and states. Moreover, there are important variations between Michoacán where La Familia focuses in large part on fighting the Federal Police, Tijuana where a succession crisis is occurring, and Juárez where competition for control among rival organizations is particularly fierce. At the same time, it has to be acknowledged that Mexico, in effect, has had all the conditions for a 'perfect storm' of drug trafficking-related violence: a strong state becoming weak then trying to reassert itself; the breakdown of tacit and sometimes overt patterns of collusion between officials and traffickers; a government and law enforcement strategy which attacked priority targets sequentially rather than consecutively, creating new opportunities and greater turbulence in the criminal world; and an emphasis on family and a culture of machismo which transformed business competition into personal feuds. All this suggests that organized crime violence in Mexico is more concentrated and virulent but not qualitatively different from that in most other places. It also cautions against narrow comparisons with Colombia while neglecting similarities with the experiences of organized crime in Russia and Italy or the recognition of some of the unintended but damaging consequences of Mexico's own policies.

**Informing policy**

Differences between drug violence in Mexico and Colombia do not diminish the need for adequate policy responses to the increasing violence in Mexico. The Colombia analogy offers a strategic shorthand to assess and respond to events in Mexico. However, the differences between the two cases also need to be understood. The long-running drug violence in Colombia has been perpetrated by differing actors in different contexts. Unique international and historical conditions helped give impetus to successive US responses to the situation in Colombia which cannot be replicated in Mexico. During the Cold War, American support for counter-narcotics operations was subsumed in the anti-communist crusade. When the Clinton Administration subsequently developed Plan Colombia, counterinsurgency operations were conducted under the cloak of counter-narcotics operations. In the post September 11 world, counter-narcotics needs were accommodated under the rubric of counter-terrorism. American presidents were able to adjust the relative profile of Colombia's struggle against drug traffickers to the changing international environment – which was then used to justify funding from Congress. This option is not available for Mexico. In fact, there is already some Congressional push back on the cost of the Mérida

Initiative.[23] The long term sustainability of such funding cannot be secured by adjusting the role of counter-narcotics plays in other international struggles. Justifying spending will depend on its contribution to greater safety for US citizens at home and the reliability of Mexico as a partner. This is likely to be an abiding debate in the halls of Congress.

Against this background, the Mérida Initiative should not be seen as the equivalent of Plan Colombia. Colombia's Democratic Security Policy (DSP) is designed to restore state control to areas that have long been beyond the authority of the government in Bogota because of the presence of non-state armed groups. Colombia's DSP is designed to expand the government's presence in these areas while fostering the rule of law and upholding human rights. Often this has meant the use of military force against guerrillas. Rather than securing territory from insurgents, Mexico has a far more vexing problem – the areas that the government seeks to reclaim from trafficker violence are cities nominally under government control. The Mexican government must vouch for those already in positions of power and authority who are ostensibly charged with combating narcotics trafficking and its associated violence in areas where drug trafficking organizations are most active. The use of the Mexican military notwithstanding, the country is still a federal system with a patchwork of competing legal authorities and jurisdictions that greatly complicates efforts to gain the upper hand against organized crime. Although drug trafficking is a federal crime, for example, kidnapping is a state police matter.

In addition, it is not clear that the Mexican army is designed for the lengthy operations that may be required to reestablish order. This raises several important questions: Would the Mexican government sanction the long term garrisoning of the Mexican army in the cities with the highest levels of homicides? Would this solve the underlying problems of capacity gaps and functional holes that have enabled the drug trafficking organizations to flourish? On the other hand, if the use of the Mexican military is a temporary measure to reduce the violence, what will follow when forces are withdrawn? These are compelling and significant questions. They highlight the need for responses which draw on the unique features of the challenge in Mexico as well as possible lessons that can be discerned from the experiences in Russia and Italy.

**Different responses**

Efforts to reduce drug-related violence in Mexico should be based on some core principles to guide strategy. In part, these are matters of appropriate conceptualizations; but they also include the need for fundamental reforms to enhance state authority, legitimacy, and reach. Yet other measures need to erode a culture which reinforces the mystique surrounding drug trafficking and establish a culture of lawfulness and outrage. Among the most important of these conceptualizations, principles, and approaches are the following:

- *View Mexican drug violence as a law and order issue and not counter-insurgency or counter-terrorism.* Drug trafficking violence is a challenge to the state, no matter where or when it occurs. Nevertheless, when devising an appropriate strategy, high intensity crime should not be confused with low intensity conflict. 'Ink blot' counterinsurgency strategies of sending in troops to re-establish order in one town and then expanding zones of control outward are short-term expedients but risk further militarizing the situation in Mexico. A military is not a police force. Citizens have a lower threshold of tolerance for collateral damage in law and order operations than they do in war.[24] During wartime, civil rights can be sacrificed in the name of state security. In a police action, civil rights are inviolable. To sacrifice them at this stage means a significant climb on the escalatory ladder of state coercion from which it would be difficult to recover. All too often governments and militaries frustrated by strategic stalemate merely escalate their tactics rather than adjust their strategy. Such an outcome would have lasting damage on Mexican civil society. Even at this stage, Mexico has not been wracked by the caliber of drug violence of the early 1990s such as the killing of Cardinal Ocampo at Guadalajara Airport in 1993 and the assassination of PRI presidential candidate Luis Donaldo Colosio in 1994. This is something that is often ignored in so many gloomy assessments of trends in drug trafficking violence in Mexico.
- *Avoid further militarization of the situation in the near term.* There are several reasons for this. Militaries with long-term and sustained exposure to counter-narcotics operations invariably suffer from institutional corruption. Moreover, given the proximity of violence to the US border, long term use of the Mexican army might lead to more accidental border incursions and accidental use of force. Deaths of US law enforcement officers at the hands of Mexican soldiers or vice versa would have severe implications for both countries. Having two militaries operating on either side of the border could diminish commerce and further erode the economies on either side. This would create a deeper reservoir from which traffickers draw recruits within Mexico and entice more Americans to become straw purchasers and mules for the gun trade going south.
- *Strengthen the state in ways which enhance legitimacy, meet needs, and remove impunity.* Mexico, like other developing states, suffers from capacity gaps and functional holes, resulting in failure to provide essential services and maintain an adequate degree of social control. Indeed, the weakness of the criminal justice system has created an environment of impunity for drug traffickers. In Mexico, only 5% of crimes are solved.[25] As a result, there is no inhibition to participation in ever-escalating levels of violence. Without punishment for criminality on the one side and the celebration of a criminal lifestyle on the other,

community support for drug trafficking organizations is facilitated. The danger is the emergence of grassroots populism in support of drug trafficking organizations, further thwarting Mexican state authority and policy approaches designed to constrain the violence. There are troubling signs of this already.[26] Building and reinforcing state institutions, particularly in the area of criminal justice, therefore, is critical to the destruction of the culture of impunity. Higher priority also needs to be given to targeting the proceeds of drug trafficking. Timing, however, is critical. In this connection, it is possible that a modus vivendi will be established among competing drug trafficking organizations, particularly if they conclude that violence has become highly counter-productive and hurts profit levels. One of the reasons that Putin's reassertion of state power in Russia succeeded was because it came at a time when spheres of influence had been clearly demarcated and a degree of stability and predictability had re-emerged in Russia's criminal world. A similar window of opportunity might appear in Mexico in the next few years. This, however, also requires a shift in the way the Mexican government targets drug trafficking organizations.

- *Weaken drug trafficking organizations simultaneously rather than sequentially.* It was suggested above that one of the lessons from Mexico's own experience of attacking drug trafficking organizations is the need to avoid creating instabilities and opportunities in the criminal world which encourage rather than discourage violence. In effect, it is necessary to adopt a broad targeting strategy which incrementally weakens groups across the board but does not create major perturbations in the criminal world. Efforts should be made to create short rather than long 'vacancy chains' and avoid asymmetric reductions in the power of one or two drug trafficking organizations which then make attractive targets for rivals to attack.

- *Mobilize outrage against drug trafficking violence.* One of the difficulties in Mexico is that violence has increased without creating a sense of outrage. One of the lessons of Sicily is that when the population is outraged and is mobilized against organized crime, the criminals become more vulnerable. The killings of Falcone and Borsellino transformed public apathy and acceptance into overt animosity towards the Sicilian Mafia. This was subsequently translated into further measures by the government to dismantle well-established structures of collusion and corruption. Replicating this elsewhere is difficult: civil society is at an inherent disadvantage when trying to deal with uncivil society. Moreover in large parts of Mexico, trafficking is deeply embedded both economically and socially in ways which help to sustain support for the drug business. This is where the Mexican government has to work hardest to inject alternative economic stimulants which can sustain growth and wean people away from what in some areas is the only form of economic subsistence. The battle for hearts and minds has to be accompanied by the battle for wallets and pocket-books. It is also a battle, however, which needs to facilitate and empower cross-border ties between US and Mexican border communities to combat narco-culture and the narco-economy.

- *Think of narco-cities rather than a narco-state.* Compared to Colombia which was challenged by powerful insurgencies operating freely in large swaths of territory and by the successful co-option of political leaders, the challenge to the Mexican state is more modest. Much of the violence is confined to three cities and three or four states. Policy options must focus not only on the most violent cities, but also on those in which there is little violence. Developing proactive measures to contain balloon or pillow effects is essential.

In sum, the situation in Mexico is serious, but not hopeless. Mexican strategies and policies which take into account the uniqueness of the situation, yet are informed about past practices, and incorporate lessons from elsewhere are essential. So too are US efforts to nudge Mexico in appropriate directions as well as to reduce the profitability of its own drug markets. The United States also needs to acknowledge that measures to enhance the authority and legitimacy of the Mexican state are ultimately far more important than the supply of military equipment. Even with such sensitivity, this will be a long arduous struggle; without a refined discriminating approach which eschews facile analogies, however, it will be doomed to certain failure.

**Notes**

1.  McCaffrey, 'After Action Report – VISIT MEXICO – 5–7 December 2008', 4.
2.  Carpenter, 'Mexico is Becoming the Next Colombia'.
3.  The authors are grateful for this observation to Robert Jervis, Columbia University.
4.  Bowden, *Killing Pablo*, 33.
5.  Chepesiuk, *Drug Lords*, 131.
6.  Mueller, *Remnants of War*, 6.
7.  Conant and Campo-Flores, 'The Enemy Within'.
8.  Msnbc.com, 'Over 200 Americans Killed in Mexico since '04'. See also Cuevas-Nazario, 'Americans Beaten, Shot to Death in Mexico'.
9.  McKinley, 'Mexican Cartels Lure American Teens as Killers'.
10. Stratfor.com, 'Organized Crime in Mexico'.
11. See Quinones, 'State of War', 78. For an example of this narco-culture, go to: http://www.youtube.com/watch?v=d0GSXbC8wEA and http://www.youtube.com/watch?v=iKC6OHY97uQ. For an excellent study on the popular music style that pays tribute to drug traffickers, smugglers, and dealers, see Wald, *Narcocorrido: A Journey into the Music of Drugs, Guns and Guerrillas*.
12. Quinones, 'State of War', 78.
13. Hersh, 'The Wild East'.
14. Astorga, 'Drug Trafficking in Mexico'.
15. Pimentel, 'The Nexus of Organized Crime and Politics'.
16. Godson, 'Political-Criminal Nexus: Overview'.
17. Friman, 'Forging the Vacancy Chain'.

18.  Grant, *God's Middle Finger*.
19.  'Sedena Statistics'.
20.  Rotella, *Twilight on the Line*, 7.
21.  Falcone, *Men of Honor*, 3 and 7.
22.  Creechan, 'Gomorrah and Mexican Cartel Violence'.
23.  Hsu and Sheridan, 'Anti-Drug Effort at US Border Readied', A1.
24.  This seems to be occurring in Mexico. See Ellingwood, 'Mexico Under Siege: Abuse Allegations against Army Mount Dramatically', A-27; and Fainaru and Booth, 'Mexico Accused of Torture in Drug War'.
25.  *The Times of London*, 'Mexican Crimewave', 2.
26.  Lacey, 'Drug Tie Seen to Protests in Mexico', A12; and Emmott, 'Mexicans Protest Army Campaign against Drug Cartels'.

## Bibliography

Bowden, Mark. *Killing Pablo*. New York: Atlantic Monthly Press, 2001.

Carpenter, Ted Galen. 'Mexico is Becoming the Next Colombia'. CATO Institute Foreign Policy Briefing no. 87, 15 November 2005.

Chepesiuk, Ron. *Drug Lords*. Preston: Milo Books, 2007.

Conant, Eve and Adrian Campo-Flores. 'The Enemy Within'. *Newsweek.com*, 23 March 2009.

Cuevas-Nazario, Marya. 'Americans Beaten, Shot to Death in Mexico'. *CNN.com*, http://www.cnn.com/2009/WORLD/Americas/07/09/mexico.killings/index.html (accessed 9 July 2009).

Ellingwood, Ken. 'Mexico under Siege: Abuse Allegations against Army Mount Dramatically'. *Los Angeles Times*, 21 March 2009.

Emmott, Robin. 'Mexicans Protest Army Campaign against Drug Cartels'. *Reuters*, 18 February 2009.

Fainaru, Steve and William Booth. 'Mexico Accused of Torture in Drug War'. *MSNBC.com*, 9 July 2009, http://www.msnbc.com/id/31822017/ns/world-news-washington_post (accessed 9 July 2009).

Lacey, Marc. 'Drug Tie Seen to Protests in Mexico'. *New York Times*, 19 February 2009.

McCaffrey, Barry. 'After Action Report – VISIT MEXICO – 5–7 December 2008'. 29 December 2008.

McKinley, James. 'Mexican Cartels Lure American Teens as Killers'. *New York Times*, 23 June 2009, http://www.nytimes.com/2009/06/23/23killers.html?_r=1&ref+world&pagewanted=print.

*Msnbc.com*. 'Over 200 Americans Killed in Mexico since '04'. 9 February 2009, http://www.msnbc.msn.com/id/29095730/ (accessed 19 March 2009).

Mueller, John. *Remnants of War*. New York: Cornell University Press, 2004.

Quinones, Sam. 'State of War'. *Foreign Policy*, March/April 2009, http://www.foreignpolicy.com/articles/2009/02/16/state_of_war.

*Stratfor.com*. 'Organized Crime in Mexico'. 11 March 2008, www.stratfor.com/analysis/organized_crime_mexico (accessed 11 February 2009).

*The Times of London*. 'Mexican Crimewave'. 1 September 2008.

Wald, Elijah. *Narcocorrido: A Journey into the Music of Drugs, Guns and Guerrillas*. New York: Rayo, 2001.

# Index

Page numbers in *Italics* represent tables.
Page numbers in **Bold** represent figures.
Page numbers followed by n represent endnotes.

# Cold War History

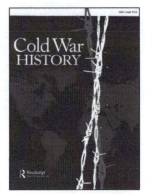

*Cold War History* is based in the Cold War Studies Centre at the London School
of Economics. It aims to make available to the general public the results of recent
research on the origins and development of the Cold War and its impact on
nations, alliances and regions at various levels of statecraft, as well as in areas such as the military and intelligence, the
economy, and social and intellectual developments. The new history of the Cold War is a fascinating example of how
experts – often working across national and disciplinary boundaries – are able to use newly available information to refine,
or in some cases destroy, old images and interpretations. *Cold War History* aims at publishing the best of this emerging
scholarship, from a perspective that attempts to de-centre the era through paying special attention to the role of Europe
and the Third World. The journal welcomes contributions from historians and representatives of other disciplines on all
aspects of the global Cold War and its present repercussions.